GO:
with Microsoft®

Office 2010
Getting Started

**Shelley Gaskin, Robert L. Ferrett,
Alicia Vargas, and Carolyn McLellan**

Prentice Hall
Boston Columbus Indianapolis New York San Francisco Upper Saddle River
Amsterdam Cape Town Dubai London Madrid Milan Munich Paris Montreal Toronto
Delhi Mexico City Sao Paulo Sydney Hong Kong Seoul Singapore Taipei Tokyo

Associate VP/Executive Acquisitions Editor, Print: Stephanie Wall

Editorial Project Manager: Laura Burgess

Editor in Chief: Michael Payne

Product Development Manager: Eileen Bien Calabro

Development Editor: Ginny Munroe

Editorial Assistant: Nicole Sam

Director of Marketing: Kate Valentine

Marketing Manager: Tori Olson Alves

Marketing Coordinator: Susan Osterlitz

Marketing Assistant: Darshika Vyas

Senior Managing Editor: Cynthia Zonneveld

Associate Managing Editor: Camille Trentacoste

Production Project Manager: Mike Lackey

Operations Director: Alexis Heydt

Operations Specialist: Natacha Moore

Senior Art Director: Jonathan Boylan

Cover Photo: © Ben Durrant

Text and Cover Designer: Blair Brown

Manager, Cover Visual Research & Permissions: Karen Sanatar

Manager, Rights and Permissions: Zina Arabia

AVP/Director of Online Programs, Media: Richard Keaveny

AVP/Director of Product Development, Media: Lisa Strite

Media Project Manager, Editorial: Alana Coles

Media Project Manager, Production: John Cassar

Full-Service Project Management: PreMediaGlobal

Composition: PreMediaGlobal

Printer/Binder: Quebecor World Book Services

Cover Printer: Lehigh-Phoenix Color

Text Font: Bookman Light

Credits and acknowledgments borrowed from other sources and reproduced, with permission, in this textbook appear on appropriate page within text. Photos appearing in Word chapter 1 supplied by Robert Ferrett and used with permission. Photos appearing in PowerPoint chapter 1 supplied by Alicia Vargas and used with permission.

Microsoft® and Windows® are registered trademarks of the Microsoft Corporation in the U.S.A. and other countries. Screen shots and icons reprinted with permission from the Microsoft Corporation. This book is not sponsored or endorsed by or affiliated with the Microsoft Corporation.

Many of the designations by manufacturers and seller to distinguish their products are claimed as trademarks. Where those designations appear in this book, and the publisher was aware of a trademark claim, the designations have been printed in initial caps or all caps.

Library of Congress Cataloging-in-Publication Data

Go! with Microsoft Office 2010, getting started / Shelley Gaskin . . . [et al.].
   p. cm.
 ISBN-13: 978-0-13-508865-4
 ISBN-10: 0-13-508865-8
 1. Microsoft Office. 2. Business—Computer programs. I. Gaskin, Shelley.
 HF5548.4.M525G6256 2011
 005.5—dc22

                                   2010020031

10 9 8 7 6 5 4 3 2 1

Prentice Hall
is an imprint of

www.pearsonhighered.com

ISBN 10: 0-13-508865-8
ISBN 13: 978-0-13-508865-4

Brief Contents

Contents

Word

Chapter 1   Creating Documents with Microsoft Word 2010 49

Excel

Chapter 1 Creating a Worksheet and Charting Data 105

Access

Chapter 1   Getting Started with Access Databases **171**

PowerPoint

Chapter 1   Getting Started with Microsoft Office PowerPoint 237

GO! System Contributors

We thank the following people for their hard work and support in making the GO! System all that it is!

Instructor Resource Authors

Adickes, Erich	Parkland College	Holland, Susan	Southeast Community College-Nebraska
Baray, Carrie	Ivy Tech Community College		
Clausen, Jane	Western Iowa Tech Community College	Landenberger, Toni	Southeast Community College-Nebraska
Crossley, Connie	Cincinnati State Technical and Community College	McMahon, Richard	University of Houston—Downtown
		Miller, Sandra	Wenatchee Valley College
Emrich, Stefanie	Metropolitan Community College of Omaha, Nebraska	Niebur, Katherine	Dakota County Technical College
		Nowakowski, Anthony	Buffalo State
Faix, Dennis	Harrisburg Area Community College	Pierce, Tonya	Ivy Tech Community College
Hadden, Karen	Western Iowa Tech Community College	Roselli, Diane	Harrisburg Area Community College
		St. John, Steve	Tulsa Community College
Hammerle, Patricia	Indiana University/Purdue University at Indianapolis	Sterr, Jody	Blackhawk Technical College
		Thompson, Joyce	Lehigh Carbon Community College
Hines, James	Tidewater Community College	Tucker, William	Austin Community College

Technical Editors

Matthew Bisi	Barbara Edington	Joyce Nielsen	Jan Snyder
Mary Corcoran	Sarah Evans	Janet Pickard	Mara Zebest
Lori Damanti	Adam Layne	Sean Portnoy	

Student Reviewers

Albinda, Sarah Evangeline	Phoenix College	Innis, Tim	Tulsa Community College
Allen, John	Asheville-Buncombe Tech Community College	Jarboe, Aaron	Central Washington University
		Key, Penny	Greenville Technical College
Alexander, Steven	St. Johns River Community College	Klein, Colleen	Northern Michigan University
Alexander, Melissa	Tulsa Community College	Lloyd, Kasey	Ivy Tech Bloomington
Bolz, Stephanie	Northern Michigan University	Moeller, Jeffrey	Northern Michigan University
Berner, Ashley	Central Washington University	Mullen, Sharita	Tidewater Community College
Boomer, Michelle	Northern Michigan University	Nelson, Cody	Texas Tech University
Busse, Brennan	Northern Michigan University	Nicholson, Regina	Athens Tech College
Butkey, Maura	Central Washington University	Niehaus, Kristina	Northern Michigan University
Cates, Concita	Phoenix College	Nisa, Zaibun	Santa Rosa Community College
Charles, Marvin	Harrisburg Area Community College	Nunez, Nohelia	Santa Rosa Community College
		Oak, Samantha	Central Washington University
Christensen, Kaylie	Northern Michigan University	Oberly, Sara	Harrisburg Area Community College Lancaster
Clark, Glen D. III	Harrisburg Area Community College		
		Oertii, Monica	Central Washington University
Cobble, Jan N.	Greenville Technical College	Palenshus, Juliet	Central Washington University
Connally, Brianna	Central Washington University	Pohl, Amanda	Northern Michigan University
Davis, Brandon	Northern Michigan University	Presnell, Randy	Central Washington University
Davis, Christen	Central Washington University	Reed, Kailee	Texas Tech University
De Jesus Garcia, Maria	Phoenix College	Ritner, April	Northern Michigan University
Den Boer, Lance	Central Washington University	Roberts, Corey	Tulsa Community College
Dix, Jessica	Central Washington University	Rodgers, Spencer	Texas Tech University
Moeller, Jeffrey	Northern Michigan University	Rodriguez, Flavia	Northwestern State University
Downs, Elizabeth	Central Washington University	Rogers, A.	Tidewater Community College
Elser, Julie	Harrisburg Area Community College	Rossi, Jessica Ann	Central Washington University
		Rothbauer, Taylor	Trident Technical College
Erickson, Mike	Ball State University	Rozelle, Lauren	Texas Tech University
Frye, Alicia	Phoenix College	Schmadeke, Kimberly	Kirkwood Community College
Gadomski, Amanda	Northern Michigan University	Shafapay, Natasha	Central Washington University
Gassert, Jennifer	Harrisburg Area Community College	Shanahan, Megan	Northern Michigan University
		Sullivan, Alexandra Nicole	Greenville Technical College
Gross, Mary Jo	Kirkwood Community College	Teska, Erika	Hawaii Pacific University
Gyselinck, Craig	Central Washington University	Torrenti, Natalie	Harrisburg Area Community College
Harrison, Margo	Central Washington University		
Hatt, Patrick	Harrisburg Area Community College	Traub, Amy	Northern Michigan University
Heacox, Kate	Central Washington University	Underwood, Katie	Central Washington University
Hedgman, Shaina	Tidewater College	Walters, Kim	Central Washington University
Hill, Cheretta	Northwestern State University	Warren, Jennifer L.	Greenville Technical College
Hochstedler, Bethany	Harrisburg Area Community College Lancaster	Wilson, Kelsie	Central Washington University
		Wilson, Amanda	Green River Community College
Homer, Jean	Greenville Technical College	Wylie, Jimmy	Texas Tech University

Contributors continued

Series Reviewers

Abraham, Reni — Houston Community College
Addison, Paul — Ivy Tech Community College
Agatston, Ann — Agatston Consulting Technical College
Akuna, Valeria, Ph.D. — Estrella Mountain Community College
Alexander, Melody — Ball Sate University
Alejandro, Manuel — Southwest Texas Junior College
Alger, David — Tidewater Community College Chesapeake Campus
Allen, Jackie — Rowan-Cabarrus Community College
Ali, Farha — Lander University
Amici, Penny — Harrisburg Area Community College
Anderson, Patty A. — Lake City Community College
Andrews, Wilma — Virginia Commonwealth College, Nebraska University
Anik, Mazhar — Tiffin University
Armstrong, Gary — Shippensburg University
Arnold, Linda L. — Harrisburg Area Community College
Ashby, Tom — Oklahoma City Community College
Atkins, Bonnie — Delaware Technical Community College
Aukland, Cherie — Thomas Nelson Community College
Bachand, LaDonna — Santa Rosa Community College
Bagui, Sikha — University of West Florida
Beecroft, Anita — Kwantlen University College
Bell, Paula — Lock Haven College
Belton, Linda — Springfield Tech. Community College
Bennett, Judith — Sam Houston State University
Bhatia, Sai — Riverside Community College
Bishop, Frances — DeVry Institute—Alpharetta (ATL)
Blaszkiewicz, Holly — Ivy Tech Community College/Region 1
Boito, Nancy — HACC Central Pennsylvania's Community College
Borger-Boglin, Grietje L. — San Antonio College/Northeast Lakeview College
Branigan, Dave — DeVry University
Bray, Patricia — Allegany College of Maryland
Britt, Brenda K. — Fayetteville Technical Community College
Brotherton, Cathy — Riverside Community College
Brown, Judy — Western Illinois University
Buehler, Lesley — Ohlone College
Buell, C — Central Oregon Community College
Burns, Christine — Central New Mexico Community College
Byars, Pat — Brookhaven College
Byrd, Julie — Ivy Tech Community College
Byrd, Lynn — Delta State University, Cleveland, Mississippi
Cacace, Richard N. — Pensacola Junior College
Cadenhead, Charles — Brookhaven College
Calhoun, Ric — Gordon College
Cameron, Eric — Passaic Community College
Canine, Jill — Ivy Tech Community College of Indiana
Cannamore, Madie — Kennedy King

Cannon, Kim — Greenville Technical College
Carreon, Cleda — Indiana University—Purdue University, Indianapolis
Carriker, Sandra — North Shore Community College
Casey, Patricia — Trident Technical College
Cates, Wally — Central New Mexico Community College
Chaffin, Catherine — Shawnee State University
Chauvin, Marg — Palm Beach Community College, Boca Raton
Challa, Chandrashekar — Virginia State University
Chamlou, Afsaneh — NOVA Alexandria
Chapman, Pam — Wabaunsee Community College
Christensen, Dan — Iowa Western Community College
Clay, Betty — Southeastern Oklahoma State University
Collins, Linda D. — Mesa Community College
Cone, Bill — Northern Arizona University
Conroy-Link, Janet — Holy Family College
Conway, Ronald — Bowling Green State University
Cornforth, Carol G. — WVNCC
Cosgrove, Janet — Northwestern CT Community
Courtney, Kevin — Hillsborough Community College
Coverdale, John — Riverside Community College
Cox, Rollie — Madison Area Technical College
Crawford, Hiram — Olive Harvey College
Crawford, Sonia — Central New Mexico Community College
Crawford, Thomasina — Miami-Dade College, Kendall Campus
Credico, Grace — Lethbridge Community College
Crenshaw, Richard — Miami Dade Community College, North
Crespo, Beverly — Mt. San Antonio College
Crooks, Steven — Texas Tech University
Crossley, Connie — Cincinnati State Technical Community College
Curik, Mary — Central New Mexico Community College
De Arazoza, Ralph — Miami Dade Community College
Danno, John — DeVry University/Keller Graduate School
Davis, Phillip — Del Mar College
Davis, Richard — Trinity Valley Community College
Davis, Sandra — Baker College of Allen Park
Dees, Stephanie D. — Wharton County Junior College
DeHerrera, Laurie — Pikes Peak Community College
Delk, Dr. K. Kay — Seminole Community College
Denton, Bree — Texas Tech University
Dix, Jeanette — Ivy Tech Community College
Dooly, Veronica P. — Asheville-Buncombe Technical Community College
Doroshow, Mike — Eastfield College
Douglas, Gretchen — SUNYCortland
Dove, Carol — Community College of Allegheny
Dozier, Susan — Tidewater Community College, Virginia Beach Campus
Driskel, Loretta — Niagara Community College
Duckwiler, Carol — Wabaunsee Community College
Duhon, David — Baker College
Duncan, Mimi — University of Missouri-St. Louis
Duthie, Judy — Green River Community College
Duvall, Annette — Central New Mexico Community College

Ecklund, Paula — Duke University
Eilers, Albert — Cincinnati State Technical and Community College
Eng, Bernice — Brookdale Community College
Epperson, Arlin — Columbia College
Evans, Billie — Vance-Granville Community College
Evans, Jean — Brevard Community College
Feuerbach, Lisa — Ivy Tech East Chicago
Finley, Jean — ABTCC
Fisher, Fred — Florida State University
Foster, Nancy — Baker College
Foster-Shriver, Penny L. — Anne Arundel Community College
Foster-Turpen, Linda — CNM
Foszcz, Russ — McHenry County College
Fry, Susan — Boise State University
Fustos, Janos — Metro State
Gallup, Jeanette — Blinn College
Gelb, Janet — Grossmont College
Gentry, Barb — Parkland College
Gerace, Karin — St. Angela Merici School
Gerace, Tom — Tulane University
Ghajar, Homa — Oklahoma State University
Gifford, Steve — Northwest Iowa Community College
Glazer, Ellen — Broward Community College
Gordon, Robert — Hofstra University
Gramlich, Steven — Pasco-Hernando Community College
Graviett, Nancy M. — St. Charles Community College, St. Peters, Missouri
Greene, Rich — Community College of Allegheny County
Gregoryk, Kerry — Virginia Commonwealth State
Griggs, Debra — Bellevue Community College
Grimm, Carol — Palm Beach Community College
Guthrie, Rose — Fox Valley Technical College
Hahn, Norm — Thomas Nelson Community College
Haley-Hunter, Deb — Bluefield State College
Hall, Linnea — Northwest Mississippi Community College
Hammerschlag, Dr. Bill — Brookhaven College
Hansen, Michelle — Davenport University
Hayden, Nancy — Indiana University—Purdue University, Indianapolis
Hayes, Theresa — Broward Community College
Headrick, Betsy — Chattanooga State
Helfand, Terri — Chaffey College
Helms, Liz — Columbus State Community College
Hernandez, Leticia — TCI College of Technology
Hibbert, Marilyn — Salt Lake Community College
Hinds, Cheryl — Norfolk State University
Hines, James — Tidewater Community College
Hoffman, Joan — Milwaukee Area Technical College
Hogan, Pat — Cape Fear Community College
Holland, Susan — Southeast Community College
Holliday, Mardi — Community College of Philadelphia
Hollingsworth, Mary Carole — Georgia Perimeter College
Hopson, Bonnie — Athens Technical College
Horvath, Carrie — Albertus Magnus College
Horwitz, Steve — Community College of Philadelphia

Hotta, Barbara — Leeward Community College
Howard, Bunny — St. Johns River Community
Howard, Chris — DeVry University
Huckabay, Jamie — Austin Community College
Hudgins, Susan — East Central University
Hulett, Michelle J. — Missouri State University
Humphrey, John — Asheville Buncombe Technical Community College
Hunt, Darla A. — Morehead State University, Morehead, Kentucky
Hunt, Laura — Tulsa Community College
Ivey, Joan M. — Lanier Technical College
Jacob, Sherry — Jefferson Community College
Jacobs, Duane — Salt Lake Community College
Jauken, Barb — Southeastern Community
Jerry, Gina — Santa Monica College
Johnson, Deborah S. — Edison State College
Johnson, Kathy — Wright College
Johnson, Mary — Kingwood College
Johnson, Mary — Mt. San Antonio College
Jones, Stacey — Benedict College
Jones, Warren — University of Alabama, Birmingham
Jordan, Cheryl — San Juan College
Kapoor, Bhushan — California State University, Fullerton
Kasai, Susumu — Salt Lake Community College
Kates, Hazel — Miami Dade Community College, Kendall
Keen, Debby — University of Kentucky
Keeter, Sandy — Seminole Community College
Kern-Blystone, Dorothy Jean — Bowling Green State
Kerwin, Annette — College of DuPage
Keskin, Ilknur — The University of South Dakota
Kinney, Mark B. — Baker College
Kirk, Colleen — Mercy College
Kisling, Eric — East Carolina University
Kleckner, Michelle — Elon University
Kliston, Linda — Broward Community College, North Campus
Knuth, Toni — Baker College of Auburn Hills
Kochis, Dennis — Suffolk County Community College
Kominek, Kurt — Northeast State Technical Community College
Kramer, Ed — Northern Virginia Community College
Kretz, Daniel — Fox Valley Technical College
Laird, Jeff — Northeast State Community College
Lamoureaux, Jackie — Central New Mexico Community College
Lange, David — Grand Valley State
LaPointe, Deb — Central New Mexico Community College
Larsen, Jacqueline Anne — A-B Tech
Larson, Donna — Louisville Technical Institute
Laspina, Kathy — Vance-Granville Community College
Le Grand, Dr. Kate — Broward Community College
Lenhart, Sheryl — Terra Community College
Leonard, Yvonne — Coastal Carolina Community College
Letavec, Chris — University of Cincinnati
Lewis, Daphne L, Ed.D. — Wayland Baptist University
Lewis, Julie — Baker College-Allen Park
Liefert, Jane — Everett Community College

Lindaman, Linda	Black Hawk Community College
Lindberg, Martha	Minnesota State University
Lightner, Renee	Broward Community College
Lindberg, Martha	Minnesota State University
Linge, Richard	Arizona Western College
Logan, Mary G.	Delgado Community College
Loizeaux, Barbara	Westchester Community College
Lombardi, John	South University
Lopez, Don	Clovis-State Center Community College District
Lopez, Lisa	Spartanburg Community College
Lord, Alexandria	Asheville Buncombe Tech
Lovering, LeAnne	Augusta Technical College
Lowe, Rita	Harold Washington College
Low, Willy Hui	Joliet Junior College
Lucas, Vickie	Broward Community College
Luna, Debbie	El Paso Community College
Luoma, Jean	Davenport University
Luse, Steven P.	Horry Georgetown Technical College
Lynam, Linda	Central Missouri State University
Lyon, Lynne	Durham College
Lyon, Pat Rajski	Tomball College
Macarty, Matthew	University of New Hampshire
MacKinnon, Ruth	Georgia Southern University
Macon, Lisa	Valencia Community College, West Campus
Machuca, Wayne	College of the Sequoias
Mack, Sherri	Butler County Community College
Madison, Dana	Clarion University
Maguire, Trish	Eastern New Mexico University
Malkan, Rajiv	Montgomery College
Manning, David	Northern Kentucky University
Marcus, Jacquie	Niagara Community College
Marghitu, Daniela	Auburn University
Marks, Suzanne	Bellevue Community College
Marquez, Juanita	El Centro College
Marquez, Juan	Mesa Community College
Martin, Carol	Harrisburg Area Community College
Martin, Paul C.	Harrisburg Area Community College
Martyn, Margie	Baldwin-Wallace College
Marucco, Toni	Lincoln Land Community College
Mason, Lynn	Lubbock Christian University
Matutis, Audrone	Houston Community College
Matkin, Marie	University of Lethbridge
Maurel, Trina	Odessa College
May, Karen	Blinn College
McCain, Evelynn	Boise State University
McCannon, Melinda	Gordon College
McCarthy, Marguerite	Northwestern Business College
McCaskill, Matt L.	Brevard Community College
McClellan, Carolyn	Tidewater Community College
McClure, Darlean	College of Sequoias
McCrory, Sue A.	Missouri State University
McCue, Stacy	Harrisburg Area Community College
McEntire-Orbach, Teresa	Middlesex County College
McKinley, Lee	Georgia Perimeter College
McLeod, Todd	Fresno City College
McManus, Illyana	Grossmont College
McPherson, Dori	Schoolcraft College
Meck, Kari	HACC
Meiklejohn, Nancy	Pikes Peak Community College
Menking, Rick	Hardin-Simmons University
Meredith, Mary	University of Louisiana at Lafayette
Mermelstein, Lisa	Baruch College
Metos, Linda	Salt Lake Community College
Meurer, Daniel	University of Cincinnati
Meyer, Colleen	Cincinnati State Technical and Community College
Meyer, Marian	Central New Mexico Community College
Miller, Cindy	Ivy Tech Community College, Lafayette, Indiana
Mills, Robert E.	Tidewater Community College, Portsmouth Campus
Mitchell, Susan	Davenport University
Mohle, Dennis	Fresno Community College
Molki, Saeed	South Texas College
Monk, Ellen	University of Delaware
Moore, Rodney	Holland College
Morris, Mike	Southeastern Oklahoma State University
Morris, Nancy	Hudson Valley Community College
Moseler, Dan	Harrisburg Area Community College
Nabors, Brent	Reedley College, Clovis Center
Nadas, Erika	Wright College
Nadelman, Cindi	New England College
Nademlynsky, Lisa	Johnson & Wales University
Nagengast, Joseph	Florida Career College
Nason, Scott	Rowan Cabarrus Community College
Ncube, Cathy	University of West Florida
Newsome, Eloise	Northern Virginia Community College Woodbridge
Nicholls, Doreen	Mohawk Valley Community College
Nicholson, John R.	Johnson County Community College
Nielson, Phil	Salt Lake Community College
Nunan, Karen L.	Northeast State Technical Community College
O'Neal, Lois Ann	Rogers State University
Odegard, Teri	Edmonds Community College
Ogle, Gregory	North Community College
Orr, Dr. Claudia	Northern Michigan University South
Orsburn, Glen	Fox Valley Technical College
Otieno, Derek	DeVry University
Otton, Diana Hill	Chesapeake College
Oxendale, Lucia	West Virginia Institute of Technology
Paiano, Frank	Southwestern College
Pannell, Dr. Elizabeth	Collin College
Patrick, Tanya	Clackamas Community College
Paul, Anindya	Daytona State College
Peairs, Deb	Clark State Community College
Perez, Kimberly	Tidewater Community College
Porter, Joyce	Weber State University
Prince, Lisa	Missouri State University-Springfield Campus
Proietti, Kathleen	Northern Essex Community College
Puopolo, Mike	Bunker Hill Community College
Pusins, Delores	HCCC
Putnam, Darlene	Thomas Nelson Community College

Raghuraman, Ram — Joliet Junior College
Rani, Chigurupati — BMCC/CUNY
Reasoner, Ted Allen — Indiana University—Purdue
Reeves, Karen — High Point University
Remillard, Debbie — New Hampshire Technical Institute
Rhue, Shelly — DeVry University
Richards, Karen — Maplewoods Community College
Richardson, Mary — Albany Technical College
Rodgers, Gwen — Southern Nazarene University
Rodie, Karla — Pikes Peak Community College
Roselli, Diane Maie — Harrisburg Area Community College
Ross, Dianne — University of Louisiana in Lafayette
Rousseau, Mary — Broward Community College, South
Rovetto, Ann — Horry-Georgetown Technical College
Rusin, Iwona — Baker College
Sahabi, Ahmad — Baker College of Clinton Township
Samson, Dolly — Hawaii Pacific University
Sams, Todd — University of Cincinnati
Sandoval, Everett — Reedley College
Santiago, Diana — Central New Mexico Community College
Sardone, Nancy — Seton Hall University
Scafide, Jean — Mississippi Gulf Coast Community College
Scheeren, Judy — Westmoreland County Community College
Scheiwe, Adolph — Joliet Junior College
Schneider, Sol — Sam Houston State University
Schweitzer, John — Central New Mexico Community College
Scroggins, Michael — Southwest Missouri State University
Sedlacek, Brenda — Tidewater Community College
Sell, Kelly — Anne Arundel Community College
Sever, Suzanne — Northwest Arkansas Community College
Sewell, John — Florida Career College
Sheridan, Rick — California State University-Chico
Silvers, Pamela — Asheville Buncombe Tech
Sindt, Robert G. — Johnson County Community College
Singer, Noah — Tulsa Community College
Singer, Steven A. — University of Hawai'i, Kapi'olani Community College
Sinha, Atin — Albany State University
Skolnick, Martin — Florida Atlantic University
Smith, Kristi — Allegany College of Maryland
Smith, Patrick — Marshall Community and Technical College
Smith, Stella A. — Georgia Gwinnett College
Smith, T. Michael — Austin Community College
Smith, Tammy — Tompkins Cortland Community Collge
Smolenski, Bob — Delaware County Community College
Smolenski, Robert — Delaware Community College
Southwell, Donald — Delta College
Spangler, Candice — Columbus State
Spangler, Candice — Columbus State Community College
Stark, Diane — Phoenix College
Stedham, Vicki — St. Petersburg College, Clearwater
Stefanelli, Greg — Carroll Community College
Steiner, Ester — New Mexico State University
Stenlund, Neal — Northern Virginia Community College, Alexandria
St. John, Steve — Tulsa Community College
Sterling, Janet — Houston Community College
Stoughton, Catherine — Laramie County Community College
Sullivan, Angela — Joliet Junior College

Sullivan, Denise — Westchester Community College
Sullivan, Joseph — Joliet Junior College
Swart, John — Louisiana Tech University
Szurek, Joseph — University of Pittsburgh at Greensburg
Taff, Ann — Tulsa Community College
Taggart, James — Atlantic Cape Community College
Tarver, Mary Beth — Northwestern State University
Taylor, Michael — Seattle Central Community College
Terrell, Robert L. — Carson-Newman College
Terry, Dariel — Northern Virginia Community College
Thangiah, Sam — Slippery Rock University
Thayer, Paul — Austin Community College
Thompson, Joyce — Lehigh Carbon Community College
Thompson-Sellers, Ingrid — Georgia Perimeter College
Tomasi, Erik — Baruch College
Toreson, Karen — Shoreline Community College
Townsend, Cynthia — Baker College
Trifiletti, John J. — Florida Community College at Jacksonville
Trivedi, Charulata — Quinsigamond Community College, Woodbridge
Tucker, William — Austin Community College
Turgeon, Cheryl — Asnuntuck Community College
Turpen, Linda — Central New Mexico Community College
Upshaw, Susan — Del Mar College
Unruh, Angela — Central Washington University
Vanderhoof, Dr. Glenna — Missouri State University-Springfield Campus
Vargas, Tony — El Paso Community College
Vicars, Mitzi — Hampton University
Villarreal, Kathleen — Fresno
Vitrano, Mary Ellen — Palm Beach Community College
Vlaich-Lee, Michelle — Greenville Technical College
Volker, Bonita — Tidewater Community College
Waddell, Karen — Butler Community College
Wahila, Lori (Mindy) — Tompkins Cortland Community College
Wallace, Melissa — Lanier Technical College
Walters, Gary B. — Central New Mexico Community College
Waswick, Kim — Southeast Community College, Nebraska
Wavle, Sharon M. — Tompkins Cortland Community College
Webb, Nancy — City College of San Francisco
Webb, Rebecca — Northwest Arkansas Community College
Weber, Sandy — Gateway Technical College
Weissman, Jonathan — Finger Lakes Community College
Wells, Barbara E. — Central Carolina Technical College
Wells, Lorna — Salt Lake Community College
Welsh, Jean — Lansing Community College Nebraska
White, Bruce — Quinnipiac University
Willer, Ann — Solano Community College
Williams, Mark — Lane Community College
Williams, Ronald D. — Central Piedmont Community College
Wilms, Dr. G. Jan — Union University
Wilson, Kit — Red River College
Wilson, MaryLou — Piedmont Technical College
Wilson, Roger — Fairmont State University
Wimberly, Leanne — International Academy of Design and Technology

Winters, Floyd	Manatee Community College	Yip, Thomas	Passaic Community College
Worthington, Paula	Northern Virginia Community College	Zavala, Ben	Webster Tech
		Zaboski, Maureen	University of Scranton
Wright, Darrell	Shelton State Community College	Zlotow, Mary Ann	College of DuPage
Wright, Julie	Baker College	Zudeck, Steve	Broward Community College, North
Yauney, Annette	Herkimer County Community College	Zullo, Matthew D.	Wake Technical Community College

About the Authors

Shelley Gaskin, Series Editor, is a professor in the Business and Computer Technology Division at Pasadena City College in Pasadena, California. She holds a bachelor's degree in Business Administration from Robert Morris College (Pennsylvania), a master's degree in Business from Northern Illinois University, and a doctorate in Adult and Community Education from Ball State University. Before joining Pasadena City College, she spent 12 years in the computer industry where she was a systems analyst, sales representative, and Director of Customer Education with Unisys Corporation. She also worked for Ernst & Young on the development of large systems applications for their clients. She has written and developed training materials for custom systems applications in both the public and private sector, and has written and edited numerous computer application textbooks.

This book is dedicated to my students, who inspire me every day.

Robert L. Ferrett recently retired as the Director of the Center for Instructional Computing at Eastern Michigan University, where he provided computer training and support to faculty. He has authored or co-authored more than 70 books on Access, PowerPoint, Excel, Publisher, WordPerfect, Windows, Word, OpenOffice, and Computer Fundamentals. He has been designing, developing, and delivering computer workshops for more than three decades. Before writing for the *GO! Series*, Bob was a series editor for the Learn Series. He has a bachelor's degree in Psychology, a master's degree in Geography, and a master's degree in Interdisciplinary Technology from Eastern Michigan University. His doctoral studies were in Instructional Technology at Wayne State University.

I'd like to dedicate this book to my wife Mary Jane,
whose constant support has been so important all these years.

Alicia Vargas is a faculty member in Business Information Technology at Pasadena City College. She holds a master's and a bachelor's degree in business education from California State University, Los Angeles, and has authored several textbooks and training manuals on Microsoft Word, Microsoft Excel, and Microsoft PowerPoint.

This book is dedicated with all my love to my husband Vic, who makes
everything possible; and to my children Victor, Phil, and Emmy, who are an
unending source of inspiration and who make everything worthwhile.

Carolyn McLellan is the Dean of the Division of Information Technology and Business at Tidewater Community College in Virginia Beach, Virginia. She has a master's degree in Secondary Education from Regent University and a bachelor's degree in Business Education from Old Dominion University. She taught for Norfolk Public Schools for 17 years in Business Education and served as a faculty member at Tidewater Community College for eight years teaching networking, where she developed over 23 new courses and earned the Microsoft Certified Trainer and Microsoft Certified System Engineer industry certifications. In addition to teaching, Carolyn loves to play volleyball, boogie board at the beach, bicycle, crochet, cook, and read.

This book is dedicated to my daughters, Megan and Mandy, who have my
eternal love; to my mother, Jean, who always believes in me and encouraged
me to become a teacher; to my sister Debbie, who was my first student and
who inspires me with her strength in overcoming hardships; to my niece
Jenna, for her bravery, composure, and beauty; to my grandsons, Damon
and Jordan, who bring me happiness and a renewed joie de vie; and to
the students and IT faculty at Tidewater Community College.

A Microsoft® Office textbook designed for student success!

- **Project-Based** – Students learn by creating projects that they will use in the real world.

- **Microsoft Procedural Syntax** – Steps are written to put students in the right place at the right time.

- **Teachable Moment** – Expository text is woven into the steps—at the moment students need to know it—not chunked together in a block of text that will go unread.

- **Sequential Pagination** – Students have actual page numbers instead of confusing letters and abbreviations.

Student Outcomes and Learning Objectives – Objectives are clustered around projects that result in student outcomes.

Project Activities – A project summary stated clearly and quickly.

Project Files – Clearly shows students which files are needed for the project and the names they will use to save their documents.

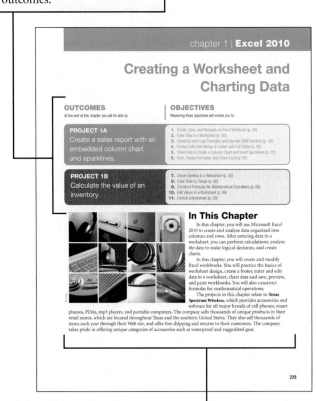

Scenario – Each chapter opens with a story that sets the stage for the projects the student will create.

Project Results – Shows students how their final outcome will appear.

Key Feature

Microsoft Procedural Syntax – Steps are written to put the student in the right place at the right time.

Color Coding

Color Coding – Color variations between the two projects in each chapter make it easy to identify which project students are working on.

Key Feature

Sequential Pagination – Students are given actual page numbers to navigate through the textbook instead of confusing letters and abbreviations.

Key Feature

Teachable Moment – Expository text is woven into the steps—at the moment students need to know it—not chunked together in a block of text that will go unread.

End-of-Chapter

Content-Based Assessments – Assessments with defined solutions.

Objective List - Every project includes a listing of covered objectives from Projects A and B.

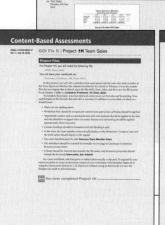

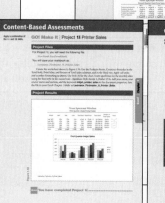

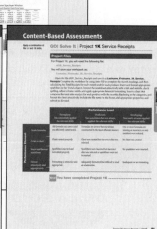

End-of-Chapter

Outcomes-Based Assessments – Assessments with open-ended solutions.

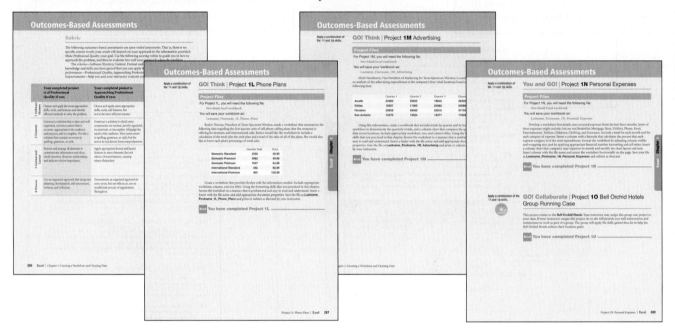

Task-Specific Rubric – A matrix specific to the **GO! Solve It** projects that states the criteria and standards for grading these defined-solution projects.

Outcomes Rubric – A matrix specific to the **GO! Think** projects that states the criteria and standards for grading these open-ended assessments.

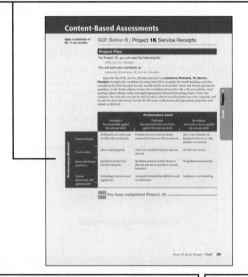

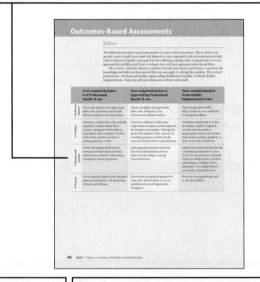

Student CD – All student data files readily available on a CD that comes with the book.

Podcasts – Videos that teach some of the more difficult topics when working with Microsoft applications.

Student Videos – A visual and audio walk-through of every A and B project in the book (see sample images on following page).

 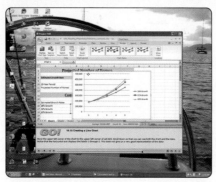 

Student Videos! –

Each chapter comes with two videos that include audio, demonstrating the objectives and activities taught in the chapter.

Instructor Materials

All Instructor materials available on the IRCD

Annotated Instructor Edition – An instructor tool includes a full copy of the student textbook annotated with teaching tips, discussion topics, and other useful pieces for teaching each chapter.

Assignment Sheets – Lists all the assignments for the chapter. Just add in the course information, due dates, and points. Providing these to students ensures they will know what is due and when.

Scripted Lectures – Classroom lectures prepared for you.

Annotated Solution Files – Coupled with the assignment tags, these create a grading and scoring system that makes grading so much easier for you.

PowerPoint Lectures – PowerPoint presentations for each chapter.

Scoring Rubrics – Can be used either by students to check their work or by you as a quick check-off for the items that need to be corrected.

Syllabus Templates – For 8-week, 12-week, and 16-week courses.

Test Bank – Includes a variety of test questions for each chapter.

Companion Website – Online content such as the Online Study Guide, Glossary, and Student Data Files are all at www.pearsonhighered.com/go.

Using the Common Features of Microsoft Office 2010

OUTCOMES

At the end of this chapter you will be able to:

OBJECTIVES

Mastering these objectives will enable you to:

PROJECT 1A

Create, save, and print
a Microsoft Office 2010 file.

1. Use Windows Explorer to Locate Files and Folders (p. 3)
2. Locate and Start a Microsoft Office 2010 Program (p. 6)
3. Enter and Edit Text in an Office 2010 Program (p. 9)
4. Perform Commands from a Dialog Box (p. 11)
5. Create a Folder, Save a File, and Close a Program (p. 13)
6. Add Document Properties and Print a File (p. 18)

PROJECT 1B

Use the Ribbon and dialog
boxes to perform common
commands in a Microsoft
Office 2010 file.

7. Open an Existing File and Save It with a New Name (p. 22)
8. Explore Options for an Application (p. 25)
9. Perform Commands from the Ribbon (p. 26)
10. Apply Formatting in Office Programs (p. 32)
11. Use the Microsoft Office 2010 Help System (p. 43)
12. Compress Files (p. 44)

olly/Shutterstock

In This Chapter

In this chapter, you will use Windows Explorer to navigate the Windows folder structure, create a folder, and save files in Microsoft Office 2010 programs. You will also practice using the features of Microsoft Office 2010 that are common across the major programs that comprise the Microsoft Office 2010 suite. These common features include creating, saving, and printing files.

Common features also include the new Paste Preview and Microsoft Office Backstage view. You will apply formatting, perform commands, and compress files. You will see that creating professional-quality documents is easy and quick in Microsoft Office 2010, and that finding your way around is fast and efficient.

The projects in this chapter relate to **Oceana Palm Grill**, which is a chain of 25 casual, full-service restaurants based in Austin, Texas. The Oceana Palm Grill owners plan an aggressive expansion program. To expand by 15 additional restaurants in North Carolina and Florida by 2018, the company must attract new investors, develop new menus, and recruit new employees, all while adhering to the company's quality guidelines and maintaining its reputation for excellent service. To succeed, the company plans to build on its past success and maintain its quality elements.

Project 1A PowerPoint File

myitlab Project 1A Training

Project Activities

In Activities 1.01 through 1.06, you will create a PowerPoint file, save it in a folder that you create by using Windows Explorer, and then print the file or submit it electronically as directed by your instructor. Your completed PowerPoint slide will look similar to Figure 1.1.

Project Files

For Project 1A, you will need the following file:

New blank PowerPoint presentation

You will save your file as:

Lastname_Firstname_1A_Menu_Plan

Project Results

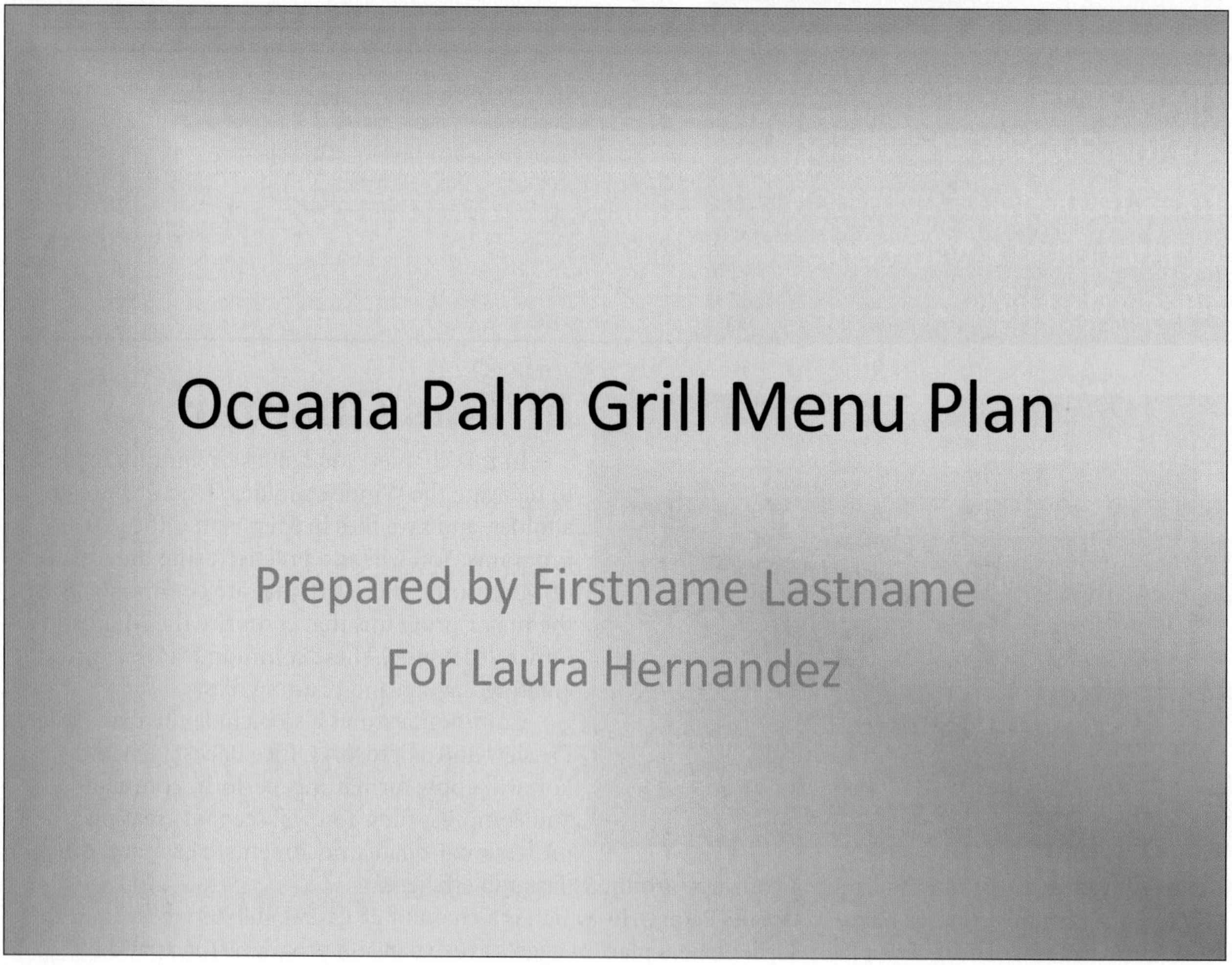
Oceana Palm Grill Menu Plan
Prepared by Firstname Lastname
For Laura Hernandez

Figure 1.1
Project 1A Menu Plan

Objective 1 | Use Windows Explorer to Locate Files and Folders

A *file* is a collection of information stored on a computer under a single name, for example, a Word document or a PowerPoint presentation. Every file is stored in a *folder*—a container in which you store files—or a *subfolder*, which is a folder within a folder. Your Windows operating system stores and organizes your files and folders, which is a primary task of an operating system.

You *navigate*—explore within the organizing structure of Windows—to create, save, and find your files and folders by using the *Windows Explorer* program. Windows Explorer displays the files and folders on your computer, and is at work anytime you are viewing the contents of files and folders in a *window*. A window is a rectangular area on a computer screen in which programs and content appear; a window can be moved, resized, minimized, or closed.

Activity 1.01 | Using Windows Explorer to Locate Files and Folders

1 Turn on your computer and display the Windows *desktop*—the opening screen in Windows that simulates your work area.

> **Note | Comparing Your Screen with the Figures in This Textbook**
>
> Your screen will match the figures shown in this textbook if you set your screen resolution to 1024 × 768. At other resolutions, your screen will closely resemble, but not match, the figures shown. To view your screen's resolution, on the Windows 7 desktop, right-click in a blank area, and then click Screen resolution. In Windows Vista, right-click a blank area, click Personalize, and then click Display Settings. In Windows XP, right-click the desktop, click Properties, and then click the Settings tab.

2 In your CD/DVD tray, insert the **Student CD** that accompanies this textbook. Wait a few moments for an **AutoPlay** window to display. Compare your screen with Figure 1.2.

> *AutoPlay* is a Windows feature that lets you choose which program to use to start different kinds of media, such as music CDs, or CDs and DVDs containing photos; it displays when you plug in or insert media or storage devices.

> **Note | If You Do Not Have the Student CD**
>
> If you do not have the Student CD, consult the inside back flap of this textbook for instructions on how to download the files from the Pearson Web site.

Figure 1.2

AutoPlay window ——

Close button ——

Windows desktop (yours may vary in color and arrangement) ——

3 In the upper right corner of the **AutoPlay** window, move your mouse over—*point* to—the **Close** button ![Close button], and then *click*—press the left button on your mouse pointing device one time.

4 On the left side of the **Windows taskbar**, click the **Start** button 🔵 to display the **Start menu**. Compare your screen with Figure 1.3.

> The *Windows taskbar* is the area along the lower edge of the desktop that contains the *Start button* and an area to display buttons for open programs. The Start button displays the *Start menu*, which provides a list of choices and is the main gateway to your computer's programs, folders, and settings.

Figure 1.3

Computer on Start menu
Start menu (your array of programs may vary)
Windows 7 taskbar
Start button

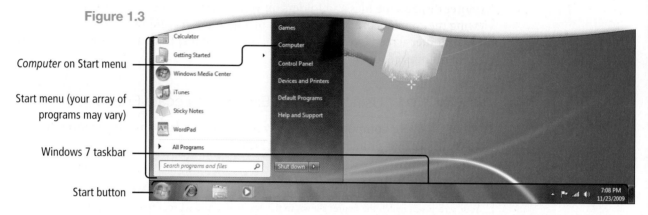

5 On the right side of the **Start menu**, click **Computer** to see the disk drives and other hardware connected to your computer. Compare your screen with Figure 1.4, and then take a moment to study the table in Figure 1.5.

> The *folder window* for *Computer* displays. A folder window displays the contents of the current folder, *library*, or device, and contains helpful parts so that you can navigate within Windows.

> In Windows 7, a library is a collection of items, such as files and folders, assembled from *various locations*; the locations might be on your computer, an external hard drive, removable media, or someone else's computer.

> The difference between a folder and a library is that a library can include files stored in *different locations*—any disk drive, folder, or other place that you can store files and folders.

Figure 1.4

Back and Forward
Address bar
File list
Navigation pane
Folder window toolbar
Views button
Search box
Preview pane button
Details pane

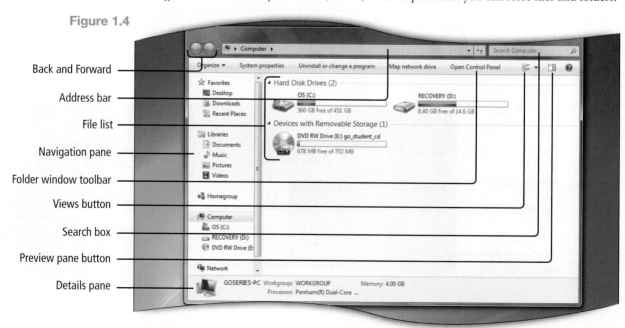

Window Part	Use to:
Address bar	Navigate to a different folder or library, or go back to a previous one.
Back and Forward buttons	Navigate to other folders or libraries you have already opened without closing the current window. These buttons work in conjunction with the address bar; that is, after you use the address bar to change folders, you can use the Back button to return to the previous folder.
Details pane	Display the most common file properties—information about a file, such as the author, the date you last changed the file, and any descriptive *tags*, which are custom file properties that you create to help find and organize your files.
File list	Display the contents of the current folder or library. In Computer, the file list displays the disk drives.
Folder window for *Computer*	Display the contents of the current folder, library, or device. The Folder window contains helpful features so that you can navigate within Windows.
Folder window toolbar	Perform common tasks, such as changing the view of your files and folders or burning files to a CD. The buttons available change to display only relevant tasks.
Navigation pane	Navigate to, open, and display favorites, libraries, folders, saved searches, and an expandable list of drives.
Preview pane button	Display (if you have chosen to open this pane) the contents of most files without opening them in a program. To open the preview pane, click the Preview pane button on the toolbar to turn it on and off.
Search box	Look for an item in the current folder or library by typing a word or phrase in the search box.
Views button	Choose how to view the contents of the current location.

Figure 1.5

6 On the toolbar of the **Computer** folder window, click the **Views button arrow** 🔲 — the small arrow to the right of the Views button—to display a list of views that you can apply to the file list. If necessary, on the list, click **Tiles**.

The Views button is a *split button*; clicking the main part of the button performs a *command* and clicking the arrow opens a menu or list. A command is an instruction to a computer program that causes an action to be carried out.

When you open a folder or a library, you can change how the files display in the file list. For example, you might prefer to see large or small *icons*—pictures that represent a program, a file, a folder, or some other object—or an arrangement that lets you see various types of information about each file. Each time you click the Views button, the window changes, cycling through several views—additional view options are available by clicking the Views button arrow.

Another Way

Point to the CD/DVD drive, right-click, and then click Open.

7 In the **file list**, under **Devices with Removable Storage**, point to your **CD/DVD Drive**, and then *double-click*—click the left mouse button two times in rapid succession—to display the list of folders on the CD. Compare your screen with Figure 1.6.

When double-clicking, keep your hand steady between clicks; this is more important than the speed of the two clicks.

Figure 1.6

Views button indicates
Details view

List of folders on the
CD in Details view

Views button arrow

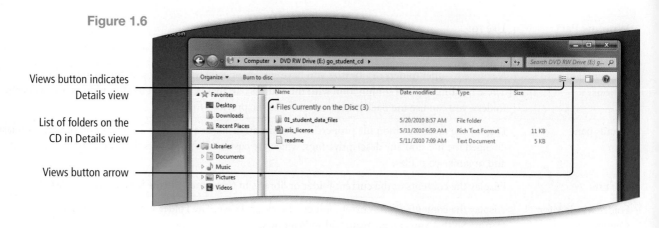

---

8 In the **file list**, point to the folder **01_student_data_files** and double-click to display the list of subfolders in the folder. Double-click to open the folder **01_common_features**. Compare your screen with Figure 1.7.

The Student Resource CD includes files that you will use to complete the projects in this textbook. If you prefer, you can also copy the **01_student_data_files** folder to a location on your computer's hard drive or to a removable device such as a *USB flash drive*, which is a small storage device that plugs into a computer USB port. Your instructor might direct you to other locations where these files are located; for example, on your learning management system.

Figure 1.7

Address bar displays
sequence of folders

One folder in the
01_common_features
folder

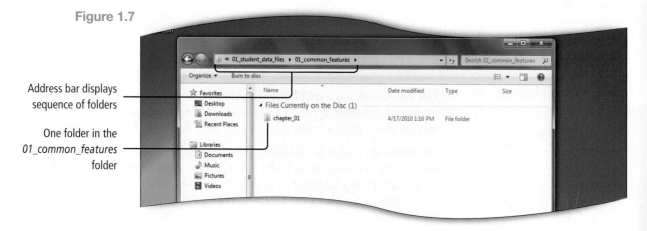

---

9 In the upper right corner of the **Computer** window, click the **Close** button to redisplay your desktop.

Objective 2 | Locate and Start a Microsoft Office 2010 Program

Microsoft Office 2010 includes programs, servers, and services for individuals, small organizations, and large enterprises. A *program*, also referred to as an *application*, is a set of instructions used by a computer to perform a task, such as word processing or accounting.

Activity 1.02 | Locating and Starting a Microsoft Office 2010 Program

1 On the **Windows taskbar**, click the **Start** button 🌐 to display the **Start** menu.

2 From the displayed **Start** menu, locate the group of **Microsoft Office 2010** programs on your computer—the Office program icons from which you can start the program may be located on your Start menu, in a Microsoft Office folder on the **All Programs** list, on your desktop, or any combination of these locations; the location will vary depending on how your computer is configured.

> *All Programs* is an area of the Start menu that displays all the available programs on your computer system.

3 Examine Figure 1.8, and notice the programs that are included in the Microsoft Office Professional Plus 2010 group of programs. (Your group of programs may vary.)

> *Microsoft Word* is a word processing program, with which you create and share documents by using its writing tools.

> *Microsoft Excel* is a spreadsheet program, with which you calculate and analyze numbers and create charts.

> *Microsoft Access* is a database program, with which you can collect, track, and report data.

> *Microsoft PowerPoint* is a presentation program, with which you can communicate information with high-impact graphics and video.

> Additional popular Office programs include *Microsoft Outlook* to manage e-mail and organizational activities, *Microsoft Publisher* to create desktop publishing documents such as brochures, and *Microsoft OneNote* to manage notes that you make at meetings or in classes and to share notes with others on the Web.

> The Professional Plus version of Office 2010 also includes *Microsoft SharePoint Workspace* to share information with others in a team environment and *Microsoft InfoPath Designer and Filler* to create forms and gather data.

Figure 1.8

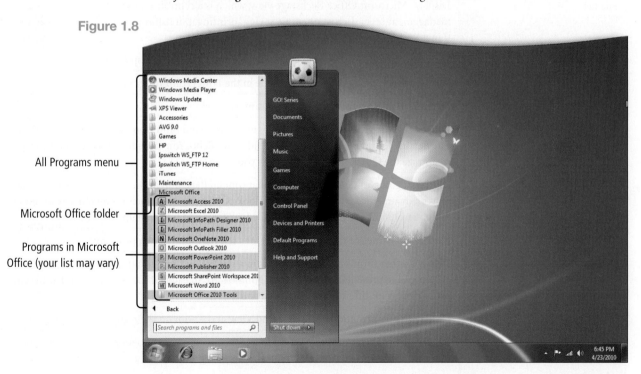

All Programs menu

Microsoft Office folder

Programs in Microsoft Office (your list may vary)

4 Click to open the program **Microsoft PowerPoint 2010**. Compare your screen with Figure 1.9, and then take a moment to study the description of these screen elements in the table in Figure 1.10.

Figure 1.9

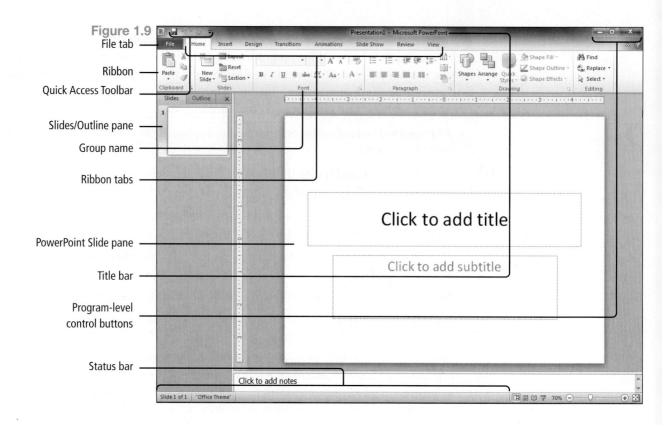

File tab

Ribbon

Quick Access Toolbar

Slides/Outline pane

Group name

Ribbon tabs

PowerPoint Slide pane

Title bar

Program-level control buttons

Status bar

Click to add title

Click to add subtitle

Screen Element	Description
File tab	Displays Microsoft Office Backstage view, which is a centralized space for all of your file management tasks such as opening, saving, printing, publishing, or sharing a file—all the things you can do *with* a file.
Group names	Indicate the name of the groups of related commands on the displayed tab.
PowerPoint Slide pane	Displays a large image of the active slide in the PowerPoint program.
Program-level control buttons	Minimizes, restores, or closes the program window.
Quick Access Toolbar	Displays buttons to perform frequently used commands and resources with a single click. The default commands include Save, Undo, and Redo. You can add and delete buttons to customize the Quick Access Toolbar for your convenience.
Ribbon	Displays a group of task-oriented tabs that contain the commands, styles, and resources you need to work in an Office 2010 program. The look of your Ribbon depends on your screen resolution. A high resolution will display more individual items and button names on the Ribbon.
Ribbon tabs	Display the names of the task-oriented tabs relevant to the open program.
Slides/Outline pane	Displays either thumbnails of the slides in a PowerPoint presentation (Slides tab) or the outline of the presentation's content (Outline tab). In each Office 2010 program, different panes display in different ways to assist you.
Status bar	Displays file information on the left and View and Zoom on the right.
Title bar	Displays the name of the file and the name of the program. The program window control buttons—Minimize, Maximize/Restore Down, and Close—are grouped on the right side of the title bar.

Figure 1.10

Objective 3 | Enter and Edit Text in an Office 2010 Program

All of the programs in Office 2010 require some typed text. Your keyboard is still the primary method of entering information into your computer. Techniques to *edit*—make changes to—text are similar among all of the Office 2010 programs.

Activity 1.03 | Entering and Editing Text in an Office 2010 Program

1 In the middle of the PowerPoint Slide pane, point to the text *Click to add title* to display the $\boxed{I}$ pointer, and then click one time.

> The *insertion point*—a blinking vertical line that indicates where text or graphics will be inserted—displays.
>
> In Office 2010 programs, the mouse *pointer*—any symbol that displays on your screen in response to moving your mouse device—displays in different shapes depending on the task you are performing and the area of the screen to which you are pointing.

2 Type **Oceana Grille Info** and notice how the insertion point moves to the right as you type. Point slightly to the right of the letter *e* in *Grille* and click to place the insertion point there. Compare your screen with Figure 1.11.

Figure 1.11

Insertion point —

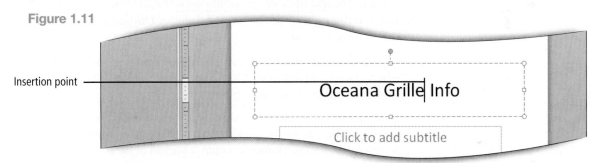

3 On your keyboard, locate and press the $\boxed{\text{Backspace}}$ key to delete the letter *e*.

> Pressing $\boxed{\text{Backspace}}$ removes a character to the left of the insertion point.

4 Point slightly to the left of the *I* in *Info* and click one time to place the insertion point there. Type **Menu** and then press $\boxed{\text{Spacebar}}$ one time. Compare your screen with Figure 1.12.

> By *default*, when you type text in an Office program, existing text moves to the right to make space for new typing. Default refers to the current selection or setting that is automatically used by a program unless you specify otherwise.

Figure 1.12

Menu inserted —

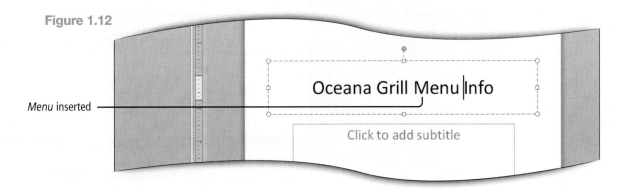

5 Press ⏍Del⏎ four times to delete *Info* and then type **Plan**

> Pressing ⏍Del⏎ removes—deletes—a character to the right of the insertion point.

6 With your insertion point blinking after the word *Plan*, on your keyboard, hold down the ⏍Ctrl⏎ key. While holding down ⏍Ctrl⏎, press ⏍←⏎ three times to move the insertion point to the beginning of the word *Grill*.

> This is a **keyboard shortcut**—a key or combination of keys that performs a task that would otherwise require a mouse. This keyboard shortcut moves the insertion point to the beginning of the previous word.
>
> A keyboard shortcut is commonly indicated as ⏍Ctrl⏎ + ⏍←⏎ (or some other combination of keys) to indicate that you hold down the first key while pressing the second key. A keyboard shortcut can also include three keys, in which case you hold down the first two and then press the third. For example, ⏍Ctrl⏎ + ⏍Shift⏎ + ⏍←⏎ selects one word to the left.

7 With the insertion point blinking at the beginning of the word *Grill*, type **Palm** and press ⏍Spacebar⏎.

8 Click anywhere in the text *Click to add subtitle*. With the insertion point blinking, type the following and include the spelling error: **Prepered by Annabel Dunham**

9 With your mouse, point slightly to the left of the *A* in *Annabel*, hold down the left mouse button, and then **drag**—hold down the left mouse button while moving your mouse—to the right to select the text *Annabel Dunham*, and then release the mouse button. Compare your screen with Figure 1.13.

> The **Mini toolbar** displays commands that are commonly used with the selected object, which places common commands close to your pointer. When you move the pointer away from the Mini toolbar, it fades from view.
>
> To **select** refers to highlighting, by dragging with your mouse, areas of text or data or graphics so that the selection can be edited, formatted, copied, or moved. The action of dragging includes releasing the left mouse button at the end of the area you want to select. The Office programs recognize a selected area as one unit, to which you can make changes. Selecting text may require some practice. If you are not satisfied with your result, click anywhere outside of the selection, and then begin again.

Figure 1.13

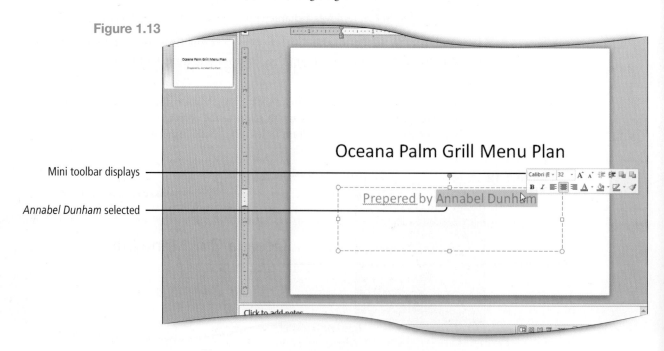

Mini toolbar displays

Annabel Dunham selected

10 With the text *Annabel Dunham* selected, type your own firstname and lastname.

In any Windows-based program, such as the Microsoft Office 2010 programs, selected text is deleted and then replaced when you begin to type new text. You will save time by developing good techniques to select and then edit or replace selected text, which is easier than pressing the Del key numerous times to delete text that you do not want.

11 Notice that the misspelled word *Prepered* displays with a wavy red underline; additionally, all or part of your name might display with a wavy red underline.

Office 2010 has a dictionary of words against which all entered text is checked. In Word and PowerPoint, words that are *not* in the dictionary display a wavy red line, indicating a possible misspelled word or a proper name or an unusual word—none of which are in the Office 2010 dictionary.

In Excel and Access, you can initiate a check of the spelling, but wavy red underlines do not display.

12 Point to *Prepered* and then ***right-click***—click your right mouse button one time.

The Mini toolbar and a ***shortcut menu*** display. A shortcut menu displays commands and options relevant to the selected text or object—known as ***context-sensitive commands*** because they relate to the item you right-clicked.

Here, the shortcut menu displays commands related to the misspelled word. You can click the suggested correct spelling *Prepared*, click Ignore All to ignore the misspelling, add the word to the Office dictionary, or click Spelling to display a ***dialog box***. A dialog box is a small window that contains options for completing a task. Whenever you see a command followed by an ***ellipsis*** (...), which is a set of three dots indicating incompleteness, clicking the command will always display a dialog box.

13 On the displayed shortcut menu, click **Prepared** to correct the misspelled word. If necessary, point to any parts of your name that display a wavy red underline, right-click, and then on the shortcut menu, click Ignore All so that Office will no longer mark your name with a wavy underline in this file.

More Knowledge | Adding to the Office Dictionary

The main dictionary contains the most common words, but does not include all proper names, technical terms, or acronyms. You can add words, acronyms, and proper names to the Office dictionary by clicking Add to Dictionary when they are flagged, and you might want to do so for your own name and other proper names and terms that you type often.

Objective 4 | Perform Commands from a Dialog Box

In a dialog box, you make decisions about an individual object or topic. A dialog box also offers a way to adjust a number of settings at one time.

Activity 1.04 | Performing Commands from a Dialog Box

1 Point anywhere in the blank area above the title *Oceana Palm Grill Menu Plan* to display the ⌖ pointer.

2 Right-click to display a shortcut menu. Notice the command *Format Background* followed by an ellipsis (...). Compare your screen with Figure 1.14.

Recall that a command followed by an ellipsis indicates that a dialog box will display if you click the command.

Figure 1.14

Shortcut menu ⸻

Ellipsis following command ⸻

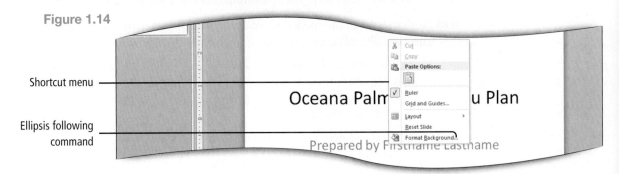

3 Click **Format Background** to display the **Format Background** dialog box, and then compare your screen with Figure 1.15.

Figure 1.15

Fill selected ⸻

Format Background dialog box ⸻

Options related to the background fill ⸻

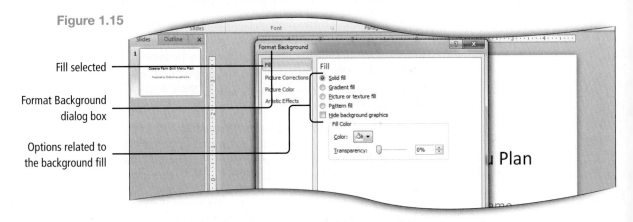

4 On the left, if necessary, click **Fill** to display the **Fill** options.

Fill is the inside color of an object. Here, the dialog box displays the option group names on the left; some dialog boxes provide a set of tabs across the top from which you can display different sets of options.

5 On the right, under **Fill**, click the **Gradient fill** option button.

The dialog box displays additional settings related to the gradient fill option. An *option button* is a round button that enables you to make one choice among two or more options. In a gradient fill, one color fades into another.

6 Click the **Preset colors arrow**—the arrow in the box to the right of the text *Preset colors*—and then in the gallery, in the second row, point to the fifth fill color to display the ScreenTip *Fog*.

A *gallery* is an Office feature that displays a list of potential results. A *ScreenTip* displays useful information about mouse actions, such as pointing to screen elements or dragging.

7 Click **Fog**, and then notice that the fill color is applied to your slide. Click the **Type arrow**, and then click **Rectangular** to change the pattern of the fill color. Compare your screen with Figure 1.16.

Figure 1.16

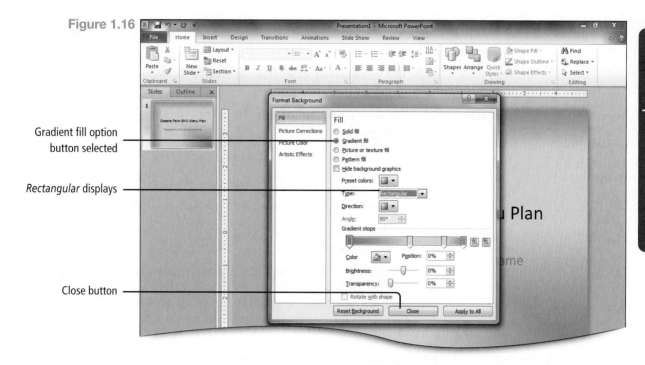

Gradient fill option button selected

Rectangular displays

Close button

8 At the bottom of the dialog box, click **Close**.

As you progress in your study of Microsoft Office, you will practice using many dialog boxes and applying dramatic effects such as this to your Word documents, Excel spreadsheets, Access databases, and PowerPoint slides.

Objective 5 | Create a Folder, Save a File, and Close a Program

A *location* is any disk drive, folder, or other place in which you can store files and folders. Where you store your files depends on how and where you use your data. For example, for your classes, you might decide to store primarily on a removable USB flash drive so that you can carry your files to different locations and access your files on different computers.

If you do most of your work on a single computer, for example your home desktop system or your laptop computer that you take with you to school or work, store your files in one of the Libraries—Documents, Music, Pictures, or Videos—provided by your Windows operating system.

Although the Windows operating system helps you to create and maintain a logical folder structure, take the time to name your files and folders in a consistent manner.

Activity 1.05 | Creating a Folder, Saving a File, and Closing a Program

A PowerPoint presentation is an example of a file. Office 2010 programs use a common dialog box provided by the Windows operating system to assist you in saving files. In this activity, you will create a folder on a USB flash drive in which to store files. If you prefer to store on your hard drive, you can use similar steps to store files in your My Documents folder in your Documents library.

1 Insert a USB flash drive into your computer, and if necessary, **Close** [×] the **AutoPlay** dialog box. If you are not using a USB flash drive, go to Step 2.

> As the first step in saving a file, determine where you want to save the file, and if necessary, insert a storage device.

2 At the top of your screen, in the title bar, notice that *Presentation1 – Microsoft PowerPoint* displays.

> Most Office 2010 programs open with a new unsaved file with a default name—*Presentation1, Document1*, and so on. As you create your file, your work is temporarily stored in the computer's memory until you initiate a Save command, at which time you must choose a file name and location in which to save your file.

3 In the upper left corner of your screen, click the **File tab** to display **Microsoft Office Backstage** view. Compare your screen with Figure 1.17.

> Microsoft Office *Backstage view* is a centralized space for tasks related to *file* management; that is why the tab is labeled *File*. File management tasks include, for example, opening, saving, printing, publishing, or sharing a file. The *Backstage tabs*—*Info, Recent, New, Print, Save & Send*, and *Help*—display along the left side. The tabs group file-related tasks together.

> Above the Backstage tabs, *Quick Commands*—*Save, Save As, Open*, and *Close*—display for quick access to these commands. When you click any of these commands, Backstage view closes and either a dialog box displays or the active file closes.

> Here, the *Info tab* displays information—*info*—about the current file. In the center panel, various file management tasks are available in groups. For example, if you click the Protect Presentation button, a list of options that you can set for this file that relate to who can open or edit the presentation displays.

> On the Info tab, in the right panel, you can also examine the *document properties*. Document properties, also known as *metadata*, are details about a file that describe or identify it, such as the title, author name, subject, and keywords that identify the document's topic or contents. On the Info page, a thumbnail image of the current file displays in the upper right corner, which you can click to close Backstage view and return to the document.

More Knowledge | Deciding Where to Store Your Files

Where should you store your files? In the libraries created by Windows 7 (Documents, Pictures, and so on)? On a removable device like a flash drive or external hard drive? In Windows 7, it is easy to find your files, especially if you use the libraries. Regardless of where you save a file, Windows 7 will make it easy to find the file again, even if you are not certain where it might be.

In Windows 7, storing all of your files within a library makes sense. If you perform most of your work on your desktop system or your laptop that travels with you, you can store your files in the libraries created by Windows 7 for your user account—Documents, Pictures, Music, and so on. Within these libraries, you can create folders and subfolders to organize your data. These libraries are a good choice for storing your files because:

- From the Windows Explorer button on the taskbar, your libraries are always just one click away.
- The libraries are designed for their contents; for example, the Pictures folder displays small images of your digital photos.
- You can add new locations to a library; for example, an external hard drive, or a network drive. Locations added to a library behave just like they are on your hard drive.
- Other users of your computer cannot access your libraries.
- The libraries are the default location for opening and saving files within an application, so you will find that you can open and save files with fewer navigation clicks.

Figure 1.17

Save command

Information about the file you are working on

Info tab selected

Backstage tabs, Info tab active

Groups

Indicates unsaved file with default name

Document Properties

Screen thumbnail

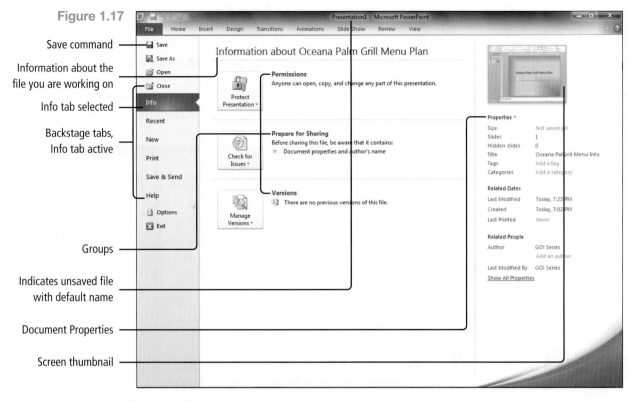

4 Above the **Backstage tabs**, click **Save** to display the **Save As** dialog box.

Backstage view closes and the Save As dialog box, which includes a folder window and an area at the bottom to name the file and set the file type, displays.

When you are saving something for the first time, for example a new PowerPoint presentation, the Save and Save As commands are identical. That is, the Save As dialog box will display if you click Save or if you click Save As.

Note | Saving Your File

After you have named a file and saved it in your desired location, the Save command saves any changes you make to the file without displaying any dialog box. The Save As command will display the Save As dialog box and let you name and save a new file based on the current one—in a location that you choose. After you name and save the new document, the original document closes, and the new document—based on the original one—displays.

---

5 In the **Save As** dialog box, on the left, locate the **navigation pane**; compare your screen with Figure 1.18.

By default, the Save command opens the Documents library unless your default file location has been changed.

Figure 1.18

Save As dialog box
Address bar

Default save location

Navigation pane

File list (yours will vary)

File name box

Save as type defaults to
PowerPoint Presentation

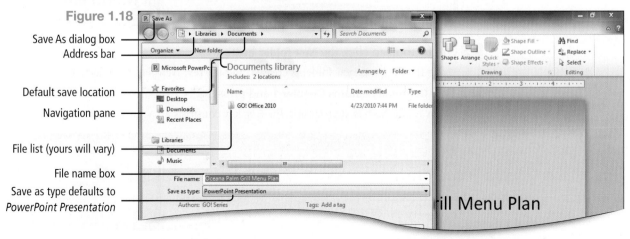

6 On the right side of the **navigation pane**, point to the **scroll bar**. Compare your screen with Figure 1.19.

A *scroll bar* displays when a window, or a pane within a window, has information that is not in view. You can click the up or down scroll arrows—or the left and right scroll arrows in a horizontal scroll bar—to scroll the contents up or down or left and right in small increments.

You can also drag the *scroll box*—the box within the scroll bar—to scroll the window in either direction.

Figure 1.19

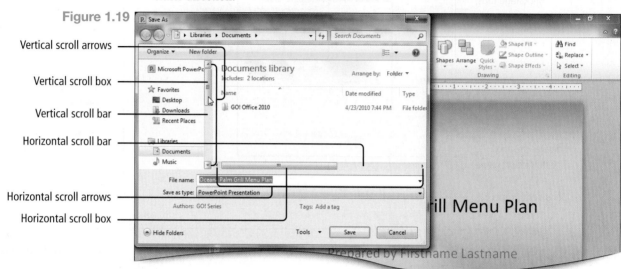

Vertical scroll arrows
Vertical scroll box
Vertical scroll bar
Horizontal scroll bar
Horizontal scroll arrows
Horizontal scroll box

7 Click the **down scroll arrow** as necessary so that you can view the lower portion of the **navigation pane**, and then click the icon for your USB flash drive. Compare your screen with Figure 1.20. (If you prefer to store on your computer's hard drive instead of a USB flash drive, in the navigation pane, click Documents.)

Figure 1.20

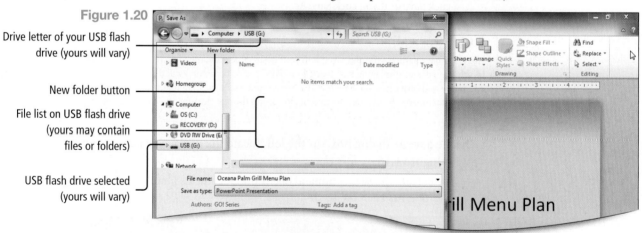

Drive letter of your USB flash drive (yours will vary)
New folder button
File list on USB flash drive (yours may contain files or folders)
USB flash drive selected (yours will vary)

8 On the toolbar, click the **New folder** button.

In the file list, a new folder is created, and the text *New folder* is selected.

9 Type **Common Features Chapter 1** and press Enter. Compare your screen with Figure 1.21.

In Windows-based programs, the Enter key confirms an action.

Figure 1.21

New folder

10 In the **file list**, double-click the name of your new folder to open it and display its name in the **address bar**.

11 In the lower portion of the dialog box, click in the **File name** box to select the existing text. Notice that Office inserts the text at the beginning of the presentation as a suggested file name.

12 On your keyboard, locate the [-] key. Notice that the Shift of this key produces the underscore character. With the text still selected, type **Lastname_Firstname_1A_ Menu_Plan** Compare your screen with Figure 1.22.

> You can use spaces in file names, however some individuals prefer not to use spaces. Some programs, especially when transferring files over the Internet, may not work well with spaces in file names. In general, however, unless you encounter a problem, it is OK to use spaces. In this textbook, underscores are used instead of spaces in file names.

Figure 1.22

File name box indicates your file name

Save as type box indicates *PowerPoint Presentation*

Save button

13 In the lower right corner, click **Save**; or press [Enter]. See Figure 1.23.

> Your new file name displays in the title bar, indicating that the file has been saved to a location that you have specified.

Figure 1.23

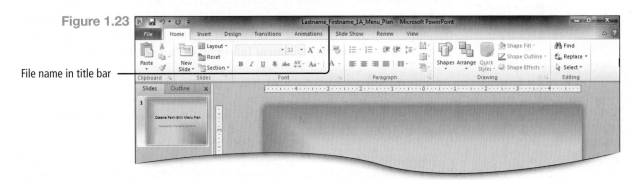

File name in title bar

14 In the text that begins *Prepared by*, click to position the insertion point at the end of your name, and then press [Enter] to move to a new line. Type **For Laura Hernandez**

15 Click the **File tab** to display **Backstage** view. At the top of the center panel, notice that the path where your file is stored displays. Above the Backstage tabs, click **Close** to close the file. In the message box, click **Save** to save the changes you made and close the file. Leave PowerPoint open.

> PowerPoint displays a message asking if you want to save the changes you have made. Because you have made additional changes to the file since your last Save operation, an Office program will always prompt you to save so that you do not lose any new data.

Objective 6 | Add Document Properties and Print a File

The process of printing a file is similar in all of the Office applications. There are differences in the types of options you can select. For example, in PowerPoint, you have the option of printing the full slide, with each slide printing on a full sheet of paper, or of printing handouts with small pictures of slides on a page.

Activity 1.06 | Adding Document Properties and Printing a File

> **Alert! | Are You Printing or Submitting Your Files Electronically?**
>
> If you are submitting your files electronically only, or have no printer attached, you can still complete this activity. Complete Steps 1-9, and then submit your file electronically as directed by your instructor.

1 In the upper left corner, click the **File tab** to display **Backstage** view. Notice that the **Recent tab** displays.

> Because no file was open in PowerPoint, Office applies predictive logic to determine that your most likely action will be to open a PowerPoint presentation that you worked on recently. Thus, the Recent tab displays a list of PowerPoint presentations that were recently open on your system.

2 At the top of the **Recent Presentations** list, click your **Lastname_Firstname_1A_Menu_Plan** file to open it.

3 Click the **File tab** to redisplay **Backstage** view. On the right, under the screen thumbnail, click **Properties**, and then click **Show Document Panel**. In the **Author** box, delete the existing text, and then type your firstname and lastname. Notice that in PowerPoint, some variation of the slide title is automatically inserted in the Title box. In the **Subject** box, type your Course name and section number. In the **Keywords** box, type **menu plan** and then in the upper right corner of the **Document Properties** panel, click the **Close the Document Information Panel** button ⊠.

> Adding properties to your documents will make them easier to search for in systems such as Microsoft SharePoint.

Another Way

Press Ctrl + P or Ctrl + F2 to display the Print tab in Backstage view.

4 Redisplay **Backstage** view, and then click the **Print tab**. Compare your screen with Figure 1.24.

> On the Print tab in Backstage view, in the center panel, three groups of printing-related tasks display—Print, Printer, and Settings. In the right panel, the *Print Preview* displays, which is a view of a document as it will appear on the paper when you print it.

> At the bottom of the Print Preview area, on the left, the number of pages and arrows with which you can move among the pages in Print Preview display. On the right, *Zoom* settings enable you to shrink or enlarge the Print Preview. Zoom is the action of increasing or decreasing the viewing area of the screen.

Figure 1.24

Your default printer (yours may differ)

Three groups of printing-related tasks: *Print, Printer, Settings*

Print tab selected in Backstage view

Print Preview (yours may display in shades of gray if a non-color printer is attached)

Color (yours may differ if a non-color printer is attached)

Zoom tools

Page navigation arrows

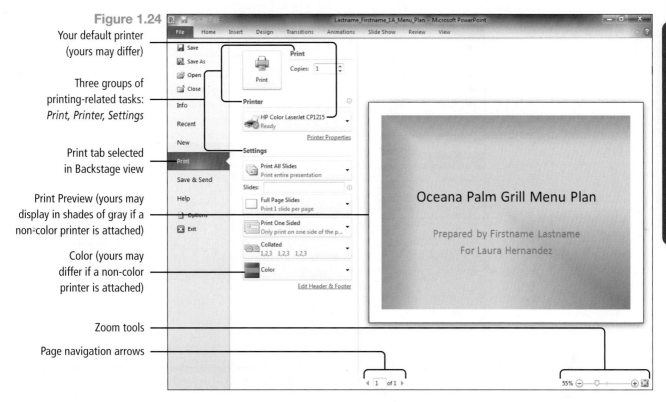

5 Locate the **Settings group**, and notice that the default setting is to **Print All Slides** and to print **Full Page Slides**—each slide on a full sheet of paper.

6 Point to **Full Page Slides**, notice that the button glows orange, and then click the button to display a gallery of print arrangements. Compare your screen with Figure 1.25.

Figure 1.25

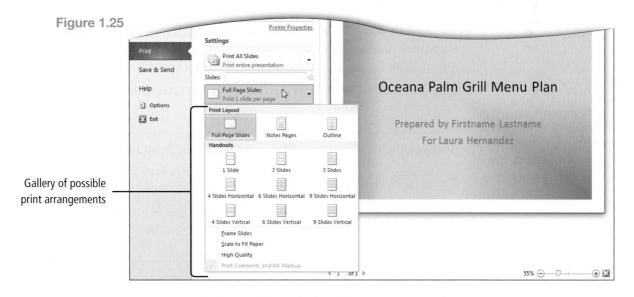

Gallery of possible print arrangements

7 In the displayed gallery, under **Handouts**, click **1 Slide**, and then compare your screen with Figure 1.26.

The Print Preview changes to show how your slide will print on the paper in this arrangement.

Figure 1.26

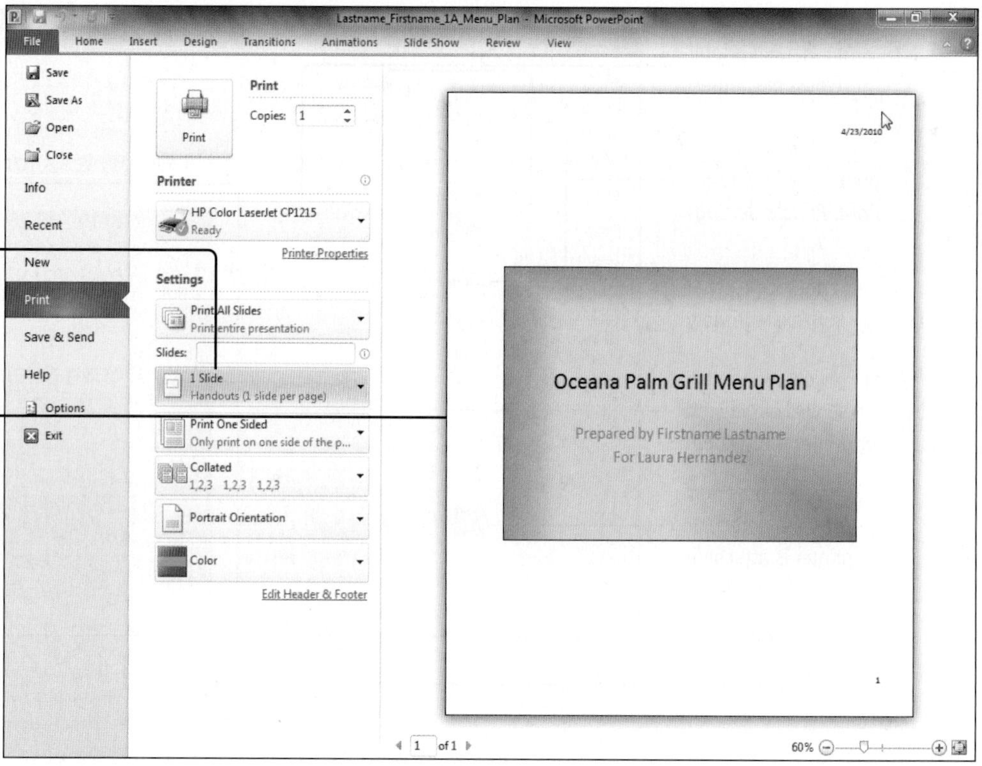

Handouts selected

Print Preview displays
the 1 slide printed as
handouts setting

8 To submit your file electronically, skip this step and move to Step 9. To print your slide, be sure your system is connected to a printer, and then in the **Print group**, click the **Print** button. On the Quick Access Toolbar, click **Save** 💾, and then move to Step 10.

> The handout will print on your default printer—on a black and white printer, the colors will print in shades of gray. Backstage view closes and your file redisplays in the PowerPoint window.

9 To submit your file electronically, above the **Backstage tabs**, click **Close** to close the file and close **Backstage** view, click **Save** in the displayed message, and then follow the instructions provided by your instructor to submit your file electronically.

Another Way

In the upper right corner of your PowerPoint window, click the red Close button.

10 Display **Backstage** view, and then below the **Backstage tabs**, click **Exit** to close your file and close PowerPoint.

More Knowledge | Creating a PDF as an Electronic Printout

From Backstage view, you can save an Office file as a *PDF file*. *Portable Document Format* (PDF) creates an image of your file that preserves the look of your file, but that cannot be easily changed. This is a popular format for sending documents electronically, because the document will display on most computers. From Backstage view, click Save & Send, and then in the File Types group, click Create PDF/XPS Document. Then in the third panel, click the Create PDF/XPS button, navigate to your chapter folder, and then in the lower right corner, click Publish.

End **You have completed Project 1A** ————————————————

Project 1B Word File

Project Activities

In Activities 1.07 through 1.16, you will open, edit, save, and then compress a Word file. Your completed document will look similar to Figure 1.27.

Project Files

For Project 1B, you will need the following file:

cf01B_Cheese_Promotion

You will save your Word document as:

Lastname_Firstname_1B_Cheese_Promotion

Project Results

Memo

TO: Laura Mabry Hernandez, General Manager

FROM: Donna Jackson, Executive Chef

DATE: December 17, 2014

SUBJECT: Cheese Specials on Tuesdays

To increase restaurant traffic between 4:00 p.m. and 6:00 p.m., I am proposing a trial cheese event in one of the restaurants, probably Orlando. I would like to try a weekly event on Tuesday evenings where the focus is on a good selection of cheese.

I envision two possibilities: a selection of cheese plates or a cheese bar—or both. The cheeses would have to be matched with compatible fruit and bread or crackers. They could be used as appetizers, or for desserts, as is common in Europe. The cheese plates should be varied and diverse, using a mixture of hard and soft, sharp and mild, unusual and familiar.

I am excited about this new promotion. If done properly, I think it could increase restaurant traffic in the hours when individuals want to relax with a small snack instead of a heavy dinner.

The promotion will require that our employees become familiar with the types and characteristics of both foreign and domestic cheeses. Let's meet to discuss the details and the training requirements, and to create a flyer that begins something like this:

Oceana Palm Grill Tuesday Cheese Tastings

Lastname_Firstname_1B_Cheese_Promotion

Figure 1.27
Project 1B Cheese Promotion

Objective 7 | Open an Existing File and Save It with a New Name

In any Office program, use the Open command to display the **Open dialog box**, from which you can navigate to and then open an existing file that was created in that same program.

The Open dialog box, along with the Save and Save As dialog boxes, are referred to as **common dialog boxes**. These dialog boxes, which are provided by the Windows programming interface, display in all of the Office programs in the same manner. Thus, the Open, Save, and Save As dialog boxes will all look and perform the same in each Office program.

Activity 1.07 | Opening an Existing File and Saving it with a New Name

In this activity, you will display the Open dialog box, open an existing Word document, and then save it in your storage location with a new name.

1 Determine the location of the student data files that accompany this textbook, and be sure you can access these files.

> For example:
>
> If you are accessing the files from the Student CD that came with this textbook, insert the CD now.
>
> If you copied the files from the Student CD or from the Pearson Web site to a USB flash drive that you are using for this course, insert the flash drive in your computer now.
>
> If you copied the files to the hard drive of your computer, for example in your Documents library, be sure you can locate the files on the hard drive.

2 Determine the location of your **Common Features Chapter 1** folder you created in Activity 1.05, in which you will store your work from this chapter, and then be sure you can access that folder.

> For example:
>
> If you created your chapter folder on a USB flash drive, insert the flash drive in your computer now. This can be the same flash drive where you have stored the student data files; just be sure to use the chapter folder you created.
>
> If you created your chapter folder in the Documents library on your computer, be sure you can locate the folder. Otherwise, create a new folder at the computer at which you are working, or on a USB flash drive.

3 Using the technique you practiced in Activity 1.02, locate and then start the **Microsoft Word 2010** program on your system.

> **Another Way**
>
> In the Word (or other program) window, press [Ctrl] + [F12] to display the Open dialog box.

4 On the Ribbon, click the **File tab** to display **Backstage** view, and then click **Open** to display the **Open** dialog box.

5 In the **navigation pane** on the left, use the scroll bar to scroll as necessary, and then click the location of your student data files to display the location's contents in the **file list**. Compare your screen with Figure 1.28.

> For example:
>
> If you are accessing the files from the Student CD that came with your book, under Computer, click the CD/DVD.
>
> If you are accessing the files from a USB flash drive, under Computer, click the flash drive name.
>
> If you are accessing the files from the Documents library of your computer, under Libraries, click Documents.

Figure 1.28

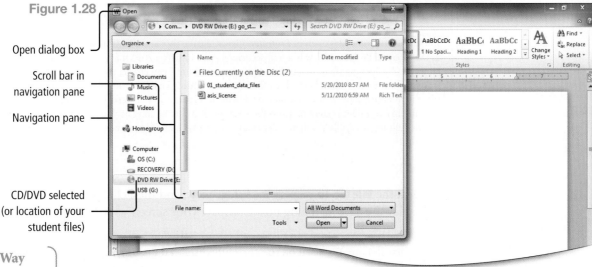

Open dialog box

Scroll bar in
navigation pane

Navigation pane

CD/DVD selected
(or location of your
student files)

Another Way

Point to a folder name,
right-click, and then
from the shortcut
menu, click Open.

6 Point to the folder **01_student_data_files** and double-click to open the folder. Point
to the subfolder **01_common_features**, double-click, and then compare your screen
with Figure 1.29.

Figure 1.29

File list displays
the contents of the
01_common_features folder

Another Way

Click one time to select
the file, and then press
Enter or click the Open
button in the lower
right corner of the
dialog box.

7 In the **file list**, point to the **chapter_01** subfolder and double-click to open it. In the
file list, point to Word file **cf01B_Cheese_Promotion** and then double-click to open
and display the file in the Word window. On the Ribbon, on the **Home tab**, in the
Paragraph group, if necessary, click the **Show/Hide** button ¶ so that it is active—
glowing orange. Compare your screen with Figure 1.30.

On the title bar at the top of the screen, the file name displays. If you opened the document
from the Student CD, (*Read-Only*) will display. If you opened the document from another
source to which the files were copied, (*Read-Only*) might not display. **Read-Only** is a property
assigned to a file that prevents the file from being modified or deleted; it indicates that you
cannot save any changes to the displayed document unless you first save it with a new name.

Figure 1.30

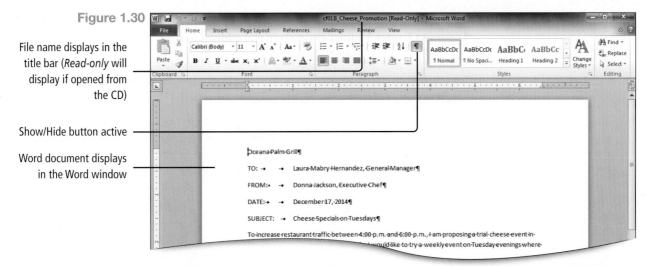

File name displays in the
title bar (*Read-only* will
display if opened from
the CD)

Show/Hide button active

Word document displays
in the Word window

Another Way

Press F12 to display the Save As dialog box.

8 Click the **File tab** to display **Backstage** view, and then click the **Save As** command to display the **Save As** dialog box. Compare your screen with Figure 1.31.

The Save As command displays the Save As dialog box where you can name and save a *new* document based on the currently displayed document. After you name and save the new document, the original document closes, and the new document—based on the original one—displays.

Figure 1.31

Save As dialog box

Navigation pane

Current file name selected

Default type is *Word Document*

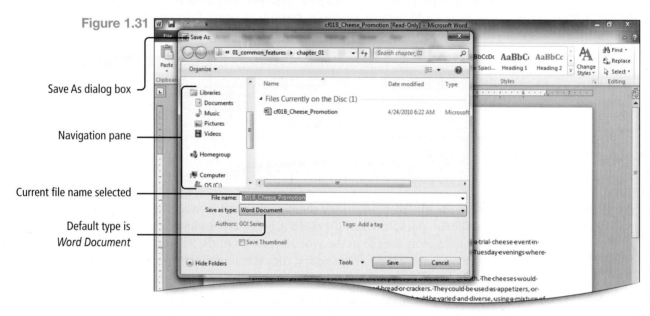

9 In the **navigation pane**, click the location in which you are storing your projects for this chapter—the location where you created your **Common Features Chapter 1** folder; for example, your USB flash drive or the Documents library.

10 In the **file list**, double-click the necessary folders and subfolders until your **Common Features Chapter 1** folder displays in the **address bar**.

11 Click in the **File name** box to select the existing file name, or drag to select the existing text, and then using your own name, type **Lastname_Firstname_1B_Cheese_Promotion** Compare your screen with Figure 1.32.

As you type, the file name from your 1A project might display briefly. Because your 1A project file is stored in this location and you began the new file name with the same text, Office predicts that you might want the same or similar file name. As you type new characters, the suggestion is removed.

Figure 1.32

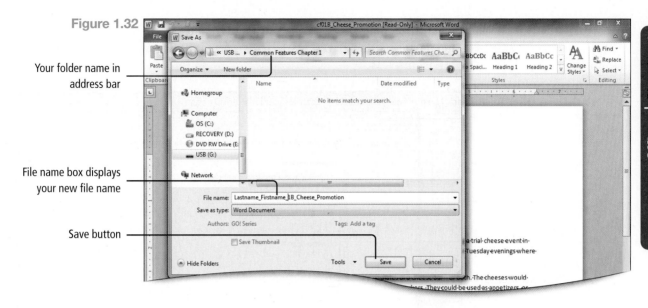

Your folder name in
address bar

File name box displays
your new file name

Save button

12 In the lower right corner of the **Save As** dialog box, click **Save**; or press Enter. Compare your screen with Figure 1.33.

> The original document closes, and your new document, based on the original, displays with the name in the title bar.

Figure 1.33

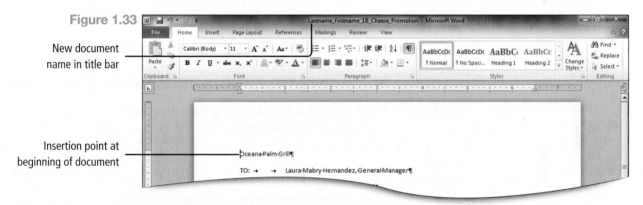

New document
name in title bar

Insertion point at
beginning of document

Objective 8 | Explore Options for an Application

Within each Office application, you can open an *Options dialog box* where you can select program settings and other options and preferences. For example, you can set preferences for viewing and editing files.

Activity 1.08 | Viewing Application Options

1 Click the **File tab** to display **Backstage** view. Under the **Help tab**, click **Options**.

2 In the displayed **Word Options** dialog box, on the left, click **Display**, and then on the right, locate the information under **Always show these formatting marks on the screen**.

> When you press Enter, Spacebar, or Tab on your keyboard, characters display to represent these keystrokes. These screen characters do not print, and are referred to as *formatting marks* or *nonprinting characters*.

3 Under **Always show these formatting marks on the screen**, be sure the last check box, **Show all formatting marks**, is selected—select it if necessary. Compare your screen with Figure 1.34.

Figure 1.34

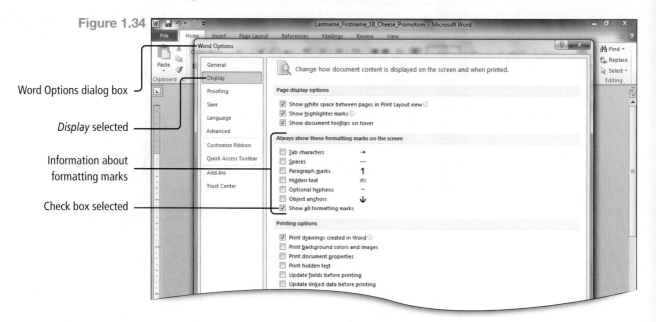

Word Options dialog box

Display selected

Information about formatting marks

Check box selected

4 In the lower right corner of the dialog box, click **OK**.

Objective 9 | Perform Commands from the Ribbon

The *Ribbon*, which displays across the top of the program window, groups commands and features in a manner that you would most logically use them. Each Office program's Ribbon is slightly different, but all contain the same three elements: *tabs*, *groups*, and *commands*.

Tabs display across the top of the Ribbon, and each tab relates to a type of activity; for example, laying out a page. Groups are sets of related commands for specific tasks. Commands—instructions to computer programs—are arranged in groups, and might display as a button, a menu, or a box in which you type information.

You can also minimize the Ribbon so only the tab names display. In the minimized Ribbon view, when you click a tab the Ribbon expands to show the groups and commands, and then when you click a command, the Ribbon returns to its minimized view. Most Office users, however, prefer to leave the complete Ribbon in view at all times.

Activity 1.09 | Performing Commands from the Ribbon

1 Take a moment to examine the document on your screen.

This document is a memo from the Executive Chef to the General Manager regarding a new restaurant promotion.

2 On the Ribbon, click the **View tab**. In the **Show group**, if necessary, click to place a check mark in the **Ruler** check box, and then compare your screen with Figure 1.35.

> When working in Word, display the rulers so that you can see how margin settings affect your document and how text aligns. Additionally, if you set a tab stop or an indent, its location is visible on the ruler.

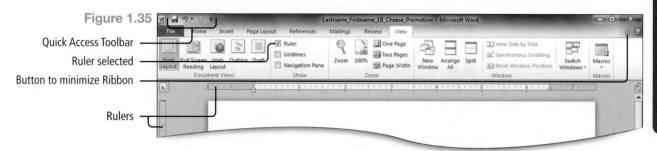

Figure 1.35

Quick Access Toolbar
Ruler selected
Button to minimize Ribbon
Rulers

3 On the Ribbon, click the **Home tab**. In the **Paragraph group**, if necessary, click the **Show/Hide** button ¶ so that it glows orange and formatting marks display in your document. Point to the button to display information about the button, and then compare your screen with Figure 1.36.

> When the Show/Hide button is active—glowing orange—formatting marks display. Because formatting marks guide your eye in a document—like a map and road signs guide you along a highway—these marks will display throughout this instruction. Many expert Word users keep these marks displayed while creating documents.

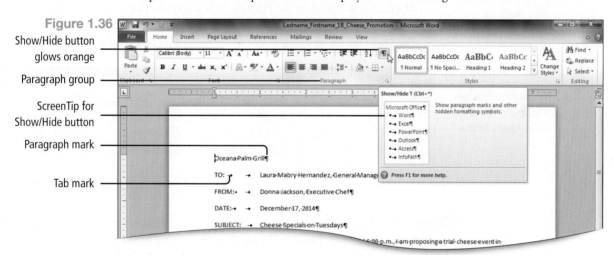

Figure 1.36

Show/Hide button glows orange
Paragraph group
ScreenTip for Show/Hide button
Paragraph mark
Tab mark

4 In the upper left corner of your screen, above the Ribbon, locate the **Quick Access Toolbar**.

> The *Quick Access Toolbar* contains commands that you use frequently. By default, only the commands Save, Undo, and Redo display, but you can add and delete commands to suit your needs. Possibly the computer at which you are working already has additional commands added to the Quick Access Toolbar.

5 At the end of the Quick Access Toolbar, click the **Customize Quick Access Toolbar** button ▾.

6 Compare your screen with Figure 1.37.

A list of commands that Office users commonly add to their Quick Access Toolbar displays, including *Open*, *E-mail*, and *Print Preview and Print*. Commands already on the Quick Access Toolbar display a check mark. Commands that you add to the Quick Access Toolbar are always just one click away.

Here you can also display the More Commands dialog box, from which you can select any command from any tab to add to the Quick Access Toolbar.

Figure 1.37

Customize Quick Access Toolbar

Popular commands to add

Existing commands checked

Displays *More Commands* dialog box

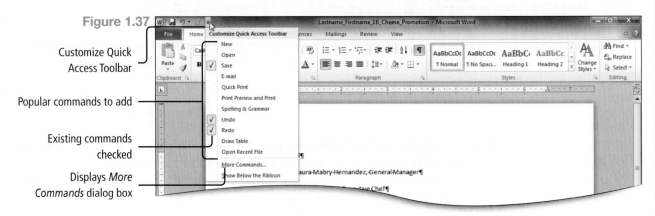

Another Way

Right-click any command on the Ribbon, and then on the shortcut menu, click Add to Quick Access Toolbar.

7 On the displayed list, click **Print Preview and Print**, and then notice that the icon is added to the **Quick Access Toolbar**. Compare your screen with Figure 1.38.

The icon that represents the Print Preview command displays on the Quick Access Toolbar. Because this is a command that you will use frequently while building Office documents, you might decide to have this command remain on your Quick Access Toolbar.

Figure 1.38

Icon for Print Preview command added to Quick Access Toolbar

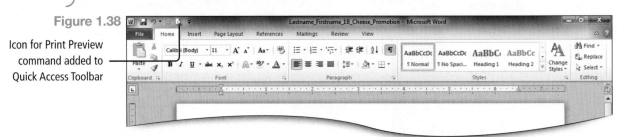

8 In the first line of the document, be sure your insertion point is blinking to the left of the *O* in *Oceana*. Press (Enter) one time to insert a blank paragraph, and then click to the left of the new paragraph mark (¶) in the new line.

The *paragraph symbol* is a formatting mark that displays each time you press (Enter).

9 On the Ribbon, click the **Insert tab**. In the **Illustrations group**, point to the **Clip Art** button to display its ScreenTip.

Many buttons on the Ribbon have this type of *enhanced ScreenTip*, which displays more descriptive text than a normal ScreenTip.

10 Click the **Clip Art** button.

The Clip Art *task pane* displays. A task pane is a window within a Microsoft Office application that enables you to enter options for completing a command.

11 In the **Clip Art** task pane, click in the **Search for** box, delete any existing text, and then type **cheese grapes** Under **Results should be:**, click the arrow at the right, if necessary click to *clear* the check mark for **All media types** so that no check boxes are selected, and then click the check box for **Illustrations**. Compare your screen with Figure 1.39.

Figure 1.39

Search term ———

Blank paragraph ———

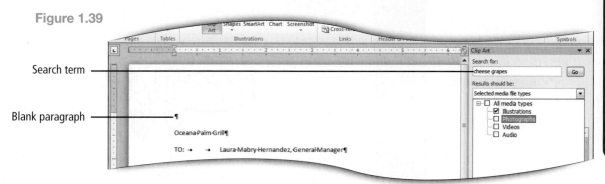

12 Click the **Results should be arrow** again to close the list, and then if necessary, click to place a check mark in the **Include Office.com content** check box.

> By selecting this check box, the search for clip art images will include those from Microsoft's online collections of clip art at www.office.com.

13 At the top of the **Clip Art** task pane, click **Go**. Wait a moment for clips to display, and then locate the clip indicated in Figure 1.40.

Figure 1.40

Check box selected ———

Locate this image ———

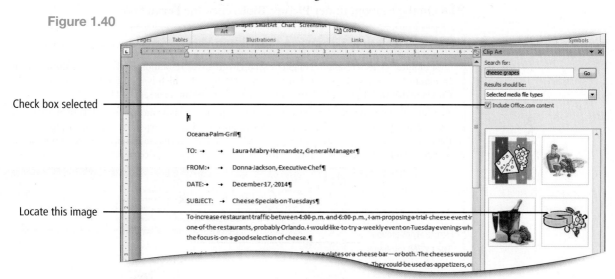

14 Click the image indicated in Figure 1.40 one time to insert it at the insertion point, and then in the upper right corner of the **Clip Art** task pane, click the **Close** ☒ button.

Alert! | If You Cannot Locate the Image

If the image shown in Figure 1.40 is unavailable, select a different cheese image that is appropriate.

---

15 With the image selected—surrounded by a border—on the Ribbon, click the **Home tab**, and then in the **Paragraph group**, click the **Center** button ☰. Click anywhere outside of the bordered picture to *deselect*—cancel the selection. Compare your screen with Figure 1.41.

Figure 1.41

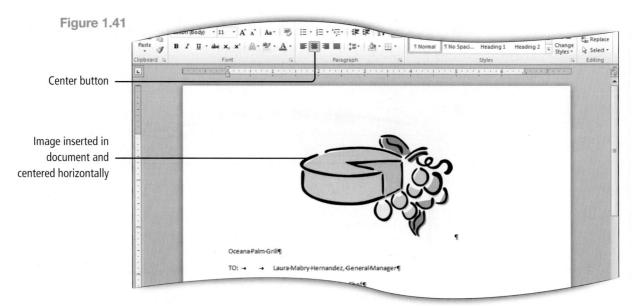

Center button

Image inserted in document and centered horizontally

Oceana·Palm·Grill¶

TO: → → Laura·Mabry·Hernandez,·General·Manager¶

16 Point to the inserted clip art image, and then watch the last tab of the Ribbon as you click the image one time to select it.

The *Picture Tools* display and an additional tab—the *Format* tab—is added to the Ribbon. The Ribbon adapts to your work and will display additional tabs—referred to as **contextual tabs**—when you need them.

17 On the Ribbon, under **Picture Tools**, click the **Format tab**.

Alert! | The Size of Groups on the Ribbon Varies with Screen Resolution

Your monitor's screen resolution might be set higher than the resolution used to capture the figures in this book. In Figure 1.42 below, the resolution is set to 1024 × 768, which is used for all of the figures in this book. Compare that with Figure 1.43 below, where the screen resolution is set to 1280 × 1024.

At a higher resolution, the Ribbon expands some groups to show more commands than are available with a single click, such as those in the Picture Styles group. Or, the group expands to add descriptive text to some buttons, such as those in the Arrange group. Regardless of your screen resolution, all Office commands are available to you. In higher resolutions, you will have a more robust view of the commands.

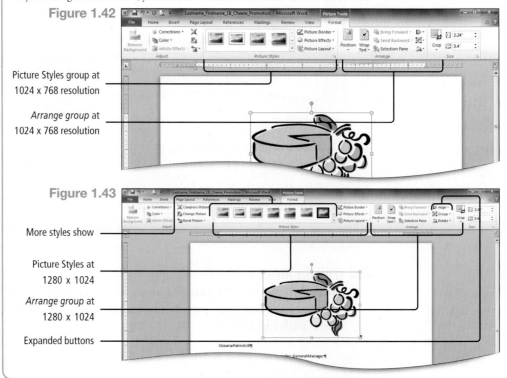

Figure 1.42

Picture Styles group at 1024 x 768 resolution

Arrange group at 1024 x 768 resolution

Figure 1.43

More styles show

Picture Styles at 1280 x 1024

Arrange group at 1280 x 1024

Expanded buttons

18 In the **Picture Styles group**, point to the first style to display the ScreenTip *Simple Frame, White*, and notice that the image displays with a white frame.

19 Watch the image as you point to the second picture style, and then to the third, and then to the fourth.

This is *Live Preview*, a technology that shows the result of applying an editing or formatting change as you point to possible results—*before* you actually apply it.

20 In the **Picture Styles group**, click the fourth style—**Drop Shadow Rectangle**—and then click anywhere outside of the image to deselect it. Notice that the Picture Tools no longer display on the Ribbon. Compare your screen with Figure 1.44.

Contextual tabs display only when you need them.

Figure 1.44

Picture Tools no longer display on the Ribbon

Drop Shadow Rectangle picture style applied to image

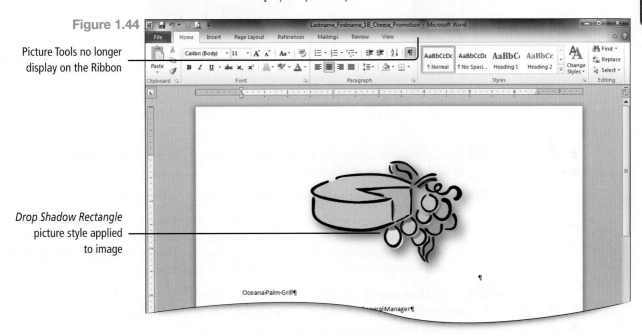

21 In the upper left corner of your screen, on the Quick Access Toolbar, click the **Save** button to save the changes you have made.

Activity 1.10 | Minimizing and Using the Keyboard to Control the Ribbon

Instead of a mouse, some individuals prefer to navigate the Ribbon by using keys on the keyboard. You can activate keyboard control of the Ribbon by pressing the Alt key. You can also minimize the Ribbon to maximize your available screen space.

1 On your keyboard, press the Alt key, and then on the Ribbon, notice that small labels display. Press N to activate the commands on the **Insert tab**, and then compare your screen with Figure 1.45.

Each label represents a *KeyTip*—an indication of the key that you can press to activate the command. For example, on the Insert tab, you can press F to activate the Clip Art task pane.

Figure 1.45

KeyTips indicate that
keyboard control
of the Ribbon is active

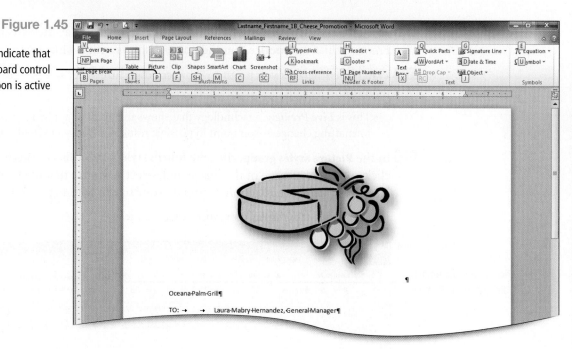

2 Press Esc to redisplay the KeyTips for the tabs. Then, press Alt again to turn off keyboard control of the Ribbon.

3 Point to any tab on the Ribbon and right-click to display a shortcut menu.

> Here you can choose to display the Quick Access Toolbar below the Ribbon or minimize the Ribbon to maximize screen space. You can also customize the Ribbon by adding, removing, renaming, or reordering tabs, groups, and commands on the Ribbon, although this is not recommended until you become an expert Office user.

> **Another Way**
>
> Double-click the active tab; or, click the Minimize the Ribbon button at the right end of the Ribbon.

4 Click **Minimize the Ribbon**. Notice that only the Ribbon tabs display. Click the **Home tab** to display the commands. Click anywhere in the document, and notice that the Ribbon reverts to its minimized view.

> **Another Way**
>
> Double-click any tab to redisplay the full Ribbon.

5 Right-click any Ribbon tab, and then click **Minimize the Ribbon** again to turn the minimize feature off.

> Most expert Office users prefer to have the full Ribbon display at all times.

6 Point to any tab on the Ribbon, and then on your mouse device, roll the mouse wheel. Notice that different tabs become active as your roll the mouse wheel.

> You can make a tab active by using this technique, instead of clicking the tab.

Objective 10 | Apply Formatting in Office Programs

Formatting is the process of establishing the overall appearance of text, graphics, and pages in an Office file—for example, in a Word document.

Activity 1.11 | Formatting and Viewing Pages

In this activity, you will practice common formatting techniques used in Office applications.

1 On the Ribbon, click the **Insert tab**, and then in the **Header & Footer group**, click the **Footer** button.

Another Way

On the Design tab, in the Insert group, click Quick Parts, click Field, and then under Field names, click FileName.

2 At the top of the displayed gallery, under **Built-In**, click **Blank**. At the bottom of your document, with *Type text* highlighted in blue, using your own name type the file name of this document **Lastname_Firstname_1B_Cheese_Promotion** and then compare your screen with Figure 1.46.

> Header & Footer Tools are added to the Ribbon. A **footer** is a reserved area for text or graphics that displays at the bottom of each page in a document. Likewise, a **header** is a reserved area for text or graphics that displays at the top of each page in a document. When the footer (or header) area is active, the document area is inactive (dimmed).

Figure 1.46

Design tab added

Header & Footer Tools active

Document area inactive (dimmed) when footer area is active

Close Header and Footer button

Your file name

Footer area displays

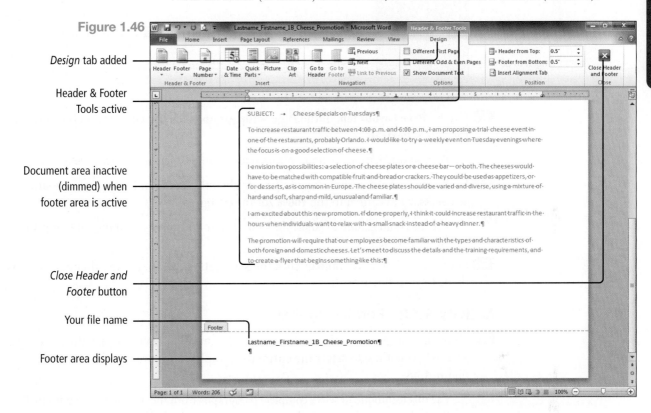

3 On the Ribbon, on the **Design tab**, in the **Close group**, click the **Close Header and Footer** button.

4 On the Ribbon, click the **Page Layout tab**. In the **Page Setup group**, click the **Orientation** button, and notice that two orientations display—*Portrait* and *Landscape*. Click **Landscape**.

> In **portrait orientation**, the paper is taller than it is wide. In **landscape orientation**, the paper is wider than it is tall.

5 In the lower right corner of the screen, locate the **Zoom control** buttons.

> To **zoom** means to increase or decrease the viewing area. You can zoom in to look closely at a section of a document, and then zoom out to see an entire page on the screen. You can also zoom to view multiple pages on the screen.

6 Drag the **Zoom slider** to the left until you have zoomed to approximately *60%*. Compare your screen with Figure 1.47.

Figure 1.47

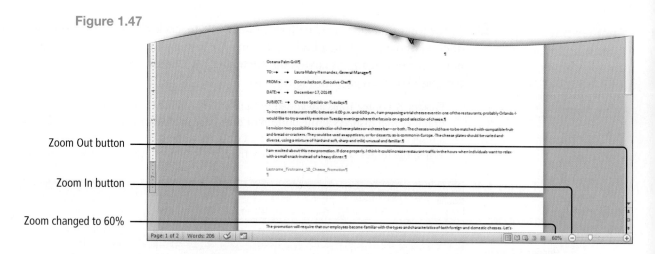

Zoom Out button

Zoom In button

Zoom changed to 60%

7 On the **Page Layout tab**, in the **Page Setup group**, click the **Orientation** button, and then click **Portrait**.

Portrait orientation is commonly used for business documents such as letters and memos.

8 In the lower right corner of your screen, click the **Zoom In** button ⊕ as many times as necessary to return to the **100%** zoom setting.

Use the zoom feature to adjust the view of your document for editing and for your viewing comfort.

9 On the Quick Access Toolbar, click the **Save** button 🖫 to save the changes you have made to your document.

Activity 1.12 | Formatting Text

1 To the left of *Oceana Palm Grill*, point in the margin area to display the 🔏 pointer and click one time to select the entire paragraph. Compare your screen with Figure 1.48.

Use this technique to select complete paragraphs from the margin area. Additionally, with this technique you can drag downward to select multiple-line paragraphs—which is faster and more efficient than dragging through text.

Figure 1.48

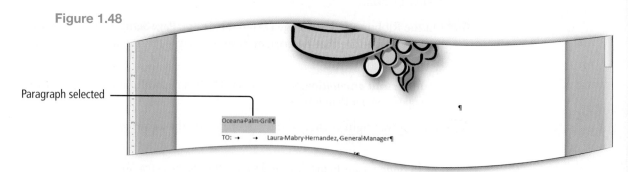

Paragraph selected

2 On the Ribbon, click the **Home tab**, and then in the **Paragraph group**, click the **Center** button ☰ to center the paragraph.

Alignment refers to the placement of paragraph text relative to the left and right margins. *Center alignment* refers to text that is centered horizontally between the left and right margins. You can also align text at the left margin, which is the default alignment for text in Word, or at the right margin.

3 On the **Home tab**, in the **Font group**, click the **Font button arrow** [Calibri (Body) ▼]. At the top of the list, point to **Cambria**, and as you do so, notice that the selected text previews in the Cambria font.

> A *font* is a set of characters with the same design and shape. The default font in a Word document is Calibri, which is a *sans serif* font—a font design with no lines or extensions on the ends of characters.
>
> The Cambria font is a *serif* font—a font design that includes small line extensions on the ends of the letters to guide the eye in reading from left to right.
>
> The list of fonts displays as a gallery showing potential results. For example, in the Font gallery, you can see the actual design and format of each font as it would look if applied to text.

4 Point to several other fonts and observe the effect on the selected text. Then, at the top of the **Font** gallery, under **Theme Fonts**, click **Cambria**.

> A *theme* is a predesigned set of colors, fonts, lines, and fill effects that look good together and that can be applied to your entire document or to specific items.
>
> A theme combines two sets of fonts—one for text and one for headings. In the default Office theme, Cambria is the suggested font for headings.

5 With the paragraph *Oceana Palm Grill* still selected, on the **Home tab**, in the **Font group**, click the **Font Size button arrow** [11 ▼], point to **36**, and then notice how Live Preview displays the text in the font size to which you are pointing. Compare your screen with Figure 1.49.

Figure 1.49

Font Size button

Font button

Font Size list

Pointing to 36 pt font size

Oceana Palm Grill centered,
Cambria font applied

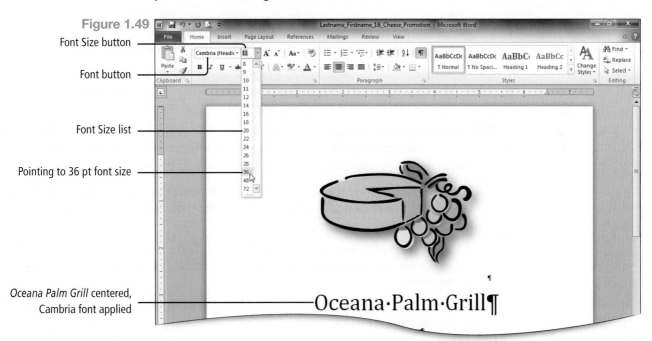

6 On the displayed list of font sizes, click **20**.

> Fonts are measured in *points*, with one point equal to 1/72 of an inch. A higher point size indicates a larger font size. Headings and titles are often formatted by using a larger font size. The word *point* is abbreviated as *pt*.

7 With *Oceana Palm Grill* still selected, on the **Home tab**, in the **Font group**, click the **Font Color button arrow** [A ▼]. Under **Theme Colors**, in the seventh column, click the last color—**Olive Green, Accent 3, Darker 50%**. Click anywhere to deselect the text.

8 To the left of *TO:*, point in the left margin area to display the ⟮🔖⟯ pointer, hold down the left mouse button, and then drag down to select the four memo headings. Compare your screen with Figure 1.50.

> Use this technique to select complete paragraphs from the margin area—dragging downward to select multiple-line paragraphs—which is faster and more efficient than dragging through text.

Figure 1.50

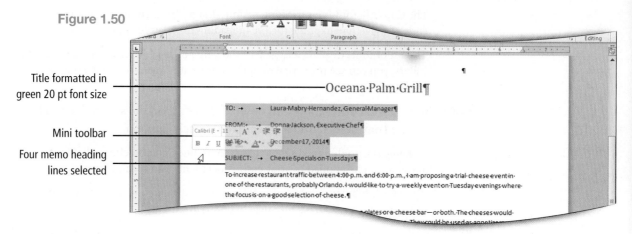

Title formatted in green 20 pt font size

Mini toolbar

Four memo heading lines selected

9 With the four paragraphs selected, on the Mini toolbar, click the **Font Color** button ⟮🅰⟯, which now displays a dark green bar instead of a red bar.

> The font color button retains its most recently used color—Olive Green, Accent 3, Darker 50%. As you progress in your study of Microsoft Office, you will use other buttons that behave in this manner; that is, they retain their most recently used format.

> The purpose of the Mini toolbar is to place commonly used commands close to text or objects that you select. By selecting a command on the Mini toolbar, you reduce the distance that you must move your mouse to access a command.

10 Click anywhere in the paragraph that begins *To increase*, and then ***triple-click***—click the left mouse button three times—to select the entire paragraph. If the entire paragraph is not selected, click in the paragraph and begin again.

11 With the entire paragraph selected, on the Mini toolbar, click the **Font Color button arrow** ⟮🅰⟯, and then under **Theme Colors**, in the sixth column, click the first color— **Red, Accent 2**.

> It is convenient to have commonly used commands display on the Mini toolbar so that you do not have to move your mouse to the top of the screen to access the command from the Ribbon.

12 Select the text *TO:* and then on the displayed Mini toolbar, click the **Bold** button ⟮B⟯ and the **Italic** button ⟮I⟯.

> ***Font styles*** include bold, italic, and underline. Font styles emphasize text and are a visual cue to draw the reader's eye to important text.

13 On the displayed Mini toolbar, click the **Italic** button ⟮I⟯ again to turn off the Italic formatting. Notice that the Italic button no longer glows orange.

> A button that behaves in this manner is referred to as a ***toggle button***, which means it can be turned on by clicking it once, and then turned off by clicking it again.

14 With *TO:* still selected, on the Mini toolbar, click the **Format Painter** button 🖌. Then, move your mouse under the word *Laura*, and notice the 🔲I mouse pointer. Compare your screen with Figure 1.51.

> You can use the ***Format Painter*** to copy the formatting of specific text or of a paragraph and then apply it in other locations in your document.

> The pointer takes the shape of a paintbrush, and contains the formatting information from the paragraph where the insertion point is positioned. Information about the Format Painter and how to turn it off displays in the status bar.

Figure 1.51

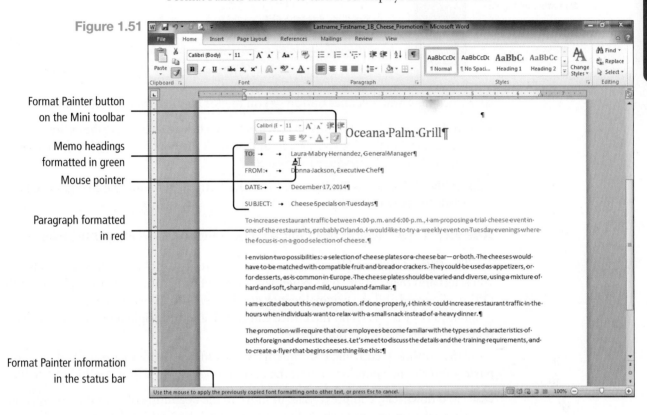

Format Painter button on the Mini toolbar

Memo headings formatted in green

Mouse pointer

Paragraph formatted in red

Format Painter information in the status bar

15 With the 🔲I pointer, drag to select the text *FROM:* and notice that the Bold formatting is applied. Then, point to the selected text *FROM:* and on the Mini toolbar, *double-click* the **Format Painter** button 🖌.

16 Select the text *DATE:* to copy the Bold formatting, and notice that the pointer retains the 🔲I shape.

> When you *double-click* the Format Painter button, the Format Painter feature remains active until you either click the Format Painter button again, or press [Esc] to cancel it—as indicated on the status bar.

17 With Format Painter still active, select the text *SUBJECT:*, and then on the Ribbon, on the **Home tab**, in the **Clipboard group**, notice that the **Format Painter** button 🖌 is glowing orange, indicating that it is active. Compare your screen with Figure 1.52.

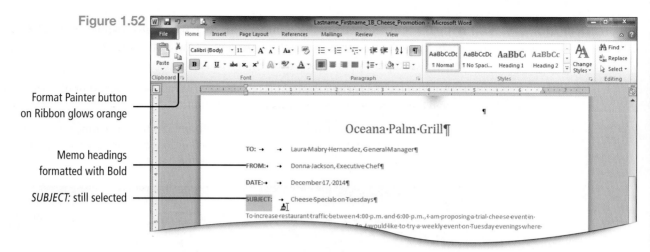

Figure 1.52

Format Painter button on Ribbon glows orange

Memo headings formatted with Bold

SUBJECT: still selected

18 Click the **Format Painter** button on the Ribbon to turn the command off.

19 In the paragraph that begins *To increase*, triple-click again to select the entire paragraph. On the displayed Mini toolbar, click the **Bold** button and the **Italic** button . Click anywhere to deselect.

20 On the Quick Access Toolbar, click the **Save** button to save the changes you have made to your document.

Activity 1.13 | Using the Office Clipboard to Cut, Copy, and Paste

The *Office Clipboard* is a temporary storage area that holds text or graphics that you select and then cut or copy. When you *copy* text or graphics, a copy is placed on the Office Clipboard and the original text or graphic remains in place. When you *cut* text or graphics, a copy is placed on the Office Clipboard, and the original text or graphic is removed—cut—from the document.

After cutting or copying, the contents of the Office Clipboard are available for you to *paste*—insert—in a new location in the current document, or into another Office file.

1 Hold down Ctrl and press Home to move to the beginning of your document, and then take a moment to study the table in Figure 1.53, which describes similar keyboard shortcuts with which you can navigate quickly in a document.

To Move	Press
To the beginning of a document	Ctrl + Home
To the end of a document	Ctrl + End
To the beginning of a line	Home
To the end of a line	End
To the beginning of the previous word	Ctrl + ←
To the beginning of the next word	Ctrl + →
To the beginning of the current word (if insertion point is in the middle of a word)	Ctrl + ←
To the beginning of a paragraph	Ctrl + ↑
To the beginning of the next paragraph	Ctrl + ↓
To the beginning of the current paragraph (if insertion point is in the middle of a paragraph)	Ctrl + ↑
Up one screen	PgUp
Down one screen	PageDown

Figure 1.53

2 To the left of *Oceana Palm Grill*, point in the left margin area to display the pointer, and then click one time to select the entire paragraph. On the **Home tab**, in the **Clipboard group**, click the **Copy** button.

Because anything that you select and then copy—or cut—is placed on the Office Clipboard, the Copy command and the Cut command display in the Clipboard group of commands on the Ribbon.

There is no visible indication that your copied selection has been placed on the Office Clipboard.

3 On the **Home tab**, in the **Clipboard group**, to the right of the group name *Clipboard*, click the **Dialog Box Launcher** button, and then compare your screen with Figure 1.54.

The Clipboard task pane displays with your copied text. In any Ribbon group, the *Dialog Box Launcher* displays either a dialog box or a task pane related to the group of commands.

It is not necessary to display the Office Clipboard in this manner, although sometimes it is useful to do so. The Office Clipboard can hold 24 items.

Figure 1.54

Copy button
Dialog Box Launcher in Clipboard group
Clipboard task pane displays
Selected text on the Office Clipboard

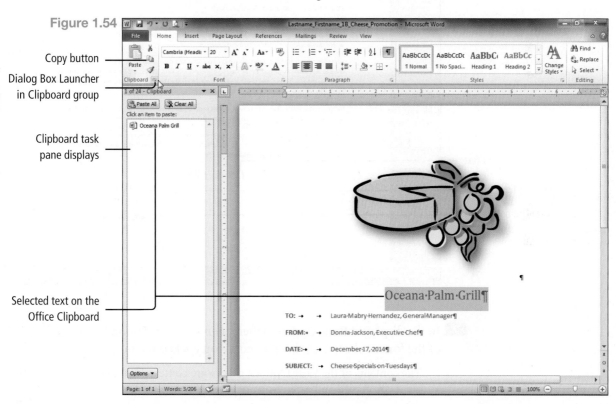

4 In the upper right corner of the **Clipboard** task pane, click the **Close** button.

5 Press Ctrl + End to move to the end of your document. Press Enter one time to create a new blank paragraph. On the **Home tab**, in the **Clipboard group**, point to the **Paste** button, and then click the *upper* portion of this split button.

The Paste command pastes the most recently copied item on the Office Clipboard at the insertion point location. If you click the lower portion of the Paste button, a gallery of Paste Options displays.

6 Click the **Paste Options** button ⬚ that displays below the pasted text as shown in Figure 1.55.

Here you can view and apply various formatting options for pasting your copied or cut text. Typically you will click Paste on the Ribbon and paste the item in its original format. If you want some other format for the pasted item, you can do so from the *Paste Options gallery*.

The Paste Options gallery provides a Live Preview of the various options for changing the format of the pasted item with a single click. The Paste Options gallery is available in three places: on the Ribbon by clicking the lower portion of the Paste button—the Paste button arrow; from the Paste Options button that displays below the pasted item following the paste operation; or, on the shortcut menu if you right-click the pasted item.

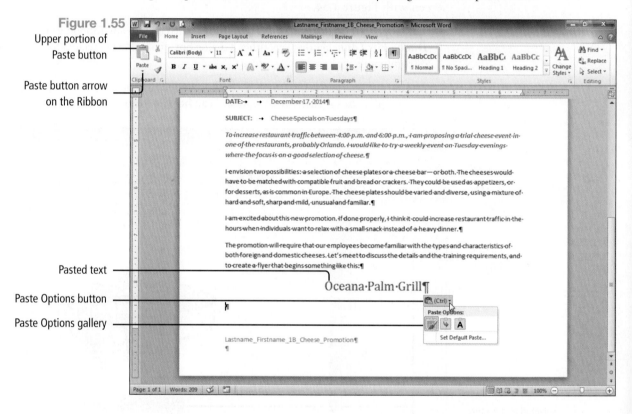

Figure 1.55
Upper portion of Paste button
Paste button arrow on the Ribbon
Pasted text
Paste Options button
Paste Options gallery

7 In the displayed **Paste Options** gallery, *point* to each option to see the Live Preview of the format that would be applied if you clicked the button.

The contents of the Paste Options gallery are contextual; that is, they change based on what you copied and where you are pasting.

8 Press [Esc] to close the gallery; the button will remain displayed until you take some other screen action.

Another Way

On the Home tab, in the Clipboard group, click the Cut button; or, use the keyboard shortcut [Ctrl] + [X].

9 Press [Ctrl] + [Home] to move to the top of the document, and then click the **cheese image** one time to select it. While pointing to the selected image, right-click, and then on the shortcut menu, click **Cut**.

Recall that the Cut command cuts—removes—the selection from the document and places it on the Office Clipboard.

10 Press Del one time to remove the blank paragraph from the top of the document, and then press Ctrl + End to move to the end of the document.

11 With the insertion point blinking in the blank paragraph at the end of the document, right-click, and notice that the **Paste Options** gallery displays on the shortcut menu. Compare your screen with Figure 1.56.

Figure 1.56

Paste Options on shortcut menu

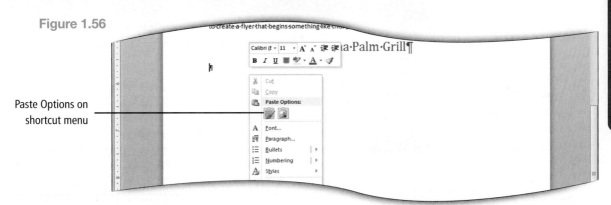

12 On the shortcut menu, under **Paste Options**, click the first button—**Keep Source Formatting** .

13 Click the picture to select it. On the **Home tab**, in the **Paragraph group**, click the **Center** button .

14 Above the cheese picture, click to position the insertion point at the end of the word *Grill*, press Spacebar one time, and then type **Tuesday Cheese Tastings** Compare your screen with Figure 1.57.

Figure 1.57

Heading

Picture inserted and centered

Activity 1.14 | Viewing Print Preview and Printing a Word Document

1 Press Ctrl + Home to move to the top of your document. Select the text *Oceana Palm Grill*, and then replace the selected text by typing **Memo**

2 Display **Backstage** view, on the right, click **Properties**, and then click **Show Document Panel**. Replace the existing author name with your first and last name. In the **Subject** box, type your course name and section number, and then in the **Keywords** box, type **cheese promotion** and then **Close** the **Document Information Panel**.

Another Way

Press Ctrl + F2 to display Print Preview.

3 On the Quick Access Toolbar, click **Save** 🖫 to save the changes you have made to your document.

4 On the Quick Access Toolbar, click the **Print Preview** button 🔍 that you added. Compare your screen with Figure 1.58.

Figure 1.58

Memo typed

If no printer is attached to your system, OneNote is the default printer

Print tab active in Backstage view

Print Preview (if you have a non-color printer as your default printer, the preview may display in shades of gray)

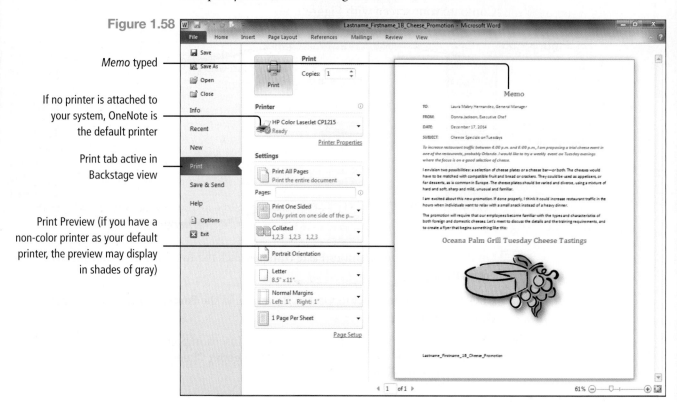

5 Examine the **Print Preview**. Under **Settings**, notice that in **Backstage** view, several of the same commands that are available on the Page Layout tab of the Ribbon also display.

For convenience, common adjustments to Page Layout display here, so that you can make last-minute adjustments without closing Backstage view.

6 If you need to make any corrections, click the Home tab to return to the document and make any necessary changes.

It is good practice to examine the Print Preview before printing or submitting your work electronically. Then, make any necessary corrections, re-save, and redisplay Print Preview.

7 If you are directed to do so, click Print to print the document; or, above the Info tab, click Close, and then submit your file electronically according to the directions provided by your instructor.

If you click the Print button, Backstage view closes and the Word window redisplays.

8 On the Quick Access Toolbar, point to the **Print Preview icon** 🔍 you placed there, right-click, and then click **Remove from Quick Access Toolbar**.

If you are working on your own computer and you want to do so, you can leave the icon on the toolbar; in a lab setting, you should return the software to its original settings.

9 At the right end of the title bar, click the program **Close** button ▣.

10 If a message displays asking if you want the text on the Clipboard to be available after you quit Word, click **No**.

> This message most often displays if you have copied some type of image to the Clipboard. If you click Yes, the items on the Clipboard will remain for you to use.

Objective 11 | Use the Microsoft Office 2010 Help System

Within each Office program, the Help feature provides information about all of the program's features and displays step-by-step instructions for performing many tasks.

Activity 1.15 | Using the Microsoft Office 2010 Help System in Excel

In this activity, you will use the Microsoft Help feature to find information about formatting numbers in Excel.

Another Way

Press F1 to display Help.

1 **Start** the **Microsoft Excel 2010** program. In the upper right corner of your screen, click the **Microsoft Excel Help** button ⊙.

2 In the **Excel Help** window, click in the white box in upper left corner, type **formatting numbers** and then click **Search** or press Enter.

3 On the list of results, click **Display numbers as currency**. Compare your screen with Figure 1.59.

Figure 1.59

Excel Help window —
Search term —
Print button —
Search button —
Help information —
Excel Help button —

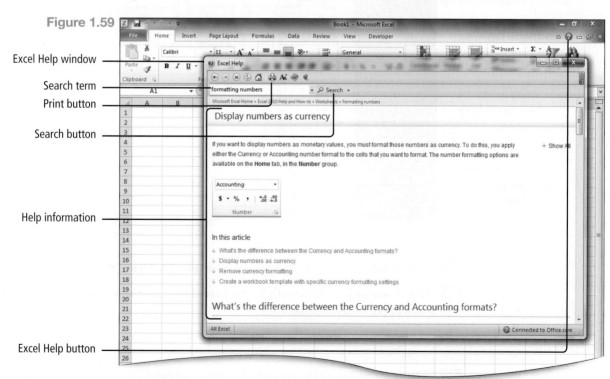

4 If you want to do so, on the toolbar at the top of the **Excel Help** window, click the Print 🖶 button to print a copy of this information for your reference.

5 On the title bar of the Excel Help window, click the **Close** button 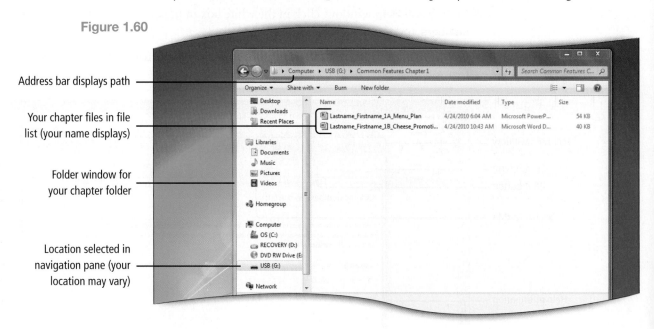. On the right side of the Microsoft Excel title bar, click the **Close** button to close Excel.

Objective 12 | Compress Files

A *compressed file* is a file that has been reduced in size. Compressed files take up less storage space and can be transferred to other computers faster than uncompressed files. You can also combine a group of files into one compressed folder, which makes it easier to share a group of files.

Activity 1.16 | Compressing Files

In this activity, you will combine the two files you created in this chapter into one compressed file.

1 On the Windows taskbar, click the **Start** button, and then on the right, click **Computer**.

2 On the left, in the **navigation pane**, click the location of your two files from this chapter—your USB flash drive or other location—and display the folder window for your **Common Features Chapter 1** folder. Compare your screen with Figure 1.60.

Figure 1.60

Address bar displays path

Your chapter files in file list (your name displays)

Folder window for your chapter folder

Location selected in navigation pane (your location may vary)

3 In the **file list**, click your **Lastname_Firstname_1A_Menu_Plan** file one time to select it.

4 Hold down Ctrl, and then click your **Lastname_Firstname_1B_Cheese_Promotion** file to select both files. Release Ctrl.

In any Windows-based program, holding down Ctrl while selecting enables you to select multiple items.

5 Point anywhere over the two selected files and right-click. On the shortcut menu, point to **Send to**, and then compare your screen with Figure 1.61.

Figure 1.61

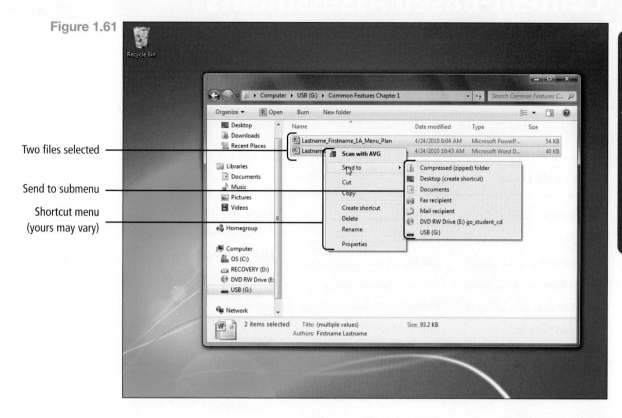

Two files selected

Send to submenu

Shortcut menu
(yours may vary)

6 On the shortcut submenu, click **Compressed (zipped) folder**.

Windows creates a compressed folder containing a *copy* of each of the selected files. The folder name is the name of the file or folder to which you were pointing, and is selected—highlighted in blue—so that you can rename it.

7 Using your own name, type **Lastname_Firstname_Common_Features_Ch1** and press Enter.

The compressed folder is now ready to attach to an e-mail or share in some other electronic format.

8 **Close** ☒ the folder window. If directed to do so by your instructor, submit your compressed folder electronically.

More Knowledge | Extracting Compressed Files

Extract means to decompress, or pull out, files from a compressed form. When you extract a file, an uncompressed copy is placed in the folder that you specify. The original file remains in the compressed folder.

End You have completed Project 1B ——————————————

Content-Based Assessments

Summary

In this chapter, you used Windows Explorer to navigate the Windows file structure. You also used features that are common across the Microsoft Office 2010 programs.

Key Terms

Content-Based Assessments

Matching

Match each term in the second column with its correct definition in the first column by writing the letter of the term on the blank line in front of the correct definition.

A Address bar
B Command
C File
D Folder
E Folder window
F Icons
G Keyboard shortcut
H Library
I Microsoft Excel
J Program
K Ribbon
L Start menu
M Subfolder
N Title bar
O Windows Explorer

_____ 1. A collection of information stored on a computer under a single name.

_____ 2. A container in which you store files.

_____ 3. A folder within a folder.

_____ 4. The program that displays the files and folders on your computer.

_____ 5. The Windows menu that is the main gateway to your computer.

_____ 6. In Windows 7, a window that displays the contents of the current folder, library, or device, and contains helpful parts so that you can navigate.

_____ 7. In Windows, a collection of items, such as files and folders, assembled from various locations that might be on your computer.

_____ 8. The bar at the top of a folder window with which you can navigate to a different folder or library, or go back to a previous one.

_____ 9. An instruction to a computer program that carries out an action.

_____ 10. Small pictures that represent a program, a file, a folder, or an object.

_____ 11. A set of instructions that a computer uses to perform a specific task.

_____ 12. A spreadsheet program used to calculate numbers and create charts.

_____ 13. The user interface that groups commands on tabs at the top of the program window.

_____ 14. A bar at the top of the program window displaying the current file and program name.

_____ 15. One or more keys pressed to perform a task that would otherwise require a mouse.

Multiple Choice

Circle the correct answer.

1. A small toolbar with frequently used commands that displays when selecting text or objects is the:
    A. Quick Access Toolbar   B. Mini toolbar   C. Document toolbar

2. In Office 2010, a centralized space for file management tasks is:
    A. a task pane   B. a dialog box   C. Backstage view

3. The commands Save, Save As, Open, and Close in Backstage view are located:
    A. above the Backstage tabs   B. below the Backstage tabs   C. under the screen thumbnail

4. The tab in Backstage view that displays information about the current file is the:
    A. Recent tab   B. Info tab   C. Options tab

5. Details about a file, including the title, author name, subject, and keywords are known as:
    A. document properties   B. formatting marks   C. KeyTips

6. An Office feature that displays a list of potential results is:
    A. Live Preview   B. a contextual tab   C. a gallery

7. A type of formatting emphasis applied to text such as bold, italic, and underline, is called:

   A. a font style   **B.** a KeyTip   **C.** a tag

8. A technology showing the result of applying formatting as you point to possible results is called:

   A. Live Preview   **B.** Backstage view   **C.** gallery view

9. A temporary storage area that holds text or graphics that you select and then cut or copy is the:

   A. paste options gallery   **B.** ribbon   **C.** Office clipboard

10. A file that has been reduced in size is:

   A. a compressed file   **B.** an extracted file   **C.** a PDF file

Creating Documents with Microsoft Word 2010

Joy Brown/Shutterstock

In This Chapter

In this chapter, you will use Microsoft Word, which is one of the most common programs found on computers and one that almost everyone has a reason to use. You will use many of the new tools found in Word 2010. When you learn word processing, you are also learning skills and techniques that you need to work efficiently on a computer. You can use Microsoft Word to perform basic word processing tasks such as writing a memo, a report, or a letter. You can also use Word to complete complex word processing tasks, such as creating sophisticated tables, embedding graphics, writing blogs, creating publications, and inserting links into other documents and the Internet. Word is a program that you can learn gradually, and then add more advanced skills one at a time.

The projects in this chapter relate to **Laurel College**. The college offers this diverse geographic area a wide range of academic and career programs, including associate degrees, certificate programs, and non-credit continuing education and personal development courses. The college makes positive contributions to the community through cultural and athletic programs and partnerships with businesses and nonprofit organizations. The college also provides industry-specific training programs for local businesses through its growing Economic Development Center.

Project 1A Flyer

Project Activities

In Activities 1.01 through 1.12, you will create a flyer announcing a new rock climbing class offered by the Physical Education Department at Laurel College. Your completed document will look similar to Figure 1.1.

Project Files

For Project 1A, you will need the following files:

New blank Word document
w01A_Fitness_Flyer
w01A_Rock_Climber

You will save your document as:

Lastname_Firstname_1A_Fitness_Flyer

Project Results

Figure 1.1
Project 1A Fitness Flyer

Objective 1 | Create a New Document and Insert Text

When you create a new document, you can type all of the text, or you can type some of the text and then insert additional text from another source.

Activity 1.01 | Starting a New Word Document and Inserting Text

1 **Start** Word and display a new blank document. On the **Home tab**, in the **Paragraph group**, if necessary click the Show/Hide button ¶ so that it is active (glows orange) to display the formatting marks. If the rulers do not display, click the View tab, and then in the Show group, select the Ruler check box.

2 Type **Rock Climbing 101** and then press Enter two times. As you type the following text, press the Spacebar only one time at the end of a sentence: **Increase your fitness level by learning basic rock climbing using the new Laurel College Gymnasium rock climbing wall. The Physical Education Department is offering Rock Climbing 101 as part of its Recreational Fitness Program.**

As you type, the insertion point moves to the right, and when it approaches the right margin, Word determines whether the next word in the line will fit within the established right margin. If the word does not fit, Word moves the entire word down to the next line. This feature is called *wordwrap* and means that you press Enter *only* when you reach the end of a paragraph—it is not necessary to press Enter at the end of each line of text.

> **Note** | Spacing Between Sentences
>
> Although you might have learned to add two spaces following end-of-sentence punctuation, the common practice now is to space only one time at the end of a sentence.

3 Press Enter one time. Take a moment to study the table in Figure 1.2 to become familiar with the default document settings in Microsoft Word, and then compare your screen with Figure 1.3.

When you press Enter, Spacebar, or Tab on your keyboard, characters display in your document to represent these keystrokes. These characters do not print and are referred to as *formatting marks* or *nonprinting characters*. These marks will display throughout this instruction.

Default Document Settings in a New Word Document

Setting	Default format
Font and font size	The default font is Calibri and the default font size is 11.
Margins	The default left, right, top, and bottom page margins are 1 inch.
Line spacing	The default line spacing is 1.15, which provides slightly more space between lines than single spacing does—an extra 1/6 of a line added between lines than single spacing.
Paragraph spacing	The default spacing after a paragraph is 10 points, which is slightly less than the height of one blank line of text.
View	The default view is Print Layout view, which displays the page borders and displays the document as it will appear when printed.

Figure 1.2

Figure 1.3

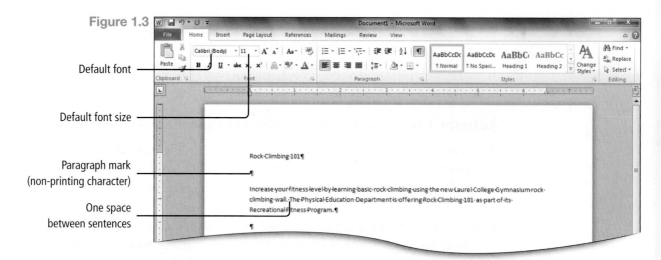

Default font

Default font size

Paragraph mark
(non-printing character)

One space
between sentences

4 On the Ribbon, click the **Insert tab**. In the **Text group**, click the **Object button arrow**, and then click **Text from File**.

> **Alert! | Does the Object Dialog Box Display?**
>
> If the Object dialog box displays, you probably clicked the Object *button* instead of the Object *button arrow*. Close the Object dialog box, and then in the Text group, click the Object button arrow, as shown in Figure 1.4. Click *Text from File*, and then continue with Step 5.

Another Way

Open the file, copy the required text, close the file, and then paste the text into the current document.

5 In the **Insert File** dialog box, navigate to the student files that accompany this textbook, locate and select **w01A_Fitness_Flyer**, and then click **Insert**. Compare your screen with Figure 1.4.

A *copy* of the text from the w01A_Fitness_Flyer file displays at the insertion point location; the text is not removed from the original file.

Figure 1.4

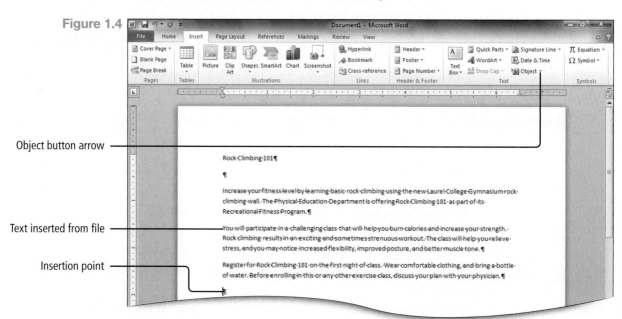

Object button arrow

Text inserted from file

Insertion point

6 On the **Quick Access Toolbar**, click the **Save** button. In the **Save As** dialog box, navigate to the location where you are saving your files for this chapter, and then create and open a new folder named **Word Chapter 1** In the **File name** box, replace the existing text with **Lastname_Firstname_1A_Fitness_Flyer** and then click **Save**.

> **More Knowledge** | Word's Default Settings Are Easier to Read Online
>
> Until just a few years ago, word processing programs used single spacing, an extra blank paragraph to separate paragraphs, and 12 pt Times New Roman as the default formats. Now, studies show that individuals find the Word default formats described in Figure 1.2 to be easier to read online, where many documents are now viewed and read.

Objective 2 | Insert and Format Graphics

To add visual interest to a document, insert **graphics**. Graphics include pictures, clip art, charts, and **drawing objects**—shapes, diagrams, lines, and so on. For additional visual interest, you can convert text to an attractive graphic format; add, resize, move, and format pictures; and add an attractive page border.

Activity 1.02 | Formatting Text Using Text Effects

Text effects are decorative formats, such as shadowed or mirrored text, text glow, 3-D effects, and colors that make text stand out.

1 Including the paragraph mark, select the first paragraph of text—*Rock Climbing 101*. On the **Home tab**, in the **Font group**, click the **Text Effects** button [A▾].

2 In the displayed **Text Effects** gallery, in the first row, point to the second effect to display the ScreenTip *Fill - None, Outline - Accent 2* and then click this effect.

3 With the text still selected, in the **Font group**, click in the **Font Size** box [11 ▾] to select the existing font size. Type **60** and then press [Enter].

> When you want to change the font size of selected text to a size that does not display in the Font Size list, type the number in the Font Size button box and press [Enter] to confirm the new font size.

4 With the text still selected, in the **Paragraph group**, click the **Center** button [≡] to center the text. Compare your screen with Figure 1.5.

Figure 1.5

Text Effects button

Center button glowing orange indicates centering applied

Text effects applied to title (title selected)

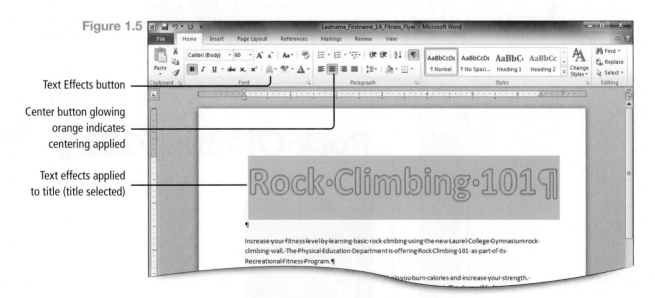

5 With the text still selected, in the **Font group**, click the **Text Effects** button [A▾]. Point to **Shadow**, and then under **Outer**, in the second row, click the third style—**Offset Left**.

6 With the text still selected, in the **Font group**, click the **Font Color button arrow** [A▾]. Under **Theme Colors**, in the fourth column, click the first color—**Dark Blue, Text 2**.

7 Click anywhere in the document to deselect the text, and then compare your screen with Figure 1.6.

Figure 1.6

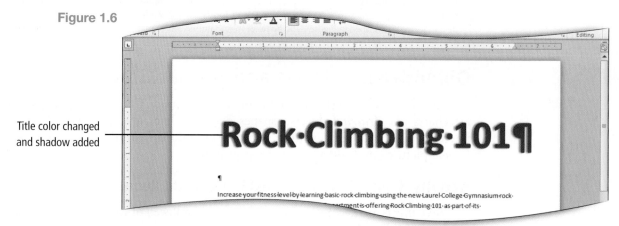

Title color changed and shadow added ———

8 **Save** 🖫 your document.

Activity 1.03 | Inserting and Resizing Pictures

1 In the paragraph that begins *Increase your fitness*, click to position the insertion point at the beginning of the paragraph.

2 On the **Insert tab**, in the **Illustrations group**, click the **Picture** button. In the **Insert Picture** dialog box, navigate to your student data files, locate and click **w01A_Rock_Climber**, and then click **Insert**.

> Word inserts the picture as an ***inline object***; that is, the picture is positioned directly in the text at the insertion point, just like a character in a sentence. Sizing handles surround the picture indicating it is selected.

3 If necessary, scroll to view the entire picture. Notice the round and square sizing handles around the border of the selected picture, as shown in Figure 1.7.

> The round corner sizing handles resize the graphic proportionally. The square sizing handles resize a graphic vertically or horizontally only; however, sizing with these will distort the graphic. A green rotate handle, with which you can rotate the graphic to any angle, displays above the top center sizing handle.

Figure 1.7

Center sizing handle ———

Rotate handle ———

Corner sizing handles ———

4 At the lower right corner of the picture, point to the round sizing handle until the ⬈ pointer displays. Drag upward and to the left until the bottom of the graphic is aligned at approximately **4 inches on the vertical ruler**. Compare your screen with Figure 1.8. Notice that the graphic is proportionally resized.

Figure 1.8

Picture resized

4-inch mark on the vertical ruler

5 On the **Format tab**, in the **Adjust group**, click the **Reset Picture button arrow** 🖼, and then click **Reset Picture & Size**.

6 In the **Size group**, click the **Shape Height spin box up arrow** as necessary to change the height of the picture to **4.5"**. Scroll down to view the entire picture on your screen, compare your screen with Figure 1.9, and then **Save** 💾 your document.

When you use the Height and Width *spin boxes* to change the size of a graphic, the graphic will always resize proportionally; that is, the width adjusts as you change the height and vice versa.

Figure 1.9

Picture height increased to 4.5 inches

Activity 1.04 | Wrapping Text Around a Picture

Graphics inserted as inline objects are treated like characters in a sentence, which can result in unattractive spacing. You can change an inline object to a *floating object*—a graphic that can be moved independently of the surrounding text characters.

1 Be sure the picture is selected—you know it is selected if the sizing handles display.

2 On the **Format tab**, in the **Arrange group**, click the **Wrap Text** button to display a gallery of text wrapping arrangements.

> *Text wrapping* refers to the manner in which text displays around an object.

3 From the gallery, click **Square** to wrap the text around the graphic, and then notice the *anchor* symbol to the left of the first line of the paragraph. Compare your screen with Figure 1.10.

> Select square text wrapping when you want to wrap the text to the left or right of the image. When you apply text wrapping, the object is always associated with—anchored to—a specific paragraph.

Figure 1.10

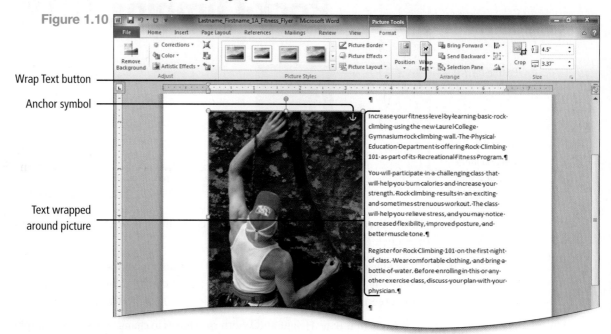

Wrap Text button

Anchor symbol

Text wrapped around picture

4 **Save** 💾 your document.

Activity 1.05 | Moving a Picture

1 Point to the rock climber picture to display the 🔸 pointer.

2 Hold down Shift and drag the picture to the right until the right edge of the picture aligns at approximately **6.5 inches on the horizontal ruler**. Notice that the picture moves in a straight line when you hold down Shift. Compare your screen with Figure 1.11.

Figure 1.11

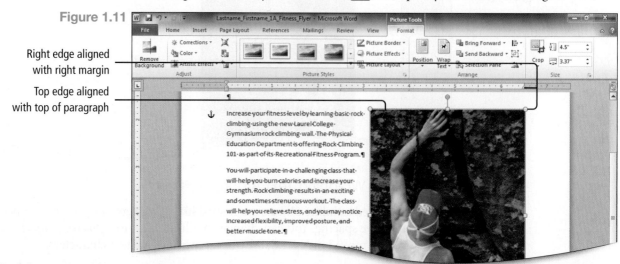

Right edge aligned with right margin

Top edge aligned with top of paragraph

3 If necessary, press any of the arrow keys on your keyboard to *nudge*—move in small increments—the picture in any direction so that the text wraps to match Figure 1.11. **Save** 🖫 your document.

Activity 1.06 | Applying Picture Styles and Artistic Effects

Picture styles include shapes, shadows, frames, borders, and other special effects with which you can stylize an image. *Artistic effects* are formats that make pictures look more like sketches or paintings.

1 Be sure the rock climber picture is selected. On the **Format tab**, in the **Picture Styles group**, click the **Picture Effects** button. Point to **Soft Edges**, and then click **5 Point**.

The Soft Edges feature fades the edges of the picture. The number of points you choose determines how far the fade goes inward from the edges of the picture.

2 On the **Format tab**, in the **Adjust group**, click the **Artistic Effects** button. In the first row of the gallery, point to, but do not click, the third effect—**Pencil Grayscale**.

Live Preview displays the picture with the *Pencil Grayscale* effect added.

3 In the second row of the gallery, click the third effect—**Paint Brush**. Notice that the picture looks like a painting, rather than a photograph, as shown in Figure 1.12. **Save** 🖫 your document.

Figure 1.12

Paint Brush artistic effect applied to picture

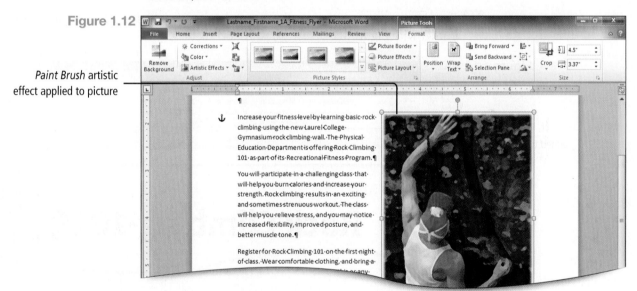

Activity 1.07 | Adding a Page Border

Page borders frame a page and help to focus the information on the page.

1 Click anywhere outside the picture to deselect it. On the **Page Layout tab**, in the **Page Background group**, click the **Page Borders** button.

2 In the **Borders and Shading** dialog box, under **Setting**, click **Box**. Under **Style**, scroll down the list about a third of the way and click the heavy top line with the thin bottom line—check the **Preview** area to be sure the heavier line is the nearest to the edges of the page.

3 Click the **Color arrow**, and then in the fourth column, click the first color—**Dark Blue, Text 2**.

4 Under **Apply to**, be sure *Whole document* is selected, and then compare your screen with Figure 1.13.

Figure 1.13

Page Borders button

Page border preview

Box setting

Border style

Border color

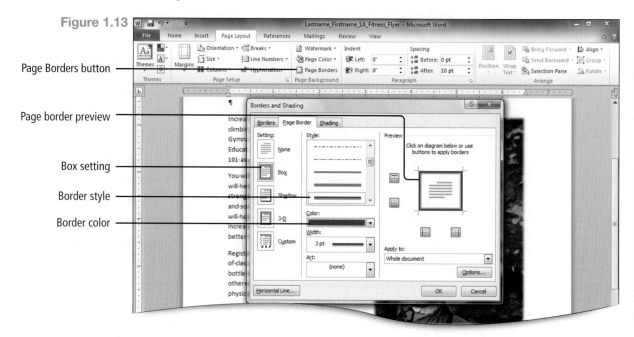

5 At the bottom of the **Borders and Shading** dialog box, click **OK**.

6 Press Ctrl + Home to move to the top of the document, and then compare your page border with Figure 1.14. **Save** your document.

Figure 1.14

Page Border added to document

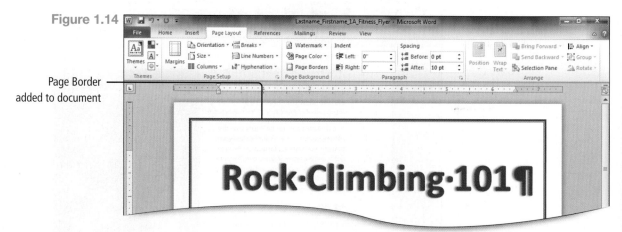

Objective 3 | Insert and Modify Text Boxes and Shapes

Word provides predefined **shapes** and **text boxes** that you can add to your documents. A shape is an object such as a line, arrow, box, callout, or banner. A text box is a movable, resizable container for text or graphics. Use these objects to add visual interest to your document.

Activity 1.08 | Inserting a Shape

1 Press ↓ one time to move to the blank paragraph below the title. Press Enter four times to make space for a text box, and notice that the picture anchored to the paragraph moves with the text.

2 Press Ctrl + End to move to the bottom of the document, and notice that your insertion point is positioned in the empty paragraph at the end of the document.

3 Click the **Insert tab**, and then in the **Illustrations group**, click the **Shapes** button to display the gallery. Compare your screen with Figure 1.15.

Figure 1.15

Shapes button

Rounded Rectangle shape

Shapes gallery

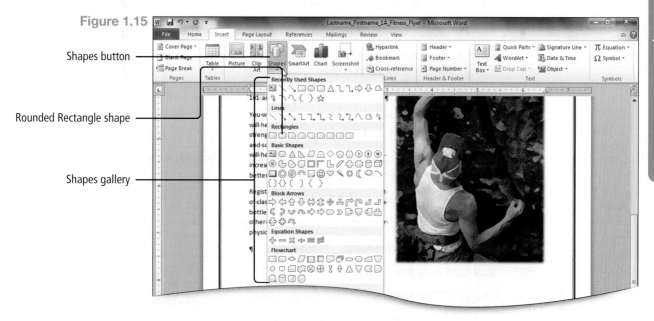

4 Under **Rectangles**, click the second shape—**Rounded Rectangle**, and then move your pointer. Notice that the ⊞ pointer displays.

5 Position the ⊞ pointer just under the lower left corner of the picture, and then drag down approximately **1 inch** and to the right edge of the picture.

6 Point to the shape and right-click, and then from the shortcut menu, click **Add Text**.

7 With the insertion point blinking inside the shape, point inside the shape and right-click, and then on the Mini toolbar, change the **Font Size** to **16**, and be sure **Center** ≣ alignment is selected.

8 Click inside the shape again, and then type **Improve your strength, balance, and coordination** If necessary, use the lower middle sizing handle to enlarge the shape to view your text. Compare your screen with Figure 1.16. **Save** 🖫 your document.

Figure 1.16

Rounded Rectangle
shape inserted and
formatted, text added

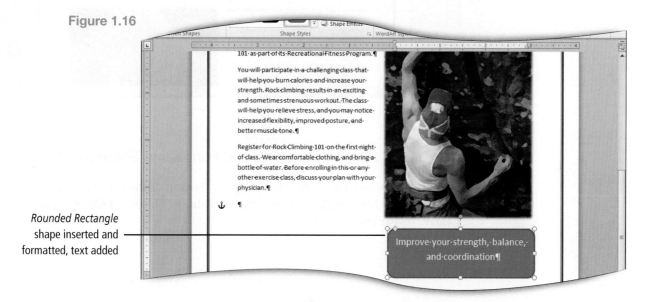

Activity 1.09 | Inserting a Text Box

A text box is useful to differentiate portions of text from other text on the page. You can move a text box anywhere on the page.

1 Press Ctrl + Home to move to the top of the document.

2 On the **Insert tab**, in the **Text group**, click the **Text Box** button. At the bottom of the gallery, click **Draw Text Box**.

3 Position the ✛ pointer below the letter *k* in *Rock*—at approximately **1.5 inches on the vertical ruler**. Drag down and to the right to create a text box approximately **1.5 inches** high and **3 inches** wide—the exact size and location need not be precise.

4 With the insertion point blinking in the text box, type the following, pressing Enter after each line to create a new paragraph:

> **Meets Tuesdays and Thursdays, 7-9 p.m.**
>
> **Begins September 13, ends December 16**
>
> **College Gymnasium, Room 104**

5 Compare your screen with Figure 1.17.

Figure 1.17

Text box with inserted text

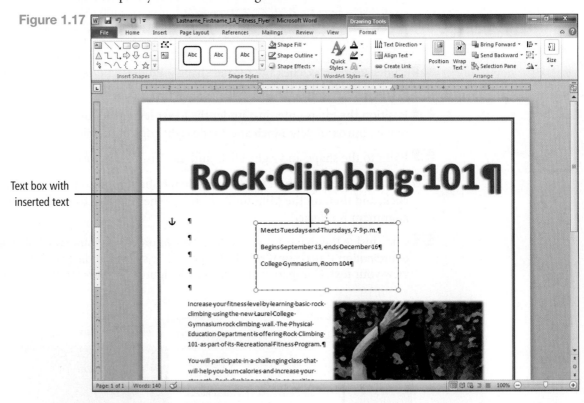

6 **Save** 🖫 your document.

Activity 1.10 | Moving, Resizing, and Formatting Shapes and Text Boxes

1 In the text box you just created in the upper portion of the flyer, select all of the text. From the Mini toolbar, change the **Font Size** to **14**, apply **Bold** **B**, and then **Center** **≡** the text.

2 On the **Format tab**, in the **Size group**, if necessary, click the **Size** button. Click the **Shape Height spin arrows** ⌷ 1.5" ⌄ as necessary to set the height of the text box to **1.2"**. Click the **Shape Width spin arrows** ⌷ 1.37" ⌄ as necessary to set the width of the text box to **4"**.

3 In the **Shape Styles group**, click the **Shape Effects** button. Point to **Shadow**, and then under **Outer**, in the first row, click the first style—**Offset Diagonal Bottom Right**.

4 In the **Shape Styles group**, click the **Shape Outline button arrow**. In the fourth column, click the first color—**Dark Blue, Text 2** to change the color of the text box border.

5 Click the **Shape Outline button arrow** again, point to **Weight**, and then click **3 pt**.

6 Click anywhere in the document to deselect the text box. Notice that with the text box deselected, you can see all the measurements on the horizontal ruler.

7 Click anywhere in the text box and point to the text box border to display the ⌖ pointer. By dragging, visually center the text box vertically and horizontally in the space below the *Rock Climbing 101* title. Then, if necessary, press any of the arrow keys on your keyboard to nudge the text box in precise increments to match Figure 1.18.

Figure 1.18

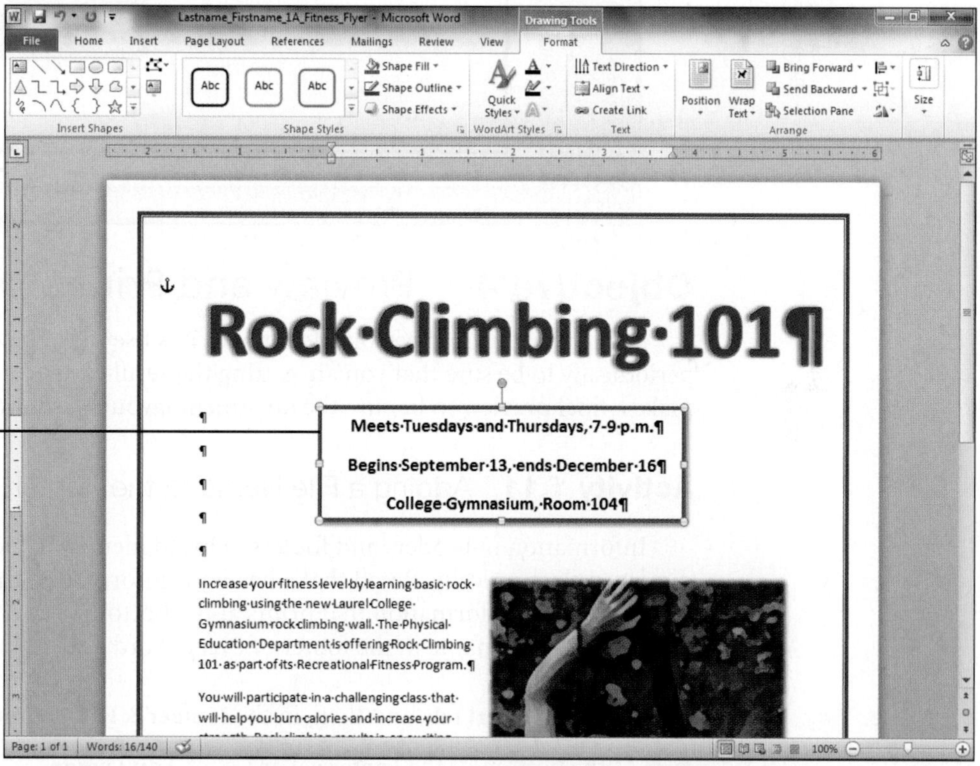

Text formatted and centered in text box, shadow added, border color and weight changed

8 Press ⌃Ctrl + ⌅End to move to the bottom of the document. Click on the border of the rounded rectangular shape to select it.

9 On the **Format tab**, in the **Size group**, if necessary, click the **Size** button. Click the **Shape Height spin arrows** ⌷ 1.5" ⌄ as necessary to change the height of the shape to **0.8"**.

10 In the **Shape Styles group**, click the **Shape Fill button arrow**, and then at the bottom of the gallery, point to **Gradient**. Under **Dark Variations**, in the third row click the first gradient—**Linear Diagonal - Bottom Left to Top Right**.

11 In the **Shape Styles group**, click the **Shape Outline button arrow**. In the sixth column, click the first color—**Red, Accent 2**.

12 Click the **Shape Outline button arrow** again, point to **Weight**, and then click **1 1/2 pt**. Click anywhere in the document to deselect the shape. Compare your screen with Figure 1.19, and then **Save** 🖫 your document.

Figure 1.19

Gradient fill added, shape outline formatted

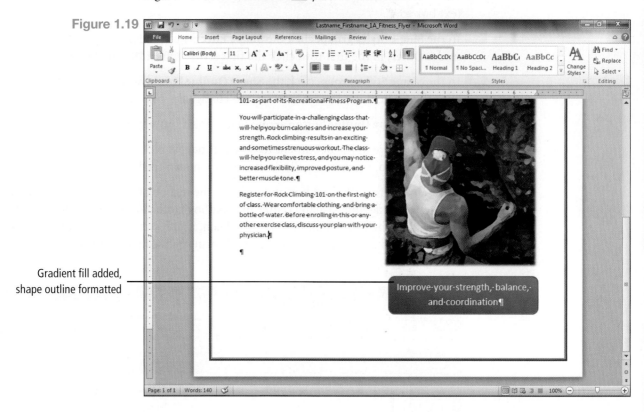

Objective 4 | Preview and Print a Document

While you are creating your document, it is useful to preview your document periodically to be sure that you are getting the result you want. Then, before printing, make a final preview to be sure the document layout is what you intended.

Activity 1.11 | Adding a File Name to the Footer

Information in headers and footers helps to identify a document when it is printed or displayed electronically. Recall that a header is information that prints at the top of every page; a footer is information that prints at the bottom of every page. In this textbook, you will insert the file name in the footer of every Word document.

Another Way

At the bottom edge of the page, right-click; from the shortcut menu, click Edit Footer.

1 Click the **Insert tab**, and then, in the **Header & Footer group**, click the **Footer** button.

2 At the bottom of the **Footer** gallery, click **Edit Footer**.

The footer area displays with the insertion point blinking at the left edge, and on the Ribbon, the Header & Footer Tools display and add the Design tab.

3 On the **Design tab**, in the **Insert group**, click the **Quick Parts** button, and then click **Field**. In the **Field** dialog box, under **Field names**, use the vertical scroll bar to examine the items that you can insert in a header or footer.

A *field* is a placeholder that displays preset content such as the current date, the file name, a page number, or other stored information.

4 In the **Field names** list, scroll as necessary to locate and then click **FileName**. Compare your screen with Figure 1.20.

Figure 1.20

Quick Parts button

Field dialog box

FileName field

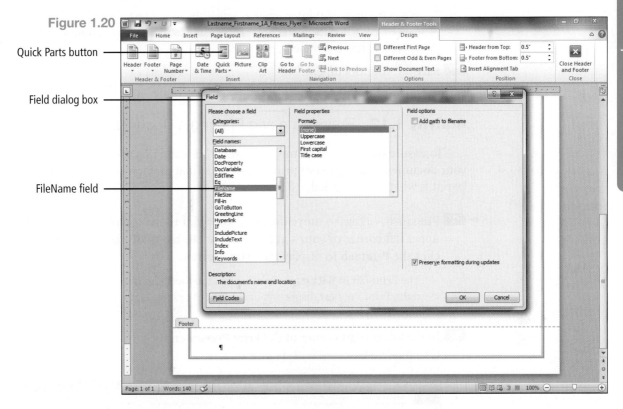

5 In the lower right corner of the **Field** dialog box, click **OK**, and then compare your screen with Figure 1.21.

Figure 1.21

Document text and image dimmed when footer is open

File name in footer

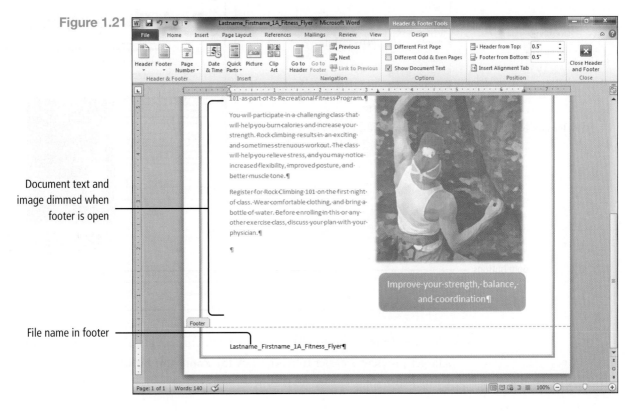

Another Way

Double-click anywhere in the document to close the footer area.

6 On the **Design tab**, at the far right in the **Close group**, click the **Close Header and Footer** button.

When the body of the document is active, the footer text is dimmed—displays in gray. Conversely, when the footer area is active, the footer text is not dimmed; instead, the document text is dimmed.

7 **Save** 🔲 your document.

Activity 1.12 | Previewing and Printing a Document

To ensure that you are getting the result you want, it is useful to periodically preview your document. Then, before printing, make a final preview to be sure the document layout is what you intended.

Another Way

Press Ctrl + F2 to display Print Preview.

1 Press Ctrl + Home to move the insertion point to the top of the document. In the upper left corner of your screen, click the **File tab** to display **Backstage** view, and then click the **Print tab** to display the **Print Preview**.

The Print tab in Backstage view displays the tools you need to select your settings. On the right, Print Preview displays your document exactly as it will print; the formatting marks do not display.

2 In the lower right corner of the **Print Preview**, notice the zoom buttons that display. Compare your screen with Figure 1.22.

Figure 1.22

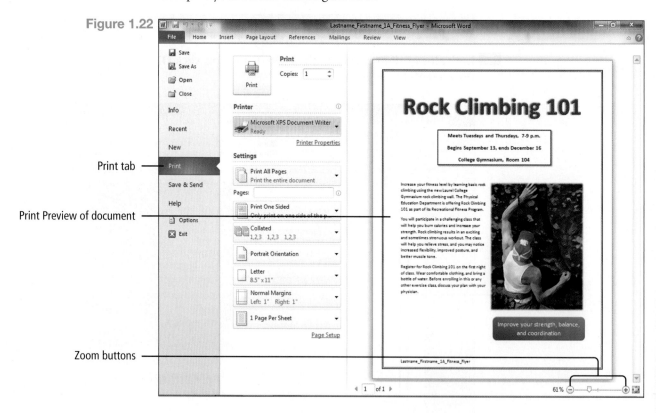

Print tab

Print Preview of document

Zoom buttons

3 Click the **Zoom In** button ⊕ to view the document at full size, and notice that a larger preview is easier to read. Click the **Zoom Out** button ⊖ to view the entire page.

4 Click the **Info tab**. On the right, under the screen thumbnail, click **Properties**, and then click **Show Document Panel**.

Here you can adjust the document properties.

5 In the **Author** box, delete any text and then type your firstname and lastname. In the **Subject** box type your course name and section number, and in the **Keywords** box type **fitness, rock climbing Close**  the Document Panel.

6 **Save** 💾 your document. To print, display **Backstage** view, and then on the **navigation bar**, click **Print**. In the **Settings** group, be sure the correct printer is selected, and then in the **Print group**, click the **Print** button. Or, submit your document electronically as directed by your instructor.

7 In **Backstage** view, click **Exit** to close the document and exit Word.

End You have completed Project 1A ————————————————————

Project 1B Information Handout

Project Activities

In Activities 1.13 through 1.23, you will format and add lists to an information handout that describes student activities at Laurel College. Your completed document will look similar to Figure 1.23.

Project Files

For Project 1B, you will need the following file:

w01B_Student_Activities

You will save your document as:

Lastname_Firstname_1B_Student_Activities

Project Results

Every spring, students vote for the President, Vice President, Treasurer, Secretary, and Student Trustee for the following year. Executive Officers work with the college administration to manage campus activities and to make changes to policies and procedures. For example, the Student Trustee is a ...h consists of elected members from the ...college budget, and employee hiring. ...the Board to vote for a proposal to ...ocations in Laurelton and outlying areas.

...clubs and academic organizations vote for ...n information and applications on the ...mpus and in the student newspaper.

...f interests, including academic, political, ...currently in existence at Laurel College. A ...oin a club, you may enjoy being a member ...or you may decide to take a leadership role

...fice in the Campus Center, Room CC208, or ...d complete the form online. Clubs accept ...e following are the first meeting dates and

... October 8, 2:00 p.m., Room CC214
...ctober 5, 5:00 p.m., Computer Café
...7, 3:00 p.m., Field House, Room 2A
... October 6, 2:00 p.m., Room CC212
...6, 4:00 p.m., Math Tutoring Lab, L35
... October 8, 3:00 p.m., Room CC214
...4, 5:30 p.m., Photo Lab, Foster Hall
...........October 8, 5:00 p.m., Room L24
... October 7, 4:30 p.m., Room CC214
...October 4, 3:00 p.m., Little Theater

...listed here, are great, but your goals are ...ing a degree or certificate. Maybe you want ...ou leave Laurel College. Whatever your ...ur education, work experience, and ...lly ones in which you had a leadership role,

Associated Students of Laurel College

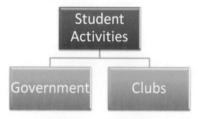

Get Involved in Student Activities

Your experience at Laurel College will be richer and more memorable if you get involved in activities that take you beyond the classroom. You will have the opportunity to meet other students, faculty, and staff members and will participate in organizations that make valuable contributions to your college and to the community.

Consider becoming involved in student government or joining a club. You might take part in activities such as these:

- ✓ Volunteering to help with a blood drive
- ✓ Traveling to a foreign country to learn about other cultures
- ✓ Volunteering to assist at graduation
- ✓ Helping to organize a community picnic
- ✓ Planning and implementing advertising for a student event
- ✓ Meeting with members of the state legislature to discuss issues that affect college students—for example, tuition costs and financial aid

Student Government

As a registered student, you are eligible to attend meetings of the Executive Officers of the Associated Students of Laurel College. At the meetings, you will have the opportunity to learn about college issues that affect students. At the conclusion of each meeting, the Officers invite students to voice their opinions. Eventually, you might decide to run for an office yourself. Running for office is a three-step process:

1. Pick up petitions at the Student Government office.
2. Obtain 100 signatures from current students.
3. Turn in petitions and start campaigning.

Lastname_Firstname_1B_Student_Activities

Figure 1.23
Project 1B Student Activities

Objective 5 | Change Document and Paragraph Layout

Document layout includes *margins*—the space between the text and the top, bottom, left, and right edges of the paper. Paragraph layout includes line spacing, indents, and tabs. In Word, the information about paragraph formats is stored in the paragraph mark at the end of a paragraph. When you press the ⌷Enter⌷, the new paragraph mark contains the formatting of the previous paragraph, unless you take steps to change it.

Activity 1.13 | Setting Margins

1 **Start** Word. From **Backstage** view, display the **Open** dialog box. From your student files, locate and open the document **w01B_Student_Activities**. On the **Home tab**, in the **Paragraph group**, be sure the **Show/Hide** button ⌷¶⌷ is active—glows orange—so that you can view the formatting marks.

2 From **Backstage** view, display the **Save As** dialog box. Navigate to your **Word Chapter 1** folder, and then **Save** the document as **Lastname_Firstname_1B_Student_Activities**

3 Click the **Page Layout tab**. In the **Page Setup group**, click the **Margins** button, and then take a moment to study the buttons in the Margins gallery.

The top button displays the most recent custom margin settings, while the other buttons display commonly used margin settings.

4 At the bottom of the **Margins** gallery, click **Custom Margins**.

5 In the **Page Setup** dialog box, press ⌷Tab⌷ as necessary to select the value in the **Left** box, and then, with *1.25"* selected, type **1**

This action will change the left margin to 1 inch on all pages of the document. You do not need to type the inch (") mark.

6 Press ⌷Tab⌷ to select the margin in the **Right** box, and then type **1** At the bottom of the dialog box, notice that the new margins will apply to the **Whole document**. Compare your screen with Figure 1.24.

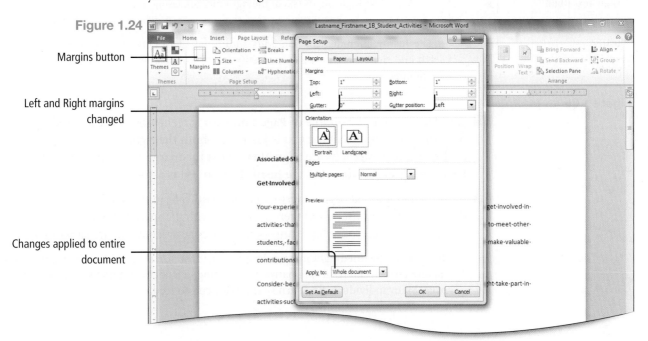

Figure 1.24

Margins button

Left and Right margins changed

Changes applied to entire document

Another Way

Click the View tab, and then in the Show group, select the Ruler check box.

7 Click **OK** to apply the new margins and close the dialog box. If the ruler below the Ribbon is not displayed, at the top of the vertical scroll bar, click the View Ruler button [icon].

8 Scroll to view the bottom of **Page 1** and the top of **Page 2**. Notice that the page edges display, and the page number and total number of pages display on the left side of the status bar.

9 Near the bottom edge of **Page 1**, point anywhere in the margin area, right-click, and then click **Edit Footer** to display the footer area.

10 On the **Design tab**, in the **Insert group**, click the **Quick Parts** button, and then click **Field**. In the **Field** dialog box, under **Field names**, locate and click **FileName**, and then click **OK**.

11 Double-click anywhere in the document to close the footer area, and then **Save** [icon] your document.

Activity 1.14 | Aligning Text

Alignment refers to the placement of paragraph text relative to the left and right margins. Most paragraph text uses *left alignment*—aligned at the left margin, leaving the right margin uneven. Three other types of paragraph alignment are: *center alignment*—centered between the left and right margins; *right alignment*—aligned at the right margin with an uneven left margin; and *justified alignment*—text aligned evenly at both the left and right margins. See the table in Figure 1.25.

Paragraph Alignment Options

Alignment	Button	Description and Example
Align Text Left	[icon]	Align Text Left is the default paragraph alignment in Word. Text in the paragraph aligns at the left margin, and the right margin is uneven.
Center	[icon]	Center alignment aligns text in the paragraph so that it is centered between the left and right margins.
Align Text Right	[icon]	Align Text Right aligns text at the right margin. Using Align Text Right, the left margin, which is normally even, is uneven.
Justify	[icon]	The Justify alignment option adds additional space between words so that both the left and right margins are even. Justify is often used when formatting newspaper-style columns.

Figure 1.25

1 Scroll to position the middle of **Page 2** on your screen, look at the left and right margins, and notice that the text is justified—both the right and left margins of multiple-line paragraphs are aligned evenly at the margins. On the **Home tab**, in the **Paragraph group**, notice that the **Justify** button [icon] is active.

2 In the paragraph that begins *Every spring, students vote*, in the first line, look at the space following the word *Every*, and then compare it with the space following the word *Trustee* in the second line. Notice how some of the spaces between words are larger than others.

To achieve a justified right margin, Word adjusts the size of spaces between words in this manner, which can result in unattractive spacing in a document that spans the width of a page. Many individuals find such spacing difficult to read.

Another Way

On the Home tab, in the Editing group, click the Select button, and then click Select All.

3 Press Ctrl + A to select all of the text in the document, and then on the **Home tab**, in the **Paragraph group**, click the **Align Text Left** button.

4 Press Ctrl + Home. At the top of the document, in the left margin area, point to the left of the first paragraph—*Associated Students of Laurel College*—until the pointer displays, and then click one time to select the paragraph. On the Mini toolbar, change the **Font Size** to **26**.

Use this technique to select entire lines of text.

5 Point to the left of the first paragraph—*Associated Students of Laurel College*—to display the pointer again, and then drag down to select the first two paragraphs, which form the title and subtitle of the document.

6 On the Mini toolbar, click the **Center** button to center the title and subtitle between the left and right margins, and then compare your screen with Figure 1.26.

Figure 1.26

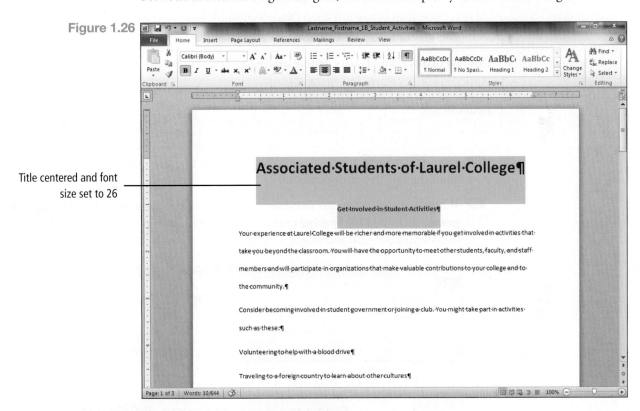

Title centered and font size set to 26

7 Scroll down to view the bottom of **Page 1**, and then locate the first bold subheading—*Student Government*. Point to the left of the paragraph to display the pointer, and then click one time.

8 With *Student Government* selected, use your mouse wheel or the vertical scroll bar to bring the lower portion of **Page 2** into view. Locate the subheading *Clubs*. Move the pointer to the left of the paragraph to display the pointer, hold down Ctrl, and then click one time.

Two subheadings are selected; in Windows-based programs, you can hold down Ctrl to select multiple items.

9 On the Mini toolbar, click the **Center** button to center both subheadings, and then click **Save**.

Activity 1.15 | Changing Line Spacing

Line spacing is the distance between lines of text in a paragraph. Three of the most commonly used line spacing options are shown in the table in Figure 1.27.

Line Spacing Options	
Alignment	**Description, Example, and Information**
Single spacing	**This text in this example uses single spacing**. Single spacing was once the most commonly used spacing in business documents. Now, because so many documents are read on a computer screen rather than on paper, single spacing is becoming less popular.
Multiple 1.15 spacing	**This text in this example uses multiple 1.15 spacing**. The default line spacing in Microsoft Word 2010 is 1.15, which is equivalent to single spacing with an extra 1/6 line added between lines to make the text easier to read on a computer screen. Many individuals now prefer this spacing, even on paper, because the lines of text appear less crowded.
Double spacing	**This text in this example uses double spacing**. College research papers and draft documents that need space for notes are commonly double-spaced; there is space for a full line of text between each document line.

Figure 1.27

1 Press Ctrl + Home to move to the beginning of the document. Press Ctrl + A to select all of the text in the document.

2 With all of the text in the document selected, on the **Home tab**, in the **Paragraph group**, click the **Line Spacing** button, and notice that the text in the document is double spaced—**2.0** is checked. Compare your screen with Figure 1.28.

Figure 1.28

Document text double-spaced

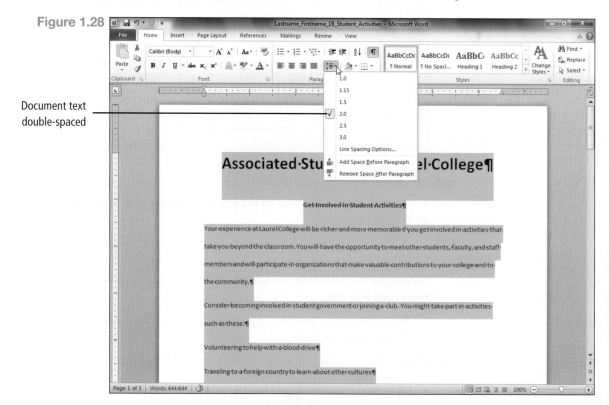

3 On the **Line Spacing** menu, click the *second* setting—**1.15**—and then click anywhere in the document. Compare your screen with Figure 1.29, and then **Save** 🖫 your document.

> Double spacing is most commonly used in research papers and rough draft documents. Recall that 1.15 is the default line spacing for new Word documents. Line spacing of 1.15 has slightly more space between the lines than single spacing. On a computer screen, spacing of 1.15 is easier to read than single spacing. Because a large percentage of Word documents are read on a computer screen, 1.15 is the default spacing for a new Word document.

Figure 1.29

Line spacing changed to 1.15

Activity 1.16 | Indenting Text and Adding Space After Paragraphs

Common techniques to distinguish paragraphs include adding space after each paragraph, indenting the first line of each paragraph, or both.

1 Below the title and subtitle of the document, click anywhere in the paragraph that begins *Your experience*.

2 On the **Home tab**, in the **Paragraph group**, click the **Dialog Box Launcher** 🖪.

3 In the **Paragraph** dialog box, on the **Indents and Spacing tab**, under **Indentation**, click the **Special arrow**, and then click **First line** to indent the first line by 0.5", which is the default indent setting. Compare your screen with Figure 1.30.

Figure 1.30

First line indent applied

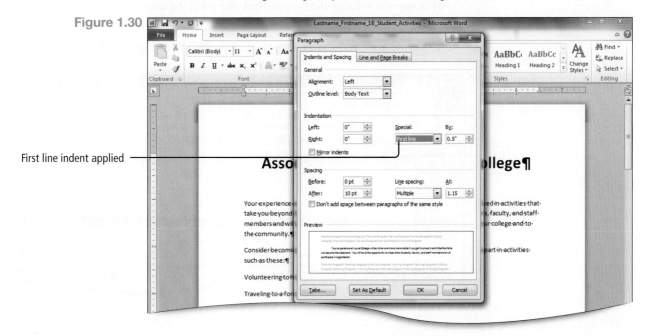

4 Click **OK**, and then click anywhere in the next paragraph, which begins *Consider becoming*. On the ruler under the Ribbon, drag the **First Line Indent** button ▽ to **0.5 inches on the horizontal ruler**, and then compare your screen with Figure 1.31.

Figure 1.31

First line Indent button

First lines indented

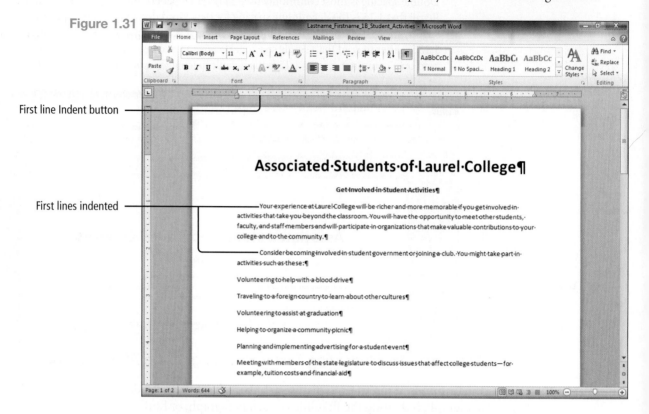

5 By using either of the techniques you just practiced, or by using the Format Painter, apply a first line indent of **0.5″** in the paragraph that begins *As a registered* to match the indent of the remaining paragraphs in the document.

Another Way

On either the Home tab or the Page Layout tab, display the Paragraph dialog box from the Paragraph group, and then under Spacing, click the spin box arrows as necessary.

6 Press Ctrl + A to select all of the text in the document. Click the **Page Layout tab**, and then in the **Paragraph group**, under **Spacing**, click the **After spin box down arrow** one time to change the value to **6 pt**.

> To change the value in the box, you can also select the existing number, type a new number, and then press Enter. This document will use 6 pt spacing after paragraphs.

7 Press Ctrl + Home, and then compare your screen with Figure 1.32.

Figure 1.32

Spacing After set to 6 pt

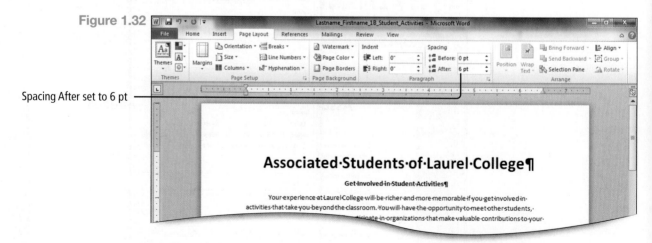

8 Scroll to view the lower portion of **Page 1**. Select the subheading *Student Government*, including the paragraph mark following it, hold down Ctrl, and then select the subheading *Clubs*.

9 With both subheadings selected, in the **Paragraph group**, under **Spacing**, click the **Before up spin box arrow** two times to set the **Spacing Before** to **12 pt**. Compare your screen with Figure 1.33, and then **Save** 💾 your document.

This action increases the amount of space above each of the two subheadings, which will make them easy to distinguish in the document. The formatting is applied only to the two selected paragraphs.

Figure 1.33
Spacing before set to 12 pt.

12-point spacing before paragraphs

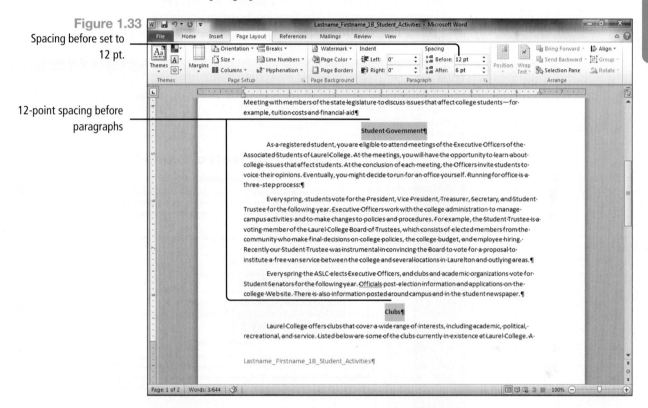

Objective 6 | Create and Modify Lists

To display a list of information, you can choose a *bulleted list*, which uses *bullets*—text symbols such as small circles or check marks—to introduce each item in a list. You can also choose a *numbered list*, which uses consecutive numbers or letters to introduce each item in a list.

Use a bulleted list if the items in the list can be introduced in any order; use a numbered list for items that have definite steps, a sequence of actions, or are in chronological order.

Activity 1.17 | Creating a Bulleted List

1 In the upper portion of **Page 1**, locate the paragraph that begins *Volunteering to help*, and then point to this paragraph from the left margin area to display the 🔠 pointer. Drag down to select this paragraph and the next five paragraphs.

2 On the **Home tab**, in the **Paragraph group**, click the **Bullets** button ⊞▾ to change the selected text to a bulleted list.

> The spacing between each of the bulleted points changes to the spacing between lines in a paragraph—in this instance, 1.15 line spacing. The spacing after the last item in the list is the same as the spacing after each paragraph—in this instance, 6 pt. Each bulleted item is automatically indented.

3 On the ruler, point to the **First Line Indent** button ▽ and read the ScreenTip, and then point to the **Hanging Indent** button △. Compare your screen with Figure 1.34.

> By default, Word formats bulleted items with a first line indent of 0.25″ and adds a Hanging Indent at 0.5″. The hanging indent maintains the alignment of text when a bulleted item is more than one line, for example, the last bulleted item in this list.

Figure 1.34

Hanging Indent button on ruler

Bulleted list

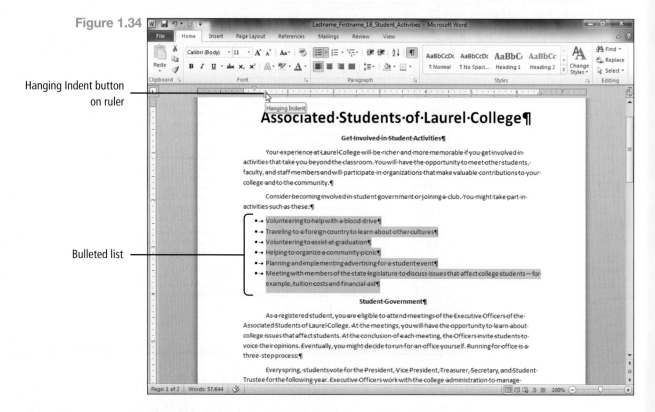

4 Scroll down to view **Page 2**. By using the pointer from the left margin area, select all of the paragraphs that indicate the club names and meeting dates, beginning with *Chess Club* and ending with *Theater Club*.

5 In the **Paragraph group**, click the **Bullets** button ⊞▾, and then **Save** 🖫 your document.

Activity 1.18 | Creating a Numbered List

1 Scroll to view **Page 1**, and then under the subheading *Student Government*, in the paragraph that begins *As a registered student*, click to position the insertion point at the *end* of the paragraph following the colon. Press Enter to create a blank paragraph.

2 Notice that the paragraph is indented, because the First Line Indent from the previous paragraph carried over to the new paragraph.

3 To change the indent formatting for this paragraph, on the ruler, drag the **First Line Indent** button ▽ to the left so that it is positioned directly above the lower button. Compare your screen with Figure 1.35.

Figure 1.35

First Line Indent button

Paragraph with no first line indent

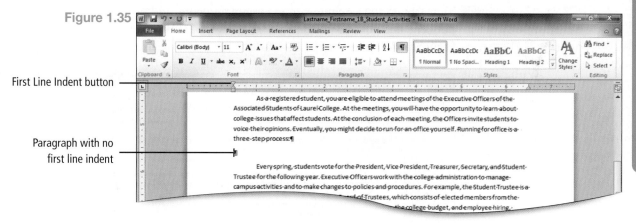

4 Being sure to include the period, type **1.** and press [Spacebar].

Word determines that this paragraph is the first item in a numbered list and formats the new paragraph accordingly, indenting the list in the same manner as the bulleted list. The space after the number changes to a tab, and the AutoCorrect Options button displays to the left of the list item. The tab is indicated by a right arrow formatting mark.

Alert! | **Activating Automatic Numbered Lists**

If a numbered list does not begin automatically, display Backstage view, and then click the Options tab. On the left side of the Word Options dialog box, click Proofing. Under AutoCorrect options, click the AutoCorrect Options button. In the AutoCorrect dialog box, click the AutoFormat As You Type tab. Under *Apply as you type*, select the *Automatic numbered lists* check box, and then click OK two times to close both dialog boxes.

---

5 Click the **AutoCorrect Options** button 🏷️ ▾, and then compare your screen with Figure 1.36.

From the displayed list, you can remove the automatic formatting here, or stop using the automatic numbered lists option in this document. You also have the option to open the AutoCorrect dialog box to *Control AutoFormat Options*.

Figure 1.36

AutoCorrect Options button

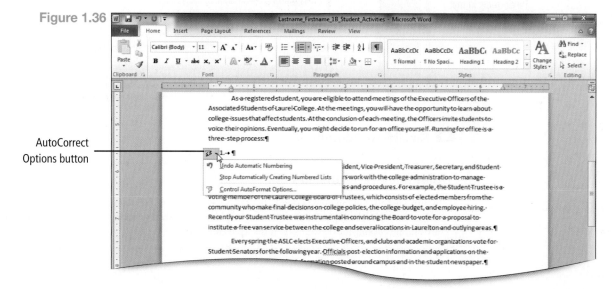

6 Click the **AutoCorrect Options** button again to close the menu without selecting any of the commands. Type **Pick up petitions at the Student Government office.** and press Enter. Notice that the second number and a tab are added to the next line.

7 Type **Obtain 100 signatures from current students.** and press Enter. Type **Turn in petitions and start campaigning.** and press Enter. Compare your screen with Figure 1.37.

Figure 1.37

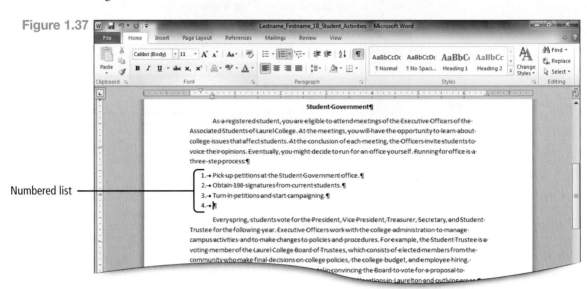

Numbered list

8 Press ←Bksp to turn off the list numbering. Then, press ←Bksp three more times to remove the blank paragraph. Compare your screen with Figure 1.38.

Figure 1.38

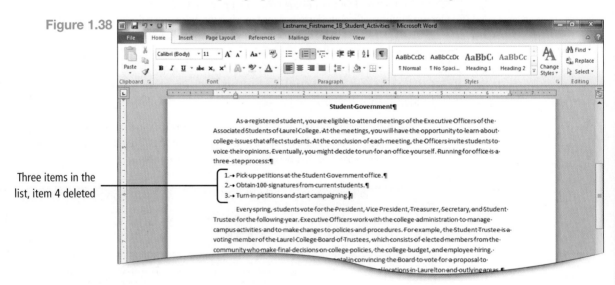

Three items in the list, item 4 deleted

9 **Save** 🖫 your document.

> **More Knowledge** | **To End a List**
>
> To turn a list off, you can press ←Bksp, click the Numbering or Bullets button, or press Enter a second time. Both list buttons—Numbering and Bullets—act as *toggle buttons*; that is, clicking the button one time turns the feature on, and clicking the button again turns the feature off.

Activity 1.19 | Customizing Bullets

1 Press Ctrl + End to move to the end of the document, and then scroll up as necessary to display the bulleted list containing the list of clubs.

2 Point to the left of the first list item to display the ⤹ pointer, and then drag down to select all the clubs in the list—the bullet symbols are not highlighted.

3 Point to the selected list and right-click. From the shortcut menu, point to **Bullets**, and then compare your screen with Figure 1.39.

Figure 1.39

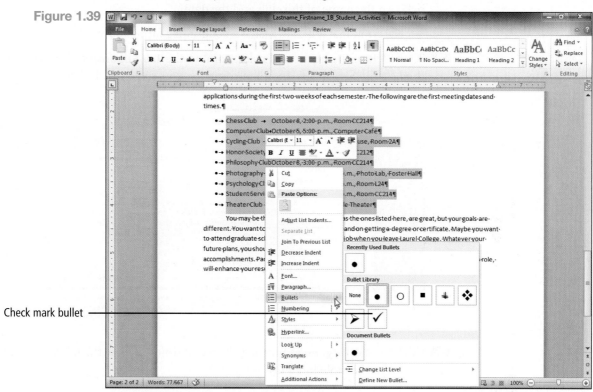

Check mark bullet

4 Under **Bullet Library**, click the **check mark** symbol. If the check mark is not available, choose another bullet symbol.

5 With the bulleted list still selected, right-click over the list, and then on the Mini toolbar, click the **Format Painter** button ⤸.

6 Use the vertical scroll bar or your mouse wheel to scroll to view **Page 1**. Move the pointer to the left of the first item in the bulleted list to display the ⤹ pointer, and then drag down to select all of the items in the list and to apply the format of the second bulleted list to this list. Compare your screen with Figure 1.40, and then **Save** ⤸ your document.

Figure 1.40

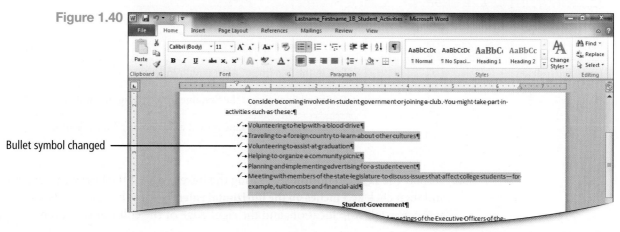

Bullet symbol changed

Objective 7 | Set and Modify Tab Stops

Tab stops mark specific locations on a line of text. Use tab stops to indent and align text, and use the ⟨Tab⟩ key to move to tab stops.

Activity 1.20 | Setting Tab Stops

1 Scroll to view the middle of **Page 2**, and then by using the 🔏 pointer at the left of the first item, select all of the items in the bulleted list. Notice that there is a tab mark between the name of the club and the date.

> The arrow that indicates a tab is a nonprinting formatting mark.

2 To the left of the horizontal ruler, point to the **Tab Alignment** button 🔳 to display the *Left Tab* ScreenTip, and then compare your screen with Figure 1.41.

Figure 1.41

Tab Alignment button ——

Left Tab ScreenTip ——

Tab mark ——

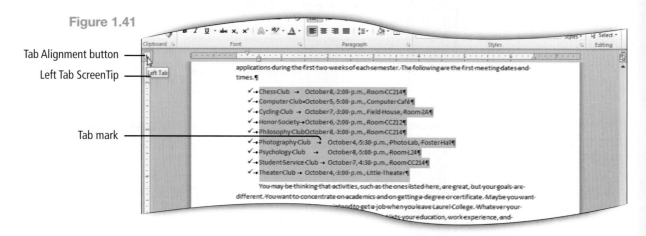

3 Click the **Tab Alignment** button 🔳 several times to view the tab alignment options shown in the table in Figure 1.42.

Tab Alignment Options

Type	Tab Alignment Button Displays This Marker	Description
Left	🔳	Text is left aligned at the tab stop and extends to the right.
Center	🔳	Text is centered around the tab stop.
Right	🔳	Text is right aligned at the tab stop and extends to the left.
Decimal	🔳	The decimal point aligns at the tab stop.
Bar	🔳	A vertical bar displays at the tab stop.
First Line Indent	▽	Text in the first line of a paragraph indents.
Hanging Indent	△	Text in all lines except the first line in the paragraph indents.
Left Indent	⊔	Moves both the First Line Indent and Hanging Indent buttons.

Figure 1.42

4 Display the **Left Tab** button 🔳. Along the lower edge of the horizontal ruler, point to and then click at **3 inches on the horizontal ruler**. Notice that all of the dates left align at the new tab stop location, and the right edge of the column is uneven.

5 Compare your screen with Figure 1.43, and then **Save** 🖫 your document.

Figure 1.43

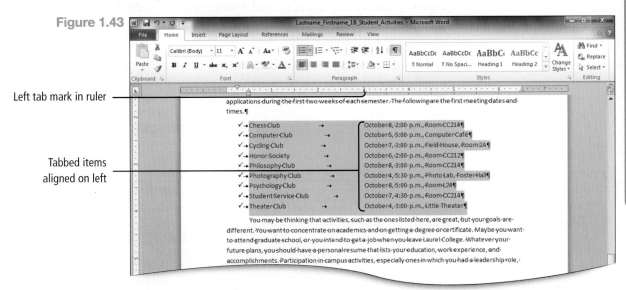

Left tab mark in ruler

Tabbed items aligned on left

Activity 1.21 | Modifying Tab Stops

Tab stops are a form of paragraph formatting, and thus, the information about tab stops is stored in the paragraph mark in the paragraphs to which they were applied.

1 With the bulleted list still selected, on the ruler, point to the new tab marker, and then when the *Left Tab* ScreenTip displays, drag the tab marker to **3.5 inches on the horizontal ruler**.

In all of the selected lines, the text at the tab stop left aligns at 3.5 inches.

2 On the ruler, point to the tab marker to display the ScreenTip, and then double-click to display the **Tabs** dialog box.

3 In the **Tabs** dialog box, under **Tab stop position**, if necessary select *3.5"* and then type **6**

4 Under **Alignment**, click the **Right** option button. Under **Leader**, click the **2** option button. Near the bottom of the **Tabs** dialog box, click **Set**.

Because the Right tab will be used to align the items in the list, the tab stop at 3.5" is no longer necessary.

5 In the **Tabs** dialog box, in the **Tab stop position** box, click **3.5"** to select this tab stop, and then in the lower portion of the **Tabs** dialog box, click the **Clear** button to delete this tab stop, which is no longer necessary. Compare your screen with Figure 1.44.

> **Another Way**
>
> On the Home tab, in the Paragraph group, click the Dialog Box Launcher. At the bottom of the Paragraph dialog box, click the Tabs button.

Figure 1.44

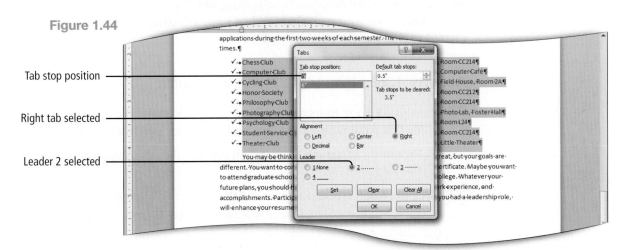

Tab stop position

Right tab selected

Leader 2 selected

6 Click **OK**. On the ruler, notice that the left tab marker at *3.5″* no longer displays, a right tab marker displays at *6″*, and a series of dots—a ***dot leader***—displays between the columns of the list. Notice also that the right edge of the column is even. Compare your screen with Figure 1.45.

> A ***leader character*** creates a solid, dotted, or dashed line that fills the space to the left of a tab character and draws the reader's eyes across the page from one item to the next. When the character used for the leader is a dot, it is commonly referred to as a dot leader.

Figure 1.45

Right tab marker

Tabbed items aligned right

Dot leader

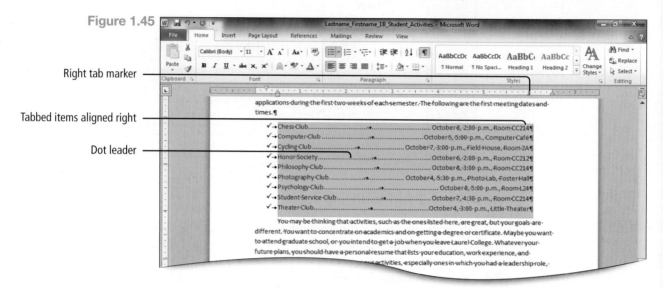

7 In the bulleted list that uses dot leaders, locate the *Honor Society* item, and then click to position the insertion point at the end of that line. Press Enter to create a new blank bullet item.

8 Type **Math Club** and press Tab. Notice that a dot leader fills the space to the tab marker location.

9 Type **October 6, 4:00 p.m., Math Tutoring Lab, L35** and notice that the text moves to the left to maintain the right alignment of the tab stop.

10 **Save** 🖫 your document.

Objective 8 | Insert a SmartArt Graphic

SmartArt graphics are designer-quality visual representations of information, and Word provides many different layouts from which you can choose. A SmartArt graphic can communicate your messages or ideas more effectively than plain text and adds visual interest to a document or Web page.

Activity 1.22 | Inserting a SmartArt Graphic

1 Press Ctrl + Home to move to the top of the document. Press End to move to the end of the first paragraph—the title—and then press Enter to create a blank paragraph.

> Because the paragraph above is 26 pt font size, the new paragraph mark displays in that size.

2 Click the **Insert tab**, and then in the **Illustrations group**, point to the **SmartArt** button to display its ScreenTip. Read the ScreenTip, and then click the button.

3 In the center portion of the **Choose a SmartArt Graphic** dialog box, scroll down and examine the numerous types of SmartArt graphics available.

4 On the left, click **Hierarchy**, and then in the first row, click the first graphic—**Organization Chart**.

At the right of the dialog box, a preview and description of the graphic displays.

5 Compare your screen with Figure 1.46.

Figure 1.46

SmartArt button

Preview of selected SmartArt

Hierarchy category

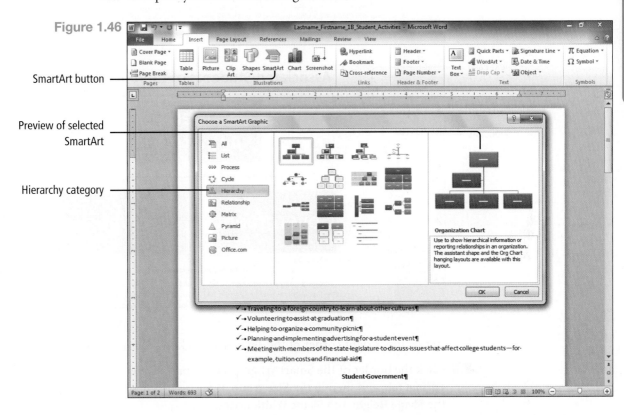

6 Click **OK**. If the pane indicating *Type your text here* does not display on the left side of the graphic, on the Design tab, in the Create Graphic group, click the Text Pane button. **Save** your document.

The SmartArt graphic displays at the insertion point location and consists of two parts—the graphic itself, and the Text Pane. On the Ribbon, the SmartArt Tools add the Design tab and the Format tab. You can type directly into the graphics, or type in the Text Pane. By typing in the Text Pane, you might find it easier to organize your layout.

Activity 1.23 | Modifying a SmartArt Graphic

1 In the SmartArt graphic, in the second row, click the border of the *[Text]* box to display a *solid* border and sizing handles, and then press Del. Repeat this procedure in the bottom row to delete the middle *[Text]* box.

> **Another Way**
>
> Close the Text Pane and type the text directly in the SmartArt boxes.

2 In the **Text Pane**, click in the top bulleted point, and then type **Student Activities** Notice that the first bulleted point aligns further to the left than the other points.

The *top-level points* are the main points in a SmartArt graphic. *Subpoints* are indented second-level bullet points.

3 Press ↓. Type **Government** and then press ↓ again. Type **Clubs** and then compare your screen with Figure 1.47.

Figure 1.47

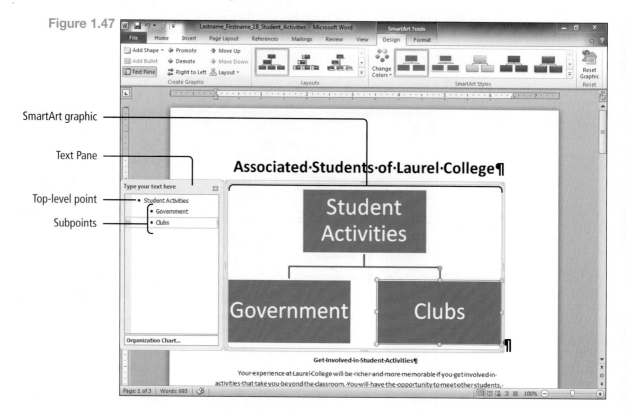

SmartArt graphic

Text Pane

Top-level point

Subpoints

4 In the upper right corner of the **Text Pane**, click the **Close** button 🗵.

5 Click the border of the SmartArt graphic—a pale border surrounds it. Click the **Format tab**, and then in the **Size group**, if necessary click the **Size** button to display the **Shape Height** and **Shape Width** boxes.

6 Set the **Height** to **2.5″** and the **Width** to **4.2″**, and then compare your screen with Figure 1.48.

Figure 1.48

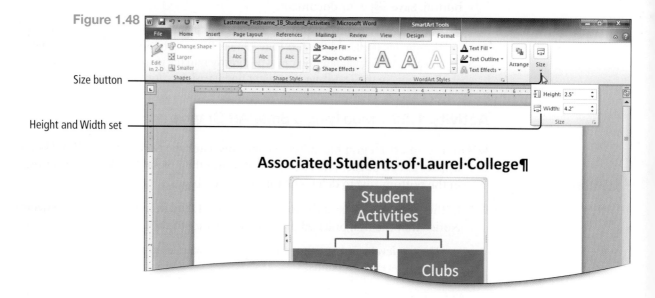

Size button

Height and Width set

7 With the SmartArt graphic still selected, click the **Design tab**, and then in the **SmartArt Styles group**, click the **Change Colors** button. Under **Colorful**, click the second style—**Colorful Range - Accent Colors 2 to 3**.

8 On the **Design tab**, in the **SmartArt Styles group**, click the **More** button ⏷. Under **3-D**, click the first style—**Polished**. Compare your screen with Figure 1.49.

Figure 1.49

Polished style selected —

SmartArt color and style changed

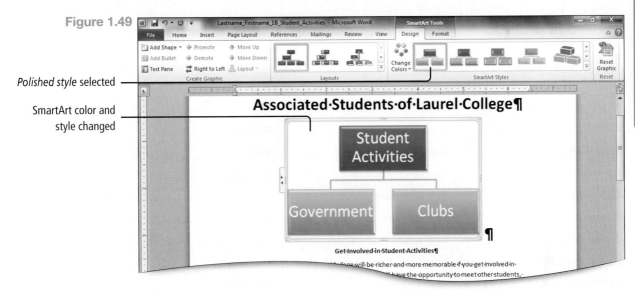

9 Click outside of the graphic to deselect it. Display **Backstage** view. On the right, under the screen thumbnail, click **Properties**, and then click **Show Document Panel**. In the **Author** box, delete any text and then type your firstname and lastname. In the **Subject** box, type your course name and section number, and in the **Keywords** box type **Student Activities, Associated Students Close** ✖ the Document Panel and **Save** 🖫 your document.

10 Display **Backstage** view, and then click **Print** to display **Print Preview**. At the bottom of the preview, click the **Next Page** 🔽 and **Previous Page** 🔼 buttons to move between pages. If necessary, return to the document and make any necessary changes.

11 As directed by your instructor, print your document or submit it electronically. **Close** ✖ Word.

More Knowledge | Changing the Bullet Level in a SmartArt Graphic

To increase or decrease the level of an item, on the Design tab, in the Create Graphic group, click either the Promote or the Demote button.

 You have completed Project 1B _____

Summary

In this chapter, you created and formatted documents using Microsoft Word 2010. You inserted and formatted graphics, created and formatted bulleted and numbered lists, and created and formatted text boxes. You also created lists using tab stops with dot leaders, and created and modified a SmartArt graphic.

Key Terms

Alignment 68	Graphics 53	Right tab stop 78
Anchor............................56	Inline object 54	Shapes 58
Artistic effects 57	Justified alignment.........68	SmartArt 80
Bar tab stop 78	Leader characters 80	Spin box 55
Bulleted list....................73	Left alignment.................68	Subpoints 81
Bullets 73	Left tab stop 78	Tab stop...........................78
Center alignment 68	Line spacing 70	Text box...........................58
Center tab stop 78	Margins 67	Text effects 53
Decimal tab stop 78	Nonprinting	Text wrapping 56
Dot leader 80	characters...................51	Toggle button 76
Drawing objects 53	Nudge 57	Top-level points 81
Field...............................62	Numbered list 73	Wordwrap 51
Floating object 55	Picture styles 57	
Formatting marks............51	Right alignment 68	

Matching

Match each term in the second column with its correct definition in the first column by writing the letter of the term on the blank line in front of the correct definition.

_____ 1. Formats that make pictures look more like sketches or paintings.

_____ 2. A small box with an upward- and downward-pointing arrow that enables you to move rapidly through a set of values by clicking.

_____ 3. Small circles in the corners of a selected graphic with which you can resize the graphic proportionally.

_____ 4. The manner in which text displays around an object.

_____ 5. An object or graphic that can be moved independently of the surrounding text.

_____ 6. The process of using the arrow keys to move an object in small precise increments.

_____ 7. An object or graphic inserted in a document that acts like a character in a sentence.

_____ 8. Frames, shapes, shadows, borders, and other special effects that can be added to an image to create an overall visual style for the image.

_____ 9. Predefined drawing objects, such as stars, banners, arrows, and callouts, included with Microsoft Office, and that can be inserted into documents.

A Artistic effects

B Bullets

C Floating object

D Inline object

E Justified alignment

F Left alignment

G Line spacing

H Nudge

I Picture styles

J Shapes

K Sizing handles

L SmartArt

M Spin box

N Tab stop

O Text wrapping

_____ 10. A commonly used alignment of text in which text is aligned at the left margin, leaving the right margin uneven.

_____ 11. An alignment of text in which the text is evenly aligned on both the left and right margins.

_____ 12. The distance between lines of text in a paragraph.

_____ 13. Text symbols such as small circles or check marks that introduce items in a list.

_____ 14. A mark on the ruler that indicates the location where the insertion point will be placed when you press the Tab key.

_____ 15. A designer-quality graphic used to create a visual representation of information.

Multiple Choice

Circle the correct answer.

1. Characters that display on the screen to show the location of paragraphs, tabs, and spaces, but that do not print, are called:
   A. text effects   **B.** bullets   **C.** formatting marks

2. The placement of paragraph text relative to the left and right margins is referred to as:
   A. alignment   **B.** spacing   **C.** indents

3. The symbol that indicates to which paragraph an image is attached is:
   A. a small arrow   **B.** an anchor   **C.** a paragraph mark

4. A movable, resizable container for text or graphics is a:
   A. text box   **B.** dialog box   **C.** SmartArt graphic

5. A banner is an example of a predefined:
   A. paragraph   **B.** format   **C.** shape

6. A placeholder that displays preset content, such as the current date, the file name, a page number, or other stored information is:
   A. a leader   **B.** a field   **C.** a tab

7. The space between the text and the top, bottom, left, and right edges of the paper are referred to as:
   A. alignment   **B.** margins   **C.** spacing

8. A group of items in which items are displayed in order to indicate definite steps, a sequence of actions, or chronological order is a:
   A. numbered list   **B.** bulleted list   **C.** outline list

9. A series of dots following a tab that serve to guide the reader's eye is a:
   A. leader   **B.** field   **C.** shape

10. Tab stops are a form of:
    A. line formatting   **B.** document formatting   **C.** paragraph formatting

Apply 1A skills from these Objectives:

- ■ Create a New Document and Insert Text
- ② Insert and Format Graphics
- ③ Insert and Modify Text Boxes and Shapes
- ④ Preview and Print a Document

Skills Review | Project **1C** Welcome Week

In the following Skills Review, you will create and edit a flyer for the Laurel College New Student Welcome Week. Your completed document will look similar to Figure 1.50.

Project Files

For Project 1C, you will need the following files:

New blank Word document
w01C_Welcome_Text
w01C_Welcome_Picture

You will save your document as:

Lastname_Firstname_1C_Welcome_Week

Project Results

Figure 1.50

(Project 1C Welcome Week continues on the next page)

Content-Based Assessments

1 **Start** Word and display a new blank document. On the **Home tab**, in the **Paragraph group**, be sure the **Show/Hide ¶** button is active so that you can view formatting marks. In the **Quick Access Toolbar**, click the **Save** button, navigate to your **Word Chapter 1** folder, and then **Save** the document as Lastname_Firstname_1C_Welcome_Week

a. Type **Welcome Week** and then press Enter two times.

b. Type **The Laurel College Student Government Association is sponsoring a week of special activities for new students. This is your opportunity to meet the people and learn about the programs that will help you succeed at Laurel College.**

c. Press Enter one time. Click the **Insert tab**. In the **Text group**, click the **Object button arrow**, and then click **Text from File**. Navigate to your student files, select the file **w01C_Welcome_Text**, and then at the bottom of the **Insert File** dialog box, click **Insert**. **Save** your document.

2 At the top of the document, in the left margin area, point to the left of the first paragraph—*Welcome Week*—until the pointer displays, and then click one time to select the paragraph. On the **Home tab**, in the **Font group**, click the **Text Effects** button. In the displayed **Text Effects** gallery, in the first row, click the fourth effect—**Fill - White, Outline - Accent 1**.

a. With the text still selected, in the **Font group**, click the **Font Size button arrow**, and then click **72**. In the **Paragraph group**, click the **Center** button.

b. With the text still selected, in the **Font group**, click the **Text Effects** button. Point to **Shadow**, and then under **Outer**, in the first row click the third style—**Offset Diagonal Bottom Left**. In the **Font group**, click the **Font Color button arrow**. Under **Theme Colors**, in the fourth column, click the first color—**Dark Blue, Text 2**.

c. In the paragraph that begins *The Laurel College*, click to position the insertion point at the beginning of the paragraph. On the **Insert tab**, in the **Illustrations group**, click the **Picture** button. From your student data files, **Insert** the file **w01C_Welcome_Picture**. On the **Format tab**, in the **Size group**, click the **Shape Height down spin arrow** as necessary to change the height of the picture to **2″**.

d. With the picture still selected, on the **Format tab**, in the **Arrange group**, click the **Wrap Text** button. From the **Wrap Text** gallery, click **Square**.

e. Hold down Shift and point anywhere in the picture to display the pointer. Drag the picture to align the right edge of the picture just to the left of the right margin.

f. On the **Format tab**, in the **Picture Styles group**, click the **Picture Effects** button. Point to **Glow**, and then under **Glow Variations**, in the third row, click the first style—**Blue, 11 pt glow, Accent color 1**. Nudge as necessary to match the picture position shown in Figure 1.50.

g. Click anywhere to deselect the picture. Click the **Page Layout tab**, and then in the **Page Background group**, click the **Page Borders** button. In the **Borders and Shading** dialog box, under **Setting**, click **Box**. Under **Style**, scroll down the list. About two-thirds down the list, click the style with a thin top and bottom line and a slightly thicker middle line.

h. Click the **Color arrow**, and then under **Theme Colors**, in the fourth column, click the first color—**Dark Blue, Text 2**. Click **OK**, and then **Save** your document.

3 Press Ctrl + End to move to the bottom of the document. On the **Insert tab**, in the **Text group**, click the **Text Box** button. At the bottom of the **Text Box** gallery, click **Draw Text Box**.

a. At the bottom of the document, position the pointer in an open area near the left margin, and then drag down and to the right to create a text box approximately **2.5 inches** high and **5.5 inches** wide; you need not be precise.

b. With the insertion point positioned in the text box, type the following:

Welcome Week Highlights

Tuesday: Campus tour and meeting with administrators

Wednesday: Open house in all academic departments

Thursday: Club meetings to recruit members

Friday: Student Government-hosted barbecue

(Project 1C Welcome Week continues on the next page)

c. In the text box, select all of the text. On the Mini toolbar, click the **Font Size button arrow**, and then click **14**. Click the **Bold** button, and then click the **Center** button.

d. On the **Format tab**, in the **Size group**, if necessary click the **Size** button. Click the **Shape Height spin arrows** as necessary to change the height of the text box to **2.5"**. Click the **Shape Width button up spin arrow** as necessary to widen the text box to **5.5"**.

e. In the **Shape Styles group**, click the **Shape Effects** button. Point to **Shadow**, and then under **Outer**, in the second row, click the second style—**Offset Center**. In the **Shape Styles group**, click the **Shape Outline button arrow**. Under **Theme Colors**, in the fourth column, click the first color—**Dark Blue, Text 2**.

f. If necessary, click anywhere inside the text box. Point to the text box border to display the 🖰 pointer. Drag the text box to align the left edge at approximately **0.5 inches on the horizontal ruler** and to align the top edge at approximately **5.5 inches on the vertical ruler**. You may have to click outside the text box several times to see the exact location on the rulers.

g. On the **Insert tab**, in the **Illustrations group**, click the **Shapes** button. Under **Basic Shapes**, in the first row, click the seventh shape—**Diamond**.

h. Position the ⊞ pointer slightly under the text box and at approximately **2 inches on the horizontal ruler**. Drag down approximately **1 inch** and to the right approximately **2 inches**. On the **Format tab**, in the **Size group**, adjust the **Shape Height** to **0.9"** and the **Shape Width** to **2"**.

i. Right-click the new shape, and then click **Add Text**. Type **Enjoy!** and then select the text you typed. On the Mini toolbar, click the **Font Size button arrow**,

and then click **20**. Click the **Bold** button, and then if necessary, click the **Center** button.

j. On the **Format tab**, in the **Shape Styles group**, click the **Shape Fill button arrow**, and then under **Theme Colors**, in the fourth column, click the first color—**Dark Blue, Text 2**.

k. Point to the shape border until the 🖰 pointer displays, and then position the shape with its widest points aligned with the lower edge of the text box and approximately centered. As necessary, move the shape in small increments by pressing the arrow keys on your keyboard. Refer to Figure 1.50 for approximate placement. **Save** your document.

4 Click the **Insert tab**, and then, in the **Header & Footer group**, click the **Footer** button. At the bottom of the **Footer** gallery, click **Edit Footer**.

a. On the **Design tab**, in the **Insert group**, click the **Quick Parts** button, and then click **Field**. In the **Field names** list, scroll as necessary to locate and click **FileName**. Click **OK**, and then double-click anywhere in the document.

b. Press Ctrl + Home to move the insertion point to the beginning of the document. Display **Backstage** view. On the right, under the screen thumbnail, click **Properties**, and then click **Show Document Panel**. In the **Author** box, delete any text and then type your firstname and lastname. In the **Subject** box, type your course name and section number, and in the **Keywords** box type **Welcome Week**

c. **Close** the Document Panel. In **Backstage** view, click the **Print tab** to display the **Print Preview**. If necessary, return to the document to make any corrections or adjustments.

d. **Save** your document, print or submit electronically as directed by your instructor, and then **Close** Word.

End You have completed Project 1C

Content-Based Assessments

Apply **1B** skills from these Objectives:

5 Change Document and Paragraph Layout

6 Create and Modify Lists

7 Set and Modify Tab Stops

8 Insert a SmartArt Graphic

Skills Review | Project **1D** Constitution

In the following Skills Review, you will edit the constitution of the Associated Students of Laurel College. Your completed document will look similar to Figure 1.51.

Project Files

For Project 1D, you will need the following file:

w01D_Constitution

You will save your document as:

Lastname_Firstname_1D_Constitution

Project Results

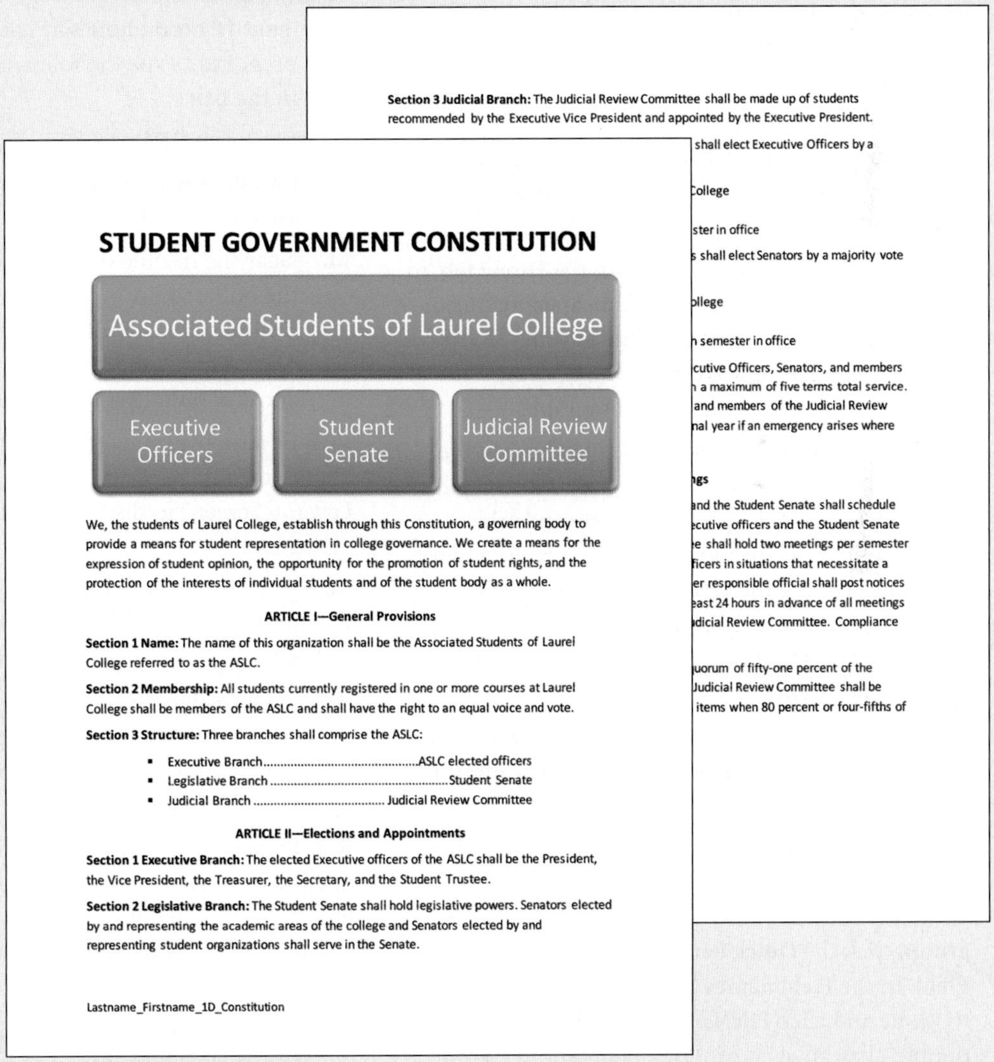

Figure 1.51

(Project 1D Constitution continues on the next page)

1 **Start** Word. From your student files, locate and open the document **w01D_Constitution**. Display **Backstage** view, click **Save As**, and then navigate to your **Word Chapter 1** folder. **Save** the document as **Lastname_Firstname_1D_Constitution**

a. On the **Home tab**, in the **Paragraph group**, be sure the **Show/Hide** button is active so you can view formatting marks. Click the **Page Layout tab**. In the **Page Setup group**, click the **Margins** button, and then at the bottom of the **Margins** gallery, at the bottom of the list, click **Custom Margins**. In the **Page Setup** dialog box, in the **Top** box, type **1** Press `Tab` as necessary to select the values in the **Bottom**, **Left**, and **Right** boxes and change all margins to **1**. Click **OK**.

b. Press `Ctrl` + `A` to select all of the text in the document. On the **Home tab**, in the **Paragraph group**, click the **Align Text Left** button to change the alignment from justified to left aligned.

c. With all of the text still selected, on the **Home tab**, in the **Paragraph group**, click the **Line Spacing** button, and then click **1.15**. Click the **Page Layout tab**, and then in the **Paragraph group**, under **Spacing**, set **After** to **6 pt** spacing after each paragraph.

d. At the top of the document, click anywhere in the title, right-click, and then on the Mini toolbar, click **Center**. Near the top of **Page 1**, locate and select the paragraph that begins *ARTICLE 1*. Hold down `Ctrl`, and then use the vertical scroll bar to scroll through the document, and then select the other two paragraphs that begin *ARTICLE*. On the Mini toolbar, click **Center**.

e. With the three subheadings that begin *ARTICLE* still selected, on the **Page Layout tab**, in the **Paragraph group**, under **Spacing**, set **Before** to **12 pt**.

f. Scroll to view the bottom of **Page 1**, point anywhere in the bottom margin area, right-click, and then click **Edit Footer**. On the **Design tab**, in the **Insert group**, click the **Quick Parts** button, and then click **Field**. In the **Field names** list, scroll as necessary to locate and click **FileName**. Click **OK**, and then double-click anywhere in the document to exit the footer area.

2 Near the middle of **Page 1**, *above* the *ARTICLE II* subheading, locate the paragraph that begins *Executive Branch*, and then move the pointer into the left margin

area to display the pointer. Drag down to select this paragraph and the next two paragraphs. On the **Home tab**, in the **Paragraph group**, click the **Bullets** button.

a. Scroll to view the bottom of **Page 1**, and then locate the paragraph that begins *Completion of at least*. Select that paragraph and the next two paragraphs. On the **Home tab**, in the **Paragraph group**, click the **Numbering** button.

b. Locate the paragraph that begins *Section 4 Elections*. Click to position the insertion point at the *end* of that paragraph after the colon, and then press `Enter`.

c. Type **1.** and press `Spacebar`. Type **Completion of at least 12 credit hours at Laurel College** and then press `Enter`. Type the following text for items 2 and 3 in the list:

Minimum GPA of 2.75

Enrollment in at least six credit hours each semester in office

d. Near the middle of **Page 1**, select the three items in the bulleted list, right-click the list, and then point to **Bullets**. Under **Bullet Library**, click the **black square** symbol. If the black square is not available, choose another bullet symbol. **Save** your document.

3 Be sure the bulleted list is still selected. Point to the left tab marker at **2″ on the horizontal ruler**. When the *Left Tab* ScreenTip displays, double-click to open the **Tabs** dialog box.

a. Under **Tab stop position**, with *2″* selected, at the bottom of the dialog box, click **Clear** to delete this tab stop. Then, type **5.5** in the **Tab stop position** box.

b. Under **Alignment**, click the **Right** option button. Under **Leader**, click the **2** option button. At the bottom of the **Tabs** dialog box, click the **Set** button, and then click **OK**.

4 Press `Ctrl` + `Home` to move to the top of the document. Click at the end of the title, and then press `Enter` to insert a blank paragraph. Click the **Insert tab**, and then in the **Illustrations group**, click the **SmartArt** button.

a. In the **Choose a SmartArt Graphic** dialog box, on the left, click **Hierarchy**, and in the second row, click the fourth style—**Table Hierarchy**. At the bottom of the **Choose a SmartArt Graphic** dialog box, click **OK**. If necessary, on the Design tab, in the Create Graphic group, activate the Text Pane button.

(Project 1D Constitution continues on the next page)

b. In the SmartArt graphic, in the second row, click the border of the first *[Text]* box, and then press Del. Press Del again to delete a second *[Text]* box. In the **Text Pane**, under **Type your text here** box, click in the last bulleted point. On the **Design tab**, in the **Create Graphic group**, click the **Promote** button to move the list item up one level.

c. In the **Text Pane**, click in the top bulleted point, type **Associated Students of Laurel College** and then press ↓. Type the following in the three remaining boxes:

Executive Officers

Student Senate

Judicial Review Committee

d. In the upper right corner of the **Text Pane**, click the **Close** button. Be sure the graphic is selected—a pale border surrounds the entire graphic, and then click the outside border one time. Click the **Format tab**, and then in the **Size group**, if necessary click the **Size** button. By clicking the spin box arrows, change the **Shape Height** to **2.6″** and the **Shape Width** to **6.5″**.

e. With the SmartArt graphic still selected, on the **Design tab**, in the **SmartArt Styles group**, click the **Change Colors** button. Scroll down, and then under **Accent 5**, click the second style—**Colored Fill - Accent 5**.

f. On the **Design tab**, in the **SmartArt Styles group**, click the **More** button. Under **3-D**, click the second style—**Inset**. Click anywhere in the document to deselect the graphic. Press Ctrl + Home to move the insertion point to the beginning of the document.

g. Display **Backstage** view, on the right, under the screen thumbnail, click **Properties**, and then click **Show Document Panel**. In the **Author** box, type your firstname and lastname. In the **Subject** box type your course name and section number, and in the **Keywords** box type **student constitution**

h. **Close** the Document Panel. Click **Save**. Display **Backstage** view and click the **Print tab**. Examine the **Print Preview**. Print or submit electronically as directed. **Close** Word.

End **You have completed Project 1D**

Content-Based Assessments

Apply **1A** skills from these Objectives:

1 Create a New Document and Insert Text

2 Insert and Format Graphics

3 Insert and Modify Text Boxes and Shapes

4 Preview and Print a Document

Mastering Word | Project **1E** Retreat

In the following Mastering Word project, you will create a flyer announcing a retreat for the Associated Students of Laurel College Board. Your completed document will look similar to Figure 1.52.

Project Files

For Project 1E, you will need the following files:

New blank Word document
w01E_Retreat_Text
w01E_Retreat_Picture

You will save your document as:

Lastname_Firstname_1E_Retreat

Project Results

Figure 1.52

(Project 1E Retreat continues on the next page)

Content-Based Assessments

1 **Start** Word and display a new blank document. **Save** the document in your **Word Chapter 1** folder as Lastname_Firstname_1E_Retreat and then add the file name to the footer. Be sure the formatting marks and rulers display.

2 Type **ASLC Board Retreat** and press Enter two times. Type **College President Diane Gilmore is pleased to announce a retreat for the Board of the Associated Students of Laurel College.** Press Enter one time. **Insert** the file **w01E_Retreat_Text**.

3 Select the title *ASLC Board Retreat*. On the **Home tab**, in the **Font group**, display the **Text Effects** gallery, and then in the third row, apply the first effect—**Fill - White, Gradient Outline - Accent 1**. Change the **Font Size** to **56** pt. Apply a **Shadow** text effect using the first effect under **Outer**—**Offset Diagonal Bottom Right**. Change the **Font Color** to **Olive Green, Accent 3, Darker 25%**—in the seventh column, the fifth color.

4 Click to position the insertion point at the beginning of the paragraph that begins *College President*, and then from your student files, **Insert** the picture **w01E_Retreat_Picture**. Change the **Shape Height** of the picture to **2″**, and then set the **Wrap Text** to **Square**. Move the picture so that the right edge aligns with the right margin, and the top edge aligns with the top edge of the text that begins *College President*. Apply a **Film Grain Artistic Effect**—the third effect in the third row. From **Picture Effects**, add a **5 Point Soft Edge**.

5 Scroll to view the lower portion of the page. **Insert** a **Text Box** beginning at the left margin and at approximately **7 inches on the vertical ruler** that is approximately 1″ high and 4.5″ wide. Then, in the **Size group**, make the measurements exact by setting the **Height** to **1″** and the **Width** to **4.6″**. Type the following text in the text box:

> **Prize drawings at lunch include concert tickets, college football jerseys, coffee mugs, and restaurant gift cards.**

6 Select the text in the text box. Change the **Font Size** to **16** pt, apply **Bold**, and **Center** the text. Add a **Shape Fill** to the text box using the theme color **Olive Green, Accent 3, Lighter 40%**. Then apply a **Gradient** fill using the **Linear Right** gradient. Change the **Shape Outline** color to **White, Background 1**. Drag the text box as necessary to center it horizontally between the left and right margins, and vertically between the last line of text and the footer.

7 Display the **Document Panel**. Type your firstname and lastname in the **Author** box, your course name and section number in the **Subject** box, and then in the **Keywords** box type **retreat, ASLC**

8 **Close** the Document Panel. **Save** and preview your document, make any necessary adjustments, and then print your document or submit it electronically as directed. **Close** Word.

End **You have completed Project 1E**

Content-Based Assessments

Apply **1B** skills from these Objectives:

5 Change Document and Paragraph Layout

6 Create and Modify Lists

7 Set and Modify Tab Stops

8 Insert a SmartArt Graphic

Mastering Word | Project **1F** Cycling Trip

In the following Mastering Word project, you will create an informational handout about a planned trip by the Laurel College Cycling Club. Your completed document will look similar to Figure 1.53.

Project Files

For Project 1F, you will need the following file:

w01F_Cycling_Trip

You will save your document as:

Lastname_Firstname_1F_Cycling_Trip

Project Results

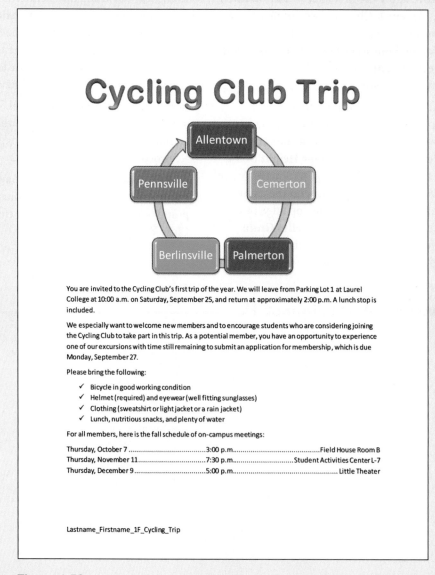

Figure 1.53

(Project 1F Cycling Trip continues on the next page)

Content-Based Assessments

Mastering Word | Project **1F** Cycling Trip (continued)

1 **Start** Word. From your student files open the document **w01F_Cycling_Trip**. **Save** the document in your **Word Chapter 1** folder as **Lastname_Firstname_1F_Cycling_Trip** Add the file name to the footer. Display formatting marks.

2 Display the **Page Setup** dialog box. Set the **Top** margin to **1.25"** and the other three margins to **1"**. Select all of the text in the document, including the title. Add **6 pt** spacing after all paragraphs. Change the **Line Spacing** to **1.15**. Change the alignment to **Align Text Left**. **Center** the document title—*Cycling Club Trip*.

3 Locate the paragraph that begins *Bicycle in good*. Select that paragraph and the three paragraphs that follow it. Create a bulleted list from the selected text. Use the shortcut menu to display bullet options, and change the bullet character to a **check mark** or another symbol if the check mark is unavailable.

4 Position the insertion point in the blank paragraph at the end of the document. Add a **Right** tab stop at **3.5"**. Display the **Tabs** dialog box and add a dot leader. **Set** the tab stop, and then add and **Set** another **Right** tab stop with a dot leader at **6.5"**.

5 Type the text shown in **Table 1**, pressing Tab between columns and Enter at the end of each line. Refer to Figure 1.53.

6 Select the first two lines in the tabbed list and change the **Space After** to **0 pt**. Near the top of the document, position the insertion point in the blank line below the title. Display the **Choose a SmartArt Graphic** dialog box, select the **Cycle** category, and then in the second row, select the first style—**Continuous Cycle**.

7 Display the **Text Pane**. Add the following cities in this order: **Allentown** and **Cemerton** and **Palmerton** and **Berlinsville** and **Pennsville**

8 **Close** the Text Pane. Click the SmartArt border. On the **Format tab**, set the **Shape Width** of the SmartArt graphic to **6.5"** and the **Shape Height** to **3"**. On the **Design tab**, from the **SmartArt Styles** gallery, apply the **Cartoon 3-D** style, and change the colors to the first color under **Colorful—Colorful – Accent Colors**.

9 Display the **Document Panel**, type your firstname and lastname in the **Author** box, your course name and section number in the **Subject** box, and then in the **Keywords** box type **cycling, cycling club**

10 **Close** the Document Panel. **Save** your document. Preview your document, check for and make any adjustments, and then print your document or submit it electronically as directed. **Close** Word.

Table 1

Thursday, October 7	3:00 p.m.	Field House Room B
Thursday, November 11	7:30 p.m.	Student Activities Center L-7
Thursday, December 9	5:00 p.m.	Little Theater

- - - ➤ (Return to Step 6)

End **You have completed Project 1F** ——————————————————

Apply a combination of **1A** and **1B** skills:

- ▪ Create a New Document and Insert Text
- ▪ Insert and Format Graphics
- ▪ Insert and Modify Text Boxes and Shapes
- ▪ Preview and Print a Document
- ▪ Change Document and Paragraph Layout
- ▪ Create and Modify Lists
- ▪ Set and Modify Tab Stops
- ▪ Insert a SmartArt Graphic

Mastering Word | Project **1G** Web Sites

In the following Mastering Word project, you will edit guidelines for club Web sites at Laurel College. Your completed document will look similar to Figure 1.54.

Project Files

For Project 1G, you will need the following files:

New blank Word document
w01G_Chess_Club_Picture
w01G_Web_Sites_Text

You will save your document as:

Lastname_Firstname_1G_Web_Sites

Project Results

Club Web Sites

Published by Student Computing Services

The Web site that your club develops will represent your club and its membership. The site can promote interest in your club and attract new members—think of it as advertising. The site is also a main source of information for current members. Always consider how others will view or interpret the content of your site. Use the guidelines listed below as you develop and update the information you publish.

The college Student Computing Services office is available to assist clubs with Web site development and maintenance. Consult the contact information, listed at the end of these guidelines, to set up a meeting with one of our staff members.

General Information Guidelines

Be sure that:

- All information on the Web site is club related.
- No personal information or links to personal information is on the Web site unless the content has a specific relationship to the club.
- Updates to the Web site are frequent enough to eliminate outdated content and to add new content.
- Instruction is available to club members regarding proper use of bulletin boards, including general etiquette rules.
- Protected information on the Web site is available only to club members who have been issued user names and passwords.
- The club's faculty advisor approves all Web site content and updates to the site.

General information about the club should include:

1. Purpose and goals of the club
2. Names of club officers and their campus email addresses
3. Dates and locations of club meetings
4. Dates and locations of special events
5. Applications for club membership
6. Information about election of officers and nomination forms

Lastname_Firstname_1G_Web_Sites

Figure 1.54

(Project 1G Web Sites continues on the next page)

Content-Based Assessments

1 **Start** Word and display a new blank document. Display formatting marks and rulers. **Save** the document in your **Word Chapter 1** folder as **Lastname_Firstname_ 1G_Web_Sites** Add the file name to the footer.

Type **Club Web Sites** and then press Enter. Select the title you just typed. From the **Text Effects** gallery, in the fourth row, apply the second effect—**Gradient Fill - Orange, Accent 6, Inner Shadow**, change the **Font Size** to **72** pt, and **Center** the title.

2 Click in the blank line below the title. Locate and insert the file **w01G_Web_Sites_Text**. *Except* for the document title, select all of the document text. **Align Text Left**, change the **Line Spacing** to **1.15**, and change the **Spacing After** to **6 pt**. Locate and **Center** the document subtitle that begins *Published by*.

3 In the middle of **Page 1**, under the subheading *Be sure that*, select the six paragraphs down to, but not including, the *General information* subheading. Format the selected text as a bulleted list. Near the bottom of **Page 1** and the top of **Page 2**, under the *Web Site Design Guidelines* subheading, select all of the paragraphs to the end of the document—not including the blank paragraph mark—and create another bulleted list.

4 Under the subheading that begins *General information*, select the six paragraphs and apply **Numbering** to create a numbered list.

Near the top of the document, position the insertion point to the left of the paragraph that begins The Web site. **Insert** the picture **w01G_Chess_Club_Picture**. Set the **Wrap Text** to **Square**. Decrease the picture **Width** to **2.7″**. From the **Picture Effects** gallery, apply the **Soft Edges** effect using **5 Point**.

5 Press Ctrl + End to move to the blank line at the end of the document. Type **For assistance, Student Computing Services hours are:** and then press Enter. Set a **Left** tab stop at **1.5″**. Display the **Tabs** dialog box. At **5″** add a **Right** tab stop with a **dot leader** and click **Set**. Click **OK** to close the dialog box, press Tab to begin, and then type the following information; be sure to press Tab to

begin each line and press Tab between the days and the times and press Enter at the end of each line:

Monday–Thursday	8 a.m. to 10 p.m.
Friday	8 a.m. to 5 p.m.
Saturday	8 a.m. to 12 noon

6 At the top of **Page 2**, position the insertion point to the left of the subheading *Web Site Design Guidelines*. Press Enter one time, and then click in the blank paragraph you just created. **Insert** a **SmartArt** graphic, and then from the **Process** group, select the **Basic Chevron Process**—in the fourth row, the third graphic. Click the border of the graphic, and then on the **Format tab**, set the **Shape Height** of the graphic to **1″** and the **Shape Width** of the graphic to **6.5″**. From the **Design tab**, display the **Text Pane**, and then type **Club** and **Web Site** and **New Members Close** the **Text Pane**. Change style to **3-D Inset** and the colors to **Colored Fill – Accent 6**, which is in the last set of colors.

7 At the bottom of **Page 2**, **Insert** a **Text Box** and set the height to **0.7″** and the width to **5″**. In the text box, type: **The Student Computing Services office is located in the Cedar Building, Room 114, call (215) 555-0932.**

Select the text in the text box. From the Mini toolbar, change the **Font Size** to **16** pt, apply **Bold**, and **Center** the text. Change the **Shape Fill** to **Orange, Accent 6, Darker 25%**. From the **Shape Effects** gallery, apply a **Circle Bevel**. By using the pointer, visually center the text box horizontally between the left and right margins and vertically between the tabbed list and the footer.

8 As the document properties, type your firstname and lastname in the **Author** box, your course name and section number in the **Subject** box, and then in the **Keywords** box type **Web sites, guidelines, Student Computing Services Save** your document, examine the Print Preview, check for and make any adjustments, and then print your document or submit it electronically as directed. **Close** Word.

End You have completed Project 1G

Content-Based Assessments

GO! Fix It | Project **1H** Guidelines

Project Files

For Project 1H, you will need the following file:

w01H_Guidelines

You will save your document as:

Lastname_Firstname_1H_Guidelines

From the student files that accompany this textbook, locate and open the file w01H_More_Guidelines, and then save the file in your Word Chapter 1 folder as **Lastname_Firstname_1H_Guidelines**

This document contains errors that you must find and correct. Read and examine the document, and then edit to correct any errors that you find and to improve the overall document format. Types of errors could include, but are not restricted to:

- Wasted space due to text not wrapping around pictures
- Inconsistent line spacing in paragraphs
- Inconsistent spacing between paragraphs
- Inconsistent paragraph indents
- Inconsistent indenting of lists
- Titles that do not extend across the page
- Text boxes that are too small
- Tabbed lists with wide spaces that do not contain leaders
- Spaces between paragraphs created using empty paragraphs rather than space after paragraphs

Things you should know to complete this project:

- Displaying formatting marks will assist in locating spacing errors.
- There are no errors in the fonts, although the title font size is too small.
- The final flyer should fit on one page.

Save your document and add the file name to the footer. In the Document Panel, type your firstname and lastname in the Author box and your course name and section number in the Subject box. In the Keywords box type **Web site guidelines** and then save your document and submit as directed.

End **You have completed Project 1H** ——————————

Apply a combination of the **1A** and **1B** skills.

GO! Make It | Project 1I Flyer

Project Files

For Project 1I, you will need the following files:

    w01I_Team_Building   w01I_Park_Picture

You will save your document as:

    Lastname_Firstname_1I_Team_Building

From the student files that accompany this textbook, locate and open the file w01I_Team_Building, and then save the file in your chapter folder as **Lastname_Firstname_1I_Team_Building**

Use the skills you have practiced, create the document shown in Figure 1.55. The title uses Gradient Fill – Blue, Accent 1, 48 pt. The SmartArt graphic uses the Radial Cycle with an Intense Effect style, is 3″ high and 6.5″ wide, has the Colorful Range – Accent Colors 2 to 3 applied. The w01I_Park_Picture picture has a 2.5 pt soft edge, and is 2.5″ wide. The page border uses Dark Blue, Text 2.

Add the file name to the footer; in the Document Panel, add your name and course information and the Keywords **team building**; save your document; and then submit as directed.

Project Results

Figure 1.55

Team Building Session

The administration at Laurel College is organizing a retreat for the ASLC Board, consisting of the Executive Officers and their appointed directors, Student Senators, Club Presidents, and members of the Judicial Review Committee. The retreat will be held at the Fogelsville campus of Penn State University on Friday, November 12.

The afternoon session will begin at 1:30 p.m. When the retreat was first organized, the afternoon session was to include small group work sessions for the sharing and development of goals and a series of exercises to facilitate group interaction. However, we have been fortunate to secure the services of F. B Lewis, the nationally-renowned team-building expert. Therefore, the afternoon session will consist of an outdoor team-building exercise.

The exercise will be held in Westfield Park, which is shown in the picture, and will enable each participant to:

- Decide when teams are appropriate, and when they are not
- Devise new conflict resolution strategies
- Strengthen leadership skills
- Strengthen interpersonal skills
- Value and understand diversity

Lastname_Firstname_1I_Team_Building

End You have completed Project 1I

Content-Based Assessments

GO! Solve It | Project **1J** Food Drive

Project Files

For Project 1J, you will need the following file:

New blank Word document
w01J_Food_Drive

You will save your document as:

Lastname_Firstname_1J_Food_Drive

Create a new document and save it in your Word Chapter 1 folder as **Lastname_Firstname_1J_Food_Drive** Use the following information to create a flyer that includes a title that uses Text Effects, introductory text, two lists of an appropriate type, one text box, and a picture with appropriate formatting and text wrapping. Use your own picture or w01J_Food_Drive.

This Thanksgiving, the Associated Students of Laurel College is sponsoring a food drive for the local community. All college clubs are invited to participate. Results will be adjusted for club membership by measuring the results in pounds of food per member. Three kinds of food are acceptable: canned goods, non-perishable dry goods, and boxed or canned dry drink mixes, such as coffee, tea, or lemonade.

To participate, a club must follow this procedure: fill out a competition form, collect the goods, and then turn the food in on November 13. The address and telephone number for the ASLC is the Cedar Building, Room 222, Laurelton, PA 19100, (215) 555-0902.

Add the file name to the footer. To the Properties area, add your name, your course name and section number, and the keywords **food drive, clubs**

<table>
<tr><td rowspan="2"></td><td colspan="3">Performance Level</td></tr>
<tr><td>Exemplary:
You consistently applied the relevant skills</td><td>Proficient:
You sometimes, but not always, applied the relevant skills</td><td>Developing:
You rarely or never applied the relevant skills</td></tr>
<tr><td>Create and format lists</td><td>Both lists use the proper list type and are formatted correctly.</td><td>One of the lists is formatted correctly.</td><td>Neither of the lists are formatted correctly.</td></tr>
<tr><td>Insert and format a picture</td><td>The picture is inserted and positioned correctly, and text is wrapped around the picture.</td><td>The picture is inserted but not formatted properly.</td><td>No picture is inserted.</td></tr>
<tr><td>Insert a text box</td><td>A text box with appropriate information is inserted and formatted.</td><td>A text box is adequately formatted but is difficult to read or unattractive.</td><td>No text box is inserted.</td></tr>
<tr><td>Insert introductory text</td><td>Introductory text explains the reason for the flyer, with no spelling or grammar errors.</td><td>Some introductory text is included, but does not contain sufficient information and/or includes spelling or grammar errors.</td><td>No introductory text, or insufficient introductory text.</td></tr>
<tr><td>Insert title using Text Effects</td><td>Text Effects title inserted and centered on the page.</td><td>Text Effects title is inserted, but not centered or formatted attractively on the page.</td><td>No Text Effects title is included.</td></tr>
</table>

Performance Criteria

End You have completed Project 1J

Content-Based Assessments

Apply a combination of the **1A** and **1B** skills..

GO! Solve It | Project **1K** Fitness Services

Project Files

For Project 1K, you will need the following files:

New blank Word document
w01K_Volleyball

You will save your document as:

Lastname_Firstname_1K_Fitness_Services

Create a new file and save it as **Lastname_Firstname_1K_Fitness Services** Use the following information to create a flyer that includes introductory text, a SmartArt graphic, a title that uses Text Effects, and a picture that has an artistic effect applied and uses text wrapping. Use your own picture or w01K_Volleyball.

The Associated Students of Laurel College sponsors fitness activities. These take place both on campus and off campus. The activities fall into two categories: Fitness Services and Intramural Sports. Fitness Services are noncompetitive activities, with the most popular being Kickboxing, Jogging, and Aerobics. The most popular Intramural Sports activities—which include competitive team and club sports—are Field Hockey, Volleyball, and Basketball.

Add the file name to the footer, and add your name, your course name and section number, and the keywords **fitness, sports** to the Properties area.

	Performance Level		
	Exemplary: You consistently applied the relevant skills	Proficient: You sometimes, but not always, applied the relevant skills	Developing: You rarely or never applied the relevant skills
Insert title using Text Effects	Text Effects title inserted and centered on the page.	Text Effects title is inserted, but not centered on the page.	No Text Effects title is included.
Insert introductory text	Introductory text explains the reason for the flyer, with no spelling or grammar errors.	Some introductory text is included, but does not sufficiently explain the topic and/or includes spelling or grammar errors.	No or insufficient introductory text is included.
Insert and format a picture	The picture is inserted and positioned correctly, an artistic effect is applied, and text is wrapped around the picture.	The picture is inserted but not formatted properly.	No picture is inserted in the document.
Insert and format SmartArt	The SmartArt graphic displays both categories of fitness activities and examples of each type.	The SmartArt graphic does not display fitness activities by category.	No SmartArt graphic inserted.

Performance Criteria (left side label)

End You have completed Project 1K

Outcomes-Based Assessments

Rubric

The following outcomes-based assessments are *open-ended assessments*. That is, there is no specific correct result; your result will depend on your approach to the information provided. Make *Professional Quality* your goal. Use the following scoring rubric to guide you in *how* to approach the problem and then to evaluate *how well* your approach solves the problem.

The *criteria*—Software Mastery, Content, Format and Layout, and Process—represent the knowledge and skills you have gained that you can apply to solving the problem. The *levels of performance*—Professional Quality, Approaching Professional Quality, or Needs Quality Improvements—help you and your instructor evaluate your result.

	Your completed project is of Professional Quality if you:	Your completed project is Approaching Professional Quality if you:	Your completed project Needs Quality Improvements if you:
1-Software Mastery	Choose and apply the most appropriate skills, tools, and features and identify efficient methods to solve the problem.	Choose and apply some appropriate skills, tools, and features, but not in the most efficient manner.	Choose inappropriate skills, tools, or features, or are inefficient in solving the problem.
2-Content	Construct a solution that is clear and well organized, contains content that is accurate, appropriate to the audience and purpose, and is complete. Provide a solution that contains no errors in spelling, grammar, or style.	Construct a solution in which some components are unclear, poorly organized, inconsistent, or incomplete. Misjudge the needs of the audience. Have some errors in spelling, grammar, or style, but the errors do not detract from comprehension.	Construct a solution that is unclear, incomplete, or poorly organized; contains some inaccurate or inappropriate content; and contains many errors in spelling, grammar, or style. Do not solve the problem.
3-Format and Layout	Format and arrange all elements to communicate information and ideas, clarify function, illustrate relationships, and indicate relative importance.	Apply appropriate format and layout features to some elements, but not others. Overuses features, causing minor distraction.	Apply format and layout that does not communicate information or ideas clearly. Do not use format and layout features to clarify function, illustrate relationships, or indicate relative importance. Use available features excessively, causing distraction.
4-Process	Use an organized approach that integrates planning, development, self-assessment, revision, and reflection.	Demonstrate an organized approach in some areas, but not others; or, uses an insufficient process of organization throughout.	Do not use an organized approach to solve the problem.

Outcomes-Based Assessments

Apply a combination of the **1A** and **1B** skills..

GO! Think | Project **1L** Academic Services

Project Files

For Project 1L, you will need the following file:

New blank Word document

You will save your document as:

Lastname_Firstname_1L_Academic_Services

The Services Coordinator of the Associated Students of Laurel College needs to create a flyer to inform students of academic services available at the ASLC office. Referrals are available for medical, legal, and counseling services, as well as tutoring and volunteer organizations. Among the services offered at the ASLC office are free printing (up to 250 pages per semester), help with minor legal issues, housing information, bicycle repair, minor computer repair, and help placing students with volunteer organizations.

Create a flyer with basic information about the services provided. Be sure the flyer is easy to read and understand and has an attractive design. If you need more information about student services available at other colleges, search the Web for **student government** and add whatever services you think might be (or should be) available at your college. Add appropriate information to the Document Panel. Save the document as **Lastname_Firstname_1L_Academic_Services** and submit it as directed.

End **You have completed Project 1L** ————————————

Apply a combination of the **1A** and **1B** skills.

GO! Think | Project **1M** Campus Bookstore

Project Files

For Project 1M, you will need the following files:

New blank Word document
w01L_Campus_Bookstore

You will save your document as:

Lastname_Firstname_1M_Campus_Bookstore

The manager of the Laurel College Bookstore needs to create a flyer that can be handed out by the ASLC to students during Welcome Week. The bookstore gives students attending Welcome Week a discount of 20% on special items such as sweatshirts and other college-related clothing, coffee mugs, calendars, and similar items. Door prizes will also be awarded. The bookstore is open Monday and Thursday from 8 a.m. to 10 p.m., Tuesday and Wednesday from 8 a.m. to 8 p.m., and Friday from 8 a.m. to 5 p.m.

Using your own campus bookstore as an example, create a flyer that gives general information about the bookstore, provides one or more lists of items that are on sale, displays the picture w01M_ Campus_Bookstore, and has a highlighted area that gives the store hours.

Add appropriate information to the Document Panel. Save the document as **Lastname_Firstname_1M_Campus_Bookstore** and submit it as directed.

End **You have completed Project 1M** ————————————

Outcomes-Based Assessments

You and GO! | Project **1N** Family Flyer

Project Files

For Project 1N, you will need the following file:

New blank Word document

You will save your document as

Lastname_Firstname_1N_Family_Flyer

In this project, you will create a one-page flyer that you can send to your family. Include any information that may interest your family members, such as work-related news, school events, vacation plans, and the activities and accomplishments of you, your spouse, your friends, or other family members. Choose any writing style that suits you—chatty, newsy, entertaining, or humorous.

To complete the assignment, be sure to include a title, at least one list, a picture, and either a SmartArt graphic or a text box or shape. Before you submit the flyer, be sure to check it for grammar and spelling errors, and also be sure to format the document in an attractive manner, using the skills you practiced in this chapter.

Save the file as **Lastname_Firstname_1N_Family_Flyer** Add the file name to the footer, and add your name, your course name and section number, and the keywords **flyer** and **family** to the Properties area. Submit your file as directed.

End **You have completed Project 1N** ————————————————

Creating a Worksheet and Charting Data

OUTCOMES
At the end of this chapter you will be able to:

OBJECTIVES
Mastering these objectives will enable you to:

PROJECT 1A
Create a sales report with an embedded column chart and sparklines.

1. Create, Save, and Navigate an Excel Workbook (p. 107)
2. Enter Data in a Worksheet (p. 110)
3. Construct and Copy Formulas and Use the SUM Function (p. 116)
4. Format Cells with Merge & Center and Cell Styles (p. 120)
5. Chart Data to Create a Column Chart and Insert Sparklines (p. 122)
6. Print, Display Formulas, and Close Excel (p. 127)

PROJECT 1B
Calculate the value of an inventory.

7. Check Spelling in a Worksheet (p. 133)
8. Enter Data by Range (p. 135)
9. Construct Formulas for Mathematical Operations (p. 136)
10. Edit Values in a Worksheet (p. 141)
11. Format a Worksheet (p. 142)

kwest/Shutterstock

In This Chapter

In this chapter, you will use Microsoft Excel 2010 to create and analyze data organized into columns and rows. After entering data in a worksheet, you can perform calculations, analyze the data to make logical decisions, and create charts.

In this chapter, you will create and modify Excel workbooks. You will practice the basics of worksheet design, create a footer, enter and edit data in a worksheet, chart data, and then save, preview, and print workbooks. You will also construct formulas for mathematical operations.

The projects in this chapter relate to **Texas Spectrum Wireless**, which provides accessories and software for all major brands of cell phones, smart phones, PDAs, mp3 players, and portable computers. The company sells thousands of unique products in their retail stores, which are located throughout Texas and the southern United States. They also sell thousands of items each year through their Web site, and offer free shipping and returns to their customers. The company takes pride in offering unique categories of accessories such as waterproof and ruggedized gear.

Project 1A Sales Report with Embedded Column Chart and Sparklines

Project Activities

In Activities 1.01 through 1.16, you will create an Excel worksheet for Roslyn Thomas, the President of Texas Spectrum Wireless. The worksheet displays the first quarter sales of wireless accessories for the current year, and includes a chart to visually represent the data. Your completed worksheet will look similar to Figure 1.1.

Project Files

For Project 1A, you will need the following file:

New blank Excel workbook

You will save your workbook as:

Lastname_Firstname_1A_Quarterly_Sales

Project Results

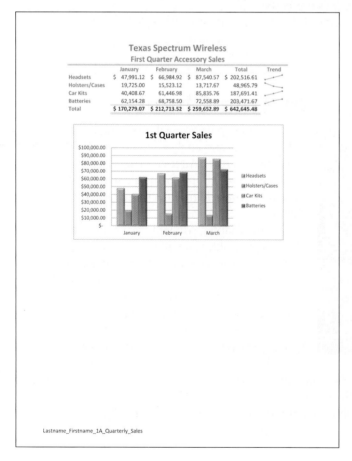

Figure 1.1
Project 1A Quarterly Sales

Objective 1 | Create, Save, and Navigate an Excel Workbook

On startup, Excel displays a new blank **workbook**—the Excel document that stores your data—which contains one or more pages called a **worksheet**. A worksheet—or **spreadsheet**—is stored in a workbook, and is formatted as a pattern of uniformly spaced horizontal rows and vertical columns. The intersection of a column and a row forms a box referred to as a **cell**.

Activity 1.01 | Starting Excel and Naming and Saving a Workbook

1 **Start** Excel. In the lower right corner of the window, if necessary, click the Normal button ▦, and then to the right, locate the zoom—magnification—level.

> Your zoom level should be 100%, although some figures in this textbook may be shown at a higher zoom level.

Another Way

Use the keyboard shortcut F12 to display the Save As dialog box.

2 In the upper left corner of your screen, click the **File tab** to display **Backstage** view, click **Save As**, and then in the **Save As** dialog box, navigate to the location where you will store your workbooks for this chapter.

3 In your storage location, create a new folder named **Excel Chapter 1** Open the new folder to display its folder window, and then in the **File name** box, notice that *Book1* displays as the default file name.

4 In the **File name** box, click *Book1* to select it, and then using your own name, type **Lastname_Firstname_1A_Quarterly_Sales** being sure to include the underscore (Shift + -) instead of spaces between words. Compare your screen with Figure 1.2.

Figure 1.2

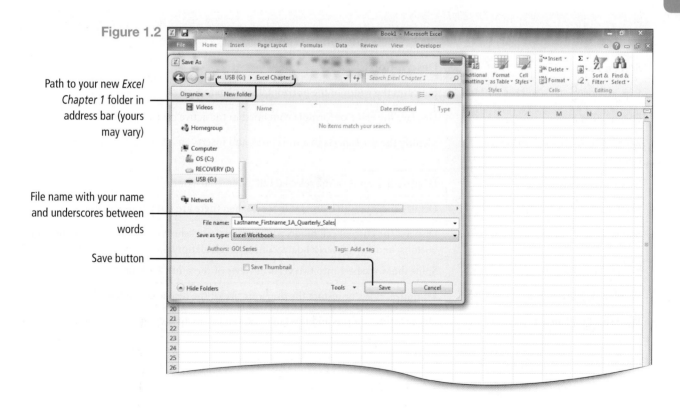

Path to your new *Excel Chapter 1* folder in address bar (yours may vary)

File name with your name and underscores between words

Save button

5 Click **Save**. Compare your screen with Figure 1.3, and then take a moment to study the Excel window parts in the table in Figure 1.4.

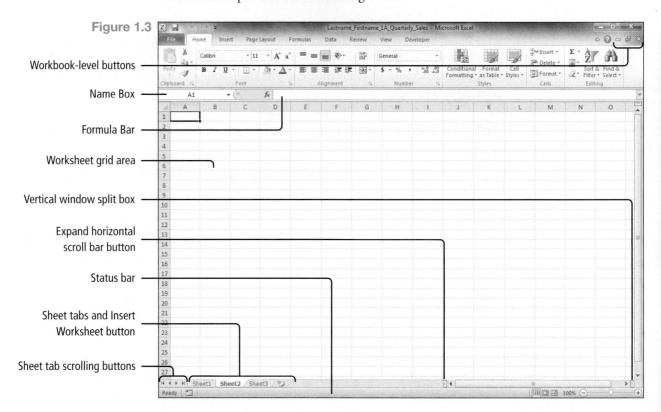

Figure 1.3

- Workbook-level buttons
- Name Box
- Formula Bar
- Worksheet grid area
- Vertical window split box
- Expand horizontal scroll bar button
- Status bar
- Sheet tabs and Insert Worksheet button
- Sheet tab scrolling buttons

Parts of the Excel Window

Screen Part	Description
Expand horizontal scroll bar button	Increases the width of the horizontal scroll bar.
Formula Bar	Displays the value or formula contained in the active cell; also permits entry or editing.
Sheet tabs and Insert Worksheet button	Identify the worksheets in a workbook and inserts an additional worksheet.
Name Box	Displays the name of the selected cell, table, chart, or object.
Sheet tab scrolling buttons	Display sheet tabs that are not in view when there are numerous sheet tabs.
Status bar	Displays the current cell mode, page number, worksheet information, view and zoom buttons, and for numerical data, common calculations such as Sum and Average.
Vertical window split box	Splits the worksheet into two vertical views of the same worksheet.
Workbook-level buttons	Minimize, close, or restore the previous size of the displayed workbook.
Worksheet grid area	Displays the columns and rows that intersect to form the worksheet's cells.

Figure 1.4

Activity 1.02 | Navigating a Worksheet and a Workbook

1 Take a moment to study Figure 1.5 and the table in Figure 1.6 to become familiar with the Excel workbook window.

Figure 1.5

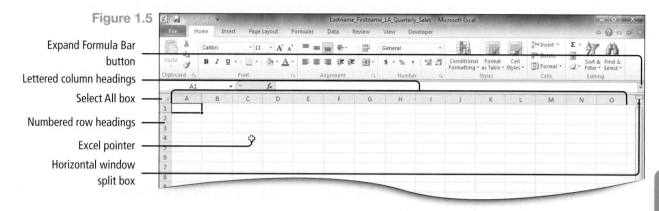

Expand Formula Bar button
Lettered column headings
Select All box
Numbered row headings
Excel pointer
Horizontal window split box

Excel Workbook Window Elements

Workbook Window Element	Description
Excel pointer	Displays the pointer in Excel.
Expand Formula Bar button	Increases the height of the Formula Bar to display lengthy cell content.
Horizontal window split box	Splits the worksheet into two horizontal views of the same worksheet.
Lettered column headings	Indicate the column letter.
Numbered row headings	Indicate the row number.
Select All box	Selects all the cells in a worksheet.

Figure 1.6

2 In the lower right corner of the screen, in the horizontal scroll bar, click the **right scroll arrow** one time to shift **column A** out of view.

A *column* is a vertical group of cells in a worksheet. Beginning with the first letter of the alphabet, *A*, a unique letter identifies each column—this is called the *column heading*. Clicking one of the horizontal scroll bar arrows shifts the window either left or right one column at a time.

3 Point to the **right scroll arrow**, and then hold down the left mouse button until the columns begin to scroll rapidly to the right; release the mouse button when you begin to see pairs of letters as the column headings.

4 Slowly drag the horizontal scroll box to the left, and notice that just above the scroll box, ScreenTips with the column letters display as you drag. Drag the horizontal scroll box left or right—or click the left or right scroll arrow—as necessary to position **column Z** near the center of your screen.

Column headings after column Z use two letters starting with AA, AB, and so on through ZZ. After that, columns begin with three letters beginning with AAA. This pattern provides 16,384 columns. The last column is XFD.

5 In the lower left portion of your screen, click the **Sheet2 tab**.

The second worksheet displays and is the active sheet. Column A displays at the left.

6 In the vertical scroll bar, click the **down scroll arrow** one time to move **Row 1** out of view.

> A *row* is a horizontal group of cells. Beginning with number 1, a unique number identifies each row—this is the *row heading*, located at the left side of the worksheet. A single worksheet has 1,048,576 rows.

7 In the lower left corner, click the **Sheet1 tab**.

> The first worksheet in the workbook becomes the active worksheet. By default, new workbooks contain three worksheets. When you save a workbook, the worksheets are contained within it and do not have separate file names.

8 Use the skills you just practiced to scroll horizontally to display **column A**, and if necessary, **row 1**.

Objective 2 | Enter Data in a Worksheet

Cell content, which is anything you type in a cell, can be one of two things: either a *constant value*—referred to simply as a *value*—or a *formula*. A formula is an equation that performs mathematical calculations on values in your worksheet. The most commonly used values are *text values* and *number values*, but a value can also include a date or a time of day.

Activity 1.03 | Entering Text and Using AutoComplete

A text value, also referred to as a *label*, usually provides information about number values in other worksheet cells. For example, a title such as First Quarter Accessory Sales gives the reader an indication that the data in the worksheet relates to information about sales of accessories during the three-month period January through March.

1 Click the **Sheet1 tab** to make it the active sheet. Point to and then click the cell at the intersection of **column A** and **row 1** to make it the *active cell*—the cell is outlined in black and ready to accept data.

> The intersecting column letter and row number form the *cell reference*—also called the *cell address*. When a cell is active, its column letter and row number are highlighted. The cell reference of the selected cell, *A1*, displays in the Name Box.

2 With cell **A1** as the active cell, type the worksheet title **Texas Spectrum Wireless** and then press Enter. Compare your screen with Figure 1.7.

> Text or numbers in a cell are referred to as *data*. You must confirm the data you type in a cell by pressing Enter or by some other keyboard movement, such as pressing Tab or an arrow key. Pressing Enter moves the selection to the cell below.

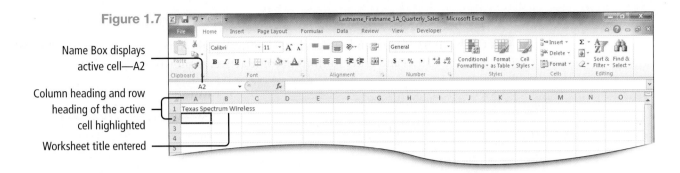

Figure 1.7

Name Box displays
active cell—A2

Column heading and row
heading of the active
cell highlighted

Worksheet title entered

---

3 In cell **A1**, notice that the text does not fit; the text spills over and displays in cells **B1** and **C1** to the right.

> If text is too long for a cell and cells to the right are empty, the text will display. If the cells to the right contain other data, only the text that will fit in the cell displays.

4 In cell **A2**, type the worksheet subtitle **First Quarter Accessory Sales** and then press Enter. Compare your screen with Figure 1.8.

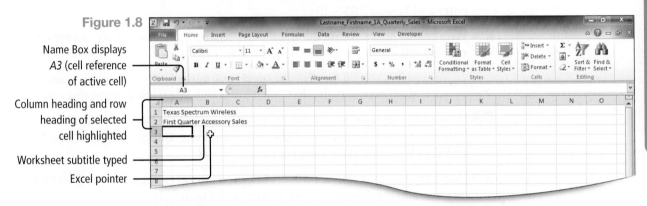

Figure 1.8

Name Box displays
A3 (cell reference
of active cell)

Column heading and row
heading of selected
cell highlighted

Worksheet subtitle typed

Excel pointer

---

5 Press Enter again to make cell **A4** the active cell. In cell **A4**, type **Headsets** which will form the first row title, and then press Enter.

> The text characters that you typed align at the left edge of the cell—referred to as *left alignment*—and cell A5 becomes the active cell. Left alignment is the default for text values.

6 In cell **A5**, type **H** and notice the text from the previous cell displays.

> If the first characters you type in a cell match an existing entry in the column, Excel fills in the remaining characters for you. This feature, called *AutoComplete*, assists only with alphabetic values.

7 Continue typing the remainder of the row title **olsters/Cases** and press Enter.

> The AutoComplete suggestion is removed when the entry you are typing differs from the previous value.

Another Way

Use the keyboard shortcut Ctrl + S to Save changes to your workbook.

8 In cell **A6**, type **Car Kits** and press Enter. In cell **A7**, type **Batteries** and press Enter. In cell **A8**, type **Total** and press Enter. On the Quick Access Toolbar, click **Save** 🔲.

Activity 1.04 | Using Auto Fill and Keyboard Shortcuts

1 Click cell **B3**. Type **J** and notice that when you begin to type in a cell, on the **Formula Bar**, the **Cancel** and **Enter** buttons become active, as shown in Figure 1.9.

Figure 1.9

Cancel and Enter buttons

Row titles entered

Excel pointer when entering text in a cell

2 Continue to type **anuary** On the **Formula Bar**, notice that values you type in a cell also display there. Then, on the **Formula Bar**, click the **Enter** button ✓ to confirm the entry and keep cell **B3** active.

3 With cell **B3** active, locate the small black square in the lower right corner of the selected cell.

> You can drag this *fill handle*—the small black square in the lower right corner of a selected cell—to adjacent cells to fill the cells with values based on the first cell.

4 Point to the **fill handle** until the ➕ pointer displays, hold down the left mouse button, drag to the right to cell **D3**, and as you drag, notice the ScreenTips *February* and *March*. Release the mouse button.

5 Under the text that you just filled, click the **Auto Fill Options** button 🔳▾ that displays, and then compare your screen with Figure 1.10.

> *Auto Fill* generates and extends a *series* of values into adjacent cells based on the value of other cells. A series is a group of things that come one after another in succession; for example, *January, February, March*.

> The Auto Fill Options button displays options to fill the data; options vary depending on the content and program from which you are filling, and the format of the data you are filling.

> *Fill Series* is selected, indicating the action that was taken. Because the options are related to the current task, the button is referred to as being *context sensitive*.

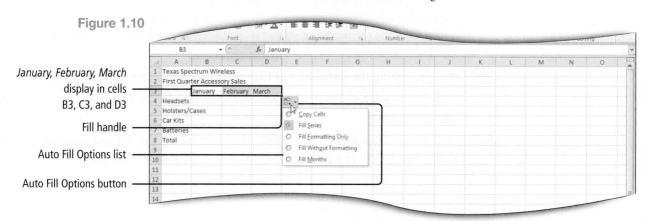

Figure 1.10

January, February, March display in cells B3, C3, and D3

Fill handle

Auto Fill Options list

Auto Fill Options button

6 Click in any cell to cancel the display of the Auto Fill Options list.

> The list no longer displays; the button will display until you perform some other screen action.

7 Press `Ctrl` + `Home`, which is the keyboard shortcut to make cell **A1** active.

8 On the Quick Access Toolbar, click **Save** 🖫 to save the changes you have made to your workbook, and then take a moment to study the table in Figure 1.11 to become familiar with additional keyboard shortcuts with which you can navigate the Excel worksheet.

Keyboard Shortcuts to Navigate the Excel Window

To Move the Location of the Active Cell:	Press:
Up, down, right, or left one cell	`↑`,`↓`,`→`,`←`
Down one cell	`Enter`
Up one cell	`Shift` + `Enter`
Up one full screen	`Page Up`
Down one full screen	`PageDown`
To column A of the current row	`Home`
To the last cell in the last column of the active area (the rectangle formed by all the rows and columns in a worksheet that contain entries)	`Ctrl` + `End`
To cell A1	`Ctrl` + `Home`
Right one cell	`Tab`
Left one cell	`Shift` + `Tab`

Figure 1.11

Activity 1.05 | Aligning Text and Adjusting the Size of Columns

1 In the **column heading area**, point to the vertical line between **column A** and **column B** to display the ⊞ pointer, press and hold down the left mouse button, and then compare your screen with Figure 1.12.

A ScreenTip displays information about the width of the column. The default width of a column is 64 *pixels*. A pixel, short for *picture element*, is a point of light measured in dots per square inch. Sixty-four pixels equal 8.43 characters, which is the average number of digits that will fit in a cell using the default font. The default font in Excel is Calibri and the default font size is 11.

Figure 1.12

Column heading area ——
Mouse pointer ——
ScreenTip ——

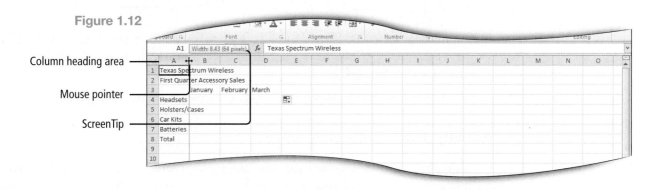

2 Drag to the right, and when the number of pixels indicated in the ScreenTip reaches **100 pixels**, release the mouse button. If you are not satisfied with your result, click Undo 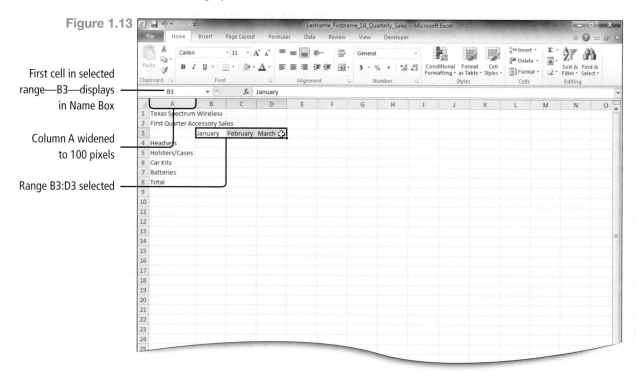 on the Quick Access Toolbar and begin again.

> This width accommodates the longest row title in cells A4 through A8—*Holsters/Cases*. The worksheet title and subtitle in cells A1 and A2 span more than one column and still do not fit in column A.

3 Point to cell **B3** and then drag across to select cells **B3**, **C3**, and **D3**. Compare your screen with Figure 1.13; if you are not satisfied with your result, click anywhere and begin again.

> The three cells, B3 through D3, are selected and form a *range*—two or more cells on a worksheet that are adjacent (next to each other) or nonadjacent (not next to each other). This range of cells is referred to as *B3:D3*. When you see a colon (:) between two cell references, the range includes all the cells between the two cell references.

> A range of cells that is selected in this manner is indicated by a dark border, and Excel treats the range as a single unit so you can make the same changes to more than one cell at a time. The selected cells in the range are highlighted except for the first cell in the range, which displays in the Name Box.

Figure 1.13

First cell in selected range—B3—displays in Name Box

Column A widened to 100 pixels

Range B3:D3 selected

4 With the range **B3:D3** selected, point anywhere over the selected range, right-click, and then on the Mini toolbar, click the **Center** button. On the Quick Access Toolbar, click **Save**.

> The column titles *January*, *February*, *March* align in the center of each cell.

Activity 1.06 | Entering Numbers

To type number values, use either the number keys across the top of your keyboard or the numeric keypad if you have one—laptop computers may not have a numeric keypad.

1 Under *January*, click cell **B4**, type **47991.12** and then on the **Formula Bar**, click the **Enter** button ☑ to maintain cell **B4** as the active cell. Compare your screen with Figure 1.14.

> By default, *number* values align at the right edge of the cell. The default **number format**—a specific way in which Excel displays numbers—is the **general format**. In the default general format, whatever you type in the cell will display, with the exception of trailing zeros to the right of a decimal point. For example, in the number 237.50 the *0* following the *5* is a trailing zero.
>
> Data that displays in a cell is the **displayed value**. Data that displays in the Formula Bar is the **underlying value**. The number of digits or characters that display in a cell—the displayed value—depends on the width of the column. Calculations on numbers will always be based on the underlying value, not the displayed value.

Figure 1.14

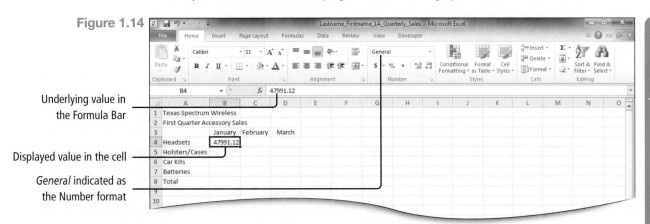

Underlying value in the Formula Bar

Displayed value in the cell

General indicated as the Number format

2 Press `Tab` to make cell **C4** active. Then, enter the remaining sales numbers as shown by using the following technique: Press `Tab` to confirm your entry and move across the row, and then press `Enter` at the end of a row to move to the next row.

	January	February	March
Headsets	47991.12	66984.92	87540.57
Holsters/Cases	19725	15523.12	13717.67
Car Kits	40408.67	61446.98	85835.76
Batteries	62154.28	68758.50	72558.89

3 Compare the numbers you entered with Figure 1.15 and then **Save** 🖫 your workbook.

> In the default general format, trailing zeros to the right of a decimal point will not display. For example, when you type *68758.50*, the cell displays 68758.5 instead.

Figure 1.15

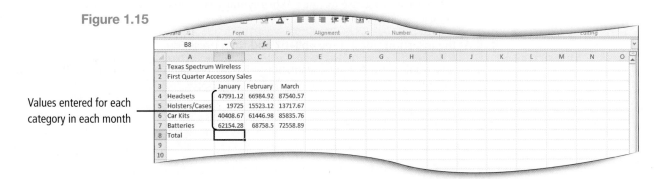

Values entered for each category in each month

Objective 3 | Construct and Copy Formulas and Use the SUM Function

A cell contains either a constant value (text or numbers) or a formula. A formula is an equation that performs mathematical calculations on values in other cells, and then places the result in the cell containing the formula. You can create formulas or use a **function**—a prewritten formula that looks at one or more values, performs an operation, and then returns a value.

Activity 1.07 | Constructing a Formula and Using the SUM Function

In this activity, you will practice three different ways to sum a group of numbers in Excel.

1 Click cell **B8** to make it the active cell and type **=**

The equal sign (=) displays in the cell with the insertion point blinking, ready to accept more data.

All formulas begin with the = sign, which signals Excel to begin a calculation. The Formula Bar displays the = sign, and the Formula Bar Cancel and Enter buttons display.

2 At the insertion point, type **b4** and then compare your screen with Figure 1.16.

A list of Excel functions that begin with the letter *B* may briefly display—as you progress in your study of Excel, you will use functions of this type. A blue border with small corner boxes surrounds cell B4, which indicates that the cell is part of an active formula. The color used in the box matches the color of the cell reference in the formula.

Figure 1.16

Cell B4 outlined in blue to show it is part of an active formula

Cell B8 displays the beginning of the formula, with *b4* in blue to match outlined cell

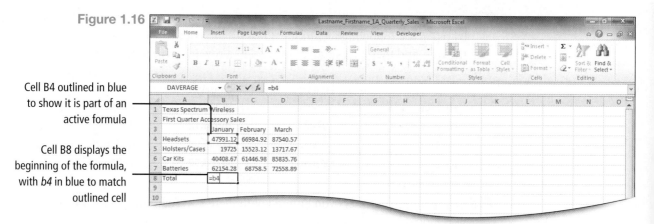

3 At the insertion point, type **+** and then type **b5**

A border of another color surrounds cell B5, and the color matches the color of the cell reference in the active formula. When typing cell references, it is not necessary to use uppercase letters.

4 At the insertion point, type **+b6+b7** and then press Enter.

The result of the formula calculation—*170279.1*—displays in the cell. Recall that in the default General format, trailing zeros do not display.

5 Click cell **B8** again, look at the **Formula Bar**, and then compare your screen with Figure 1.17.

> The formula adds the values in cells B4 through B7, and the result displays in cell B8. In this manner, you can construct a formula by typing. Although cell B8 displays the *result* of the formula, the formula itself displays in the Formula Bar. This is referred to as the ***underlying formula***.
>
> Always view the Formula Bar to be sure of the exact content of a cell—*a displayed number may actually be a formula*.

Figure 1.17

Formula displays in Formula Bar

Total of values in cells B4:B7 displays in cell B8

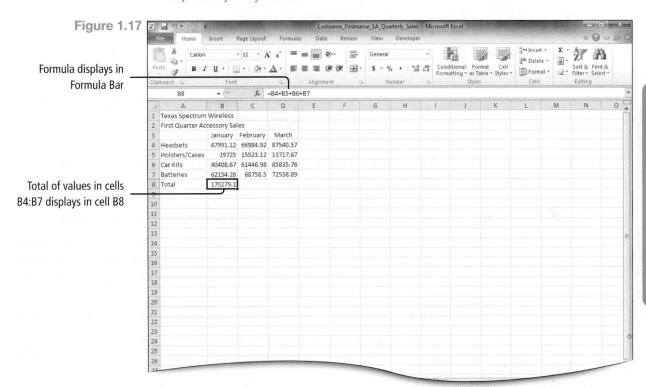

6 Click cell **C8** and type **=** to signal the beginning of a formula. Then, point to cell **C4** and click one time.

> The reference to the cell C4 is added to the active formula. A moving border surrounds the referenced cell, and the border color and the color of the cell reference in the formula are color coded to match.

7 At the insertion point, type **+** and then click cell **C5**. Repeat this process to complete the formula to add cells **C4** through **C7**, and then press Enter.

> The result of the formula calculation—*212713.5*—displays in the cell. This method of constructing a formula is the ***point and click method***.

Another Way

Use the keyboard shortcut Alt + =; or, on the Formulas tab, in the Function Library group, click the AutoSum button.

8 Click cell **D8**. On the **Home tab**, in the **Editing group**, click the **Sum** button Σ, and then compare your screen with Figure 1.18.

> *SUM* is an Excel function—a prewritten formula. A moving border surrounds the range D4:D7 and *=SUM(D4:D7)* displays in cell D8.
>
> The = sign signals the beginning of a formula, *SUM* indicates the type of calculation that will take place (addition), and *(D4:D7)* indicates the range of cells on which the sum calculation will be performed. A ScreenTip provides additional information about the action.

Figure 1.18

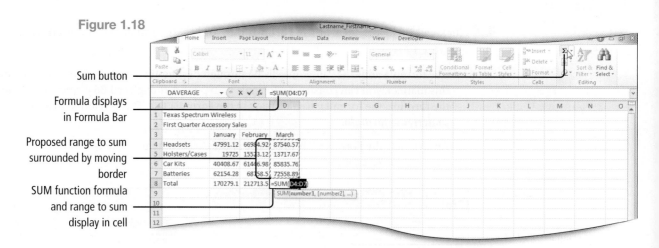

Sum button

Formula displays
in Formula Bar

Proposed range to sum
surrounded by moving
border

SUM function formula
and range to sum
display in cell

9 Look at the **Formula Bar**, and notice that the formula also displays there. Then, look again at the cells surrounded by the moving border.

> When you activate the Sum function, Excel first looks *above* the active cell for a range of cells to sum. If no range is above the active cell, Excel will look to the *left* for a range of cells to sum. If the proposed range is not what you want to calculate, you can select a different group of cells.

10 Press Enter to construct a formula by using the prewritten SUM function.

> Your total is *259652.9*. Because the Sum function is frequently used, it has its own button in the Editing group on the Home tab of the Ribbon. A larger version of the button also displays on the Formulas tab in the Function Library group. This button is also referred to as *AutoSum*.

11 Notice that the totals in the range **B8:D8** display only *one* decimal place. Click **Save** 🖫.

> Number values that are too long to fit in the cell do *not* spill over into the unoccupied cell to the right in the same manner as text values. Rather, Excel rounds the number to fit the space.

> *Rounding* is a procedure that determines which digit at the right of the number will be the last digit displayed and then increases it by one if the next digit to its right is 5, 6, 7, 8, or 9.

Activity 1.08 | Copying a Formula by Using the Fill Handle

You have practiced three ways to create a formula—by typing, by using the point-and-click technique, and by using a Function button from the Ribbon. You can also copy formulas. When you copy a formula from one cell to another, Excel adjusts the cell references to fit the new location of the formula.

1 Click cell **E3**, type **Total** and then press Enter.

> The text in cell E3 is centered because the centered format continues from the adjacent cell.

2 With cell **E4** as the active cell, hold down Alt, and then press =. Compare your screen with Figure 1.19.

> Alt + = is the keyboard shortcut for the Sum function. Recall that Excel first looks above the selected cell for a proposed range of cells to sum, and if no data is detected, Excel looks to the left and proposes a range of cells to sum.

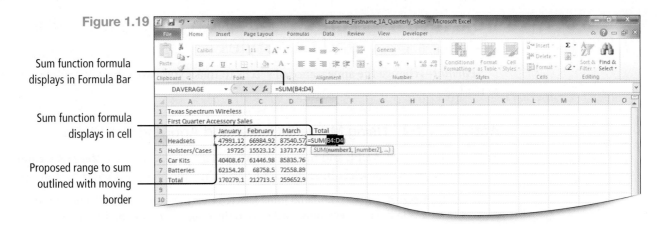

Figure 1.19

Sum function formula displays in Formula Bar

Sum function formula displays in cell

Proposed range to sum outlined with moving border

3 On the **Formula Bar**, click the **Enter** button ✔ to display the result and keep cell **E4** active.

> The total dollar amount of *Headsets* sold in the quarter is *202516.6*. In cells E5:E8, you can see that you need a formula similar to the one in E4, but formulas that refer to the cells in row 5, row 6, and so on.

4 With cell **E4** active, point to the fill handle in the lower right corner of the cell until the ⊞ pointer displays. Then, drag down through cell **E8**; if you are not satisfied with your result, on the Quick Access Toolbar, click Undo ↺ and begin again. Compare your screen with Figure 1.20.

Figure 1.20

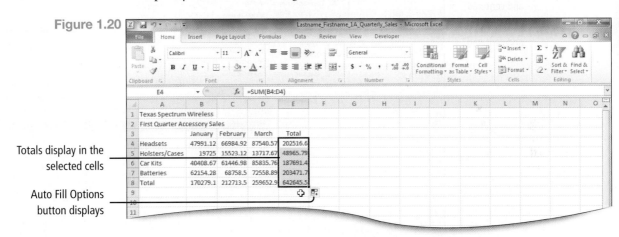

Totals display in the selected cells

Auto Fill Options button displays

5 Click cell **E5**, look at the **Formula Bar**, and notice the formula *=SUM(B5:D5)*. Click cell **E6**, look at the **Formula Bar**, and then notice the formula *=SUM(B6:D6)*.

> In each row, Excel copied the formula but adjusted the cell references *relative to* the row number. This is called a ***relative cell reference***—a cell reference based on the relative position of the cell that contains the formula and the cells referred to.

> The calculation is the same, but it is performed on the cells in that particular row. Use this method to insert numerous formulas into spreadsheets quickly.

6 Click cell **F3,** type **Trend** and then press Enter. **Save** 💾 your workbook.

Objective 4 | Format Cells with Merge & Center and Cell Styles

Format—change the appearance of—cells to make your worksheet attractive and easy to read.

Activity 1.09 | Using Merge & Center and Applying Cell Styles

Another Way

Select the range, right-click over the selection, and then on the Mini toolbar, click the Merge & Center button.

1 Select the range **A1:F1**, and then in the **Alignment group**, click the **Merge & Center** button 🔲. Then, select the range **A2:F2** and click the **Merge & Center** button 🔲.

> The *Merge & Center* command joins selected cells into one larger cell and centers the contents in the new cell; individual cells in the range B1:F1 and B2:F2 can no longer be selected—they are merged into cell A1 and A2 respectively.

2 Click cell **A1**. In the **Styles group**, click the **Cell Styles** button, and then compare your screen with Figure 1.21.

> A *cell style* is a defined set of formatting characteristics, such as font, font size, font color, cell borders, and cell shading.

Figure 1.21

Cell Styles button
Cell A1 merged and centered
Cell A2 merged and centered
Cell Styles gallery

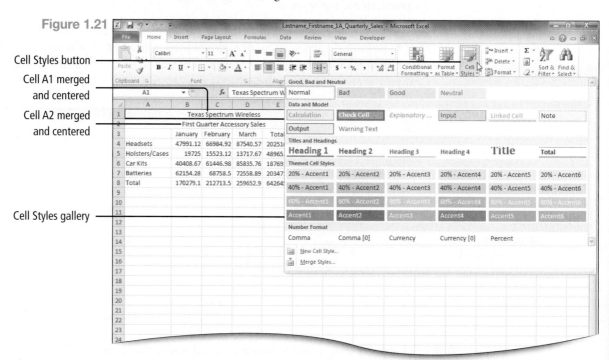

3 In the displayed gallery, under **Titles and Headings**, click **Title** and notice that the row height adjusts to accommodate this larger font size.

4 Click cell **A2**, display the **Cell Styles** gallery, and then under **Titles and Headings**, click **Heading 1**.

> Use cell styles to maintain a consistent look in a worksheet and across worksheets in a workbook.

5 Select the range **B3:F3**, hold down Ctrl, and then select the range **A4:A8** to select the column titles and the row titles.

> Use this technique to select two or more ranges that are nonadjacent—not next to each other.

120 **Excel** | Chapter 1: Creating a Worksheet and Charting Data

6 Display the **Cell Styles** gallery, click **Heading 4** to apply this cell style to the column titles and row titles, and then **Save** 🖫 your workbook.

Another Way

In the Name Box type b4:e4,b8:e8 and then press Enter.

Activity 1.10 | Formatting Financial Numbers

1 Select the range **B4:E4**, hold down Ctrl, and then select the range **B8:E8**.

This range is referred to as *b4:e4,b8:e8* with a comma separating the references to the two nonadjacent ranges.

Another Way

Display the Cell Styles gallery, and under Number Format, click Currency.

2 On the **Home tab**, in the **Number group**, click the **Accounting Number Format** button $ ▾. Compare your screen with Figure 1.22.

The *Accounting Number Format* applies a thousand comma separator where appropriate, inserts a fixed U.S. dollar sign aligned at the left edge of the cell, applies two decimal places, and leaves a small amount of space at the right edge of the cell to accommodate a parenthesis when negative numbers are present. Excel widens the columns to accommodate the formatted numbers.

Figure 1.22

Accounting Number Format button

Nonadjacent ranges selected with Accounting Number Format applied

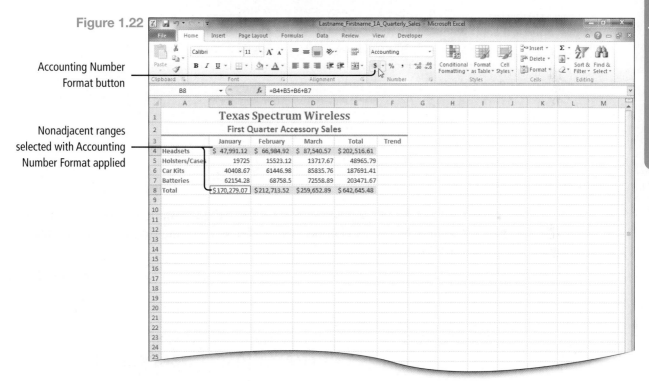

3 Select the range **B5:E7**, and then in the **Number group**, click the **Comma Style** button ▾.

The *Comma Style* inserts thousand comma separators where appropriate and applies two decimal places. Comma Style also leaves space at the right to accommodate a parenthesis when negative numbers are present.

When preparing worksheets with financial information, the first row of dollar amounts and the total row of dollar amounts are formatted in the Accounting Number Format; that is, with thousand comma separators, dollar signs, two decimal places, and space at the right to accommodate a parenthesis for negative numbers, if any. Rows that are *not* the first row or the total row should be formatted with the Comma Style.

4 Select the range **B8:E8**. From the **Styles group**, display the **Cell Styles** gallery, and then under **Titles and Headings**, click **Total**. Click any blank cell to cancel the selection, and then compare your screen with Figure 1.23.

> This is a common way to apply borders to financial information. The single border indicates that calculations were performed on the numbers above, and the double border indicates that the information is complete. Sometimes financial documents do not display values with cents; rather, the values are rounded up. You can do this by selecting the cells, and then clicking the Decrease Decimal button two times.

Figure 1.23

Comma style applied to range B5:E7

Total format applied to total row

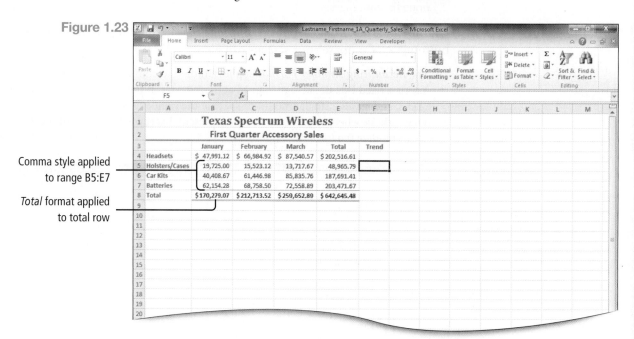

5 Click the **Page Layout tab**, and then in the **Themes group**, click **Themes**. Click the **Composite** theme, and notice that the cell styles change to match the new theme. Click **Save** .

> Recall that a theme is a predefined set of colors, fonts, lines, and fill effects that look good together.

Objective 5 | Chart Data to Create a Column Chart and Insert Sparklines

A ***chart*** is a graphic representation of data in a worksheet. Data presented as a chart is easier to understand than a table of numbers. ***Sparklines*** are tiny charts embedded in a cell and give a visual trend summary alongside your data. A sparkline makes a pattern more obvious to the eye.

Activity 1.11 | Charting Data in a Column Chart

In this activity, you will create a ***column chart*** showing the monthly sales of accessories by category during the first quarter. A column chart is useful for illustrating comparisons among related numbers. The chart will enable the company president, Rosalyn Thomas, to see a pattern of overall monthly sales.

1 Select the range **A3:D7**. Click the **Insert tab**, and then in the **Charts group**, click **Column** to display a gallery of Column chart types.

When charting data, typically you should *not* include totals—include only the data you want to compare. By using different *chart types*, you can display data in a way that is meaningful to the reader—common examples are column charts, pie charts, and line charts.

2 On the gallery of column chart types, under **2-D Column**, point to the first chart to display the ScreenTip *Clustered Column*, and then click to select it. Compare your screen with Figure 1.24.

A column chart displays in the worksheet, and the charted data is bordered by colored lines. Because the chart object is selected—surrounded by a border and displaying sizing handles—contextual tools named *Chart Tools* display and add contextual tabs next to the standard tabs on the Ribbon.

Figure 1.24

Chart Tools display three additional tabs—*Design, Layout, Format*

Border and sizing handles indicate chart is selected

Charted data range bordered by colored lines (green = legend, blue = columns, purple = category labels)

Clustered column chart displays in worksheet

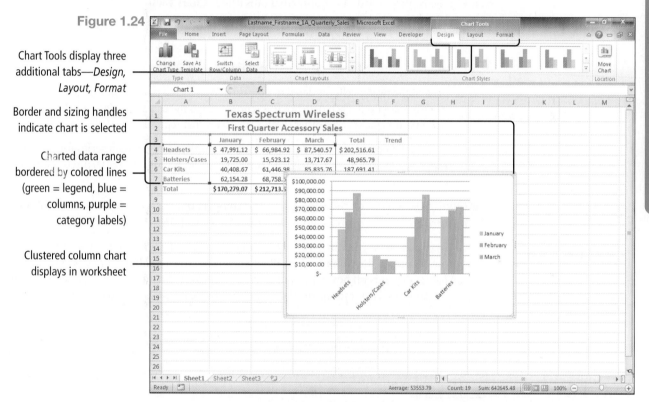

3 Point to the top border of the chart to display the ⌖ pointer, and then drag the upper left corner of the chart just inside the upper left corner of cell **A10**, approximately as shown in Figure 1.25.

Based on the data you selected in your worksheet, Excel constructs a column chart and adds *category labels*—the labels that display along the bottom of the chart to identify the category of data. This area is referred to as the *category axis* or the *x-axis*. Excel uses the row titles as the category names.

On the left, Excel includes a numerical scale on which the charted data is based; this is the *value axis* or the *y-axis*. On the right, a *legend*, which identifies the patterns or colors that are assigned to the categories in the chart, displays.

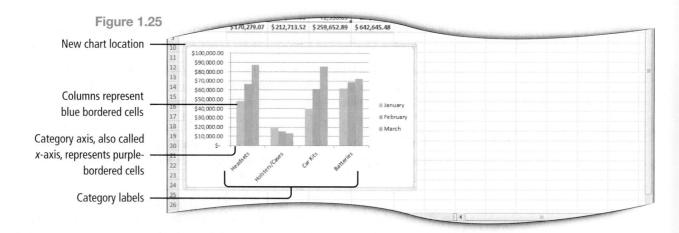

Figure 1.25

New chart location

Columns represent blue bordered cells

Category axis, also called x-axis, represents purple-bordered cells

Category labels

4 On the Ribbon, locate the contextual tabs under **Chart Tools—Design**, **Layout**, and **Format**.

When a chart is selected, Chart Tools become available and three tabs provide commands for working with the chart.

5 Locate the group of cells bordered in blue.

Each of the twelve cells bordered in blue is referred to as a ***data point***—a value that originates in a worksheet cell. Each data point is represented in the chart by a ***data marker***—a column, bar, area, dot, pie slice, or other symbol in a chart that represents a single data point.

Related data points form a ***data series***; for example, there is a data series for *January*, for *February*, and for *March*. Each data series has a unique color or pattern represented in the chart legend.

6 On the **Design tab** of the Ribbon, in the **Data group**, click the **Switch Row/Column** button, and then compare your chart with Figure 1.26.

In this manner, you can easily change the categories of data from the row titles, which is the default, to the column titles. Whether you use row or column titles as your category names depends on how you want to view your charted data. Here, the president wants to see monthly sales and the breakdown of product categories within each month.

Figure 1.26

Each value in selected range is a data point

Value axis (y-axis) based on total quarterly sales

Data series switched to row names (accessory types) as defined in legend

Categories switched to column names (months)

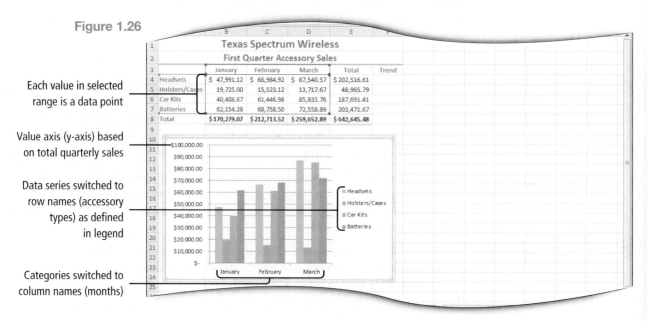

7 On the **Design tab**, in the **Chart Layouts group**, locate and click the **More** button ⊡. Compare your screen with Figure 1.27.

> In the **Chart Layouts gallery**, you can select a predesigned **chart layout**—a combination of chart elements, which can include a title, legend, labels for the columns, and the table of charted cells.

Figure 1.27

Chart Layouts gallery

More buttons in Chart Styles group

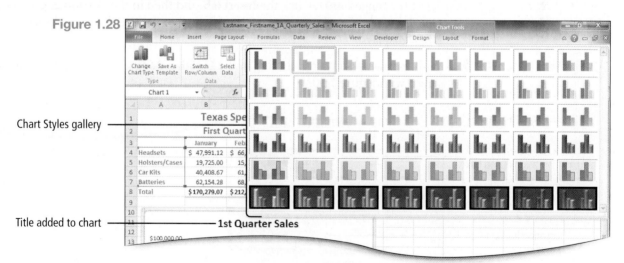

8 Click several different layouts to see the effect on your chart, and then using the ScreenTips as your guide, locate and click **Layout 1**.

9 In the chart, click anywhere in the text *Chart Title* to select the title box, watch the **Formula Bar** as you type **1st Quarter Sales** and then press Enter to display the new chart title.

10 Click in a white area just slightly *inside* the chart border to deselect the chart title. On the **Design tab**, in the **Chart Styles group**, click the **More** button ⊡. Compare your screen with Figure 1.28.

> The **Chart Styles gallery** displays an array of pre-defined **chart styles**—the overall visual look of the chart in terms of its colors, backgrounds, and graphic effects such as flat or beveled columns.

Figure 1.28

Chart Styles gallery

Title added to chart

11 Using the ScreenTips as your guide, locate and click **Style 26**.

> This style uses a white background, formats the columns with theme colors, and applies a beveled effect. With this clear visual representation of the data, the president can see the sales of all product categories in each month, and can see that the sale of headsets and car kits has risen quite markedly during the quarter.

12 Click any cell to deselect the chart, and notice that the *Chart Tools* no longer display in the Ribbon. Click **Save** 🔲, and then compare your screen with Figure 1.29.

Contextual tabs display when an object is selected, and then are removed from view when the object is deselected.

Figure 1.29

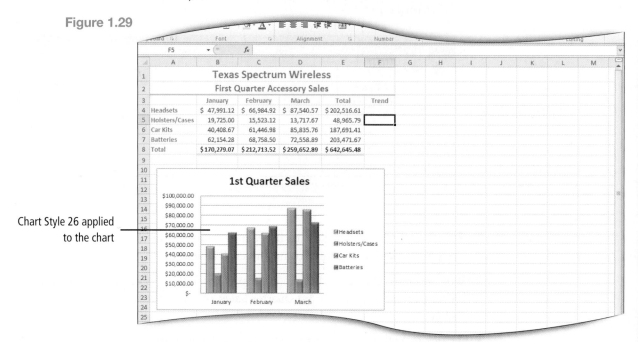

Chart Style 26 applied to the chart

Activity 1.12 | Creating and Formatting Sparklines

By creating sparklines, you provide a context for your numbers. Your readers will be able to see the relationship between a sparkline and its underlying data quickly.

> **Another Way**
>
> In the worksheet, select the range F4:F7 to insert it into the Location Range box.

1 Select the range **B4:D7**. Click the **Insert tab**, and then in the **Sparklines group**, click **Line**. In the displayed **Create Sparklines** dialog box, notice that the selected range *B4:D7* displays.

2 With the insertion point blinking in the **Location Range** box, type **f4:f7** Compare your screen with Figure 1.30.

Figure 1.30

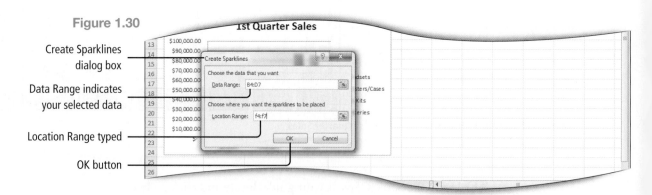

Create Sparklines dialog box

Data Range indicates your selected data

Location Range typed

OK button

3 Click **OK** to insert the trend lines in the range F4:F7, and then on the **Design tab**, in the **Show group**, click the **Markers** check box to select it.

Alongside each row of data, the sparkline provides a quick visual trend summary for sales of each accessory item over the three-month period. For example, you can see instantly that of the four items, only Holsters/Cases had declining sales for the period.

4 In the **Style group**, click the **More** button ⬇. In the second row, click the fourth style—**Sparkline Style Accent 4, Darker 25%**. Click cell **A1** to deselect the range. Click **Save** 💾. Compare your screen with Figure 1.31.

> Use markers, colors, and styles in this manner to further enhance your sparklines.

Figure 1.31

Sparklines inserted and formatted

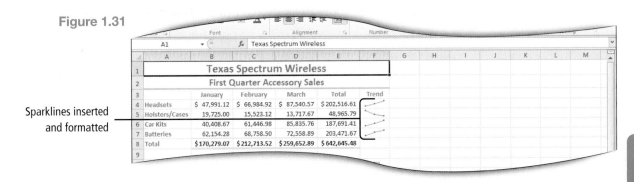

Objective 6 | Print, Display Formulas, and Close Excel

Use *Page Layout view* and the commands on the Page Layout tab to prepare for printing.

Activity 1.13 | Changing Views, Creating a Footer, and Using Print Preview

For each Excel project in this textbook, you will create a footer containing your name and the project name.

1 Be sure the chart is *not* selected. Click the **Insert tab**, and then in the **Text group**, click the **Header & Footer** button to switch to Page Layout view and open the **Header area**. Compare your screen with Figure 1.32.

> In Page Layout view, you can see the edges of the paper of multiple pages, the margins, and the rulers. You can also insert a header or footer by typing in the areas indicated and use the Header & Footer Tools.

Figure 1.32

Go to Footer button

Rulers

Header area with three sections open; center section selected

Margin

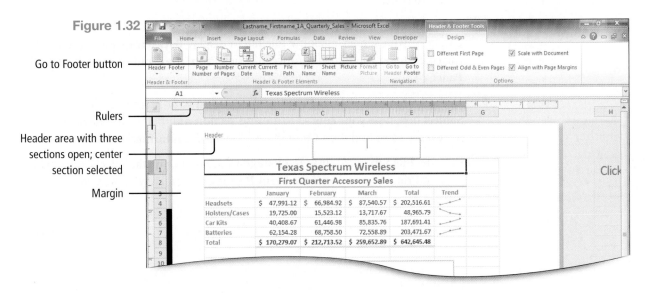

2 On the **Design tab**, in the **Navigation group**, click **Go to Footer** to open the **Footer area**, and then click just above the word *Footer* to place the insertion point in the **left section** of the **Footer area**.

3 In the **Header & Footer Elements group**, click the **File Name** button to add the name of your file to the footer—&*[File]* displays in the left section of the **Footer area**. Then, click in a cell just above the footer to exit the **Footer area** and view your file name.

4 Scroll up to see your chart, click a corner of the chart to select it, and then see if the chart is centered under the data. *Point* to the small dots on the right edge of the chart; compare your screen with Figure 1.33.

Figure 1.33

Horizontal resize pointer

Border indicates chart is selected

5 Drag the ↔ pointer to the right so that the right border of the chart is just inside the right border of **column F**. Be sure the left and right borders of the chart are just slightly **inside** the left border of **column A** and the right border of **column F**—adjust as necessary.

6 Click any cell to deselect the chart. Click the **Page Layout tab**, in the **Page Setup group**, click the **Margins** button, and then at the bottom of the **Margins** gallery, click **Custom Margins**. In the **Page Setup** dialog box, under **Center on page**, select the **Horizontally** check box.

> This action will center the data and chart horizontally on the page, as shown in the Preview area.

7 In the lower right corner of the **Page Setup** dialog box, click **OK**. In the upper left corner of your screen, click the **File tab** to display **Backstage** view. On the **Info tab**, on the right under the screen thumbnail, click **Properties**, and then click **Show Document Panel**.

8 In the **Author** box, replace the existing text with your firstname and lastname. In the **Subject** box, type your course name and section number. In the **Keywords** box type **accessory sales** and then **Close** ☒ the **Document Information Panel**.

Another Way
Press Ctrl + F2 to view the Print Preview.

9 Click the **File tab** to redisplay **Backstage** view, and then on the left, click the **Print tab** to view the Print commands and the **Print Preview**. Compare your screen with Figure 1.34.

Figure 1.34

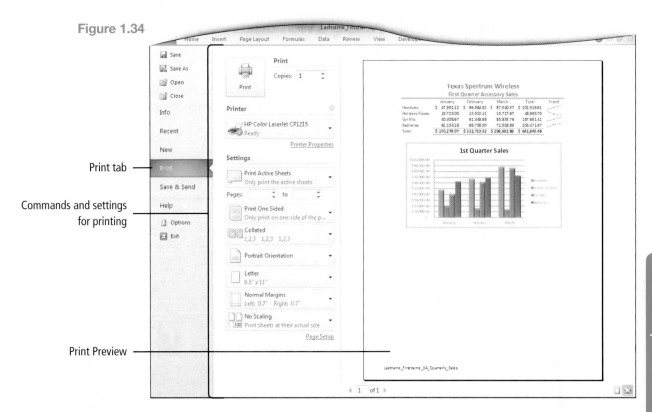

Print tab

Commands and settings for printing

Print Preview

10 Note any adjustments that need to be made, and then on the Ribbon, click the **Home tab** to close Backstage view and return to the worksheet. In the lower right corner of your screen, click the **Normal** button ⊞ to return to the Normal view, and then press Ctrl + Home to return to cell **A1**.

> The *Normal view* maximizes the number of cells visible on your screen and keeps the column letters and row numbers closer. The vertical dotted line between columns indicates that as currently arranged, only the columns to the left of the dotted line will print on the first page. The exact position of the vertical line may depend on your default printer setting.

11 Make any necessary adjustments, and then **Save** 🖫 your workbook.

Activity 1.14 | Deleting Unused Sheets in a Workbook

A new Excel workbook contains three blank worksheets. It is not necessary to delete unused sheets, but doing so saves storage space and removes any doubt that additional information is in the workbook.

1 At the bottom of your worksheet, click the **Sheet2 tab** to display the second worksheet in the workbook and make it active.

> **Another Way**
>
> On the Home tab, in the Cells group, click the Delete button arrow, and then click Delete Sheet.

2 Hold down Ctrl, and then click the **Sheet3 tab**. Release Ctrl, and then with both sheets selected (the tab background is white), point to either of the selected sheet tabs, right-click, and then on the shortcut menu, click **Delete**.

> Excel deletes the two unused sheets from your workbook. If you attempt to delete a worksheet with data, Excel will display a warning and permit you to cancel the deletion. *Sheet tabs* are labels along the lower border of the Excel window that identify each worksheet.

Activity 1.15 | Printing a Worksheet

1 Click **Save** 🖫.

2 Display **Backstage** view and on the left click the Print tab. Under **Print**, be sure **Copies** indicates *1*. Under **Settings**, verify that *Print Active Sheets* displays. Compare your screen with Figure 1.35.

Figure 1.35

Copies indicates *1*

Print Active Sheets

Print Preview

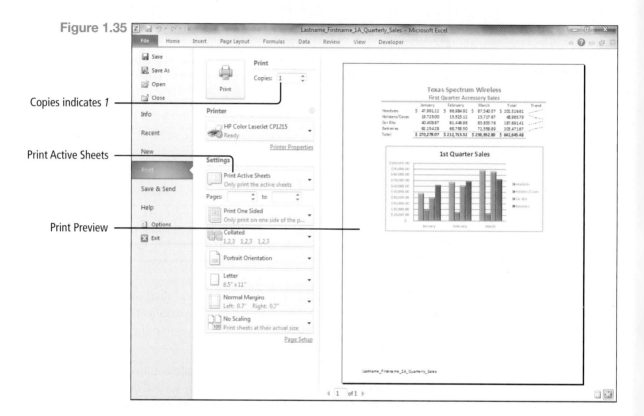

3 To print on paper, be sure that a printer is available to your system, and then in the **Print group**, click the **Print** button. To create an electronic printout, on the Backstage tabs, click the **Save & Send tab**, under **File Types** click **Create PDF/XPS Document**, and then on the right, click **Create PDF/XPS**. In the **Publish as PDF or XPS** dialog box, navigate to your storage location, and then click the **Publish** button to create the PDF file. Close the Adobe window.

Activity 1.16 | Displaying, Printing, and Hiding Formulas

When you type a formula in a cell, the cell displays the *results* of the formula calculation. Recall that this value is called the displayed value. You can view and print the underlying formulas in the cells. When you do so, a formula often takes more horizontal space to display than the result of the calculation.

1 If necessary, redisplay your worksheet. Because you will make some temporary changes to your workbook, on the Quick Access Toolbar, click **Save** 🖫 to be sure your work is saved up to this point.

Another Way

Hold down Ctrl, and then press ` (usually located below Esc).

2 On the **Formulas tab**, in the **Formula Auditing group**, click the **Show Formulas** button. Then, in the **column heading area**, point to the **column A** heading to display the ↓ pointer, hold down the left mouse button, and then drag to the right to select columns **A:F**. Compare your screen with Figure 1.36.

Figure 1.36

Dotted line shows
page break

Underlying formulas
displayed

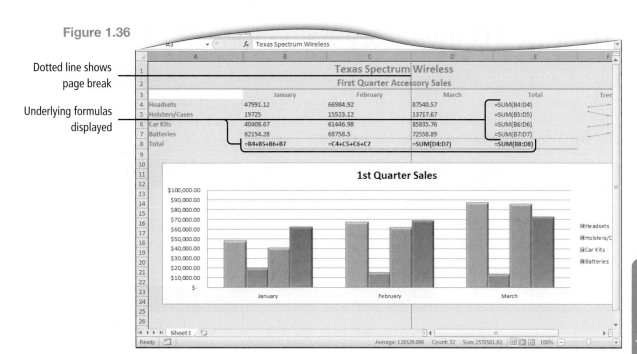

> **Note** | Turning the Display of Formulas On and Off
>
> The Show Formulas button is a toggle button. Clicking it once turns the display of formulas on—the button will glow orange. Clicking the button again turns the display of formulas off.

3 Point to the column heading boundary between any two of the selected columns to display the ⊞ pointer, and then double-click to AutoFit the selected columns.

> *AutoFit* adjusts the width of a column to fit the cell content of the *widest* cell in the column.

Another Way

In the Scale to Fit group, click the Dialog Box Launcher button to display the Page tab of the Page Setup dialog box. Then, under Scaling, click the Fit to option button.

4 On the **Page Layout tab**, in the **Page Setup group**, click **Orientation**, and then click **Landscape**. In the **Scale to Fit** group, click the **Width arrow**, and then click **1 page** to scale the data to fit onto one page.

> *Scaling* shrinks the width (or height) of the printed worksheet to fit a maximum number of pages, and is convenient for printing formulas. Although it is not always the case, formulas frequently take up more space than the actual data.

Another Way

In the Page Setup group, click the Dialog Box Launcher button to display the Page tab of the Page Setup dialog box. Then, under Orientation, click the Landscape option button.

5 In the **Page Setup group**, click the **Dialog Box Launcher** button 🖾. In the **Page Setup** dialog box, click the **Margins tab**, and then under **Center on page**, if necessary, click to select the **Horizontally** check box.

6 Click **OK** to close the dialog box. Check to be sure your chart is centered below the data and the left and right edges are slightly inside column A and column F—drag a chart edge and then deselect the chart if necessary. Display the **Print Preview**, and then submit your worksheet with formulas displayed, either printed or electronically, as directed by your instructor.

7 Click the **File tab** to display **Backstage** view, click **Close**, and when prompted, click **Don't Save** so that you do *not* save the changes you made—displaying formulas, changing column widths and orientation, and scaling—to print your formulas.

8 In the upper right corner of your screen, click the **Close** button ⬛ to exit Excel.

End You have completed Project 1A _____

Project 1B Inventory Valuation

myitlab
Project 1B Training

Project Activities

In Activities 1.17 through 1.24, you will create a workbook for Josette Lovrick, Operations Manager, which calculates the retail value of an inventory of car convenience products. Your completed worksheet will look similar to Figure 1.37.

Project Files

For Project 1B, you will need the following file:

New blank Excel workbook

You will save your workbook as:

Lastname_Firstname_1B_Car_Products

Project Results

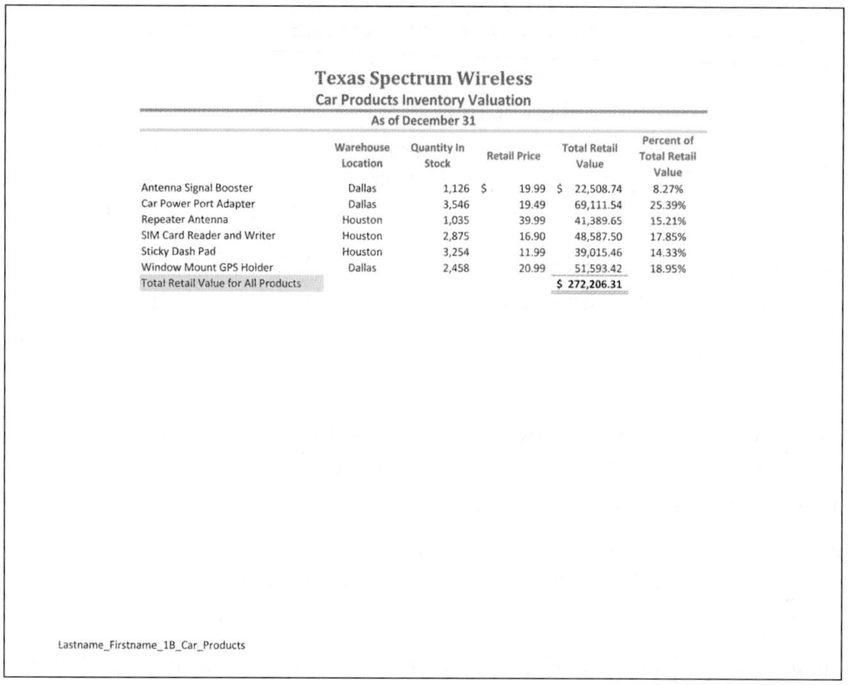

Texas Spectrum Wireless
Car Products Inventory Valuation
As of December 31

	Warehouse Location	Quantity In Stock	Retail Price	Total Retail Value	Percent of Total Retail Value
Antenna Signal Booster	Dallas	1,126	$ 19.99	$ 22,508.74	8.27%
Car Power Port Adapter	Dallas	3,546	19.49	69,111.54	25.39%
Repeater Antenna	Houston	1,035	39.99	41,389.65	15.21%
SIM Card Reader and Writer	Houston	2,875	16.90	48,587.50	17.85%
Sticky Dash Pad	Houston	3,254	11.99	39,015.46	14.33%
Window Mount GPS Holder	Dallas	2,458	20.99	51,593.42	18.95%
Total Retail Value for All Products				$ 272,206.31	

Lastname_Firstname_1B_Car_Products

Figure 1.37
Project 1B Car Products

Objective 7 | Check Spelling in a Worksheet

In Excel, the spelling checker performs similarly to the other Microsoft Office programs.

Activity 1.17 | Checking Spelling in a Worksheet

1 **Start** Excel and display a new blank workbook. In cell **A1**, type **Texas Spectrum Wireless** and press Enter. In cell **A2**, type **Car Products Inventory** and press Enter.

2 On the Ribbon, click the **File tab** to display **Backstage** view, click **Save As**, and then in the **Save As** dialog box, navigate to your **Excel Chapter 1** folder. As the **File name**, type **Lastname_Firstname_1B_Car_Products** and then click **Save**.

3 Press Tab to move to cell **B3**, type **Quantity** and press Tab. In cell **C3**, type **Average Cost** and press Tab. In cell **D3**, type **Retail Price** and press Tab.

4 Click cell **C3**, and then look at the **Formula Bar**. Notice that in the cell, the displayed value is cut off; however, in the **Formula Bar**, the entire text value—the underlying value—displays. Compare your screen with Figure 1.38.

> Text that is too long to fit in a cell spills over to cells on the right only if they are empty. If the cell to the right contains data, the text in the cell to the left is truncated. The entire value continues to exist, but is not completely visible.

Figure 1.38

Entire contents of C3 display in Formula Bar

Cell C3 active, text cut off

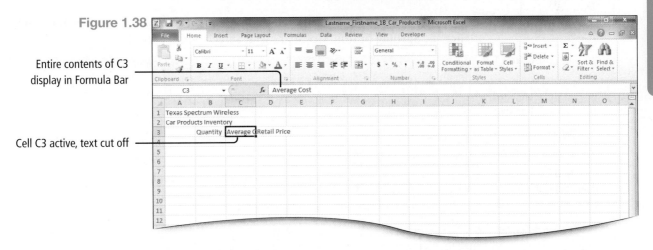

5 Click cell **E3**, type **Total Retail Value** and press Tab. In cell **F3**, type **Percent of Total Retail Value** and press Enter.

6 Click cell **A4**. *Without* correcting the spelling error, type **Antena Signal Booster** Press Enter. In the range **A5:A10**, type the remaining row titles shown below. Then compare your screen with Figure 1.39.

> **Car Power Port Adapter**
>
> **Repeater Antenna**
>
> **SIM Card Reader and Writer**
>
> **Sticky Dash Pad**
>
> **Window Mount GPS Holder**
>
> **Total Retail Value for All Products**

Figure 1.39

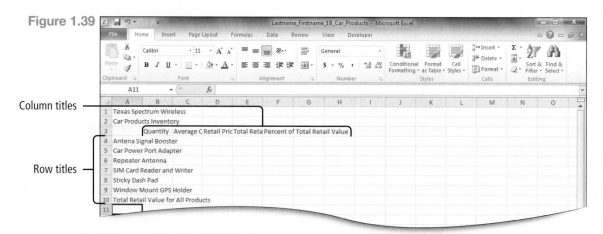

Column titles

Row titles

7 In the **column heading area**, point to the right boundary of **column A** to display the ⊞ pointer, and then drag to the right to widen **column A** to **215** pixels.

8 Select the range **A1:F1**, **Merge & Center** ▦ the text, and then from the **Cell Styles** gallery, apply the **Title** style.

9 Select the range **A2:F2**, **Merge & Center** ▦ the text, and then from the **Cell Styles** gallery, apply the **Heading 1** style. Press [Ctrl] + [Home] to move to the top of your worksheet.

Another Way

Press [F7], which is the keyboard shortcut for the Spelling command.

10 With cell **A1** as the active cell, click the **Review tab**, and then in the **Proofing group**, click the **Spelling** button. Compare your screen with Figure 1.40.

Figure 1.40

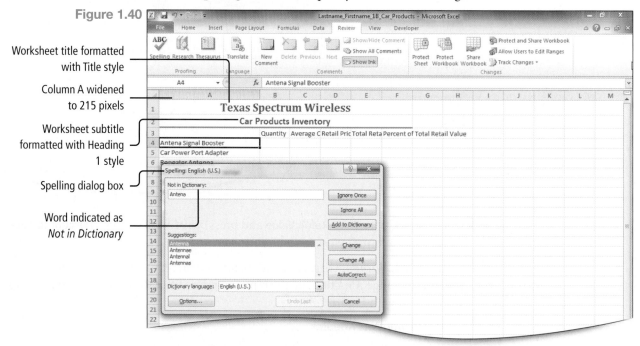

Worksheet title formatted with Title style

Column A widened to 215 pixels

Worksheet subtitle formatted with Heading 1 style

Spelling dialog box

Word indicated as *Not in Dictionary*

Alert! | **Does a Message Display Asking if You Want to Continue Checking at the Beginning of the Sheet?**

If a message displays asking if you want to continue checking at the beginning of the sheet, click Yes. The Spelling command begins its checking process with the currently selected cell and moves to the right and down. Thus, if your active cell was a cell after A4, this message may display.

11 In the **Spelling** dialog box, under **Not in Dictionary**, notice the word *Antena*.

The spelling tool does not have this word in its dictionary. Under *Suggestions*, Excel provides a list of suggested spellings.

12 Under **Suggestions**, click **Antenna**, and then click the **Change** button.

Antena, a typing error, is changed to *Antenna*. A message box displays *The spelling check is complete for the entire sheet*—unless you have additional unrecognized words. Because the spelling check begins its checking process starting with the currently selected cell, it is good practice to return to cell A1 before starting the Spelling command.

13 Correct any other errors you may have made. When the message displays, *The spelling check is complete for the entire sheet*, click **OK**. **Save** 🖫 your workbook.

Objective 8 │ Enter Data by Range

You can enter data by first selecting a range of cells. This is a time-saving technique, especially if you use the numeric keypad to enter the numbers.

Activity 1.18 │ Entering Data by Range

1 Select the range **B4:D9**, type **1126** and then press ⏎.

The value displays in cell B4, and cell B5 becomes the active cell.

2 With cell **B5** active in the range, and pressing ⏎ after each entry, type the following, and then compare your screen with Figure 1.41:

> 4226
> 1035
> 2875
> 3254
> 2458

After you enter the last value and press ⏎, the active cell moves to the top of the next column within the selected range. Although it is not required to enter data in this manner, you can see that selecting the range before you enter data saves time because it confines the movement of the active cell to the selected range.

Figure 1.41

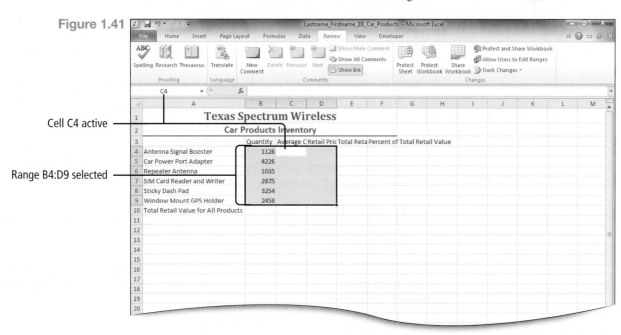

Cell C4 active

Range B4:D9 selected

3 With the selected range still active, from the following table, beginning in cell **C4** and pressing Enter after each entry, enter the data for the **Average Cost** column and then the **Retail Price** column. If you prefer, deselect the range to enter the values—typing in a selected range is optional.

Average Cost	Retail Price
9.75	19.99
9.25	19.49
16.90	39.99
9.55	16.90
4.20	12.99
10.45	20.99

Recall that the default number format for cells is the *General* number format, in which numbers display exactly as you type them and trailing zeros do not display, even if you type them.

4 Click any blank cell, and then compare your screen with Figure 1.42. Correct any errors you may have made while entering data, and then click **Save** 🖫.

Figure 1.42

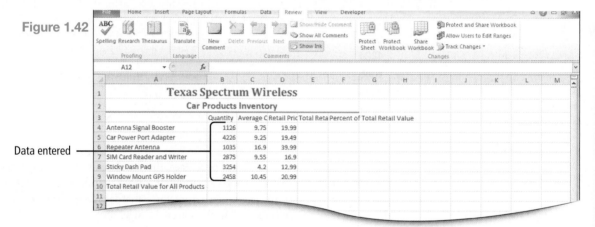

Data entered

Objective 9 | Construct Formulas for Mathematical Operations

Operators are symbols with which you can specify the type of calculation you want to perform in a formula.

Activity 1.19 | Using Arithmetic Operators

1 Click cell **E4**, type **=b4*d4** and notice that the two cells are outlined as part of an active formula. Then press Enter.

The *Total Retail Value* of all *Antenna Signal Booster* items in inventory—*22508.74*—equals the *Quantity* (1,126) times the *Retail Price* (selling price) of 19.99. In Excel, the asterisk (*) indicates multiplication.

2 Take a moment to study the symbols you will use to perform basic mathematical operations in Excel, as shown in the table in Figure 1.43, which are referred to as *arithmetic operators*.

Symbols Used in Excel for Arithmetic Operators	
Operator Symbol	**Operation**
+	Addition
-	Subtraction (also negation)
*	Multiplication
/	Division
%	Percent
^	Exponentiation

Figure 1.43

3 Click cell **E4**.

You can see that in cells E5:E9, you need a formula similar to the one in E4, but one that refers to the cells in row 5, row 6, and so forth. Recall that you can copy formulas and the cell references will change *relative to* the row number.

4 With cell **E4** selected, position your pointer over the fill handle in the lower right corner of the cell until the ⊞ pointer displays. Then, drag down through cell **E9** to copy the formula.

> **Another Way**
>
> Select the range, display the Cell Styles gallery, and then under Number Format, click Comma [0].

5 Select the range **B4:B9**, and then on the **Home tab**, in the **Number group**, click the **Comma Style** button ⟨ , ⟩. Then, in the **Number group**, click the **Decrease Decimal** button ⟨ .00→.0 ⟩ two times to remove the decimal places from these values.

Comma Style formats a number with two decimal places; because these are whole numbers referring to quantities, no decimal places are necessary.

6 Select the range **E4:E9**, and then at the bottom of your screen, in the status bar, notice the displayed values for **Average**, **Count**, and **Sum**—*48118.91833, 6* and *288713.51*.

When you select numerical data, three calculations display in the status bar by default—Average, Count, and Sum. Here, Excel indicates that if you averaged the selected values, the result would be *48118.91833*, there are 6 cells in the selection that contain values, and that if you added the values the result would be *288713.51*.

7 Click cell **E10**, in the **Editing group**, click the **Sum** button ⟨Σ⟩, notice that Excel selects a range to sum, and then press ⟨Enter⟩ to display the total *288713.5*.

8 Select the range **C5:E9** and apply the **Comma Style** ⟨ , ⟩; notice that Excel widens column E.

9 Select the range **C4:E4**, hold down ⟨Ctrl⟩, and then click cell **E10**. Release ⟨Ctrl⟩ and then apply the **Accounting Number Format** ⟨$ ▾⟩. Notice that Excel widens the columns as necessary.

10 Click cell **E10**, and then from the **Cell Styles** gallery, apply the **Total** style. Click any blank cell, and then compare your screen with Figure 1.44.

Figure 1.44

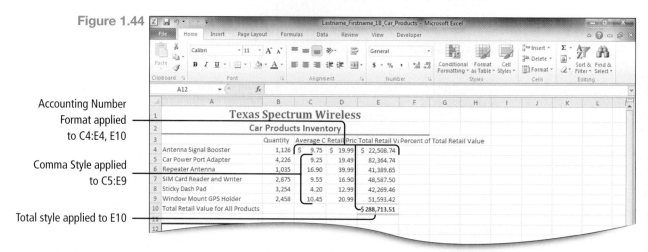

Accounting Number Format applied to C4:E4, E10

Comma Style applied to C5:E9

Total style applied to E10

11 **Save** 💾 your workbook.

More Knowledge | Multiple Status Bar Calculations

You can display a total of six calculations on the status bar. To add additional calculations—Minimum, Maximum, and Numerical Count (the number of selected cells that contain a number value)—right-click on the status bar, and then click the additional calculations that you want to display.

Activity 1.20 | Copying Formulas Containing Absolute Cell References

In a formula, a relative cell reference refers to a cell by its position *in relation to* the cell that contains the formula. An ***absolute cell reference***, on the other hand, refers to a cell by its *fixed* position in the worksheet, for example, the total in cell E10.

A relative cell reference automatically adjusts when a formula is copied. In some calculations, you do *not* want the cell reference to adjust; rather, you want the cell reference to remain the same when the formula is copied.

1 Click cell **F4**, type = and then click cell **E4**. Type **/** and then click cell **E10**.

The formula *=E4/E10* indicates that the value in cell E4 will be *divided* by the value in cell E10. Why? Because Ms. Lovrick wants to know the percentage by which each product's Total Retail Value makes up the Total Retail Value for All Products.

Arithmetically, the percentage is computed by dividing the *Total Retail Value* for each product by the *Total Retail Value for All Products*. The result will be a percentage expressed as a decimal.

2 Press Enter. Click cell **F4** and notice that the formula displays in the **Formula Bar**. Then, point to cell **F4** and double-click.

The formula, with the two referenced cells displayed in color and bordered with the same color, displays in the cell. This feature, called the ***range finder***, is useful for verifying formulas because it visually indicates which workbook cells are included in a formula calculation.

3 Press [Enter] to redisplay the result of the calculation in the cell, and notice that approximately 8% of the total retail value of the inventory is made up of Antenna Signal Boosters.

4 Click cell **F4** again, and then drag the fill handle down through cell **F9**. Compare your screen with Figure 1.45.

> Each cell displays an error message—*#DIV/0!* and a green triangle in the upper left corner of each cell indicates that Excel detects an error.

> Like a grammar checker, Excel uses rules to check for formula errors and flags errors in this manner. Additionally, the Auto Fill Options button displays, from which you can select formatting options for the copied cells.

Figure 1.45

Auto Fill Options button —

Cells F5:F9 display error message and green triangles

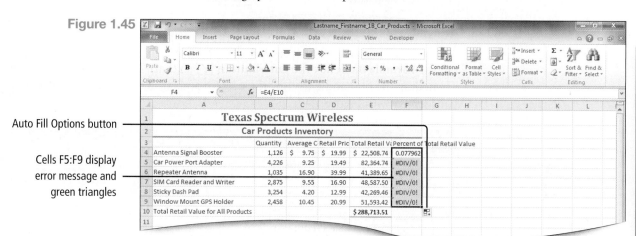

5 Click cell **F5**, and to the left of the cell, point to the **Error Checking** button ◈ to display its ScreenTip—*The formula or function used is dividing by zero or empty cells.*

> In this manner, Excel suggests the cause of an error.

6 Look at the **Formula Bar** and examine the formula.

> The formula is *=E5/E11*. The cell reference to *E5* is correct, but the cell reference following the division operator (*/*) is *E11*, and E11 is an *empty* cell.

7 Click cell **F6**, point to the **Error Checking** button ◈, and in the **Formula Bar** examine the formula.

> Because the cell references are relative, Excel builds the formulas by increasing the row number for each equation. But in this calculation, the divisor must always be the value in cell E10—the *Total Retail Value for All Products.*

8 Point to cell **F4**, and then double-click to place the insertion point within the cell.

Another Way

Edit the formula so that it indicates =E4/E10

9 Within the cell, use the arrow keys as necessary to position the insertion point to the left of *E10*, and then press [F4]. Compare your screen with Figure 1.46.

> Dollar signs ($) display, which changes the reference to cell E10 to an absolute cell reference. The use of the dollar sign to denote an absolute reference is not related in any way to whether or not the values you are working with are currency values. It is simply the symbol that Excel uses to denote an absolute cell reference.

Figure 1.46

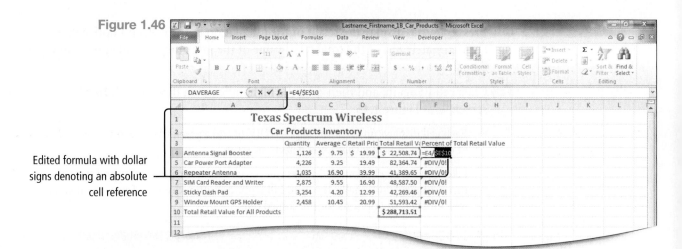

Edited formula with dollar signs denoting an absolute cell reference

10 On the **Formula Bar**, click the **Enter** button ✓ so that **F4** remains the active cell. Then, drag the fill handle to copy the new formula down through cell **F9**. Compare your screen with Figure 1.47.

Figure 1.47

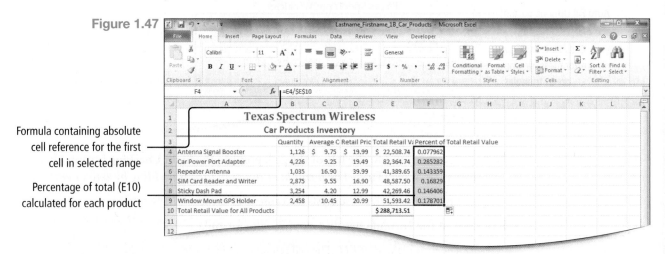

Formula containing absolute cell reference for the first cell in selected range

Percentage of total (E10) calculated for each product

11 Click cell **F5**, examine the formula in the **Formula Bar**, and then examine the formulas for cells **F6**, **F7**, **F8**, and **F9**.

> For each formula, the cell reference for the *Total Retail Value* of each product changed relative to its row; however, the value used as the divisor—*Total Retail Value for All Products* in cell F10—remained absolute. Thus, using either relative or absolute cell references, it is easy to duplicate formulas without typing them.

12 **Save** 💾 your workbook.

More Knowledge | **Calculate a Percentage if You Know the Total and the Amount**

Using the equation *amount/total = percentage*, you can calculate the percentage by which a part makes up a total—with the percentage formatted as a decimal. For example, if on a test you score 42 points correctly out of 50, your percentage of correct answers is 42/50 = 0.84 or 84%.

Objective 10 | Edit Values in a Worksheet

Excel performs calculations on numbers; that is why you use Excel. If you make changes to the numbers, Excel automatically *re*-calculates. This is one of the most powerful and valuable features of Excel.

Activity 1.21 | Editing Values in a Worksheet

You can edit text and number values directly within a cell or on the Formula Bar.

1 In cell **E10**, notice the column total *$288,713.51*. Then, click cell **B5**, and to change its value type **3546** Watch cell **E5** and press Enter.

> Excel formulas *re-calculate* if you change the value in a cell that is referenced in a formula. It is not necessary to delete the old value in a cell; selecting the cell and typing a new value replaces the old value with your new typing.

> The *Total Retail Value* of all *Car Power Port Adapters* items recalculates to *69,111.54* and the total in cell E10 recalculates to *$275,460.31*. Additionally, all of the percentages in column F recalculate.

2 Point to cell **D8**, and then double-click to place the insertion point within the cell. Use the arrow keys to move the insertion point to left or right of *2*, and use either Del or Backspace to delete *2* and then type **1** so that the new Retail Price is *11.99*.

3 Watch cell **E8** and **E10** as you press Enter, and then notice the recalculation of the formulas in those two cells.

> Excel recalculates the value in cell E8 to *39,015.46* and the value in cell E10 to *$272,206.31*. Additionally, all of the percentages in column F recalculate because the *Total Retail Value for All Products* recalculated.

4 Point to cell **A2** so that the ⊕ pointer is positioned slightly to the right of the word *Inventory*, and then double-click to place the insertion point in the cell. Edit the text to add the word **Valuation** pressing Spacebar as necessary, and then press Enter.

5 Click cell **B3**, and then in the **Formula Bar**, click to place the insertion point after the letter *y*. Press Spacebar one time, type **In Stock** and then on the **Formula Bar**, click the **Enter** button ✓. Click **Save** 🔲, and then compare your screen with Figure 1.48.

> Recall that if text is too long to fit in the cell and the cell to the right contains data, the text is truncated—cut off—but the entire value still exists as the underlying value.

Figure 1.48

In Stock added to column title

Valuation added to subtitle

New value in cell B5

New value in cell D8

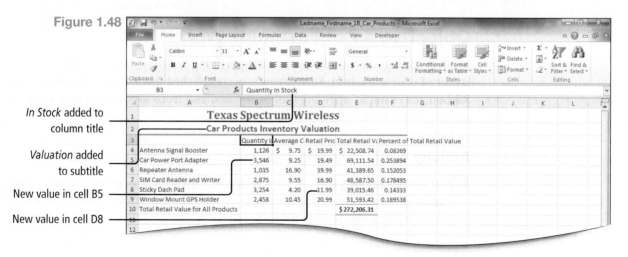

Activity 1.22 | Formatting Cells with the Percent Style

A percentage is part of a whole expressed in hundredths. For example, 75 cents is the same as 75 percent of one dollar. The Percent Style button formats the selected cell as a percentage rounded to the nearest hundredth.

1 Click cell **F4**, and then in the **Number group**, click the **Percent Style** button %.

> Your result is 8%, which is *0.08269* rounded to the nearest hundredth and expressed as a percentage. Percent Style displays the value of a cell as a percentage.

2 Select the range **F4:F9**, right-click over the selection, and then on the Mini toolbar, click the **Percent Style** button %, click the **Increase Decimal** button two times, and then click the **Center** button.

> Percent Style may not offer a percentage precise enough to analyze important financial information—adding additional decimal places to a percentage makes data more precise.

3 Click any cell to cancel the selection, **Save** your workbook, and then compare your screen with Figure 1.49.

Figure 1.49

F4:F9 formatted with Percent Style and two decimal places

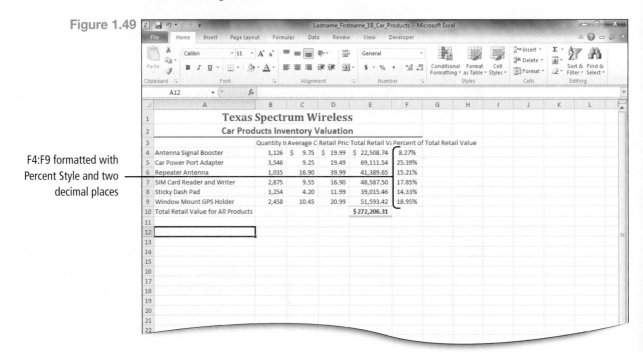

Objective 11 | Format a Worksheet

Formatting refers to the process of specifying the appearance of cells and the overall layout of your worksheet. Formatting is accomplished through various commands on the Ribbon, for example, applying Cell Styles, and also from shortcut menus, keyboard shortcuts, and the Format Cells dialog box.

Activity 1.23 | Inserting and Deleting Rows and Columns

1 In the **row heading area** on the left side of your screen, point to the row heading for **row 3** to display the pointer, and then right-click to simultaneously select the row and display a shortcut menu.

Another Way

Select the row, on the Home tab, in the Cells group, click the Insert button arrow, and then click Insert Sheet Rows. Or, select the row and click the Insert button—the default setting of the button inserts a new sheet row above the selected row.

2 On the displayed shortcut menu, click **Insert** to insert a new **row 3**.

The rows below the new row 3 move down one row, and the Insert Options button displays. By default, the new row uses the formatting of the row *above*.

3 Click cell **E11**. On the **Formula Bar**, notice that the range changed to sum the new range **E5:E10**. Compare your screen with Figure 1.50.

If you move formulas by inserting additional rows or columns in your worksheet, Excel automatically adjusts the formulas. Excel adjusted all of the formulas in the worksheet that were affected by inserting this new row.

Figure 1.50

Formula Bar displays the formula in E11

New row 3 inserted

Insert Options button

Cell E11 selected

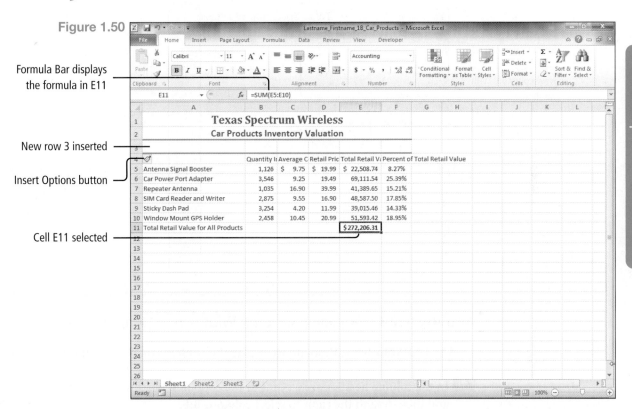

Another Way

Select the column, on the Home tab, in the Cells group, click the Insert button arrow, and then click Insert Sheet Columns. Or, select the column and click the Insert button—the default setting of the button inserts a new sheet column to the right of the selected column.

4 Click cell **A3**, type **As of December 31** and then on the **Formula Bar**, click the **Enter** button ✓ to maintain **A3** as the active cell. **Merge & Center** 🔲 the text across the range **A3:F3**, and then apply the **Heading 2** cell style.

5 In the **column heading area**, point to **column B** to display the ↓ pointer, right-click, and then click **Insert**.

By default, the new column uses the formatting of the column to the *left*.

6 Click cell **B4**, type **Warehouse Location** and then press Enter.

7 In cell **B5**, type **Dallas** and then type **Dallas** again in cells **B6** and **B10**. Use AutoComplete to speed your typing by pressing Enter as soon as the AutoComplete suggestion displays. In cells **B7**, **B8**, and **B9**, type **Houston**

8 In the **column heading area**, point to **column D**, right-click, and then click **Delete**.

The remaining columns shift to the left, and Excel adjusts all the formulas in the worksheet accordingly. You can use a similar technique to delete a row in a worksheet.

9 Compare your screen with Figure 1.51, and then **Save** your workbook.

Figure 1.51

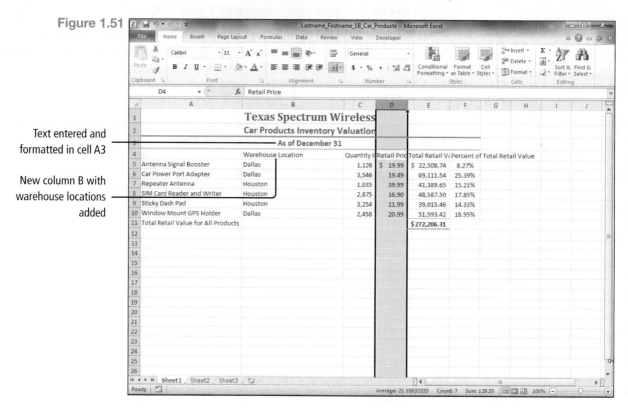

Text entered and
formatted in cell A3

New column B with
warehouse locations
added

Activity 1.24 | Adjusting Column Widths and Wrapping Text

Use the Wrap Text command to display the contents of a cell on multiple lines.

1 In the **column heading area**, point to the **column B** heading to display the ⬇ pointer, and then drag to the right to select **columns B:F**.

2 With the columns selected, in the **column heading area**, point to the right boundary of any of the selected columns to display the ⬌ pointer, and then drag to set the width to **90 pixels**.

Use this technique to format multiple columns or rows simultaneously.

3 Select the range **B4:F4** that comprises the column headings, and then on the **Home tab**, in the **Alignment group**, click the **Wrap Text** button. Notice that the row height adjusts.

4 With the range **B4:F4** still selected, in the **Alignment group**, click the **Center** button and the **Middle Align** button. With the range **B4:F4** still selected, apply the **Heading 4** cell style.

The Middle Align command aligns text so that it is centered between the top and bottom of the cell.

5 Select the range **B5:B10**, right-click, and then on the shortcut menu, click the **Center** button ▣. Click cell **A11**, and then from the **Cell Styles** gallery, under **Themed Cell Styles**, click **40% - Accent1**. Click any blank cell, and then compare your screen with Figure 1.52.

Figure 1.52

Width of columns B:F set to 90 pixels

Column headings wrapped and formatted

Warehouse locations centered

Accent applied to cell A11

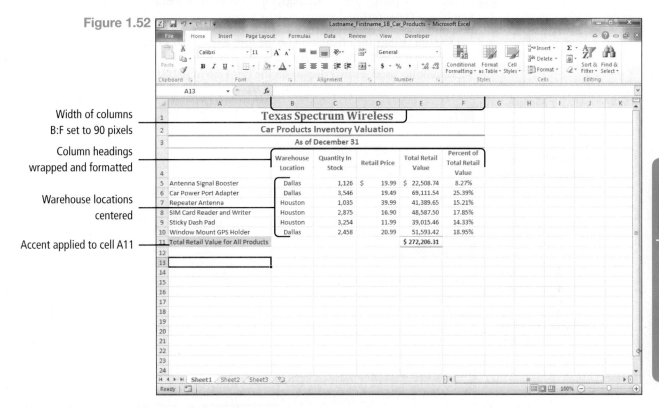

6 Click the **Insert tab**, and then in the **Text group**, click **Header & Footer** to switch to Page Layout view and open the **Header area**.

7 In the **Navigation group**, click the **Go to Footer** button to move to the bottom of the page and open the **Footer area**, and then click just above the word *Footer* to place the insertion point in the **left section** of the **Footer area**.

8 In the **Header & Footer Elements group**, click the **File Name** button to add the name of your file to the footer—&*[File]* displays in the left section of the **Footer area**. Then, click in a cell above the footer to exit the **Footer area** and view your file name.

9 Click the **Page Layout tab**, in the **Page Setup group**, click the **Margins** button, and then at the bottom of the **Margins gallery**, click **Custom Margins**. In the **Page Setup** dialog box, under **Center on page**, select the **Horizontally** check box; click **OK**.

10 In the upper left corner of your screen, click **File** to display **Backstage** view. On the **Info tab**, on the right under the screen thumbnail, click **Properties**, and then click **Show Document Panel**.

11 In the **Author** box, replace the existing text with your firstname and lastname. In the **Subject** box, type your course name and section number. In the **Keywords** box, type **car products, inventory** and then **Close** ▣ the **Document Information Panel**.

12 Press `Ctrl` + `F2` to view the **Print Preview**. At the bottom of the **Print Preview**, click the **Next Page** button ▶, and notice that as currently formatted, the worksheet occupies two pages.

13 In the center panel, under **Settings**, click **Portrait Orientation**, and then click **Landscape Orientation**. Compare your screen with Figure 1.53.

> You can change the orientation on the Page Layout tab, or here, in the Print Preview. Because it is in the Print Preview that you will often see adjustments that need to be made, commonly used settings display on the Print tab in Backstage view.

Figure 1.53

Worksheet displays in landscape orientation

Worksheet displayed in Print Preview

Landscape Orientation selected

Footer with your name

Worksheet occupies one page

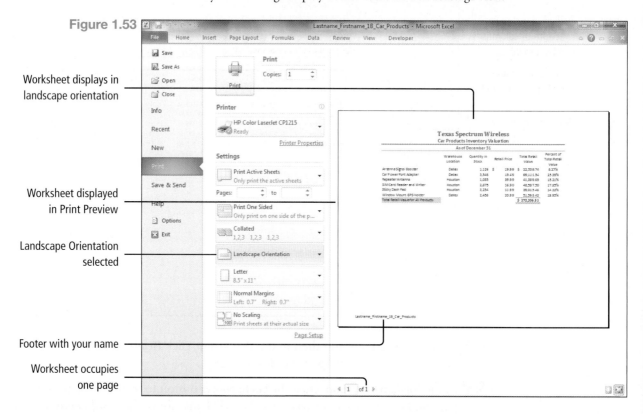

14 Note any additional adjustments or corrections that need to be made, and then on the Ribbon, click **Home** to redisplay your worksheet. In the lower right corner of your screen, on the right side of the status bar, click the **Normal** button 🔲 to return to the Normal view, and then press `Ctrl` + `Home` to return to cell **A1**.

15 Make any necessary corrections. Then, at the bottom of your worksheet, click the **Sheet2 tab** to make it the active worksheet. Hold down `Ctrl`, and then click the **Sheet3 tab**. Release `Ctrl`, and then with both sheets selected (tab background is white), point to either of the selected sheet tabs, right-click, and click **Delete** to delete the unused sheets in the workbook.

16 Save 🖫 your workbook.

17 Print or submit your worksheet electronically as directed by your instructor. If required by your instructor, print or create an electronic version of your worksheet with formulas displayed using the instructions in Activity 1.16 in Project 1A.

18 Close your workbook and close Excel.

End You have completed Project 1B ————————————————————

Content-Based Assessments

Summary

In this chapter, you used Microsoft Excel 2010 to create and analyze data organized into columns and rows and to chart and perform calculations on the data. By organizing your data with Excel, you will be able to make calculations and create visual representations of your data in the form of charts.

Key Terms

Matching

Match each term in the second column with its correct definition in the first column by writing the letter of the term on the blank line in front of the correct definition.

_____ 1. An Excel file that contains one or more worksheets.

_____ 2. Another name for a worksheet.

_____ 3. The intersection of a column and a row.

A Cell

B Cell address

C Cell content

_____ 4. The labels along the lower border of the Excel window that identify each worksheet.

_____ 5. A vertical group of cells in a worksheet.

_____ 6. A horizontal group of cells in a worksheet.

_____ 7. Anything typed into a cell.

_____ 8. Information such as numbers, text, dates, or times of day that you type into a cell.

_____ 9. Text or numbers in a cell that are not a formula.

_____ 10. An equation that performs mathematical calculations on values in a worksheet.

_____ 11. A constant value consisting of only numbers.

_____ 12. Another name for a cell reference.

_____ 13. Another name for a constant value.

_____ 14. The small black square in the lower right corner of a selected cell.

_____ 15. The graphic representation of data in a worksheet.

D Chart
E Column
F Constant value
G Data
H Fill handle
I Formula
J Number value
K Row
L Sheet tabs
M Spreadsheet
N Value
O Workbook

Multiple Choice

Circle the correct answer.

1. On startup, Excel displays a new blank:
   A. document **B.** workbook **C.** grid

2. An Excel window element that displays the value or formula contained in the active cell is the:
   A. name box **B.** status bar **C.** formula bar

3. An Excel window element that displays the name of the selected cell, table, chart, or object is the:
   A. name box **B.** status bar **C.** formula bar

4. A box in the upper left corner of the worksheet grid that selects all the cells in a worksheet is the:
   A. name box **B.** select all box **C.** split box

5. A cell surrounded by a black border and ready to receive data is the:
   A. active cell **B.** address cell **C.** reference cell

6. The feature that generates and extends values into adjacent cells based on the values of selected cells is:
   A. AutoComplete **B.** Auto Fill **C.** fill handle

7. The default format that Excel applies to numbers is the:
   A. comma format **B.** accounting format **C.** general format

8. The data that displays in the Formula Bar is referred to as the:
   A. constant value **B.** formula **C.** underlying value

9. The type of cell reference that refers to cells by their fixed position in a worksheet is:
   A. absolute **B.** relative **C.** exponentiation

10. Tiny charts embedded in a cell that give a visual trend summary alongside your data are:
   A. embedded charts **B.** sparklines **C.** chart styles

Content-Based Assessments

Apply **1A** skills from these Objectives:

1. Create, Save, and Navigate an Excel Workbook
2. Enter Data in a Worksheet
3. Construct and Copy Formulas and Use the Sum Function
4. Format Cells with Merge & Center and Cell Styles
5. Chart Data to Create a Column Chart and Insert Sparklines
6. Print, Display Formulas, and Close Excel

Skills Review | Project **1C** GPS Sales

In the following Skills Review, you will create a new Excel worksheet with a chart that summarizes the first quarter sales of GPS (Global Positioning System) navigation devices. Your completed worksheet will look similar to Figure 1.54.

Project Files

For Project 1C, you will need the following file:

New blank Excel workbook

You will save your workbook as:

Lastname_Firstname_1C_GPS_Sales

Project Results

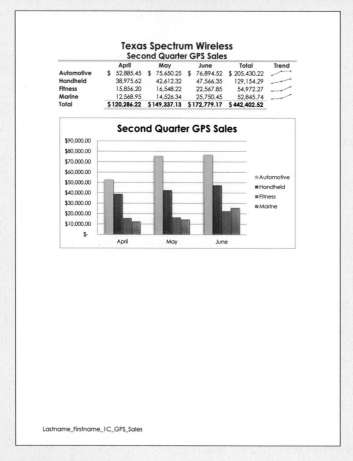

Figure 1.54

(Project 1C GPS Sales continues on the next page)

1 **Start** Excel. Click the **File tab** to display **Backstage** view, click **Save As**, and then in the **Save As** dialog box, navigate to your **Excel Chapter 1** folder. In the **File name** box, using your own name, type **Lastname_Firstname_ 1C_GPS_Sales** and then press Enter.

a. With cell **A1** as the active cell, type the worksheet title **Texas Spectrum Wireless** and then press Enter. In cell **A2**, type the worksheet subtitle **Second Quarter GPS Sales** and then press Enter.

b. Click in cell **A4**, type **Automotive** and then press Enter. In cell **A5**, type **Handheld** and then press Enter. In cell **A6**, type **Fitness** and then press Enter. In cell **A7**, type **Marine** and then press Enter. In cell **A8**, type **Total** and then press Enter.

c. Click cell **B3**. Type **April** and then in the **Formula Bar**, click the **Enter** button to keep cell **B3** the active cell. With **B3** as the active cell, point to the fill handle in the lower right corner of the selected cell, drag to the right to cell **D3**, and then release the mouse button to enter the text *May* and *June*.

d. Press Ctrl + Home, to make cell **A1** the active cell. In the **column heading area**, point to the vertical line between **column A** and **column B** to display the ⟷ pointer, hold down the left mouse button and drag to the right to increase the column width to **100 pixels**.

e. Point to cell **B3**, and then drag across to select cells **B3** and **C3** and **D3**. With the range **B3:D3** selected, point anywhere over the selected range, right-click, and then on the Mini toolbar, click the **Center** button.

f. Click cell **B4**, type **52885.45** and press Tab to make cell **C4** active. Enter the remaining values, as shown in **Table 1**, pressing Tab to move across the rows and Enter to move down the columns.

2 Click cell **B8** to make it the active cell and type =

a. At the insertion point, type **b4** and then type + Type **b5** and then type **+b6+b7** Press Enter. Your result is *120286.2*.

b. Click in cell **C8**. Type = and then click cell **C4**. Type + and then click cell **C5**. Repeat this process to complete the formula to add cells **C4** through **C7**, and then press Enter. Your result is *149337.1*.

c. Click cell **D8**. On the **Home tab**, in the **Editing group**, click the **Sum** button, and then press Enter to construct a formula by using the SUM function. Your result is *172779.2*. You can use any of these methods to add values; the Sum button is the most efficient.

d. In cell **E3** type **Total** and press Enter. With cell **E4** as the active cell, hold down Alt, and then press =. On the **Formula Bar**, click the **Enter** button to display the result and keep cell **E4** active.

e. With cell **E4** active, point to the fill handle in the lower right corner of the cell. Drag down through cell **E8**, and then release the mouse button to copy the formula with relative cell references down to sum each row.

3 Click cell **F3**. Type **Trend** and then press Enter.

a. Select the range **A1:F1**, and then on the **Home tab**, in the **Alignment group**, click the **Merge & Center** button. Select the range **A2:F2**, and then click the **Merge & Center** button.

b. Click cell **A1**. In the **Styles group**, click the **Cell Styles** button. Under **Titles and Headings**, click **Title**. Click cell **A2**, display the **Cell Styles** gallery, and then click **Heading 1**.

c. Select the range **B3:F3**, hold down Ctrl, and then select the range **A4:A8**. From the **Cell Styles** gallery, click **Heading 4** to apply this cell style to the column and row titles.

d. Select the range **B4:E4**, hold down Ctrl, and then select the range **B8:E8**. On the **Home tab**, in the **Number group**, click the **Accounting Number Format** button. Select the range **B5:E7**, and then in the **Number group**, click the **Comma Style** button. Select the range **B8:E8**. From the **Styles group**, display the **Cell Styles** gallery, and then under **Titles and Headings**, click **Total**.

Table 1

	April	May	June
Automotive	52885.45	75650.25	76894.52
Handheld	38975.62	42612.32	47566.35
Fitness	15856.20	16548.22	22567.85
Marine	12568.95	14526.34	25750.45

- - - → (Return to Step 2)

(Project 1C GPS Sales continues on the next page)

Content-Based Assessments

e. On the Ribbon, click the **Page Layout tab**, and then from the **Themes group**, click the **Themes** button to display the **Themes** gallery. Click the **Austin** theme.

4 Select the range **A3:D7**. Click the **Insert tab**, and then in the **Charts group**, click **Column**. From the gallery of column chart types, under **2-D Column**, click the first chart—**Clustered Column**.

a. On the Quick Access Toolbar, click the **Save** button to be sure that you have saved your work up to this point. Point to the top border of the chart to display the ⬚ pointer, and then drag to position the chart inside the upper left corner of cell **A10**.

b. On the **Design tab**, in the **Data group**, click the **Switch Row/Column** button so that the months display on the Horizontal (Category) axis and the types of GPS equipment display in the legend.

c. On the **Design tab**, in the **Chart Layouts group**, click the first layout—**Layout 1**.

d. In the chart, click anywhere in the text *Chart Title* to select the text box. Type **Second Quarter GPS Sales** and then press Enter.

e. Click anywhere in the chart so that the chart title text box is not selected. On the **Design tab**, in the **Chart Styles group**, click the **More** button. Using the ScreenTips as your guide, locate and click **Style 18**.

f. Point to the lower right corner of the chart to display the ⬚ pointer, and then drag down and to the right so that the lower right border of the chart is positioned just inside the lower right corner of cell **F26**.

5 Select the range **B4:D7**. Click the **Insert tab**, and then in the **Sparklines group**, click **Line**. In the **Create Sparklines** dialog box, in the **Location Range** box, type **f4:f7** and then click **OK** to insert the sparklines.

a. On the **Design tab**, in the **Show group**, select the **Markers** check box to display markers in the sparklines.

b. On the **Design tab**, in the **Style group**, click the **More** button, and then in the second row, click the fourth style—**Sparkline Style Accent 4, Darker 25%**.

6 On the **Insert tab**, in the **Text group**, click **Header & Footer** to switch to **Page Layout** view and open the **Header** area.

a. In the **Navigation group**, click the **Go to Footer** button to open the Footer area. Click just above the word *Footer* to place the insertion point in the **left section** of the Footer.

b. In the **Header & Footer Elements group**, click the **File Name** button, and then click in a cell just above the footer to exit the Footer area.

7 On the right side of the status bar, click the **Normal** button to return to Normal view, and then press Ctrl + Home to make cell **A1** active.

a. Click the **File tab**, and then on the right, click **Properties**. Click **Show Document Panel**, and then in the **Author** box, delete any text and type your firstname and lastname. In the **Subject** box, type your course name and section number, and in the **Keywords** box, type **GPS sales Close** the Document Information Panel.

b. At the bottom of your worksheet, click the **Sheet2** tab. Hold down Ctrl, and then click the **Sheet3** tab. With both sheets selected, point to either of the selected sheet tabs, right-click, and then click **Delete** to delete the sheets.

c. Click the **Page Layout tab**. In the **Page Setup group**, click the **Margins** button, and then at the bottom of the **Margins** gallery, click **Custom Margins**. In the **Page Setup** dialog box, under **Center on page**, select the **Horizontally** check box.

d. In the lower right corner of the **Page Setup** dialog box, click **OK**. On the **File tab**, click **Print** to view the **Print Preview**. Click the **Home tab** to return to Normal view and if necessary, make any necessary corrections and resize and move your chart so that it is centered under the worksheet.

e. On the Quick Access Toolbar, click the **Save** button to be sure that you have saved your work up to this point.

f. Print or submit your workbook electronically as directed by your instructor. If required by your instructor, print or create an electronic version of your worksheets with formulas displayed by using the instructions in Activity 1.16. **Exit** Excel without saving so that you do not save the changes you made to print formulas.

End You have completed Project 1C ——————

Content-Based Assessments

Apply 1B skills from these Objectives:

- **7** Check Spelling in a Worksheet
- **8** Enter Data by Range
- **9** Construct Formulas for Mathematical Operations
- **10** Edit Values in a Worksheet
- **11** Format a Worksheet

Skills Review | Project **1D** Charger Inventory

In the following Skills Review, you will create a worksheet that summarizes the inventory of cell phone chargers. Your completed worksheet will look similar to Figure 1.55.

Project Files

For Project 1D, you will need the following file:

New blank Excel workbook

You will save your workbook as:

Lastname_Firstname_1D_Charger_Inventory

Project Results

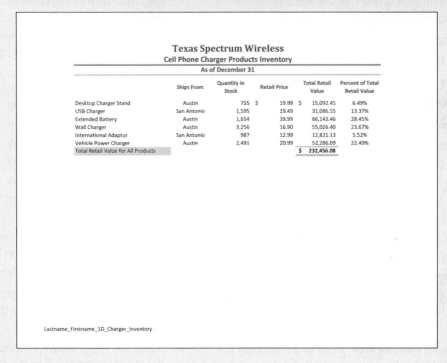

	Ships From	Quantity in Stock	Retail Price	Total Retail Value	Percent of Total Retail Value
Desktop Charger Stand	Austin	755	$ 19.99	$ 15,092.45	6.49%
USB Charger	San Antonio	1,595	19.49	31,086.55	13.37%
Extended Battery	Austin	1,654	39.99	66,143.46	28.45%
Wall Charger	Austin	3,256	16.90	55,026.40	23.67%
International Adaptor	San Antonio	987	12.99	12,821.13	5.52%
Vehicle Power Charger	Austin	2,491	20.99	52,286.09	22.49%
Total Retail Value for All Products				$ 232,456.08	

Texas Spectrum Wireless
Cell Phone Charger Products Inventory
As of December 31

Lastname_Firstname_1D_Charger_Inventory

Figure 1.55

(Project 1D Charger Inventory continues on the next page)

Content-Based Assessments

1 Start Excel and display a new blank workbook. **Save** the workbook in your **Excel Chapter 1** folder, as **Lastname_Firstname_1D_Charger_Inventory** In cell **A1** type **Texas Spectrum Wireless** and in cell **A2** type **Cell Phone Charger Products Inventory**

a. Click cell **B3**, type **Quantity in Stock** and press Tab. In cell **C3** type **Average Cost** and press Tab. In cell **D3**, type **Retail Price** and press Tab. In cell **E3**, type **Total Retail Value** and press Tab. In cell **F3** type **Percent of Total Retail Value** and press Enter.

b. Click cell **A4**, type **Desktop Charger Stand** and press Enter. In the range **A5:A10**, type the remaining row titles as shown, including the misspelled words.

USB Charger

Extended Battery

Wall Charger

International Adaptor

Vehicle Powr Charger

Total Retail Value for All Products

c. Press Ctrl + Home to move to the top of your worksheet. On the **Review tab**, in the **Proofing group**, click the **Spelling** button. Correct *Powr* to **Power** and any other spelling errors you may have made, and then when the message displays, *The spelling check is complete for the entire sheet*, click **OK**.

d. In the **column heading area**, point to the right boundary of **column A** to display the ✛ pointer, and then drag to the right to widen **column A** to **225** pixels.

e. In the **column heading area**, point to the **column B** heading to display the ↓ pointer, and then drag to the right to select **columns B:F**. With the columns selected, in the **column heading area**, point to the right boundary of any of the selected columns, and then drag to the right to set the width to **100 pixels**.

f. Select the range **A1:F1**. On the **Home tab**, in the **Alignment group**, click the **Merge & Center** button, and then from the **Cell Styles** gallery, apply the **Title** style. Select the range **A2:F2**. **Merge & Center** the text across the selection, and then from the **Cell Styles** gallery, apply the **Heading 1** style.

2 Select the empty range **B4:D9**. With cell B4 active in the range, type **755** and then press Enter.

a. With cell **B5** active in the range, and pressing Enter after each entry, type the following data in the *Quantity in Stock* column:

1595

2654

3256

987

2491

b. With the selected range still active, from the following table, beginning in cell **C4** and pressing Enter after each entry, enter the following data for the **Average Cost** column and then the **Retail Price** column. If you prefer, type without selecting the range first; recall that this is optional.

Average Cost	Retail Price
9.75	19.99
9.25	19.49
16.90	39.99
9.55	16.90
14.20	12.99
10.45	20.99

3 In cell **E4**, type **=b4*d4** and then press Enter to construct a formula that calculates the *Total Retail Value* of the *Desktop Charger Stands* (Quantity × Retail Price).

a. Click cell **E4**, position your pointer over the fill handle, and then drag down through cell **E9** to copy the formula.

b. Select the range **B4:B9**, and then on the **Home tab**, in the **Number group**, click the **Comma Style** button. Then, in the **Number group**, click the **Decrease Decimal** button two times to remove the decimal places from these non-currency values.

c. Click cell **E10**, in the **Editing group**, click the **Sum** button, and then press Enter to calculate the *Total Retail Value for All Products*. Your result is *272446.1*.

d. Select the range **C5:E9** and apply the **Comma Style**. Select the range **C4:E4**, hold down Ctrl, and then click cell **E10**. With the nonadjacent cells selected, apply the **Accounting Number Format**. Click cell **E10**, and then from the **Cell Styles** gallery, apply the **Total** style.

(Project 1D Charger Inventory continues on the next page)

e. Click cell **F4**, type **=** and then click cell **E4**. Type **/** and then click cell **E10**. Press F4 to make the reference to cell *E10* absolute, and then on the **Formula Bar**, click the **Enter** button so that **F4** remains the active cell. Drag the fill handle to copy the formula down through cell **F9**.

f. Point to cell **B6**, and then double-click to place the insertion point within the cell. Use the arrow keys to move the insertion point to left or right of *2*, and use either Del or Backspace to delete 2, and then type **1** and press Enter so that the new *Quantity in Stock* is *1654*. Notice the recalculations in the worksheet.

4 Select the range **F4:F9**, right-click over the selection, and then on the Mini toolbar, click the **Percent Style** button. Click the **Increase Decimal** button two times, and then **Center** the selection.

a. In the **row heading area** on the left side of your screen, point to **row 3** to display the → pointer, and then right-click to simultaneously select the row and display a shortcut menu. On the displayed shortcut menu, click **Insert** to insert a new **row 3**.

b. Click cell **A3**, type **As of December 31** and then on the **Formula Bar**, click the **Enter** button to keep cell **A3** as the active cell. **Merge & Center** the text across the range **A3:F3**, and then apply the **Heading 2** cell style.

5 In the **column heading area**, point to **column B**. When the ↓ pointer displays, right-click, and then click **Insert** to insert a new column.

a. Click cell **B4**, and type **Ships From** and press Enter. In cell **B5**, type **Austin** and then press Enter. In cell **B6**, type **San Antonio** and then press Enter

b. Using AutoComplete to speed your typing by pressing Enter as soon as the AutoComplete suggestion displays, in cells **B7**, **B8**, and **B10** type **Austin** and in cell **B9** type **San Antonio**

c. In the **column heading area**, point to the right boundary of **column B**, and then drag to the left and set the width to **90 pixels**. From the **column heading area**, point to **column D**, right-click, and then click **Delete**.

d. Select the range **B4:F4**, and then on the **Home tab**, in the **Alignment group**, click the **Wrap Text** button, the **Center** button, and the **Middle Align** button. With the range still selected, apply the **Heading 4** cell style.

e. Select the range **B5:B10**, right-click, and then click the **Center** button. Click cell **A11**, and then from the **Cell Styles** gallery, under **Themed Cell Styles**, click **40% - Accent1**.

6 On the **Insert tab**, in the **Text group**, click **Header & Footer**. In the **Navigation group**, click the **Go To Footer** button, and then click just above the word *Footer*. In the **Header & Footer Elements group**, click the **File Name** button to add the name of your file to the footer. Click in a cell just above the footer to exit the **Footer area**, and then return the worksheet to **Normal** view.

a. Press Ctrl + Home to move the insertion point to cell **A1**. On the **Page Layout tab**, in the **Page Setup group**, click **Orientation**, and then click **Landscape**.

b. In the **Page Setup group**, click the **Margins** button, and then at the bottom of the **Margins gallery**, click **Custom Margins**. In the **Page Setup** dialog box, under **Center on page**, select the **Horizontally** check box, and then click **OK**.

c. Click the **File tab** to display **Backstage** view, and then on the right, click **Properties**. Click **Show Document Panel**, and then in the **Author** box, delete any text and type your firstname and lastname. In the **Subject** box type your course name and section number, in the **Keywords** box type **cell phone chargers** and then **Close** the **Document Information Panel**.

d. Select **Sheet2** and **Sheet3**, and then **Delete** both sheets.

e. **Save** your file and then print or submit your workbook electronically as directed by your instructor. If required by your instructor, print or create an electronic version of your worksheet with formulas displayed by using the instructions in Activity 1.16. **Exit** Excel without saving so that you do not save the changes you made to print formulas.

End **You have completed Project 1D** ——————

Excel | Chapter 1

Mastering Excel | Project **1E** Hard Drives

In the following Mastering Excel project, you will create a worksheet comparing the sales of different types of external hard drives sold in the second quarter. Your completed worksheet will look similar to Figure 1.56.

Project Files

For Project 1E, you will need the following file:

New blank Excel workbook

You will save your workbook as:

Lastname_Firstname_1E_Hard_Drives

Project Results

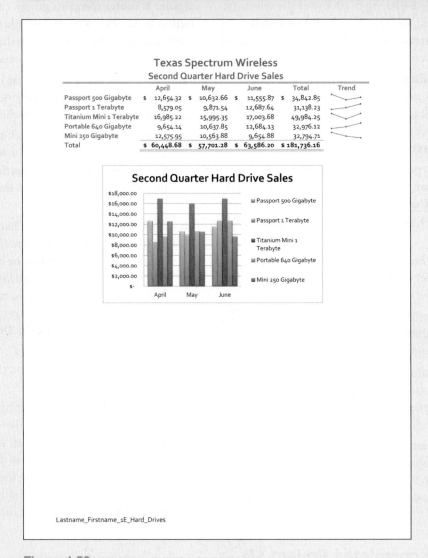

Figure 1.56

(Project 1E Hard Drives continues on the next page)

Content-Based Assessments

1 **Start** Excel. In cell **A1**, type **Texas Spectrum Wireless** and in cell **A2**, type **Second Quarter Hard Drive Sales** Change the **Theme** to **Module**, and then **Save** the workbook in your **Excel Chapter 1** folder as **Lastname_Firstname_1E_Hard_Drives**

2 In cell **B3**, type **April** and then use the fill handle to enter the months *May* and *June* in the range **C3:D3**. In cell **E3**, type **Total** and in cell **F3**, type **Trend**

3 **Center** the column titles in the range **B3:F3**. **Merge & Center** the title across the range **A1:F1**, and apply the **Title** cell style. **Merge & Center** the subtitle across the range **A2:F2**, and apply the **Heading 1** cell style.

4 Widen **column A** to **170 pixels**, and then in the range **A4:A9**, type the following row titles:

Passport 500 Gigabyte

Passport 1 Terabyte

Titanium Mini 1 Terabyte

Portable 640 Gigabyte

Mini 250 Gigabyte

Total

5 Widen columns **B:F** to **100 pixels**, and then in the range **B4:D8**, enter the monthly sales figures for each type of hard drive, as shown in **Table 1** at the bottom of the page.

6 In cell **B9**, **Sum** the *April* hard drive sales, and then copy the formula across to cells **C9:D9**. In cell **E4**, **Sum** the *Passport 500 Gigabyte sales*, and then copy the formula down to cells **E5:E9**.

7 Apply the **Heading 4** cell style to the row titles and the column titles. Apply the **Total** cell style to the totals in the range **B9:E9**. Apply the **Accounting Number Format**

to the first row of sales figures and to the total row. Apply the **Comma Style** to the remaining sales figures.

8 To compare the monthly sales of each product visually, select the range that represents the sales figures for the three months, including the month names, and for each product name—do not include any totals in the range. With this data selected, **Insert** a **2-D Clustered Column** chart. Switch the Row/Column data so that the months display on the category axis and the types of hard drives display in the legend.

9 Position the upper left corner of the chart in the approximate center of cell **A11** so that the chart is visually centered below the worksheet, as shown in Figure 1.56. Apply **Chart Style 26**, and then modify the **Chart Layout** by applying **Layout 1**. Change the **Chart Title** to **Second Quarter Hard Drive Sales**

10 In the range **F4:F8**, insert **Line** sparklines that compare the monthly data. Do not include the totals. Show the sparkline **Markers** and apply **Sparkline Style Accent 2, Darker 50%**—in the first row, the second style.

11 Insert a **Footer** with the **File Name** in the **left section**, and then return the worksheet to **Normal** view. Display the **Document Panel**, add your name, your course name and section, and the keywords **hard drives, sales** Delete the unused sheets, and then center the worksheet **Horizontally** on the page. Check your worksheet by previewing it in **Print Preview**, and then make any necessary corrections.

12 **Save** your workbook, and then print or submit electronically as directed. If required by your instructor, print or create an electronic version of your worksheets with formulas displayed by using the instructions in Activity 1.16. **Exit** Excel without saving so that you do not save the changes you made to print formulas.

Table 1

	April	May	June
Passport 500 Gigabyte	12654.32	10632.66	11555.87
Passport 1 Terabyte	8579.05	9871.54	12687.64
Titanium Mini 1 Terabyte	16985.22	15995.35	17003.68
Portable 640 Gigabyte	9654.14	10637.85	12684.13
Mini 250 Gigabyte	12575.95	10563.88	9654.88

(Return to Step 6)

End **You have completed Project 1E** ——————————

Content-Based Assessments

Apply **1B** skills from
these Objectives:

7 Check Spelling in a
Worksheet

8 Enter Data by Range

9 Construct Formulas
for Mathematical
Operations

10 Edit Values in a
Worksheet

11 Format a Worksheet

Mastering Excel | Project **1F** Camera Accessories

In the following Mastering Excel project, you will create a worksheet that summarizes the sale of digital camera accessories. Your completed worksheet will look similar to Figure 1.57.

Project Files

For Project 1F, you will need the following file:

New blank Excel workbook

You will save your workbook as:

Lastname_Firstname_1F_Camera_Accessories

Project Results

Texas Spectrum Wireless
Digital Camera Accessories Sales

	Quantity Sold	Retail Price	Total Sales	Percent of Total Sales
Month Ending August 31				
Small Cloth Gear Bag	254	$ 19.99	$ 5,077.46	10.69%
Large Cloth Gear Bag	182	24.99	4,548.18	9.58%
Lens Cap	351	6.99	2,453.49	5.17%
Lens Hood	125	5.49	686.25	1.44%
Remote Switch	750	22.50	16,875.00	35.53%
Mini Tripod	554	24.99	13,844.46	29.15%
Cleaning Kit	365	10.99	4,011.35	8.45%
Total Sales for All Products			$ 47,496.19	

Lastname_Firstname_1F_Camera_Accessories

Figure 1.57

(Project 1F Camera Accessories continues on the next page)

Content-Based Assessments

1 **Start** Excel and display a new blank workbook. **Save** the workbook in your **Excel Chapter 1** folder as Lastname_Firstname_1F_Camera_Accessories In cell **A1**, type **Texas Spectrum Wireless** In cell **A2**, type **Digital Camera Accessories Sales** and then **Merge & Center** the title and the subtitle across **columns A:F**. Apply the **Title** and **Heading 1** cell styles respectively.

2 Beginning in cell **B3**, type the following column titles: **Product Number** and **Quantity Sold** and **Retail Price** and **Total Sales** and **Percent of Total Sales**

3 Beginning in cell **A4**, type the following row titles, including misspelled words:

Small Cloth Gear Bag

Large Cloth Gear Bag

Lens Cap

Lens Hood

Remote Switch

Mini Tripod

Cleening Kit

Total Sales for All Products

4 Make cell **A1** the active cell, and then check spelling in your worksheet. Correct *Cleening* to **Cleaning**, and make any other necessary corrections. Widen **column A** to **180 pixels** and **columns B:F** to **90 pixels**.

5 In the range **B4:D10**, type the data shown in **Table 1** at the bottom of the page.

6 In cell **E4**, construct a formula to calculate the *Total Sales* of the *Small Cloth Gear Bags* by multiplying the *Quantity Sold* times the *Retail Price*. Copy the formula down for the remaining products. In cell **E11**, use the **SUM** function to calculate the *Total Sales for All Products*, and then apply the **Total** cell style to the cell.

7 Using absolute cell references as necessary so that you can copy the formula, in cell **F4**, construct a formula to calculate the *Percent of Total Sales* for the first product by dividing the *Total Sales* of the *Small Cloth Gear Bags* by the *Total Sales for All Products*. Copy the formula down for the remaining products. To the computed percentages, apply **Percent Style** with two decimal places, and then **Center** the percentages.

8 Apply the **Comma Style** with no decimal places to the *Quantity Sold* figures. To cells **D4**, **E4**, and **E11** apply the **Accounting Number Format**. To the range **D5:E10**, apply the **Comma Style**.

9 Change the *Retail Price* of the *Mini Tripod* to **24.99** and the *Quantity Sold* of the *Remote Switch* to **750** Delete **column B**, and then **Insert** a new **row 3**. In cell **A3**, type **Month Ending August 31** and then **Merge & Center** the text across the range **A3:E3**. Apply the **Heading 2** cell style. To cell **A12**, apply the **Accent1** cell style. Select the four column titles, apply **Wrap Text**, **Middle Align**, and **Center** formatting, and then apply the **Heading 3** cell style.

10 Insert a **Footer** with the **File Name** in the **left section**, and then return to **Normal** view. Display the **Document Panel**, add your name, your course name and section, and the keywords **digital camera accessories, sales**

11 Delete the unused sheets, and then center the worksheet **Horizontally** on the page. Preview the worksheet in **Print Preview**, and make any necessary corrections.

12 **Save** your workbook, and then print or submit electronically as directed. If required by your instructor, print or create an electronic version of your worksheets with formulas displayed by using the instructions in Activity 1.16. **Exit** Excel without saving so that you do not save the changes you made to print formulas.

Table 1

	Product Number	Quantity Sold	Retail Price
Small Cloth Gear Bag	CGB-3	254	19.99
Large Cloth Gear Bag	CGB-8	182	24.99
Lens Cap	LC-2	351	6.99
Lens Hood	LH-4	125	5.49
Remote Switch	RS-5	677	22.50
Mini Tripod	MTP-6	554	29.99
Cleaning Kit	CK-8	365	10.99

- - - ➤ (Return to Step 6)

End **You have completed Project 1F** ————————————

Content-Based Assessments

Apply **1A** and **1B** skills from these Objectives:

Apply 1A and 1B skills from these Objectives:

- **1** Create, Save, and Navigate an Excel Workbook
- **2** Enter Data in a Worksheet
- **3** Construct and Copy Formulas and Use the SUM Function
- **4** Format Cells with Merge & Center and Cell Styles
- **5** Chart Data to Create a Column Chart and Insert Sparklines
- **6** Print, Display Formulas, and Close Excel
- **7** Check Spelling in a Worksheet
- **8** Enter Data by Range
- **9** Construct Formulas for Mathematical Operations
- **10** Edit Values in a Worksheet
- **11** Format a Worksheet

Mastering Excel | Project **1G** Sales Comparison

In the following Mastering Excel project, you will create a new worksheet that compares annual laptop sales by store location. Your completed worksheet will look similar to Figure 1.58.

Project Files

For Project 1G, you will need the following file:

New blank Excel workbook

You will save your workbook as:

Lastname_Firstname_1G_Sales_Comparison

Project Results

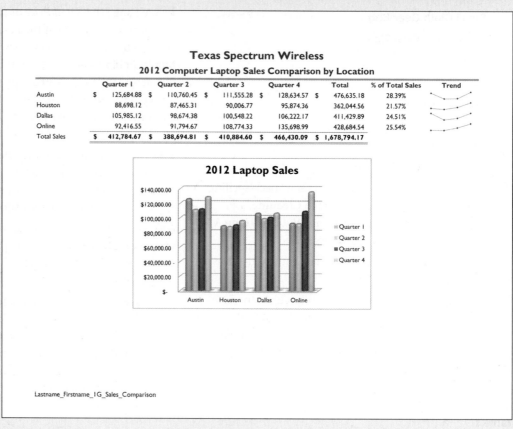

Figure 1.58

(Project 1G Sales Comparison continues on the next page)

Content-Based Assessments

Mastering Excel | Project **1G** Sales Comparison (continued)

1 **Start** Excel. In a new blank workbook, as the worksheet title, in cell **A1**, type **Texas Spectrum Wireless** As the worksheet subtitle, in cell **A2**, type **2012 Computer Laptop Sales Comparison by Location** and then **Save** the workbook in your **Excel Chapter 1** folder as **Lastname_Firstname_1G_Sales_Comparison**

2 In cell **B3**, type **Quarter 1** and then use the fill handle to enter *Quarter 2*, *Quarter 3*, and *Quarter 4* in the range **C3:E3**. In cell **F3**, type **Total** In cell **G3**, type **% of Total Sales** In cell **H3**, type **Trend**

3 In the range **A4:A7**, type the following row titles: **Austin** and **Houston** and **Online** and **Total Sales**

4 Widen columns **A:H** to **115 pixels**. **Merge & Center** the title across the range **A1:H1**, and then apply the **Title** cell style. **Merge & Center** the subtitle across the range **A2:H2**, and then apply the **Heading 1** cell style. Select the seven column titles, apply **Center** formatting, and then apply the **Heading 4** cell style.

5 In the range **B4:E6**, enter the sales values for each Quarter as shown in **Table 1** at the bottom of the page.

6 **Sum** the *Quarter 1* sales, and then copy the formula across for the remaining Quarters. **Sum** the sales for the *Austin* location, and then copy the formula down through cell **F7**. Apply the **Accounting Number Format** to the first row of sales figures and to the total row, and the **Comma Style** to the remaining sales figures. Format the totals in **row 7** with the **Total** cell style.

7 **Insert** a new **row 6** with the row title **Dallas** and the following sales figures for each quarter: **105985.12** and **98674.38** and **100548.22** and **106222.17** Copy the formula in cell **F5** down to cell **F6** to sum the new row.

8 Using absolute cell references as necessary so that you can copy the formula, in cell **G4** construct a formula to calculate the *Percent of Total Sales* for the first location by dividing the *Total* for the *Austin* location by the *Total Sales* for all Quarters. Copy the formula down for the remaining locations. To the computed percentages, apply

Percent Style with two decimal places, and then **Center** the percentages.

9 Insert **Line** sparklines in the range **H4:H7** that compare the quarterly data. Do not include the totals. Show the sparkline **Markers** and apply the second style in the second row—**Sparkline Style Accent 2, Darker 25%**.

10 **Save** your workbook. To compare the quarterly sales of each location visually, select the range that represents the sales figures for the four quarters, including the quarter names and each location—do not include any totals in the range. With this data selected, **Insert** a **Column**, **Clustered Cylinder** chart.

11 Switch the row/column data so that the locations display on the category axis. Position the top edge of the chart in **row 10** and visually center it below the worksheet data. Apply **Chart Style 26**, and then modify the **Chart Layout** by applying **Layout 1**. Change the **Chart Title** to **2012 Laptop Sales**

12 Deselect the chart. Change the **Orientation** to **Landscape**, center the worksheet **Horizontally** on the page, and then change the **Theme** to **Solstice**. Scale the worksheet so that the **Width** fits to **1 page**. Insert a **Footer** with the **File Name** in the **left section**. Return the worksheet to **Normal** view and make **A1** the active cell so that you can view the top of your worksheet.

13 Display the **Document Panel**, add your name, your course name and section, and the keywords **laptops, sales** Delete the unused sheets, preview your worksheet in **Print Preview**, and then make any necessary corrections.

14 **Save** your workbook, and then print or submit electronically as directed. If required by your instructor, print or create an electronic version of your worksheets with formulas displayed by using the instructions in Activity 1.16. **Exit** Excel without saving so that you do not save the changes you made to print formulas.

Table 1

	Quarter 1	Quarter 2	Quarter 3	Quarter 4
Austin	125684.88	110760.45	111555.28	128634.57
Houston	88698.12	87465.31	90006.77	95874.36
Online	92416.55	91794.67	108774.33	135698.99

- - - → (Return to Step 6)

End You have completed Project 1G ————————————————

Content-Based Assessments

Apply a combination of
the **1A** and **1B** skills.

GO! Fix It | Project **1H** Team Sales

Project Files

For Project 1H, you will need the following file:

e01H_Team_Sales

You will save your workbook as:

Lastname_Firstname_1H_Team_Sales

In this project, you will edit a worksheet that summarizes sales by each sales team member at the Texas Spectrum Wireless San Antonio location for the month of February. From the student files that accompany this textbook, open the file e01H_Team_Sales, and then save the file in your Excel Chapter 1 folder as **Lastname_Firstname_1H_Team_Sales**

To complete the project, you must find and correct errors in formulas and formatting. View each formula in the Formula Bar and edit as necessary. In addition to errors that you find, you should know:

- There are two spelling errors.
- Worksheet titles should be merged and centered and appropriate cell styles should be applied.
- Appropriate number and accounting format with zero decimals should be applied to the data and text should be wrapped where necessary. Percent style formatting should be applied appropriately where necessary.
- Column headings should be formatted with the Heading 4 style.
- In the chart, the team member names should display on the Horizontal (Category) axis and the week names should display in the legend.
- The chart should include the title **February Team Member Sales**
- The worksheet should be centered horizontally on one page in Landscape orientation. Remove unused sheets.
- A footer should be inserted that includes the file name, and document properties should include the keywords **team sales, San Antonio**

Save your workbook, and then print or submit electronically as directed. If required by your instructor, print or create an electronic version of your worksheets with formulas displayed by using the instructions in Activity 1.16. Exit Excel without saving so that you do not save the changes you made to print formulas.

End **You have completed Project 1H** ─────────────

Content-Based Assessments

Project Files

For Project 1I, you will need the following file:

New blank Excel workbook

You will save your workbook as:

Lastname_Firstname_1I_Printer_Sales

Create the worksheet shown in Figure 1.59. Use the Pushpin theme and change the Orientation to Landscape. Construct formulas in the Total Sold, Total Sales, and Percent of Total Sales columns, and in the Total row. Apply cell styles and number formatting as shown. Use Style 26 for the chart. Insert sparklines for the monthly data using the first style in the second row—Sparkline Style Accent 1, Darker 25%. Add your name, your course name and section, and the keywords **inkjet, printer, sales** to the document properties. Save the file in your Excel Chapter 1 folder as **Lastname_Firstname_1I_Printer_Sales**

Project Results

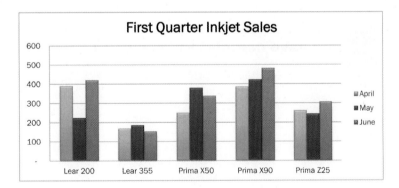

Texas Spectrum Wireless
First Quarter Inkjet Printer Sales

Model	April	May	June	Total Sold	Retail Price	Total Sales	Percent of Total Sales	Trend
Lear 200	390	224	421	1,035	$ 79.99	$ 82,789.65	8.50%	
Lear 355	168	186	153	507	169.99	86,184.93	8.85%	
Prima X50	250	379	339	968	199.99	193,590.32	19.88%	
Prima X90	386	423	482	1,291	249.99	322,737.09	33.15%	
Prima Z25	261	244	307	812	354.99	288,251.88	29.61%	
Total	1,455	1,456	1,702	4,613		$ 973,553.87		

Lastname_Firstname_1I_Printer_Sales

Figure 1.59

Excel | Chapter 1

Content-Based Assessments

GO! Solve It | Project **1J** Warranty Sales

Project Files

For Project 1J, you will need the following file:

e01J_Warranty_Sales

You will save your workbook as:

Lastname_Firstname_1J_Warranty_Sales

Open the file e01J_Warranty_Sales and save it as **Lastname_Firstname_1J_Warranty_Sales** Complete the worksheet by using Auto Fill to enter the Quarter headings, and then calculating *Total Sold*, *Total Sales*, *Total For All Products*, and *Percent of Total Sales*. Format the worksheet attractively, and apply appropriate financial formatting. Insert a chart that compares the total number of warranties sold for each item across Quarters, and format the chart to display the information appropriately. Include the file name in the footer, add appropriate document properties, and submit as directed.

		Performance Level		
		Exemplary: You consistently applied the relevant skills	Proficient: You sometimes, but not always, applied the relevant skills	Developing: You rarely or never applied the relevant skills
Performance Element	Create formulas	All formulas are correct and are efficiently constructed.	Formulas are correct but not always constructed in the most efficient manner.	One or more formulas are missing or incorrect; or only numbers were entered.
	Create a chart	Chart created properly.	Chart was created but incorrect data was selected.	No chart was created.
	Format attractively and appropriately	Formatting is attractive and appropriate.	Adequately formatted but difficult to read or unattractive.	Inadequate or no formatting.

End You have completed Project 1J ─────────────

Content-Based Assessments

Apply a combination of the **1A** and **1B** skills.

GO! Solve It | Project **1K** Service Receipts

Project Files

For Project 1K, you will need the following file:

e01K_Service_Receipts

You will save your workbook as:

Lastname_Firstname_1K_Service_Receipts

Open the file e01K_Service_Receipts and save it as **Lastname_Firstname_1K_Service_Receipts** Complete the worksheet by using Auto Fill to complete the month headings, and then calculating the Total Receipts for each month and for each product. Insert and format appropriate sparklines in the Trend column. Format the worksheet attractively with a title and subtitle, check spelling, adjust column width, and apply appropriate financial formatting. Insert a chart that compares the total sales receipts for each product with the months displaying as the categories, and format the chart attractively. Include the file name in the footer, add appropriate properties, and submit as directed.

		Performance Level		
		Exemplary: You consistently applied the relevant skills	**Proficient:** You sometimes, but not always, applied the relevant skills	**Developing:** You rarely or never applied the relevant skills
Performance Element	Create formulas	All formulas are correct and are efficiently constructed.	Formulas are correct but not always constructed in the most efficient manner.	One or more formulas are missing or incorrect; or only numbers were entered.
	Create a chart	Chart created properly.	Chart was created but incorrect data was selected.	No chart was created.
	Insert and format sparklines	Sparklines inserted and formatted properly.	Sparklines were inserted but incorrect data was selected or sparklines were not formatted.	No sparklines were inserted.
	Format attractively and appropriately	Formatting is attractive and appropriate.	Adequately formatted but difficult to read or unattractive.	Inadequate or no formatting.

End You have completed Project 1K

Outcomes-Based Assessments

Rubric

The following outcomes-based assessments are *open-ended assessments*. That is, there is no specific correct result; your result will depend on your approach to the information provided. Make *Professional Quality* your goal. Use the following scoring rubric to guide you in *how* to approach the problem, and then to evaluate *how well* your approach solves the problem.

The *criteria*—Software Mastery, Content, Format and Layout, and Process—represent the knowledge and skills you have gained that you can apply to solving the problem. The *levels of performance*—Professional Quality, Approaching Professional Quality, or Needs Quality Improvements—help you and your instructor evaluate your result.

	Your completed project is of Professional Quality if you:	Your completed project is Approaching Professional Quality if you:	Your completed project Needs Quality Improvements if you:
1-Software Mastery	Choose and apply the most appropriate skills, tools, and features and identify efficient methods to solve the problem.	Choose and apply some appropriate skills, tools, and features, but not in the most efficient manner.	Choose inappropriate skills, tools, or features, or are inefficient in solving the problem.
2-Content	Construct a solution that is clear and well organized, contains content that is accurate, appropriate to the audience and purpose, and is complete. Provide a solution that contains no errors in spelling, grammar, or style.	Construct a solution in which some components are unclear, poorly organized, inconsistent, or incomplete. Misjudge the needs of the audience. Have some errors in spelling, grammar, or style, but the errors do not detract from comprehension.	Construct a solution that is unclear, incomplete, or poorly organized; contains some inaccurate or inappropriate content; and contains many errors in spelling, grammar, or style. Do not solve the problem.
3-Format and Layout	Format and arrange all elements to communicate information and ideas, clarify function, illustrate relationships, and indicate relative importance.	Apply appropriate format and layout features to some elements, but not others. Overuse features, causing minor distraction.	Apply format and layout that does not communicate information or ideas clearly. Do not use format and layout features to clarify function, illustrate relationships, or indicate relative importance. Use available features excessively, causing distraction.
4-Process	Use an organized approach that integrates planning, development, self-assessment, revision, and reflection.	Demonstrate an organized approach in some areas, but not others; or, use an insufficient process of organization throughout.	Do not use an organized approach to solve the problem.

Outcomes-Based Assessments

Apply a combination of the **1A** and **1B** skills.

GO! Think | Project **1L** Phone Plans

Project Files

For Project 1L, you will need the following file:

New blank Excel workbook

You will save your workbook as:

Lastname_Firstname_1L_Phone_Plans

Roslyn Thomas, President of Texas Spectrum Wireless, needs a worksheet that summarizes the following data regarding the first quarter sales of cell phone calling plans that the company is offering for domestic and international calls. Roslyn would like the worksheet to include a calculation of the total sales for each plan and a total of the sales of all of the plans. She would also like to know each plan's percentage of total sales.

	Number Sold	Price
Domestic Standard	2556	29.99
Domestic Premium	3982	49.99
Domestic Platinum	1647	64.99
International Standard	582	85.99
International Premium	365	102.99

Create a worksheet that provides Roslyn with the information needed. Include appropriate worksheet, column, and row titles. Using the formatting skills that you practiced in this chapter, format the worksheet in a manner that is professional and easy to read and understand. Insert a footer with the file name and add appropriate document properties. Save the file as **Lastname_Firstname_1L_Phone_Plans** and print or submit as directed by your instructor.

End You have completed Project 1L

Outcomes-Based Assessments

GO! Think | Project **1M** Advertising

Project Files

For Project 1M, you will need the following file:

New blank Excel workbook

You will save your workbook as:

Lastname_Firstname_1M_Advertising

Eliott Verschoren, Vice President of Marketing for Texas Spectrum Wireless, is conducting an analysis of the advertising expenditures at the company's four retail locations based on the following data:

	Quarter 1	Quarter 2	Quarter 3	Quarter 4
Austin	22860	25905	18642	28405
Dallas	18557	17963	22883	25998
Houston	32609	28462	25915	31755
San Antonio	12475	15624	13371	17429

Using this information, create a workbook that includes totals by quarter and by location, sparklines to demonstrate the quarterly trends, and a column chart that compares the quarterly data across locations. Include appropriate worksheet, row, and column titles. Using the formatting skills that you practiced in this chapter, format the worksheet in a manner that is professional and easy to read and understand. Insert a footer with the file name and add appropriate document properties. Save the file as **Lastname_Firstname_1M_Advertising** and print or submit as directed by your instructor.

End **You have completed Project 1M** ———————————————————

Outcomes-Based Assessments

Apply a combination of the 1A and 1B skills.

You and GO! | Project **1N** Personal Expenses

Project Files

For Project 1N, you will need the following file:

New blank Excel workbook

You will save your workbook as:

Lastname_Firstname_1N_Personal_Expenses

Develop a worksheet that details your personal expenses from the last three months. Some of these expenses might include, but are not limited to, Mortgage, Rent, Utilities, Phone, Food, Entertainment, Tuition, Childcare, Clothing, and Insurance. Include a total for each month and for each category of expense. Insert a column with a formula that calculates the percent that each expense category is of the total expenditures. Format the worksheet by adjusting column widths and wrapping text, and by applying appropriate financial number formatting and cell styles. Insert a column chart that compares your expenses by month and modify the chart layout and style. Insert a footer with the file name and center the worksheet horizontally on the page. Save your file as **Lastname_Firstname_1N_Personal_Expenses** and submit as directed.

End **You have completed Project 1N**

Getting Started with Access Databases

OUTCOMES

At the end of this chapter you will be able to:

OBJECTIVES

Mastering these objectives will enable you to:

PROJECT 1A
Create a new database.

1. Identify Good Database Design (p. 173)
2. Create a Table and Define Fields in a New Database (p. 174)
3. Change the Structure of Tables and Add a Second Table (p. 186)
4. Create and Use a Query, Form, and Report (p. 196)
5. Save and Close a Database (p. 202)

PROJECT 1B
Create a database from a template.

6. Create a Database Using a Template (p. 204)
7. Organize Objects in the Navigation Pane (p. 208)
8. Create a New Table in a Database Created with a Template (p. 210)
9. Print a Report and a Table in a Database Created with a Template (p. 212)

Joy Brown/Shutterstock

In This Chapter

In this chapter, you will use Microsoft Access 2010 to organize a collection of related information. Access is a powerful program that enables you to organize, search, sort, retrieve, and present information in a professional-looking manner. You will create new databases, enter data into Access tables, and create a query, form, and report—all of which are Access objects that make a database useful. In this chapter, you will also create a database from a template provided with the Access program. The template creates a complete database that you can use as provided, or you can modify it to suit your needs. Additional templates are available from the Microsoft Online Web site. For your first attempt at a database, consider using a template.

The projects in this chapter relate to **Capital Cities Community College**, which is located in the Washington D. C. metropolitan area. The college provides high-quality education and professional training to residents in the cities surrounding the nation's capital. Its four campuses serve over 50,000 students and offer more than 140 certificate programs and degrees at the associate's level. CapCCC has a highly acclaimed Distance Education program and an extensive Workforce Development program. The college makes positive contributions to the community through cultural and athletic programs and partnerships with businesses and non-profit organizations.

Project 1A Contact Information Database with Two Tables

myitlab
Project 1A Training

Project Activities

In Activities 1.01 through 1.17, you will assist Dr. Justin Mitrani, Vice President of Instruction at Capital Cities Community College, in creating a new database for tracking the contact information for students and faculty members. Your completed database objects will look similar to Figure 1.1.

Project Files

For Project 1A, you will need the following files:

New blank Access database
a01A_Students (Excel workbook)
a01A_Faculty (Excel workbook)

You will save your database as:

Lastname_Firstname_1A_Contacts

Project Results

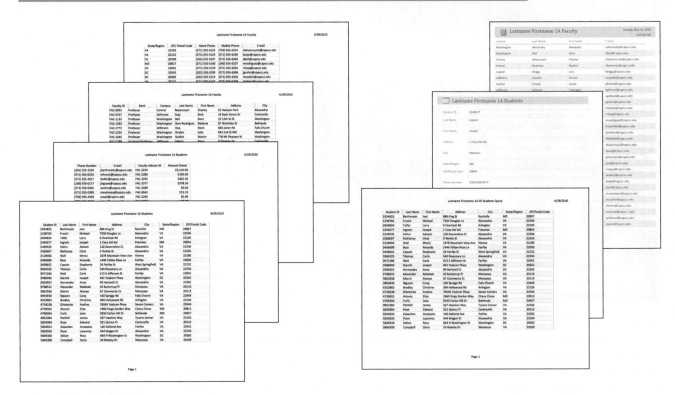

Figure 1.1
Project 1A Contacts

Objective 1 | Identify Good Database Design

A *database* is an organized collection of *data*—facts about people, events, things, or ideas—related to a specific topic or purpose. *Information* is data that is organized in a useful manner. Your personal address book is a type of database, because it is a collection of data about one topic—the people with whom you communicate. A simple database of this type is called a *flat database* because it is not related or linked to any other collection of data. Another example of a simple database is a list of movie DVDs. You do not keep information about your DVDs in your address book because the data is not related to your addresses.

A more sophisticated type of database is a *relational database*, because multiple collections of data in the database are related to one another; for example, data about the students, the courses, and the faculty members at a college. Microsoft Access 2010 is a relational *database management system*—also referred to as a *DBMS*—which is software that controls how related collections of data are stored, organized, retrieved, and secured.

Activity 1.01 | Using Good Design Techniques to Plan a Database

The first step in creating a new database is to determine the information you want to keep track of, and then ask yourself, *What questions should this database be able to answer for me?* The purpose of a database is to store the data in a manner that makes it easy for you to get the information you need by asking questions. For example, in the Contacts database for Capital Cities Community College, the questions to be answered might include:

How many students are enrolled at Capital Cities Community College?

How many faculty members teach in the Accounting Department?

Which and how many students live in Arlington, Virginia?

Which and how many students have a balance owed?

Which and how many students are majoring in Information Systems Technology?

Tables are the foundation of an Access database because all of the data is stored in one or more tables. A table is similar in structure to an Excel worksheet; that is, data is organized into rows and columns. Each table row is a *record*—all of the categories of data pertaining to one person, place, thing, event, or idea. Each table column is a *field*—a single piece of information for every record. For example, in a table storing student contact information, each row forms a record for only one student. Each column forms a field for a single piece of information for every record; for example, the student ID number for all students.

When organizing the fields of information in your database, break each piece of information into its smallest useful part. For example, create three fields for the name of a student—one field for the last name, one field for the first name, and one field for the middle name or initial.

The *first principle of good database design* is to organize data in the tables so that *redundant*—duplicate—data does not occur. For example, record the contact information for students in only *one* table, because if the address for a student changes, the change can be made in just one place. This conserves space, reduces the likelihood of errors when recording the new data, and does not require remembering all of the different places where the address is stored.

The *second principle of good database design* is to use techniques that ensure the accuracy of data when it is entered into the table. Typically, many different people enter data into a database—think of all the people who enter data at your college. When entering a state in a contacts database, one person might enter the state as *Virginia* and another might enter the state as *VA*. Use design techniques to help those who enter data into a database do so in a consistent and accurate manner.

Normalization is the process of applying design rules and principles to ensure that your database performs as expected. Taking the time to plan and create a database that is well designed will ensure that you can retrieve meaningful information from the database.

The tables of information in a relational database are linked or joined to one another by a *common field*—a field in one or more tables that stores the same data. For example, the Student Contacts table includes the Student ID, name, and address of every student. The Student Activities table includes the name of each club, and the Student ID—but not the name or address—of each student in each club. Because the two tables share a common field—Student ID—you can create a list of names and addresses of all the students in the Photography Club. The names and addresses are stored in the Student Contacts table, and the Student IDs of the Photography Club members are stored in the Student Activities table.

Objective 2 | Create a Table and Define Fields in a New Blank Database

There are two methods to create a new Access database: create a new database using a *database template*—a preformatted database designed for a specific purpose—or create a new database from a blank database. A blank database has no data and has no database tools; you create the data and the tools as you need them.

Regardless of the method you use, you must name and save the database before you can create any *objects* in it. Objects are the basic parts of a database; you create objects to store your data and to work with your data. The most common database objects are tables, forms, and reports. Think of an Access database as a container for the objects that you will create.

Activity 1.02 │ Starting with a New Database

1 **Start** Access. Take a moment to compare your screen with Figure 1.2 and study the parts of the Microsoft Access window described in the table in Figure 1.3.

From this Access starting point in Backstage view, you can open an existing database, create a new blank database, or create a new database from a template.

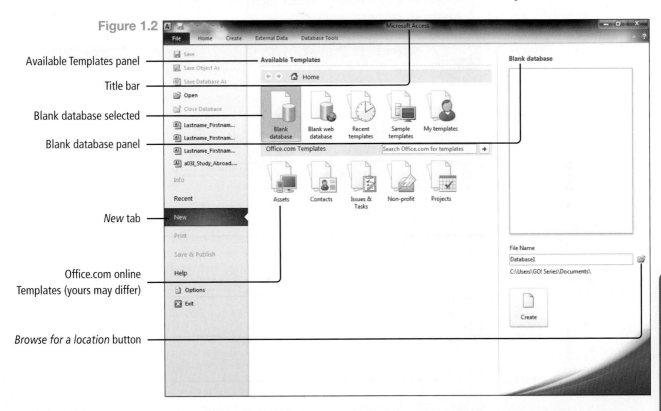

Figure 1.2

| Available Templates panel
| Title bar
| Blank database selected
| Blank database panel
| *New* tab
| Office.com online Templates (yours may differ)
| *Browse for a location* button

Microsoft Access Opening Window	
Window Part	**Description**
Available Templates panel	Displays alternative methods of creating a database.
Blank database	Starts a new blank database.
Blank database panel	Displays when *Blank database* button is selected under Available Templates.
Browse for location button	Enables you to select a storage location for the database.
New tab	Displays, when active in Backstage view, the various methods by which you can create a new database.
Office.com Templates	Displays template categories available from the Office.com Web site.
Title bar	Displays the Quick Access Toolbar, program name, and program-level buttons.

Figure 1.3

2 On the right, under **Blank database**, to the right of the **File Name** box, click the **Browse** button 📷. In the **File New Database** dialog box, navigate to the location where you are saving your databases for this chapter, create a new folder named **Access Chapter 1** and then notice that *Database1* displays as the default file name—the number at the end of your file name might differ if you have saved a database previously with the default name. In the **File New Database** dialog box, click **Open**.

3 In the **File name** box, replace the existing text with **Lastname_Firstname_1A_Contacts** Press Enter, and then compare your screen with Figure 1.4.

> On the right, the name of your database displays in the File Name box, and the drive and folder where the database is stored displays under the File Name box. An Access database has the file extension *.accdb*.

Figure 1.4

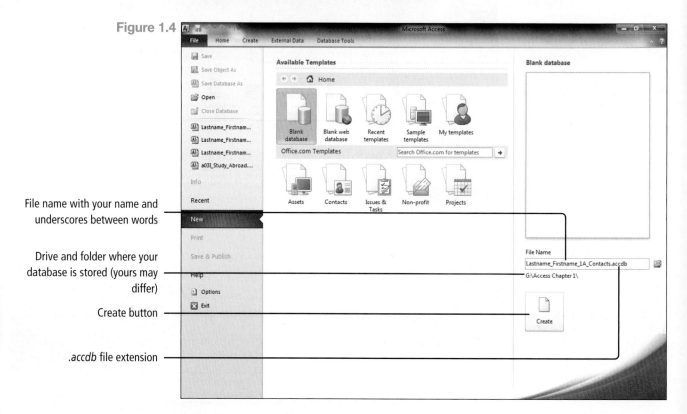

File name with your name and underscores between words

Drive and folder where your database is stored (yours may differ)

Create button

.accdb file extension

4 Under the **File Name** box, click the **Create** button, compare your screen with Figure 1.5, and then take a moment to study the screen elements described in the table in Figure 1.6.

> Access creates the new database and opens *Table1*. Recall that a *table* is an Access object that stores your data in columns and rows, similar to the format of an Excel worksheet. Table objects are the foundation of a database because tables store the actual data.

Figure 1.5

Ribbon with command groups arranged on tabs

Object tab

Table Tools active

Title bar with database name

Object window

Navigation Pane

Object window Close button

Status bar

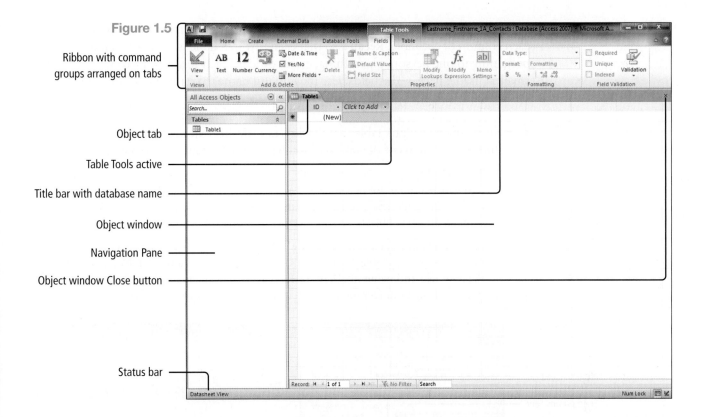

Parts of the Access Database Window

Window Part	Description
Navigation Pane	Displays the database objects; from here you open the database objects to display in the object window at the right.
Object tab	Identifies and enables you to select the open object.
Object window	Displays the active or open object (table, query, or other object).
Object window Close button	Closes the active object (table, query, or other object).
Ribbon with command groups arranged on tabs	Groups the commands for performing related database tasks on tabs.
Status bar	Indicates the active view and the status of actions occurring within the database on the left; provides buttons to switch between Datasheet view and Design view on the right.
Table Tools	Provides tools for working with a table object; Table Tools are available only when a table is displayed.
Title bar	Displays the name of your database.

Figure 1.6

Activity 1.03 | Assigning the Data Type and Name to Fields

After you have saved and named your database, the next step is to consult your database plan, and then create the tables in which to enter your data. Limit the data in each table to *one* subject. For example, in this project, your database will have two tables—one for student contact information and one for faculty contact information.

Recall that each column in a table is a field and that field names display at the top of each column of the table. Recall also that each row in a table is a record—all of the data pertaining to one person, place, thing, event, or idea. Each record is broken up into its smallest usable parts—the fields. Use meaningful names to name fields; for example, *Last Name*.

1 Notice the new blank table that displays in Datasheet view, and then take a moment to study the elements of the table's object window. Compare your screen with Figure 1.7.

The table displays in **Datasheet view**, which displays the data as columns and rows similar to the format of an Excel worksheet. Another way to view a table is in **Design view**, which displays the underlying design—the **structure**—of the table's fields. The **object window** displays the open object—in this instance, the table object.

In a new blank database, there is only one object—a new blank table. Because you have not yet named this table, the object tab displays a default name of *Table1*. Access creates the first field and names it *ID*. In the ID field, Access assigns a unique sequential number—each number incremented by one—to each record as it is entered into the table.

Figure 1.7

Navigation Pane Close button
Field names row
New record row
Object tab with default table name
First field is *ID*
Navigation Pane
Fields tab on the Ribbon

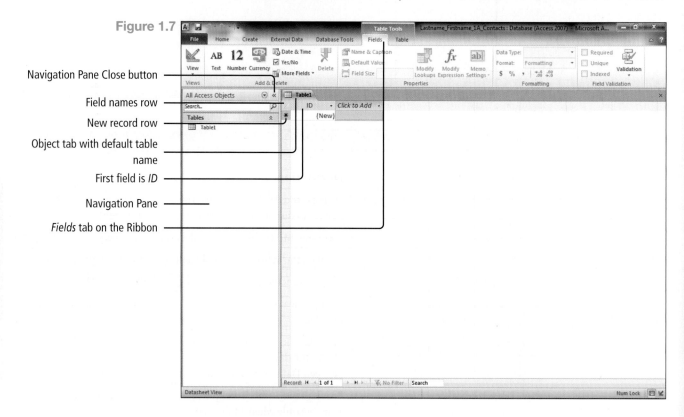

2 In the **Navigation Pane**, click the **Open/Close** button ⟪ to collapse the **Navigation Pane** to a narrow bar on the left and to display more of the table.

The **Navigation Pane** is an area of the Access window that displays and organizes the names of the objects in a database. From the Navigation Pane, you can open objects for use.

Another Way
To the right of *Click to Add*, click the arrow.

3 In the field names row, click anywhere in the text *Click to Add* to display a list of data types. Compare your screen with Figure 1.8.

Data type is the characteristic that defines the kind of data that you can type in a field, such as numbers, text, or dates. A field in a table can have only one data type. Part of your database design should include deciding on the data type of each field. After you have selected the data type, you can name the field.

Figure 1.8

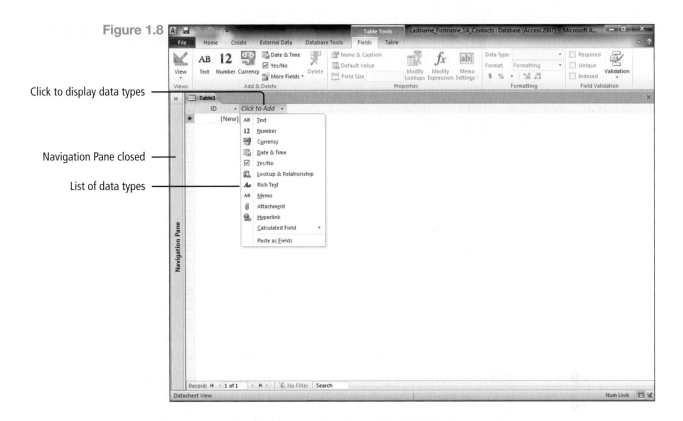

Click to display data types

Navigation Pane closed

List of data types

4 In the list of data types, click **Text**, and notice that in the second column, *Click to Add* changes to *Field1*, which is selected. Type **Last Name** and then press Enter.

The second column displays *Last Name* as the field name, and the data type list displays in the third column. The *Text data type* describes text, a combination of text and numbers, or numbers that are not used in calculations, such as a ZIP code.

Another Way

With the list of data types displayed, type *T* to select Text.

5 In the third field name box, click **Text**, type **First Name** and then press Enter. In the fourth field name box, click **Text**, type **Middle Initial** and then press Enter.

6 Using the technique you just practiced, create the remaining fields as follows by first selecting the data type, then typing the field name, and then pressing Enter. The field names in the table will display on one line.

The ZIP/Postal Code field is assigned a data type of Text because the number is never used in a calculation. The Amount Owed field is assigned a data type of Currency; the *Currency data type* describes monetary values and numeric data used in mathematical calculations involving data with one to four decimal places. Access automatically adds a U.S. dollar sign ($) and two decimal places to all of the numbers in the fields with a data type of *Currency*.

Data Type		Text	Text	Text	**Text**	**Text**	**Text**	**Text**	**Text**	**Text**	**Text**	**Currency**
Field Name	ID	Last Name	First Name	Middle Initial	**Address**	**City**	**State/ Region**	**ZIP/Postal Code**	**Phone Number**	**E-mail**	**Faculty Advisor ID**	**Amount Owed**

7 If necessary, by using the horizontal scroll bar at the bottom of the screen, scroll to the left to bring the first column into view. Compare your screen with Figure 1.9.

Access automatically created the ID field, and you created 11 additional fields in the table. The horizontal scroll bar indicates that there are additional fields that are not displayed on the screen—your screen width may vary.

Access | Chapter 1

Figure 1.9

Twelve fields created—scroll
to the left to display *ID* and
Last Name fields

Activity 1.04 │ Renaming Fields and Changing Data Types in a Table

Another Way

Right-click the field
name, and then on the
shortcut menu, click
Rename Field.

1 Click anywhere in the text *ID*. In the **Properties group**, click the **Name & Caption** button. In the **Enter Field Properties** dialog box, in the **Name** box, change *ID* to **Student ID** and then click **OK**.

The field name *Student ID* is a better description of the data in this field. In the Enter Field Properties dialog box, the **Caption** property is used to display a name for a field other than that listed as the field name. Many database designers do not use spaces in field names; instead, they might name a field LastName—with no spaces—and then create a caption for that field so it displays with spaces in tables, forms, and reports. In the Enter Field Properties dialog box, you can also provide a description for the field if you want to do so.

2 In the **Formatting group**, notice that the **Data Type** for the **Student ID** field is *AutoNumber*. Click the **Data Type arrow**, click **Text**, and then compare your screen with Figure 1.10.

In the new record row, the Student ID field is selected. By default, Access creates an ID field for all new tables and sets the data type for the field to AutoNumber. The **AutoNumber data type** describes a unique sequential or random number assigned by Access as each record is entered. By changing the data type of this field from *AutoNumber* to *Text*, you can enter a custom student ID number.

When records in a database have *no* unique value, for example the names in your address book, the AutoNumber data type is a useful way to automatically create a unique number so that you have a way to ensure that every record is different from the others.

Figure 1.10

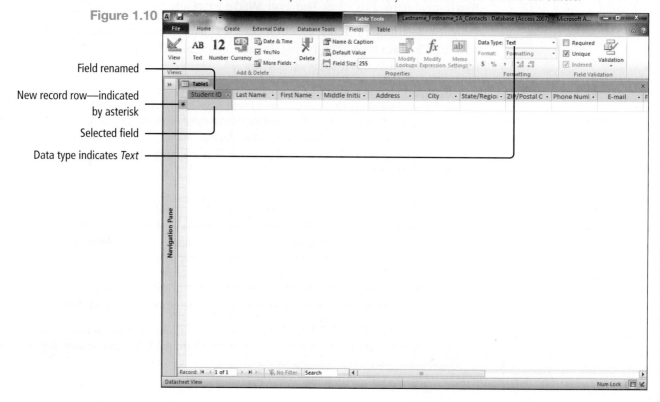

Field renamed

New record row—indicated
by asterisk

Selected field

Data type indicates *Text*

Activity 1.05 | Adding a Record to a Table

A new address book is not useful until you fill it with names, addresses, and phone numbers. Likewise, a new database is not useful until you *populate* it—fill one or more tables with data. You can populate a table with records by typing data directly into the table.

Another Way

Press Tab to move to the next field.

1 In the new record row, click in the **Student ID** field to display the insertion point, type **1238765** and then press Enter. Compare your screen with Figure 1.11.

The pencil icon  in the *record selector box*—the small box at the left of a record in Datasheet view that, when clicked, selects the entire record—indicates that a record is being entered or edited.

Figure 1.11

Pencil icon indicates record being entered or edited

Record selector box

First student ID is *1238765*

Insertion point in Last Name field

2 With the insertion point positioned in the **Last Nam**e field, type **Fresch** and then press Enter.

> **Note** | Correct Typing Errors
>
> Correct typing errors by using the techniques you have practiced in other Office applications. For example, use Backspace to remove characters to the left, Del to remove characters to the right, or select the text you want to replace and type the correct information. Press Esc to exit out of a record that has not been completely entered.

3 In the **First Name** field, type **Michael** and then press Enter.

4 In the **Middle Initial** field, type **B** and then press Enter.

5 In the **Address** field, type **7550 Douglas Ln** and then press Enter.

Do not be concerned if the data does not completely display in the column. As you progress in your study of Access, you will adjust the column widths so that you can view all of the data.

6 Continue entering data in the fields as indicated below, pressing Enter to move to the next field.

City	State/Region	ZIP/Postal Code	Phone Number	E-mail	Faculty Advisor ID
Alexandria	**VA**	**22336**	**(571) 555-0234**	**mfresch@capccc.edu**	**FAC-2289**

> **Note** | Format for Typing Telephone Numbers in Access
>
> Access does not require any specific format for typing telephone numbers in a database. The examples in this project use the format of Microsoft Outlook. Using such a format facilitates easy transfer of Outlook information to and from Access.

7 In the **Amount Owed** field, type **150** and then press [Enter]. Compare your screen with Figure 1.12.

> Pressing [Enter] or [Tab] in the last field moves the insertion point to the next row to begin a new record. As soon as you move to the next row, Access saves the record—you do not have to take any specific action to save a record.

Figure 1.12

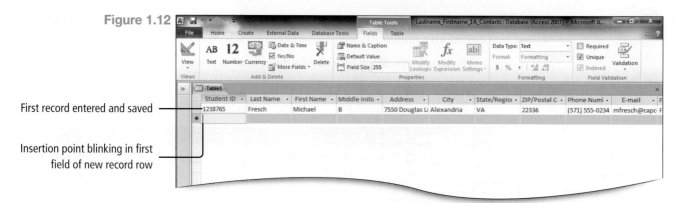

First record entered and saved

Insertion point blinking in first field of new record row

8 To give your table a meaningful name, on the Quick Access Toolbar, click the **Save** button ⊟. In the **Save As** dialog box, in the **Table Name** box, using your own name, replace the highlighted text by typing **Lastname Firstname 1A Students**

> Save each database object with a name that identifies the data that it contains. When you save objects within a database, it is not necessary to use underscores. Your name is included as part of the object name so that you and your instructor can identify your printouts or electronic files.

9 In the **Save As** dialog box, click **OK**, and then notice that the object tab displays the new table name you just typed.

> **More Knowledge** | Renaming a Table
>
> To change the name of a table, close the table, display the Navigation Pane, right-click the table name, and then on the shortcut menu, click Rename. Type the new name or edit as you would any selected text.

Activity 1.06 | Adding Additional Records to a Table

1 In the new record row, click in the **Student ID** field, and then enter the contact information for the following two additional students, pressing [Enter] or [Tab] to move from field to field. The data in each field will display on one line in the table.

Student ID	Last Name	First Name	Middle Initial	Address	City	State/Region	ZIP/Postal Code	Phone Number	E-mail	Faculty Advisor ID	Amount Owed
2345677	Ingram	Joseph	S	1 Casa Del Sol	Potomac	MD	20854	(240) 555-0177	jingram@ capccc.edu	FAC-2377	378.5
3456689	Bass	Amanda	J	1446 Yellow Rose Ln	Fairfax	VA	22030	(703) 555-0192	abass@ capccc.edu	FAC-9005	0

2 Compare your screen with Figure 1.13.

Figure 1.13

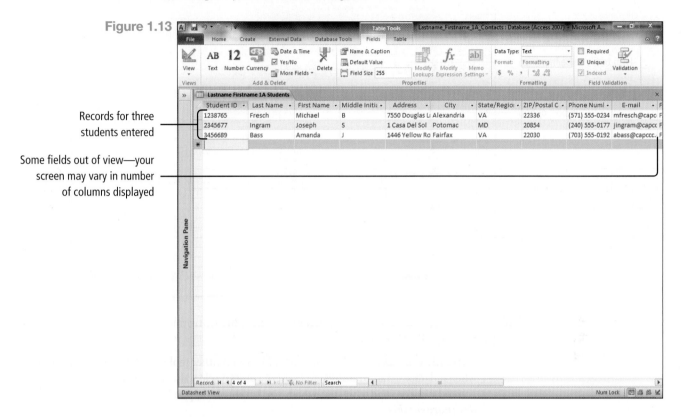

Records for three students entered

Some fields out of view—your screen may vary in number of columns displayed

Activity 1.07 │ Importing Data from an Excel Workbook into an Existing Access Table

When you create a database table, you can type the records directly into a table. You can also ***import*** data from a variety of sources. Importing is the process of copying data from one source or application to another application. For example, you can import data from a Word table or an Excel worksheet into an Access database because the data is arranged in columns and rows, similar to a table in Datasheet view.

In this activity, you will ***append***—add on—data from an Excel spreadsheet to your *1A Students* table. To append data, the table must already be created, and it must be closed.

1 In the upper right corner of the table, below the Ribbon, click the **Object Close** ☒ button to close your **1A Students** table. Notice that no objects are open.

2 On the Ribbon, click the **External Data tab**. In the **Import & Link group**, click the **Excel** button. In the **Get External Data - Excel Spreadsheet** dialog box, click the **Browse** button.

> **Another Way**
>
> Select the file name, and in the lower right area of the dialog box, click Open.

3 In the **File Open** dialog box, navigate to your student files, locate and double-click the Excel file **a01A_Students**, and then compare your screen with Figure 1.14.

The path to the ***source file***—the file being imported—displays in the File name box. There are three options for importing data from an Excel workbook—import the data into a *new* table in the current database, append a copy of the records to an existing table, or link the data from Excel to a linked table. A ***link*** is a connection to data in another file. When linking, Access creates a table that maintains a link to the source data.

Access │ Chapter 1

Figure 1.14

Path to file to be imported

Import option

Append option

Link option

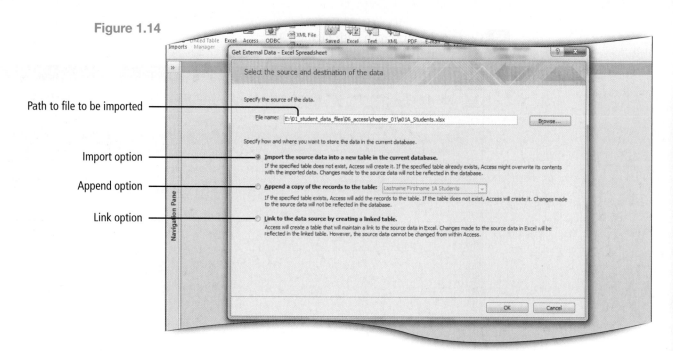

4 Click the **Append a copy of the records to the table** option button, and then in the box to its right, click the **arrow**.

Currently your database has only one table, so no other tables display on the list. However, when a database has multiple tables, here you can select the table to which you want to append records. The table into which you import or append data is referred to as the *destination table*.

5 Press Esc to cancel the list, and then in the lower right corner of the dialog box, click **OK**. Compare your screen with Figure 1.15.

The first screen of the Import Spreadsheet Wizard displays, and the presence of scroll bars indicates that records and fields are out of view in this window. To append records from an Excel worksheet to an existing database table, the field names in the Excel worksheet must be identical to the field names in the table, and that is true in this table.

Figure 1.15

Field names in Excel sheet exactly match field names in Access table

Scroll bars indicate more data

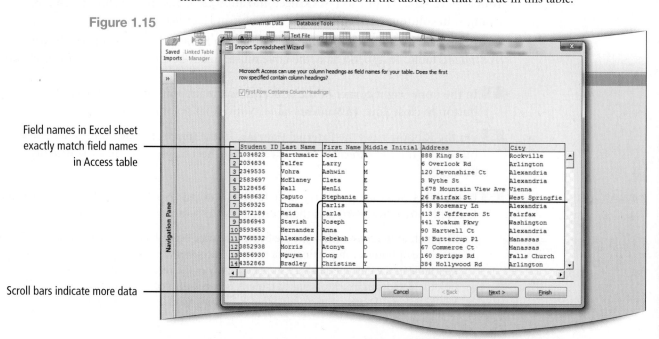

6 In the lower right corner, click **Next**. Notice that the name of your table displays under **Import to Table**. In the lower right corner, click **Finish**.

7 In the **Get External Data - Excel Spreadsheet** dialog box, click **Close**, and then **Open** ⟫ the **Navigation Pane**.

8 Point to the right edge of the **Navigation Pane** to display the ⟷ pointer. Drag to the right to widen the pane to display the entire table name, and then compare your screen with Figure 1.16.

Figure 1.16

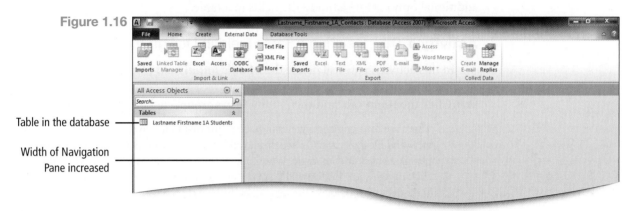

Table in the database

Width of Navigation Pane increased

Another Way

To open an object from the Navigation Pane, right-click the object name, and then on the shortcut menu, click Open.

9 In the **Navigation Pane**, double-click your **1A Students** table to open the table in Datasheet view, and then **Close** ⟪ the **Navigation Pane**.

10 At the bottom left corner of your screen, locate the navigation area, and notice that there are a total of **26** records in the table—you created three records and imported 23 additional records. Compare your screen with Figure 1.17.

The records from the Excel worksheet display in your table, and the first record is selected. The *navigation area* indicates the number of records in the table and contains controls (arrows) with which you can navigate among the records.

Figure 1.17

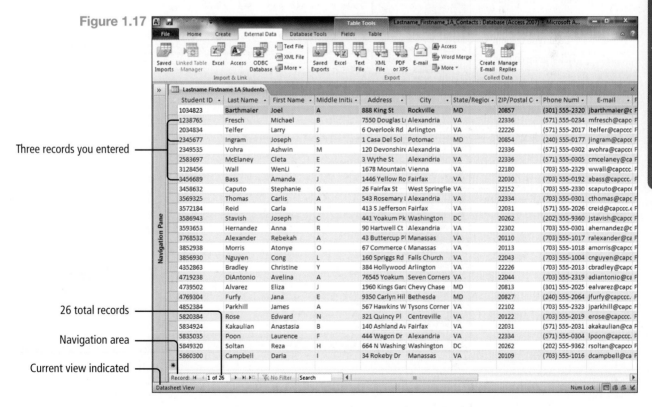

Three records you entered

26 total records

Navigation area

Current view indicated

Access | Chapter 1

Objective 3 | Change the Structure of Tables and Add a Second Table

Recall that the structure of a table is the underlying design, including field names and data types. You can create a table or modify a table in Datasheet view. To define and modify fields, many database experts prefer to work in Design view, where you have many additional options for defining the fields in a table.

Activity 1.08 | Deleting a Table Field in Design View

In this activity, you will delete the *Middle Initial* field from the table.

1 Click the **Home tab**, and then in the **Views group**, click the **View button arrow**.

There are four common views in Access, but two that you will use often are Datasheet view and Design view. On the displayed list, Design view is represented by a picture of a pencil, a ruler, and an angle. When one of these four icons is displayed on the View button, clicking the View button will display the table in the view represented by the icon. Datasheet view displays the table data in rows and columns.

2 On the list, click **Design View**, and then compare your screen with Figure 1.18.

Design view displays the underlying design—the structure—of the table and its fields. In Design view, you cannot view the data; you can view only the information about each field's characteristics. Each field name is listed, along with its data type. A column to add a Description—information about the data in the field—is provided.

In the Field Properties area, you can make additional decisions about how each individual field looks and behaves. For example, you can set a specific field size.

Figure 1.18

Delete Rows button

Data Type column

Field Name column

Row selector box for Middle Initial field

Space to add field description

Field Properties area

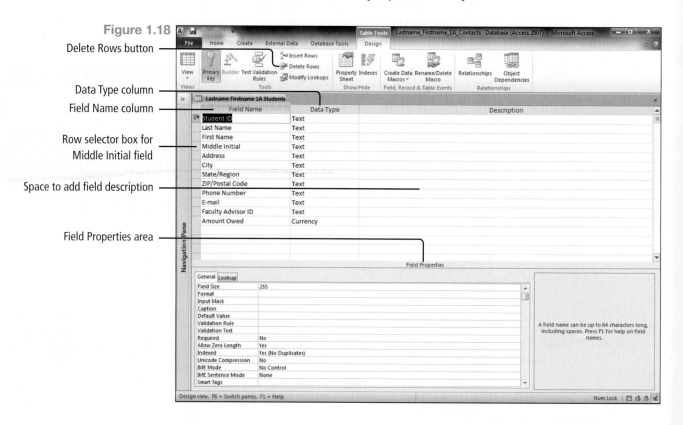

3 In the **Field Name** column, to the left of **Middle Initial**, point to the row selector box to display the ➡ pointer, and then click one time to select the entire row.

Another Way

Right-click the selected row and click Delete Rows.

- - ➤ **4** On the **Design tab**, in the **Tools group**, click the **Delete Rows** button, read the message in the message box, and then click **Yes**.

Deleting a field deletes both the field and its data; you cannot undo this action. Thus, Access prompts you to be sure you want to proceed. If you change your mind after deleting a field, you must add the field back into the table and then reenter the data in that field for every record.

Activity 1.09 | Modifying a Field Size and Adding a Description

Typically, many individuals enter data into a table. For example, at your college many Registration Assistants enter and modify student and course information daily. Two ways to help reduce errors are to restrict what can be typed in a field and to add descriptive information.

1 With your table still displayed in **Design** view, in the **Field Name** column, click anywhere in the **State/Region** field name.

2 In the lower portion of the screen, under **Field Properties**, click **Field Size** to select the text *255*, type **2** and then compare your screen with Figure 1.19.

This action limits the size of the State/Region field to no more than two characters—the size of the two-letter state abbreviations provided by the United States Postal Service. *Field properties* control how the field displays and how data can be entered in the field. You can define properties for every field in the Field Properties area.

The default field size for a text field is 255. Limiting the field size property to 2 ensures that only two characters can be entered for each state. However, this does not prevent someone from entering two characters that are incorrect. Setting the proper data type for the field and limiting the field size are two ways to *help* to reduce errors.

Figure 1.19

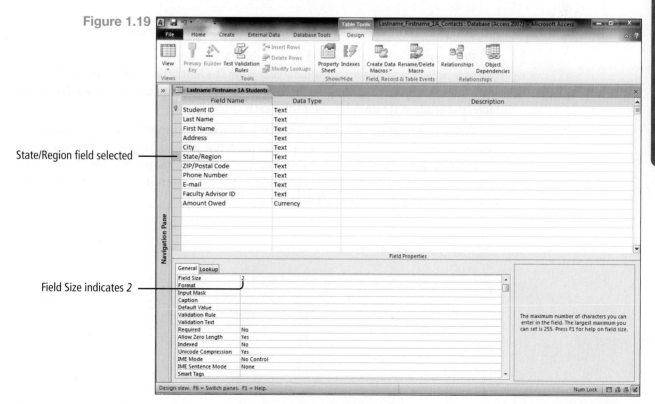

State/Region field selected

Field Size indicates *2*

3 In the **State/Region** row, click in the **Description** box, type **Two-character state abbreviation** and then press Enter.

> Descriptions for fields in a table are optional. Include a description if the field name does not provide an obvious explanation of the field. Information typed in the description area displays on the left side of the status bar in Datasheet view when the field is active, providing additional information to individuals who are entering data.

> When you enter a description for a field, a Property Update Options button displays below the text you typed, which enables you to copy the description for the field to all other database objects that use this table as an underlying source.

4 Click in the **Student ID** field name box. Using the technique you practiced, in the **Field Properties** area, change the **Field Size** to **7**

> By limiting the field size to seven characters, which is the maximum number of characters in a Student ID, you help to ensure the accuracy of the data.

5 In the **Student ID** row, click in the **Description** box, and then type **Seven-digit Student ID number**

6 Click in the **Faculty Advisor ID** field name box. In the **Field Properties** area, change the **Field Size** to **8** In the **Description** box for this field, type **Eight-character ID of faculty member assigned as advisor** and then press Enter.

7 On the Quick Access Toolbar, click the **Save** button 🖫 to save the design changes to your table, and then notice the message.

> The message indicates that the field size property of one or more fields has changed to a shorter size. If more characters are currently present in the Student ID, State/Region, or Faculty Advisor ID than you have allowed, the data could be *truncated*—cut off or shortened—because the fields were not previously restricted to a specific number of characters.

8 In the message box, click **Yes**.

Activity 1.10 | Viewing a Primary Key in Design View

Primary key refers to the field in the table that uniquely identifies a record. For example, in a college registration database, your Student ID number uniquely identifies you—no other student at the college has your exact student number. In the 1A Students table, the Student ID uniquely identifies each student.

When you create a table using the Blank database command, by default Access designates the first field as the primary key field. It is good database design practice to establish a primary key for every table, because doing so ensures that you do not enter the same record more than once. You can imagine the confusion if another student at your college had the same Student ID number as you do.

1 With your table still displayed in Design view, in the **Field Name** column, click in the **Student ID** box. To the left of the box, notice the small icon of a key, as shown in Figure 1.20.

> Access automatically designates the first field as the primary key field, but you can set any field as the primary key by clicking in the box to the left of the field name, and then clicking the Primary Key button.

Figure 1.20

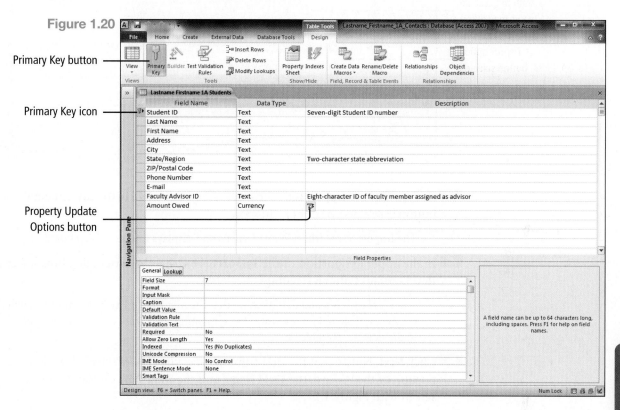

Primary Key button

Primary Key icon

Property Update Options button

2 On the **Design tab**, in the **Views group**, notice that the **View** button contains a picture of a Datasheet, indicating that clicking the button will return you to Datasheet view. Click the **View** button.

Activity 1.11 | Adding a Second Table to a Database by Importing an Excel Spreadsheet

Many Microsoft Office users track data in an Excel spreadsheet. The sorting and filtering capabilities of Excel are useful for a simple database where all the information resides in one large Excel spreadsheet. However, Excel is limited as a database management tool because it cannot *relate* the information in multiple spreadsheets in a way in which you could ask a question and get a meaningful result. Data in an Excel spreadsheet can easily become an Access table by importing the spreadsheet, because Excel's format of columns and rows is similar to that of an Access table.

1 On the Ribbon, click the **External Data tab**, and then in the **Import & Link group**, click the **Excel** button. In the **Get External Data – Excel Spreadsheet** dialog box, to the right of the **File name** box, click **Browse**.

2 In the **File Open** dialog box, navigate to your student files, and then double-click **a01A_Faculty**. Compare your screen with Figure 1.21.

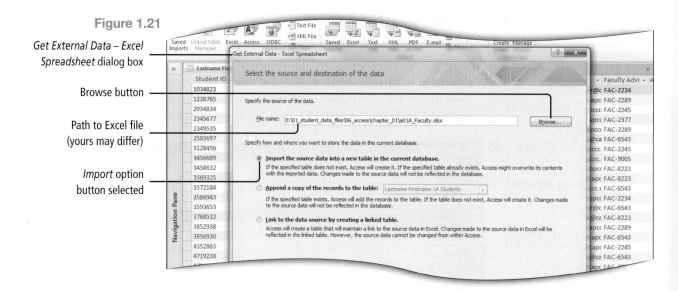

Figure 1.21

Get External Data – Excel Spreadsheet dialog box

Browse button

Path to Excel file (yours may differ)

Import option button selected

3 Be sure that the **Import the source data into a new table in the current database** option button is selected, and then click **OK**.

The Import Spreadsheet Wizard opens and displays the spreadsheet data.

4 In the upper left portion of the **Import Spreadsheet Wizard** dialog box, select the **First Row Contains Column Headings** check box.

The Excel data is framed, indicating that the first row of Excel column titles will become the Access table field names, and the remaining rows will become the individual records in the new Access table.

5 Click **Next**. Notice that the first column—*Faculty ID*—is selected, and in the upper portion of the Wizard, the **Field Name** and the **Data Type** display. Compare your screen with Figure 1.22.

Here you can review and change the field properties for each field (column). You can also identify fields in the spreadsheet that you do not want to import into the Access table by selecting the Do not import field (Skip) check box.

Figure 1.22

Import Spreadsheet Wizard dialog box

Excel column titles

Spreadsheet data—Excel rows become records

Next button

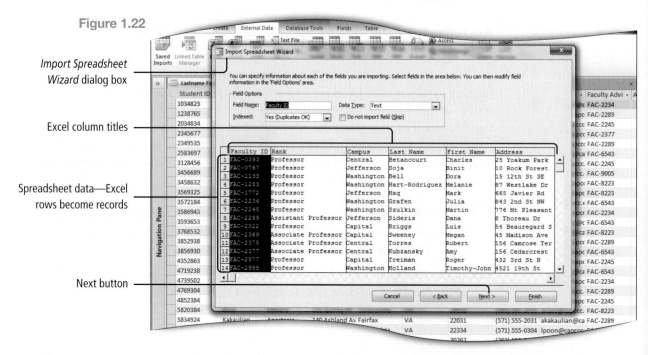

6 Click **Next**. In the upper portion of the Wizard, click the **Choose my own primary key** option button, and then be sure that **Faculty ID** displays.

> In the new table, Faculty ID will be the primary key. No two faculty members have the same Faculty ID. By default, Access selects the first field as the primary key, but you can click the arrow to select a different field.

7 Click **Next**. In the **Import to Table** box, type **Lastname Firstname 1A Faculty** and then click **Finish**.

8 In the **Get External Data – Excel Spreadsheet** dialog box, click **Close**, and then **Open** » the **Navigation Pane**.

9 In the **Navigation Pane**, double-click your **1A Faculty** table to open it in Datasheet view, and then **Close** « the **Navigation Pane**.

10 Click in the **ZIP/Postal Code** field, and then on the Ribbon, click the **Fields tab**. In the **Formatting group**, change the **Data Type** to **Text**. Compare your screen with Figure 1.23.

> The data from the *a01A_Faculty* worksheet displays in your *1A Faculty* table in the database. The navigation area indicates that there are 30 records in the table. Recall that if a field contains numbers that are not used in calculations, the data type should be set to Text. When you import data from an Excel spreadsheet, check the data types of all fields to ensure they are correct.

Figure 1.23

ZIP/Postal Code data type changed to Text

Table created by importing Excel spreadsheet

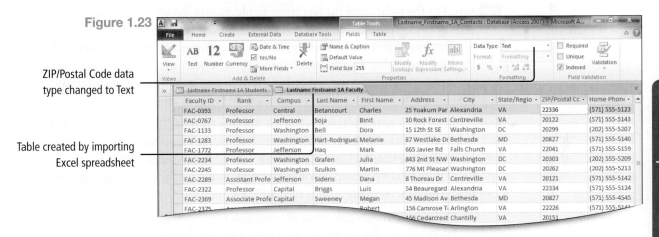

Activity 1.12 | Adjusting Column Widths

By using techniques similar to those you use for Excel worksheets, you can adjust the widths of Access fields that display in Datasheet view.

1 In the object window, click the **object tab** for your **1A Students** table.

> Clicking the object tabs along the top of the object window enables you to display open objects to work with them. All of the columns are the same width regardless of the amount of data in the field, the field size that was set, or the length of the field name. If you print the table as currently displayed, some of the data or field names will not fully print until you adjust the column widths.

2 In the field names row, point to the right edge of the **Address** field to display the ⊞
pointer, and then compare your screen with Figure 1.24.

Figure 1.24

Pointer positioned on
right edge of Address field

3 With your ⊞ pointer positioned as shown in Figure 1.24, double-click the right edge
of the **Address** field.

> The column width of the Address field widens to fully display the longest entry in the
> field. In this manner, the width of a column can be increased or decreased to fit its
> contents in the same manner as a column in an Excel worksheet. In Access this is referred
> to as *Best Fit*.

4 Point to the **Phone Number** field name to display the ↓ pointer, right-click to select
the entire column and display a shortcut menu, and then click **Field Width**. In the
Column Width dialog box, click **Best Fit**.

5 Scroll to the right until the last three fields display. Point to the **E-mail** field name to
display the ↓ pointer, hold down the left mouse button, and then drag to the right
to select this column, the **Faculty Advisor ID** column, and the **Amount Owed** column.
By double-clicking the ⊞ pointer on the right boundary of any of the selected
columns, or by displaying the Field Width dialog box from the shortcut menu, apply
Best Fit to the selected columns.

6 Scroll all the way to the left to view the **Student ID** field. To the left of the *Student ID*
field name, click the **Select All** button □. Click the **Home tab**, and in the **Records group**,
click the **More** button. Click **Field Width**, and in the **Column Width** dialog box, click
Best Fit. In the first record, scroll to the right as necessary, click in the **Amount Owed**
field, and then compare your screen with Figure 1.25.

> In this manner, you can adjust all of the column widths at one time. After applying Best
> Fit, be sure to click in any field to remove the selection from all of the records; otherwise,
> the layout changes will not be saved with the table. Adjusting the width of columns does
> not change the data in the table's records; it changes only the *display* of the data.

Figure 1.25

Select All button

More button

7 On the Quick Access Toolbar, click the **Save** button 🖫 to save the table design changes—changing the column widths.

> If you do not save the table after making design changes, Access will prompt you to save when you close the table.

Activity 1.13 | Printing a Table

Although a printed table does not look as professional as a printed report, there are times when you will want to print a table. For example, you may need a quick reference or want to proofread the data that has been entered.

1 On the Ribbon, click the **File tab** to display **Backstage** view, click the **Print** tab, click **Print Preview**, and then compare your screen with Figure 1.26.

Figure 1.26

Print Preview window

Navigation Pane

Next Page button

Page 1 displays

Navigation area—used to move from page to page

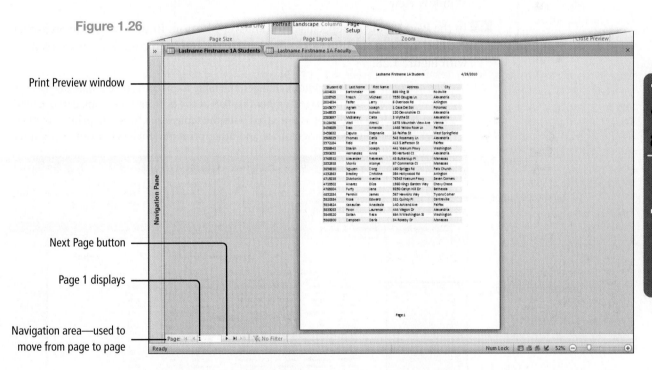

2 In the lower left corner, click the **Next Page** button ▶ two times. Point to the top of the page to display the 🔍 pointer, click one time to zoom in, and then compare your screen with Figure 1.27.

> The display enlarges, and the Zoom Out pointer displays. The third page of the table displays the last two field columns. The Next Page button is dimmed, indicating there are no more pages. The Previous Page button is darker, indicating that pages exist before this page.

Figure 1.27

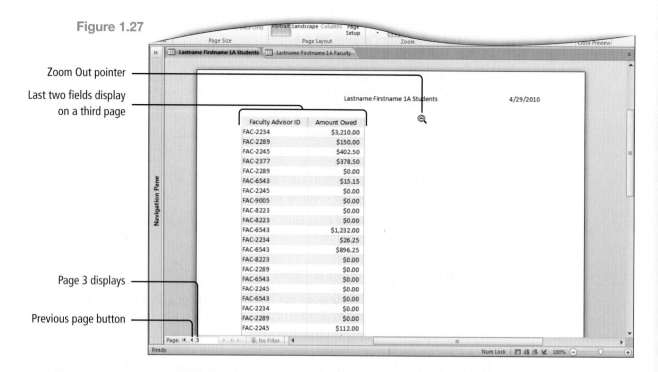

Zoom Out pointer

Last two fields display
on a third page

Page 3 displays

Previous page button

Another Way
Click the 🔍 pointer
to zoom back to Fit to
Window view.

3 On the Ribbon, in the **Zoom group**, click the **Zoom** button to zoom back to Fit to
Window view.

4 In the **Page Layout group**, click the **Landscape** button. In the navigation area, click
the **Previous Page** button ◄ to display **Page 1**, and then compare your screen
with Figure 1.28.

> The orientation of the printout changes, the table name and current date display at the
> top of the page, and the page number displays at the bottom. The change in orientation
> from portrait to landscape is not saved with the table. Each time you print, you must
> check the margins, page orientation, and other print parameters to print as you intend.

Figure 1.28

Landscape button

First page displays in
landscape orientation

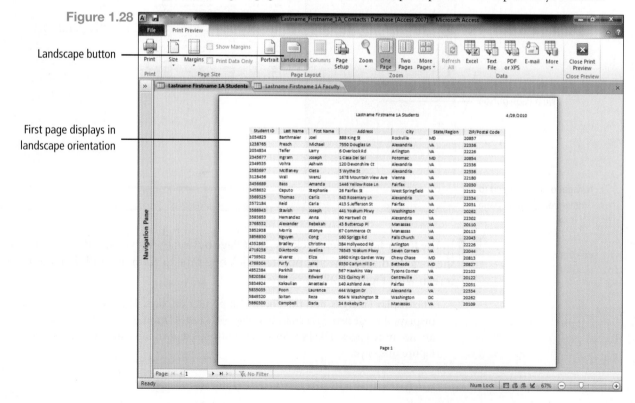

> **Note** | Headers and Footers in Access Objects
>
> The headers and footers in Access tables and queries are controlled by default settings; you cannot add additional information or edit the information. The object name displays in the center of the header area with the date on the right—that is why adding your own name to the object name is helpful to identify your paper or electronic results. The page number displays in the center of the footer area. The headers and footers in Access reports and forms, however, are more flexible; you can add to and edit the information.

5 On the **Print Preview tab**, in the **Print group**, click the **Print** button. In the **Print** dialog box, under **Print Range**, verify that the **All** option button is selected. Under **Copies**, verify that the **Number of Copies** is **1**. Compare your screen with Figure 1.29.

Figure 1.29

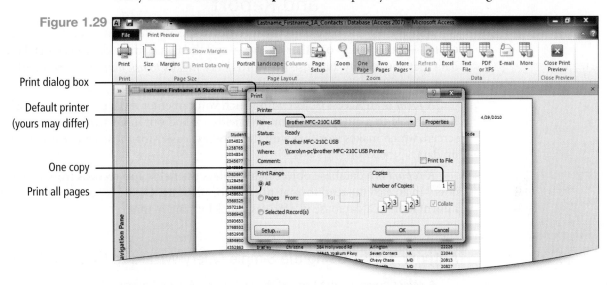

Print dialog box

Default printer (yours may differ)

One copy

Print all pages

6 Determine how your instructor wants you to submit your work for this project— on paper or electronically. If submitting electronically, determine if, in addition to submitting your Access database, you are to create and submit electronic printouts of individual database objects.

7 To print on paper, in the **Print** dialog box, click **OK**, and then in the **Close Preview group**, click the **Close Print Preview** button. This printout will have two pages. To create an electronic PDF printout of this table object, in the Print dialog box, click Cancel, and then follow the steps in the following Note—or follow the specific directions provided by your instructor.

> **Note** | To Create a PDF Electronic Printout of an Access Object
>
> Display the object (table, report, and so on) in Print Preview and adjust margins and orientation as desired. On the Print Preview tab, in the Data group, click the PDF or XPS button. In the Publish as PDF or XPS dialog box, navigate to your chapter folder. Use the default file name, or follow your instructor's directions to name the object. In the lower right corner, click Publish—the default setting is PDF. If necessary, close the Adobe Acrobat/Reader window and the Export-PDF dialog box. Click the Close Print Preview button; your electronic printout is saved.

8 At the far right edge of the object window, click the **Close Object** button ⊠ to close the **1A Students** table.

9 With your **1A Faculty** table displayed, to the left of the **Faculty ID** field name, click the **Select All** button ☐ to select all of the columns. On the **Home tab**, in the **Records group**, click the **More** button. Click **Field Width**, and in the **Column Width** dialog box, click **Best Fit**. Click in any field in the table to remove the selection, and then **Save** 🖫 the table.

10 Display the table in **Print Preview**. Change the **Orientation** to **Landscape**. If directed to do so by your instructor, create a paper or electronic printout, and then **Close Print Preview**—two pages result.

11 Click the **Close Object** button ✕.

All of your database objects—the *1A Students* table and the *1A Faculty* table—are closed; the object window is empty.

Objective 4 | Create and Use a Query, Form, and Report

A *query* is a database object that retrieves specific data from one or more database objects—either tables or other queries—and then, in a single datasheet, displays only the data that you specify. Because the word *query* means *to ask a question*, think of a query as a question formed in a manner that Access can answer.

A *form* is an Access object with which you can enter data, edit data, or display data from a table or a query. In a form, the fields are laid out in an attractive format on the screen, which makes working with the database easier for those who must enter and look up data.

A *report* is a database object that displays the fields and records from a table or a query in an easy-to-read format suitable for printing. Create reports to *summarize* information in a database in a professional-looking manner.

Activity 1.14 | Using the Simple Query Wizard to Create a Query

A *select query* is one type of Access query. A select query, also called a *simple select query*, retrieves (selects) data from one or more tables or queries and then displays the selected data in a datasheet. A select query creates subsets of data to answer specific questions; for example, *Which students live in Arlington, VA?*

The objects from which a query selects its data are referred to as the query's *data source*. In this activity, you will create a simple select query using a *wizard*. A wizard is a feature in Microsoft Office programs that walks you step by step through a process. The process involves choosing the data source, and then indicating the fields you want to include in the query result. The query—the question that you want to ask—is *What is the name, complete mailing address, and Student ID of every student?*

1 Click the **Create tab**, and then in the **Queries group**, click the **Query Wizard** button. In the **New Query** dialog box, click **Simple Query Wizard**, and then click **OK**. Compare your screen with Figure 1.30.

Figure 1.30

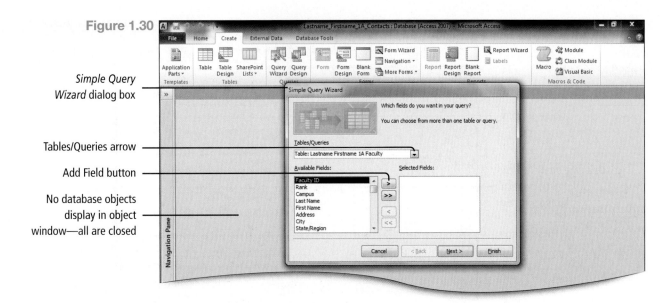

Simple Query Wizard dialog box

Tables/Queries arrow

Add Field button

No database objects display in object window—all are closed

> **2** Click the **Tables/Queries arrow**, and then click your **Table: 1A Students**.
>
> To create a query, first choose the data source—the object from which to select data. The name and complete mailing address of every student is stored in the 1A Students table, so this table will be your data source.
>
> **3** Under **Available Fields**, click **Student ID**, and then click the **Add Field** button ▣ to move the field to the **Selected Fields** list on the right. Point to the **Last Name** field, and then double-click to add the field to the **Selected Fields** list.
>
> Use either method to add fields to the Selected Fields list. Fields can be added in any order.
>
> **4** By using the **Add Field** button ▣ or by double-clicking the field name, add the following fields to the **Selected Fields** list: **First Name**, **Address**, **City**, **State/Region**, and **ZIP/Postal Code**. Compare your screen with Figure 1.31.
>
> Choosing these seven fields will answer the question, *What is the Student ID, name, and address of every student?*

Figure 1.31

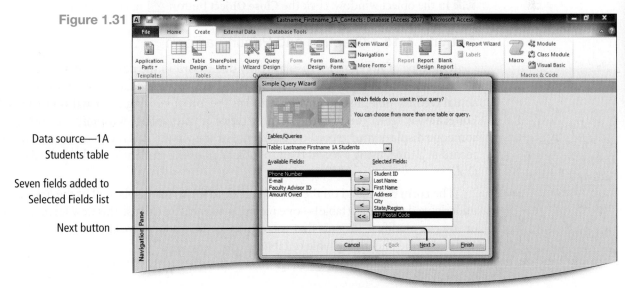

Data source—1A Students table

Seven fields added to Selected Fields list

Next button

> **5** Click **Next**. In the **Simple Query Wizard** dialog box, click in the **What title do you want for your query?** box. Edit as necessary so that the query name, using your own last and first name, is **Lastname Firstname 1A All Students Query** and then compare your screen with Figure 1.32.

Figure 1.32

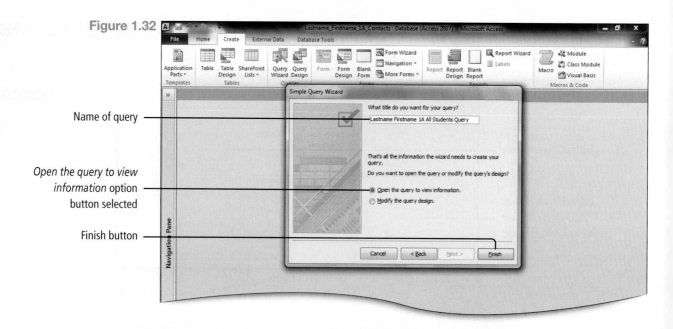

Name of query

Open the query to view information option button selected

Finish button

6 Click **Finish**.

Access *runs* the query—performs the actions indicated in your query design by searching the records in the data source you selected, and then finding the records that match specified criteria. The records that match the criteria display in a datasheet. A select query *selects*—pulls out and displays—*only* the information from the data source that you requested, including the specified fields.

In the object window, Access displays every student record in Datasheet view, but displays *only* the seven fields that you moved to the Selected Fields list in the Simple Query Wizard dialog box.

7 If necessary, apply Best Fit to the columns and then Save the query. Display the query in **Print Preview**. Change the **Orientation** to **Landscape**, and then create a paper or electronic printout as instructed. **Close** the **Print Preview**.

8 In the object window, click the **Close Object** button ☒ to close the query.

Activity 1.15 | Creating and Printing a Form

One type of Access form displays only one record in the database at a time. Such a form is useful not only to the individual who performs the data entry—typing in the actual records—but also to anyone who has the job of viewing information in a database. For example, when you visit the Records office at your college to obtain a transcript, someone displays your record on a screen. For the viewer, it is much easier to look at one record at a time, using a form, than to look at all of the student records in the database table.

The Form command on the Ribbon creates a form that displays all of the *fields* from the underlying data source (table)—one record at a time. You can use this new form immediately, or you can modify it. Records that you create or edit in a form are automatically added to or updated in the underlying table or tables.

1 **Open** ![>>] the **Navigation Pane**. Increase the width of the **Navigation Pane** so that all object names display fully. Notice that a table displays a datasheet icon, and a query displays an icon of two overlapping datasheets. Right-click your **1A Students** table to display a menu as shown in Figure 1.33.

Figure 1.33

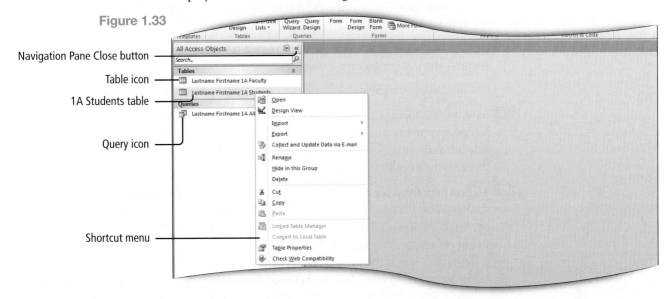

Navigation Pane Close button

Table icon

1A Students table

Query icon

Shortcut menu

2 On the shortcut menu, click **Open** to display the table in the object window, and then **Close** ![<<] the **Navigation Pane** to maximize your object space.

3 Scroll to the right, and notice that there are 11 fields in the table. On the **Create tab**, in the **Forms group**, click the **Form** button. Compare your screen with Figure 1.34.

Access creates a form based on the currently selected object—the 1A Students table. Access creates the form in a simple top-to-bottom format, with all 11 fields in the record lined up in a single column.

The form displays in *Layout view*—the Access view in which you can make changes to a form or to a report while the object is open. Each field displays the data for the first student record in the table—*Joel Barthmaier*.

Figure 1.34

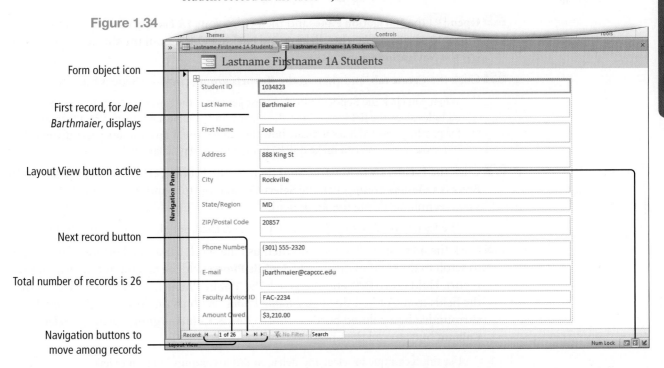

Form object icon

First record, for *Joel Barthmaier*, displays

Layout View button active

Next record button

Total number of records is 26

Navigation buttons to move among records

Access | Chapter 1

4 At the right edge of the status bar, notice that the **Layout View** button ▥ is active, indicating that the form is displayed in Layout view.

Another Way

On the Home tab, in the Views group, click the View button, which displays an icon of a form.

5 At the right edge of the status bar, click the **Form View** button ▦.

In *Form view*, you can view the records, but you cannot change the layout or design of the form.

6 In the navigation area, click the **Next record** button ▸ three times. The fourth record—for *Joseph Ingram*—displays.

You can use the navigation buttons to scroll among the records to display any single record.

7 **Save** ▤ the form with the default name—*Lastname Firstname 1A Students*. Along the left edge of the record, under ▸, click anywhere in the narrow gray bar—the *record selector bar*—to select only the record for *Joseph Ingram*. Notice that the bar turns black, indicating that the record is selected.

8 To print the form for *Joseph Ingram* only, click the **File tab**, and then click **Print**—do *not* display Print Preview. Instead, click **Print**. In the **Print** dialog box, in the lower left corner, click **Setup**. Click the **Columns tab**, change the **Width** to **7.5** so that the form prints on one page, and then click **OK**. The maximum column width that you can enter is dependent upon the printer that is installed on your system. In the lower left corner of the **Print** dialog box, click the **Selected Record(s)** option button, and then click **OK**.

> **Note | To Print a Single Form in PDF**
>
> To create a PDF electronic printout of a single record in a form, change the column width to 7.5 as described in step 8 above, and then in the Print dialog box, click Cancel. On the left edge of the form, click the Record Selector bar so that it is black—selected. On the Ribbon click the External Data tab. In the Export group, click the PDF or XPS button. Navigate to your chapter folder, and then in the lower left corner of the dialog box, if necessary, select the Open file after publishing check box. In the lower right corner of the dialog box, click the Options button. In the Options dialog box, under Range, click the Selected records option button, click OK, and then click Publish. Close the Adobe Reader or Acrobat window.

9 **Close** ☒ the form. Notice that your **1A Students** table remains open.

Activity 1.16 | Creating, Modifying, and Printing a Report

1 **Open** ⏵⏵ the **Navigation Pane**, and then open your **1A Faculty** table by double-clicking the table name or by right-clicking and clicking Open from the shortcut menu. **Close** ⏴⏴ the **Navigation Pane**.

2 Click the **Create tab**, and then in the **Reports group**, click the **Report** button.

When you click the Report button, Access generates the report in Layout view and includes all of the fields and all of the records in the table, and does so in a format suitable for printing. Dotted lines indicate how the report would break across pages if you print it. In Layout view, you can make quick changes to the report layout.

Another Way

Right-click the field. From the shortcut menu, click Select Entire Column, and then press [Del].

3 Click the **Faculty ID** field name, and then on the Ribbon, click the **Arrange tab**. In the **Rows & Columns group**, click the **Select Column** button, and then press [Del]. Using the same technique, delete the **Rank** field.

The Faculty ID and Rank fields and data are deleted, and the report readjusts the fields.

4 Click the **Address** field name, and then use the scroll bar at the bottom of the screen to scroll to the right to display the **Mobile Phone** field; be careful not to click in the report. Hold down [Shift] and then click the **Mobile Phone** field name to select all of the fields from *Address* through *Mobile Phone*. With all the field names selected—surrounded by a colored border—in the **Row & Columns group**, click the **Select Column** button, and then press [Del].

Use this technique to select and delete multiple columns in Layout view.

5 Scroll to the left, and notice that you can see all of the remaining fields. In any record, click in the **E-mail** field. Point to the right edge of the field box to display the ↔ pointer. Drag to the right slightly to increase the width of the field so that all E-mail addresses display on one line.

6 Click the **Last Name** field name. On the Ribbon, click the **Home tab**. In the **Sort & Filter group**, click the **Ascending** button. Compare your screen with Figure 1.35.

By default, tables are sorted in ascending order by the primary key field, which is the Faculty ID field. You can change the default and sort any field in either ascending order or descending order. The sort order does not change in the underlying table, only in the report.

Figure 1.35

Ascending button selected

Four fields display in report

Report sorted by Last Name field

E-mail addresses display on one line

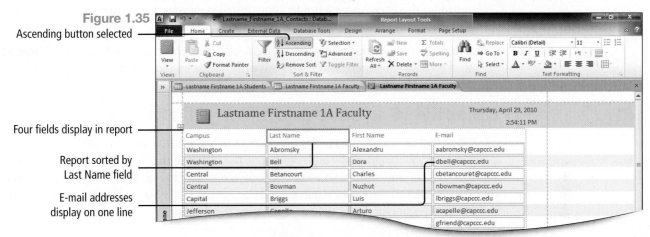

7 Click the **Save** button 🖫. In the **Report Name** box, add **Report** to the end of the suggested name, and then click **OK**.

8 Display the report in **Print Preview**. In the **Zoom group**, click the **Two Pages** button, and then compare your screen with Figure 1.36.

The report will print on two pages because the page number at the bottom of the report is located beyond the right margin of the report.

Figure 1.36

Two Pages button

Page number at bottom of second page

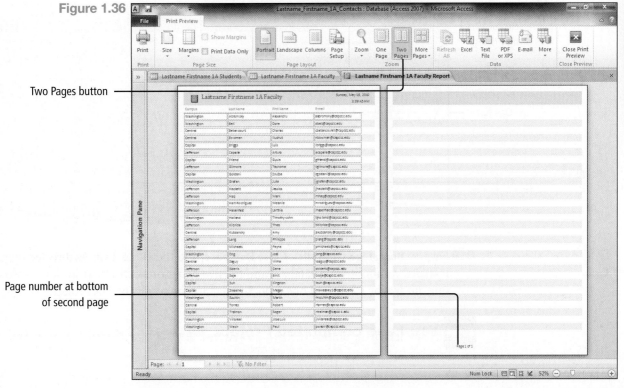

9 In the **Close Preview group**, click the **Close Print Preview button**. Scroll down to the bottom of the report, and then scroll to the right to display the page number. Click the page number—**Page 1 of 1**—and then press Del.

10 Display the report in **Print Preview** and notice that the report will print on one page. In the **Zoom group**, click the **One Page** button. **Save** 🔲 the changes to the design of the report, and then create a paper or electronic printout as instructed. At the right end of the Ribbon, click the **Close Print Preview** button.

> The default margins of a report created with the Report tool are 0.25 inch. Some printers require a greater margin so your printed report may result in two pages—you will learn to adjust this later. Also, if a printer is not installed on your system, the report may print on two pages.

11 Along the top of the object window, right-click any object tab, and then click **Close All** to close all of the open objects and leave the object window empty.

Objective 5 | Save and Close a Database

When you close an Access table, any changes made to the records are saved automatically. If you change the design of the table or change the layout of the Datasheet view, such as adjusting the column widths, you will be prompted to save the design changes. At the end of your Access session, close your database and exit Access. If the Navigation Pane is open when you close Access, it will display when you reopen the database.

Activity 1.17 | Closing and Saving a Database

1 **Open** » the **Navigation Pane**. Notice that your report object displays with a green report icon. Compare your screen with Figure 1.37.

Figure 1.37

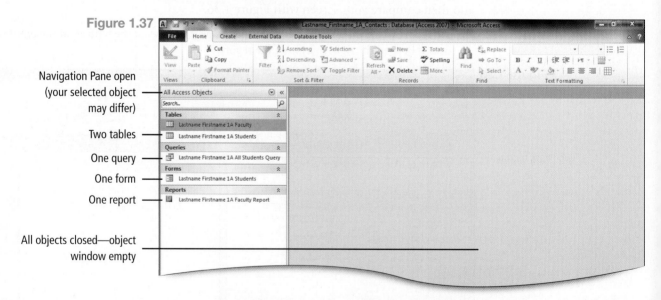

Navigation Pane open (your selected object may differ)

Two tables

One query

One form

One report

All objects closed—object window empty

Another Way

In the upper right corner of the window, click the Close button.

2 Display **Backstage** view, click **Close Database**, and then click **Exit**. As directed by your instructor, submit your database and the five paper or electronic printouts—two tables, one query, one form, and one report—that are the results of this project.

End **You have completed Project 1A**

Project 1B Student Workshops Database

myitlab
Project 1B Training

Project Activities

In Activities 1.18 through 1.23, you will assist Dr. Kirsten McCarty, Vice President of Student Services, by creating a database to store information about student workshops presented by Capital Cities Community College. You will use a database template that tracks event information, add workshop information to the database, and then print the results. Your completed report and table will look similar to Figure 1.38.

Project Files

For Project 1B, you will need the following files:

New Access database using the Events template
a01B_Workshops (Excel workbook)

You will save your database as:

Lastname_Firstname_1B_Student_Workshops

Project Results

Figure 1.38
Project 1B Student Workshops

Objective 6 | Create a Database Using a Template

A *database template* contains pre-built tables, queries, forms, and reports to perform a specific task, such as tracking a large number of events. For example, your college may hold events such as athletic contests, plays, lectures, concerts, and club meetings. Using a predefined template, your college Activities Director can quickly create a database to manage these events. The advantage of using a template to start a new database is that you do not have to create the objects—all you need to do is enter your data and modify the pre-built objects to suit your needs.

The purpose of the database in this project is to track the student workshops offered by Capital Cities Community College. The questions to be answered might include:

What workshops will be offered and when will they be offered?

In what rooms and campus locations will the workshops be held?

Which workshop locations have a computer projector for PowerPoint presentations?

Activity 1.18 | Creating a New Database Using a Template

1 **Start** Access. Under **Available Templates**, click **Sample templates**. If necessary, scroll down to locate and then click **Events**. Compare your screen with Figure 1.39.

Sample templates are stored on your computer; they are included with the Access program.

Figure 1.39

Available Sample templates stored on computer

Events template

2 On the right side of the screen, to the right of the **File Name** box, click the **Browse** button, and then navigate to your **Access Chapter 1** folder.

3 At the bottom of the **File New Database** dialog box, select the text in the **File name** box. Using your own name, type **Lastname_Firstname_1B_Student_Workshops** and then press Enter.

4 In the lower right corner of your screen, click the **Create** button.

Access creates the *1B Student Workshops* database, and the database name displays in the title bar. A predesigned *form*—Event List—displays in the object window. Although you can enter events for any date, when you open the database in the future, the Event List will display only those events for the current date and future dates.

5 Under the Ribbon, on the **Message Bar**, a Security Warning displays. On the **Message Bar**, click the **Enable Content** button.

Databases provided by Microsoft are safe to use on your computer.

Activity 1.19 │ Building a Table by Entering Records in a Multiple Items Form

The purpose of a form is to simplify the entry of data into a table—either for you or for others who enter data. In Project 1A, you created a simple form that enabled you to display or enter records in a table one record at a time. The Events template creates a *Multiple Items form*, a form that enables you to display or enter *multiple* records in a table, but still with an easier and simplified layout than typing directly into the table itself.

1 Click in the first empty **Title** field. Type **Your Cyber Reputation** and then press Tab. In the **Start Time** field, type **3/9/16 7p** and then press Tab.

Access formats the date and time. As you enter dates and times, a small calendar displays to the right of the field, which you can click to select a date instead of typing.

2 In the **End Time** field, type **3/9/16 9p** and then press Tab. In the **Description** field, type **Internet Safety** and then press Tab. In the **Location** field, type **Jefferson Campus** and then press Tab three times to move to the **Title** field in the new record row. Compare your screen with Figure 1.40.

Because the workshops have no unique value, Access uses the AutoNumber data type of the ID field to assign a unique, sequential number to each record. In the navigation area, each record is identified as a task, rather than a record or page.

Figure 1.40

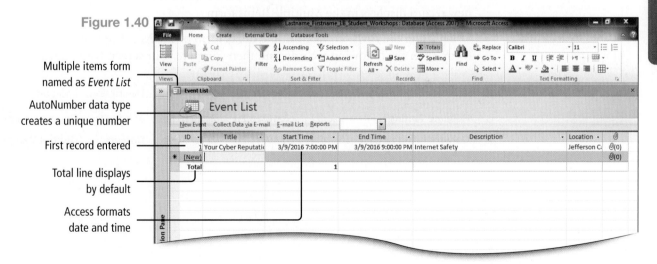

Multiple items form named as *Event List*

AutoNumber data type creates a unique number

First record entered

Total line displays by default

Access formats date and time

3 Directly above the field names row, click **New Event**.

> A *single-record form* displays, similar to the simple form you created in Project 1A. A single-record form enables you to display or enter one record at a time into a table.

4 Using [Tab] to move from field to field, enter the following record—press [Tab] three times to move from the **End Time** field to the **Description** field. Compare your screen with Figure 1.41.

Title	Location	Start Time	End Time	Description
Writing a Research Paper	**Washington Campus**	**3/10/16 4p**	**3/10/16 6p**	**Computer Skills**

Figure 1.41

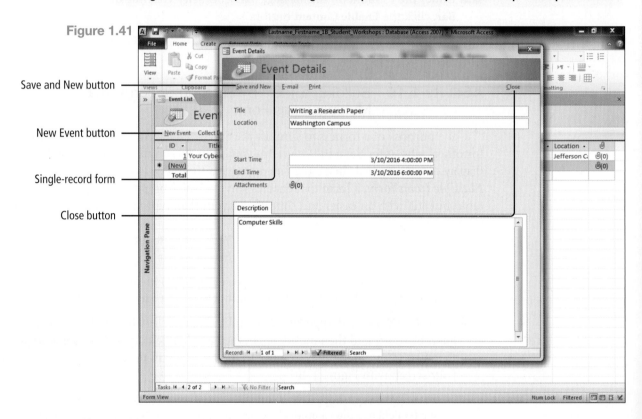

Save and New button

New Event button

Single-record form

Close button

5 In the upper right corner of the single-record form, click **Close**, and notice that the new record displays in the Multiple Items form.

6 Using either the rows on the Multiple Items form or the New Event single-record form, enter the following records, and then compare your screen with Figure 1.42.

ID	Title	Start Time	End Time	Description	Location
3	**Resume Writing**	**3/18/16 2p**	**3/18/16 4p**	**Job Skills**	**Capital Campus**
4	**Careers in the Legal Profession**	**3/19/16 2p**	**3/19/16 4p**	**Careers**	**Central Campus**

Figure 1.42

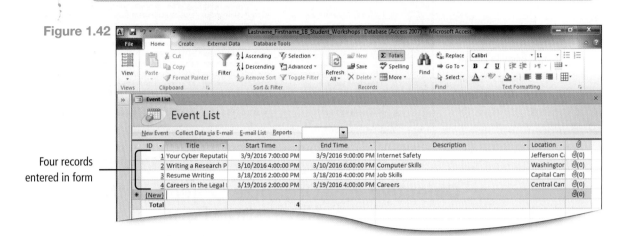

Four records entered in form

7 In the upper right corner of the object window, click **Close** ✕ to close the **Event List** form.

8 On the Ribbon, click the **External Data tab**. In the **Import & Link group**, click the **Excel** button.

Recall that you can populate a table by importing data from an Excel workbook.

9 In the **Get External Data – Excel Spreadsheet** dialog box, click the **Browse** button. Navigate to your student files, and then double-click **a01B_Workshops**.

10 Click the second option button—**Append a copy of the records to the table**—and then click **OK**.

11 Click **Next**, click **Finish**, and then **Close** the dialog box.

12 Open ❯❯ the **Navigation Pane**. Double-click **Event List** to open the form that displays data stored in the Events table, and then **Close** ❮❮ the **Navigation Pane**.

13 To the left of the **ID** field name, click the **Select All** button ⬜ to select all of the columns.

14 In the field names row, point to any of the selected field names, right-click, and then click **Field Width**. In the **Column Width** dialog box, click **Best Fit**. Notice that the widths of all of the columns are adjusted to accommodate the longest entry in the column.

15 In the first record, click in the **Title** field to deselect the columns. **Save** 🖫 the form, and then compare your screen with Figure 1.43.

Eight additional records display—those imported from the a01B_Workshops Excel workbook.

Figure 1.43

Eight additional records imported from an Excel workbook

Objective 7 | Organize Objects in the Navigation Pane

Use the Navigation Pane to organize database objects, to open them, and to perform common tasks like renaming an object.

Activity 1.20 | Organizing Database Objects in the Navigation Pane

The Navigation Pane groups and displays your database objects and can do so in predefined arrangements. In this activity, you will group your database objects using the *Tables and Related Views* category, which groups objects by the table to which they are related. This grouping is useful because you can easily determine the data source table of queries, forms, and reports.

1 Open ▷▷ the **Navigation Pane**. At the top of the **Navigation Pane**, click the **Navigation arrow** ▼. In the list, under **Navigate To Category**, click **Tables and Related Views**.

2 Confirm that *Events* displays in the bar under the Search box at the top of the **Navigation Pane**. Compare your screen with Figure 1.44.

The icons to the left of the objects listed in the Navigation Pane indicate that the Events template created a number of objects for you—among them, one table titled *Events*, one query, two forms, and five reports. The Event List Multiple Items form, which is currently displayed in the object window, is included in the Navigation Pane. All of the objects were created using the underlying data source, which is the Events table.

Figure 1.44

One table
One query
Two forms

Five reports

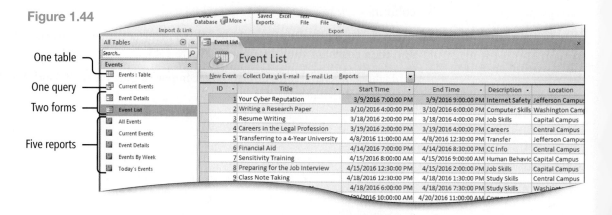

Another Way

Double-click the table name to open it in the object window.

3 In the **Navigation Pane**, point to the **Events** *table*, right-click, and then click **Open**.

The Events table is the active object in the object window. Use the Navigation Pane to open objects for use. The 12 records that you entered using the Multiple Items *form* and by importing from an Excel workbook display in the *table*. Tables are the foundation of your database because your data must be stored in a table. You can enter records directly into a table or you can use a form to enter records.

4 In the object window, click the **Event List tab** to bring the form into view and make it the active object.

Recall that a form presents a more user-friendly screen for entering records into a table.

Another Way

Double-click the report name to open it.

5 In the **Navigation Pane**, right-click the *report* (green icon) named **Current Events**, and then click **Open**. Compare your screen with Figure 1.45.

An advantage of using a template to begin a database is that many objects, such as attractively formatted reports, are already designed for you.

Figure 1.45

Three open objects

Current Events report preformatted and designed by the template

Current Events report in Navigation Pane

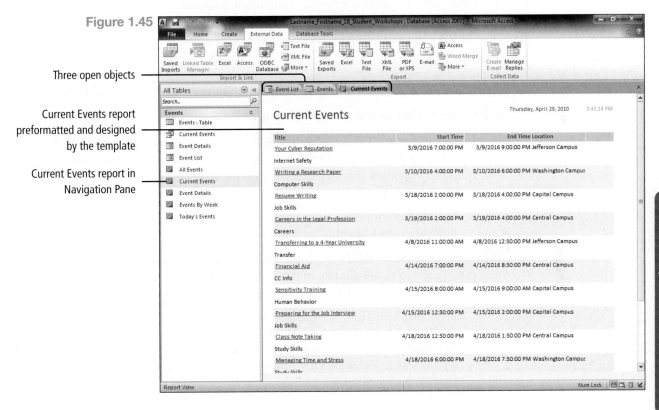

6 In the object window, **Close** ✕ the **Current Events** report.

7 From the **Navigation Pane**, open the **Events By Week** report.

In this predesigned report, the events are displayed by week. After entering records in the form or table, the preformatted reports are updated with the records from the table.

8 **Close** ✕ the **Events By Week** report, and then **Close** ✕ the remaining two open objects. **Close** « the **Navigation Pane**.

Access | Chapter 1

Objective 8 | Create a New Table in a Database Created with a Template

The Events database template created only one table—the *Events* table. Although the database was started from a template and contains other objects, you can add additional objects as needed.

Activity 1.21 | Creating a New Table and Changing Its Design

Dr. McCarty has information about the various locations where workshops are held. For example, for the Jefferson campus, she has information about the room, seating arrangements, number of seats, and audio-visual equipment. In the Events table, workshops are scheduled in rooms at each of the four campuses. It would not make sense to store information about the campus rooms multiple times in the same table. It is *not* considered good database design to have duplicate information in a table.

When data in a table becomes redundant, it is usually an indication that you need a new table to contain the information about the topic. In this activity, you will create a table to track the workshop locations and the equipment and seating arrangements in each location.

1 On the Ribbon, click the **Create tab**. In the **Tables group**, click the **Table** button.

2 Click the **Click to Add arrow**, click **Text**, type **Campus/Location** and then press [Enter].

3 In the third column, click **Text**, type **Room** and then press [Enter]. In the fourth column, click **Text**, type **Seats** and then press [Enter]. In the fifth column, click **Text**, type **Room Arrangement** and then press [Enter]. In the sixth column, click **Text**, type **Equipment** and then press [↓].

> The table has six fields. Access creates the first field in the table—the ID field—to ensure that every record has a unique value.

4 Right-click the **ID** field name, and then click **Rename Field**. Type **Room ID** and then press [Enter]. On the **Fields tab**, in the **Formatting group**, click the **Data Type arrow**, and then click **Text**. In the **Field Validation group**, notice that **Unique** is selected.

> Recall that, by default, Access creates the ID field with the AutoNumber data type so that the field can be used as the primary key. Here, this field will store a unique room ID that is a combination of letters, symbols, and numbers, so it is appropriate to change the data type to Text. In Datasheet view, the primary key field is identified by the selection of the Unique check box.

5 In the new record row, click in the **Room ID** field, type **JEFF-01** and then press Tab. In the **Campus/Location** field, type **Jefferson Campus** and then press Tab. In the **Room** field, type **J123** and then press Tab. In the **Seats** field, type **150** and then press Tab. In the **Room Arrangement** field, type **Theater** and then press Tab. In the **Equipment** field, type **Computer Projector, Surround Sound, & Microphones** and then press Tab to move to the new record row. Compare your screen with Figure 1.46.

Recall that Access saves the record when you move to another row within the table. You can press either Tab or Enter to move to another field in a table.

Figure 1.46

New table
Renamed field
First record entered
Room ID field assigned data type of *Text*
Selected field—Room ID—indicated as primary key field

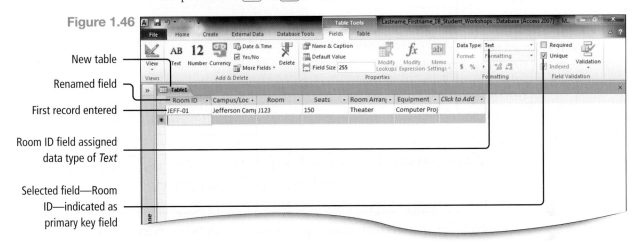

6 In the **Views group**, click the **View** button to switch to **Design** view. In the **Save As** dialog box, save the table as **Lastname Firstname 1B Workshop Locations** and then click **OK**.

7 In the **Field Name** column, to the left of the **Room ID** box, notice the key icon.

In Design view, the key icon indicates the field—Room ID—that is identified as the primary key.

8 In the **Views group**, click the **View** button to switch to **Datasheet** view.

9 Enter the following records in the table:

Room ID	Campus/Location	Room	Seats	Room Arrangement	Equipment
WASH-01	**Washington Campus**	**A15**	**35**	**Lecture/Classroom**	**Computer Projector**
CAP-01	**Capital Campus**	**C202**	**50**	**Lecture/Classroom**	**Smart Board**
CEN-01	**Central Campus**	**H248**	**20**	**U-shaped**	**White Board**
JEFF-02	**Jefferson Campus**	**A15**	**25**	**U-shaped**	**25 Computers, Projector**

10 To the left of the **Room ID** field name, click the **Select All** button ☐ to select all of the columns. On the **Home tab**, in the **Records group**, click the **More** button. Click **Field Width**, and in the **Column Width** dialog box, click **Best Fit**. Click in any field to remove the selection, and then **Save** 🖫 the changes to the table. In the object window, **Close** ☒ the **1B Workshop Locations** table.

11 Open ≫ the **Navigation Pane**, and then locate the name of your new table. Point to the right edge of the **Navigation Pane** to display the ↔ pointer. Drag to the right to display the entire table name, and then compare your screen with Figure 1.47.

Recall that as currently arranged, the Navigation Pane organizes the objects by Tables and Related Views. In Figure 1.47, the Events table is listed first, followed by its related objects, and then the Workshop Locations table is listed. In its current view, the tables are sorted in ascending order by name; therefore, your table may be listed before the Events table depending on your last name.

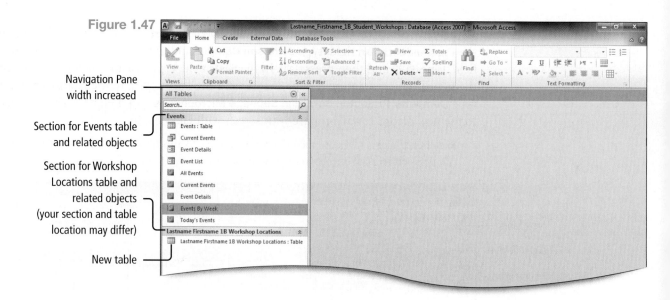

Figure 1.47

Navigation Pane width increased

Section for Events table and related objects

Section for Workshop Locations table and related objects (your section and table location may differ)

New table

Objective 9 | Print a Report and a Table in a Database Created with a Template

Recall that an advantage to starting a new database with a template, instead of from a blank database, is that many report objects are already created for you.

Activity 1.22 | Viewing and Printing a Report

1 From the **Navigation Pane**, open the **Event Details** *report* (not the form).

The pre-built Event Details report displays in an attractively arranged format.

2 **Close** ⊠ the **Event Details** report. Open the **All Events** report. In the lower right corner of the status bar, click the **Layout View** button ⊞. At the top of the report, click on the text *All Events* to display a colored border, and then click to the left of the letter *A* to place the insertion point there. Using your own name, type **Lastname Firstname** and then press ⎵Spacebar. Press ⏎Enter, and then **Save** 🖫 the report.

Each report displays the records in the table in different useful formats.

<table>
<tr><td>**Another Way**
Right-click the object tab, and then click Print Preview.</td><td>**3** Display **Backstage** view, click **Print**, and then click **Print Preview**. In the navigation area, notice that the navigation arrows are dimmed, which indicates that this report will print on one page.</td></tr>
</table>

4 Create a paper or electronic printout as instructed, **Close Print Preview**, and then **Close** ⊠ the report.

Activity 1.23 | Printing a Table

When printing a table, use the Print Preview command to determine if the table will print on one page or if you need to adjust column widths, margins, or the orientation. Recall that there will be occasions when you want to print a table for a quick reference or for proofreading. For a more professional-looking format, and for more options to format the output, create and print a report.

1 From the **Navigation Pane**, open your **1B Workshop Locations** table. **Close** ⟪ the **Navigation Pane**. Display **Backstage** view, click **Print**, and then click **Print Preview**.

The table displays in the Print Preview window, showing how it will look when it is printed. The name of the table and the date the table is printed display at the top of the page. The navigation area displays *1* in the Pages box, and the right-pointing arrow—the Next Page arrow—is active. Recall that when a table is in the Print Preview window, the navigation arrows are used to navigate from one page to the next, rather than from one record to the next.

2 In the navigation area, click the **Next Page** button ▶.

The second page of the table displays the last field column. Whenever possible, try to print all of the fields horizontally on one page. Of course, if there are many records, more than one page may be needed to print all of the records.

3 On the **Print Preview tab**, in the **Page Layout group**, click the **Landscape** button, and then compare your screen with Figure 1.48. Notice that the entire table will print on one page.

Figure 1.48

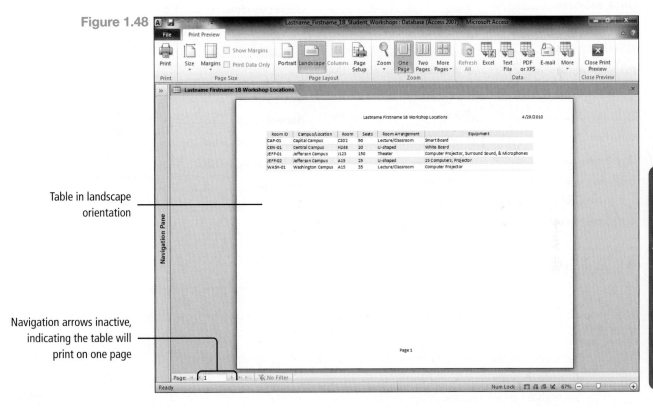

Table in landscape orientation

Navigation arrows inactive, indicating the table will print on one page

4 Create a paper or electronic printout if instructed to do so, and then **Close Print Preview**.

5 **Close** ✕ the **1B Workshop Locations** table. For the convenience of the next person opening the database, **Open** ≫ the **Navigation Pane**. In **Backstage** view, click **Close Database**, and then click **Exit** to close the Access program. As directed by your instructor, submit your database and the two paper or electronic printouts—one report and one table—that are the results of this project.

 **You have completed Project 1B** _____

Access | Chapter 1

Summary

Microsoft Access 2010 is a database management system that uses various objects—tables, forms, queries, reports—to organize information. Data is stored in tables in which you establish fields, set the data type and field size, and create a primary key. Data from a database can be reported and printed.

Key Terms

Matching

Match each term in the second column with its correct definition in the first column by writing the letter of the term on the blank line in front of the correct definition.

_____ 1. An organized collection of facts about people, events, things, or ideas related to a specific topic.

_____ 2. Facts about people, events, things, or ideas.

_____ 3. Data that is organized in a useful manner.

_____ 4. A simple database file that is not related or linked to any other collection of data.

_____ 5. The database object that stores the data, and which is the foundation of an Access database.

_____ 6. A table row that contains all of the categories of data pertaining to one person, place, thing, event, or idea.

_____ 7. A single piece of information that is stored in every record and represented by a column in a table.

_____ 8. A principle stating that data is organized in tables so that there is no redundant data.

_____ 9. A principle stating that techniques are used to ensure the accuracy of data entered into a table.

A Common field

B Data

C Database

D Field

E First principle of good database design

F Flat database

G Information

H Navigation Pane

I Normalization

J Object window

K Objects

L Populate

M Record

N Second principle of good database design

O Table

_____ 10. The process of applying design rules and principles to ensure that a database performs as expected.

_____ 11. A field in one or more tables that stores the same data.

_____ 12. The basic parts of a database; for example tables, forms, queries, and reports.

_____ 13. The window area that organizes the database objects and from which you open objects.

_____ 14. The window area that displays each open object on its own tab.

_____ 15. The action of filling a database with records.

Multiple Choice

Circle the correct answer.

1. The Access view that displays data in columns and rows like an Excel worksheet is:
   A. Datasheet view   B. Design view   C. Layout view

2. The characteristic that defines the kind of data you can enter into a field is the:
   A. data source   B. data type   C. field property

3. The box at the left of a record in Datasheet view that you click to select an entire record is the:
   A. link   B. navigation area   C. record selector box

4. To add on to the end of an object, such as to add records to the end of an existing table, is to:
   A. append   B. import   C. run

5. Characteristics of a field that control how the field displays and how data is entered are:
   A. data sources   B. data types   C. field properties

6. The field that uniquely identifies a record in a table is known as the:
   A. attachments field   B. common field   C. primary key

7. The underlying design of a table is referred to as the:
   A. caption   B. source file   C. structure

8. The object that retrieves specific data and then displays only the data that you specify is a:
   A. form   B. query   C. report

9. The object that displays fields and records from a table or query in a printable format is a:
   A. form   B. query   C. report

10. Information repeated in a database in a manner that indicates poor design is said to be:
    A. relational   B. redundant   C. truncated

Access | Chapter 1

Skills Review | Project **1C** Work Study Students Database

In the following Skills Review, you will create a database to store information about the Work Study students and the divisions in which they are employed. Your completed database objects will look similar to Figure 1.49.

Project Files

For Project 1C, you will need the following files:

New blank Access database
a01C_Student_Workers (Excel workbook)
a01C_Divisions (Excel workbook)

You will save your database as:

Lastname_Firstname_1C_Student_Workers

Project Results

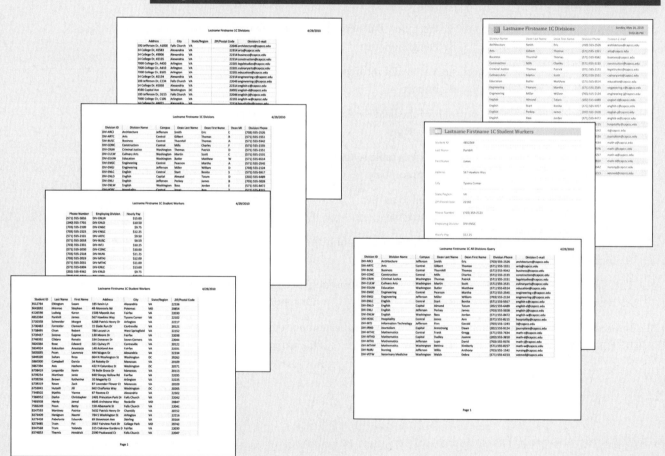

Figure 1.49

(Project 1C Work Study Students Database continues on the next page)

Content-Based Assessments

1 Start Access. Click **Blank database**, and then in the lower right corner, click the **Browse** button. In the **File New Database** dialog box, navigate to your **Access Chapter 1** folder, and then in the **File name** box, replace the existing text with **Lastname_Firstname_1C_ Student_Workers** Press Enter, and then in the lower right corner, click **Create**.

a. **Close** the **Navigation Pane**. Click in the text *Click to Add*. Click **Text**, type **Last Name** and then press Enter.

b. In the third field name box, click **Text**, type **First Name** and then press Enter. In the fourth field name box, click **Text**, type **Middle Initial** and then press Enter. Create the remaining fields as shown in **Table 1**, pressing Enter after the last field name.

c. Scroll as necessary to view the first field. Click the **ID** field name. In the **Properties group**, click the **Name & Caption** button. In the **Enter Field Properties** dialog box, in the **Name** box, change *ID* to **Student ID** and then click **OK**. In the **Formatting group**, click the **Data Type arrow**, and then click **Text**.

d. In the first record row, click in the **Student ID** field, type **3512784** and press Enter. In the **Last Name** field, type **Elkington** In the **First Name** field, type **Susan** In the **Middle Initial** field, type **A** In the **Address** field, type **185 Kevin Ln**

e. Continue entering data in the fields as shown in **Table 2**, pressing Enter to move to the next field and to the next row.

f. Click **Save**, and then in the **Table Name** box, using your own name, replace the selected text by typing **Lastname Firstname 1C Student Workers** and then click **OK**.

2 Scroll, if necessary, to view the first field. In the new record row, click in the **Student ID** field, and then enter the information for two additional students as shown in **Table 3**, pressing Enter to move from field to field.

a. **Close** your **1C Student Workers** table. On the **External Data tab**, in the **Import & Link group**, click the **Excel** button. In the **Get External Data - Excel Spreadsheet** dialog box, click the **Browse** button. In the **File Open** dialog box, navigate to your student data files, and then double-click the **a01C_Student_Workers** Excel file.

b. **Append a copy of the records to the table**, and then click **OK**. Click **Next**, click **Finish**, and then click **Close**. **Open** the **Navigation Pane**, and then widen it so that you can view the entire table name. In the **Navigation Pane**, double-click your **1C Student Workers** table to open it, and then **Close** the **Navigation Pane**—30 total records display.

Table 1

Data Type					Text	Text	Text	Text	Text	Text	Currency
Field Name	ID	Last Name	First Name	Middle Initial	Address	City	State/Region	ZIP/Postal Code	Phone Number	Employing Division	Hourly Pay

(Return to Step 1-c)

Table 2

City	State/Region	ZIP/Postal Code	Phone Number	Employing Division	Hourly Pay
Alexandria	VA	22336	(571) 555-5816	DIV-ENLW	15

(Return to Step 1-f)

Table 3

Student ID	Last Name	First Name	Middle Initial	Address	City	State/Region	ZIP/Postal Code	Phone Number	Employing Division	Hourly Pay
3641892	Monroe	Stephen	D	48 Monrovia Rd	Potomac	MD	20854	(240) 555-7701	DIV-ENLD	10.5
4126598	Ludwig	Karen	E	1508 Moonlit Ave	Fairfax	VA	22030	(703) 555-2109	DIV-ENGC	9.75

(Return to Step 2-a)

(Project 1C Work Study Students Database continues on the next page)

3 Click the **Home tab**, and then in the **Views group**, click the **View** button to switch to **Design** view.

a. To the left of **Middle Initial**, point to the row selector box, and then click to select the entire row. On the **Design tab**, in the **Tools group**, click the **Delete Rows** button, and then click **Yes**.

b. Click anywhere in the **State/Region** field name, and then under **Field Properties**, set the **Field Size** to **2** In the **State/Region** row, click in the **Description** box, and then type **Two-character state abbreviation**

c. Click in the **Student ID** field name box, set the **Field Size** to **7** and in the **Description** box, type **Seven-digit Student ID** Then **Save** the design of your table; click **Yes**. On the **Design tab**, in the **Views group**, click the **View** button to switch to **Datasheet** view.

4 On the Ribbon, click the **External Data tab**, and then in the **Import & Link group**, click the **Excel** button. In the **Get External Data – Excel Spreadsheet** dialog box, click the **Browse** button. Navigate to your student data files, and then double-click **a01C_Divisions**. Be sure that the **Import the source data into a new table in the current database** option button is selected, and then click **OK**.

a. In the **Import Spreadsheet Wizard** dialog box, click to select the **First Row Contains Column Headings** check box, and then click **Next**.

b. Click **Next** again. Click the **Choose my own primary key** option button, and to the right, be sure that *Division ID* displays. Click **Next**. In the **Import to Table** box, type **Lastname Firstname 1C Divisions** and then click **Finish**. Click **Close**, **Open** the **Navigation Pane**, and then open your **1C Divisions** table. **Close** the **Navigation Pane**—22 records display.

c. At the top of the object window, click the **1C Student Workers tab**. To the left of the **Student ID** field name, click the **Select All** button. Click the **Home tab**, and in the **Records group**, click the **More** button. Click **Field Width**, and in the **Column Width** dialog box, click **Best Fit**. Click in any field, and then **Save** the table.

d. Display **Backstage** view, click **Print**, and then click **Print Preview**. In the **Page Layout group**, click the **Landscape** button. Create a paper or electronic printout as directed by your instructor; two pages result. Click **Close Print Preview**, and then **Close** your **1C Student Workers** table.

e. With your **1C Divisions** table displayed, to the left of the **Division ID** field name, click the **Select All** button, and then apply **Best Fit** to all of the columns. Click in any field, **Save** the table, and then display the table in **Print Preview**. Change the **Orientation** to **Landscape**. Create a paper or electronic printout as directed—two pages result. **Close Print Preview**, and then **Close** your **1C Divisions** table.

5 On the **Create tab**, in the **Queries group**, click the **Query Wizard** button. In the **New Query** dialog box, click **Simple Query Wizard**, and then click **OK**. Click the **Tables/Queries arrow**, and then be sure your **Table: 1C Divisions** is selected.

a. Under **Available Fields**, click **Division ID**, and then click the **Add Field** button to move the field to the **Selected Fields** list on the right. Using either the **Add Field** button or by double-clicking, add the following fields to the **Selected Fields** list: **Division Name**, **Campus**, **Dean Last Name**, **Dean First Name**, **Division Phone**, and **Division E-mail**. The query will answer the question, *What is the Division ID, Division Name, Campus, Dean's name, Division Phone number, and Division E-mail address of every division?*

b. Click **Next**. In the **Simple Query Wizard** dialog box, change the query title to **Lastname Firstname 1C All Divisions Query** and then click **Finish** to run the query.

c. Display the query in **Print Preview**. Change the **Orientation** to **Landscape**. In the **Page Size group**, click the **Margins** button, and then click **Normal**. Create a paper or electronic printout as directed—one page results. **Close Print Preview**, and then **Close** the query.

d. **Open** the **Navigation Pane**, open your **1C Student Workers** table, and then **Close** the **Navigation Pane**. The table contains 10 fields. On the **Create tab**, in the **Forms group**, click the **Form** button. Click **Save**, and then in the **Save As** dialog box, accept the default name for the form—*Lastname Firstname 1C Student Workers*—by clicking **OK**. In the navigation area, click the **Next record** button three times to display the record for *James Parkhill*. At the left edge of the form, click the gray **record selector bar** to select only this record. By using the instructions in Activity 1.15, print or create an electronic printout of this record as directed. **Close** the form object. Your **1C Student Workers** table object remains open.

(Project 1C Work Study Students Database continues on the next page)

Content-Based Assessments

Skills Review | Project **1C** Work Study Students Database (continued)

6 **Open** the **Navigation Pane**, open your **1C Divisions** table, and then **Close** the **Navigation Pane**. On the **Create tab**, in the **Reports group**, click the **Report** button. In the field names row at the top of the report, click the **Division ID** field name. On the Ribbon, click the **Arrange tab**. In the **Rows & Columns group**, click the **Select Column** button, and then press ⎯Del⎯. Using the same technique, delete the **Campus** field.

   a. Scroll to position the **Dean MI** field at the left of your screen, and click the field name **Dean MI**. Hold down ⎯Ctrl⎯, and then click the field names for **Address**, **City**, **State/Region**, and **ZIP/Postal Code**. On the **Arrange tab**, in the **Rows & Columns group**, click the **Select Column** button, and then press ⎯Del⎯.

   b. Scroll to the left, and then click in the **Dean Last Name** field name. By using the ⟷ pointer, decrease the width of the field until there is about **0.25 inch** of space between the **Dean Last Name** field and the **Dean First Name** field. Decrease the widths of the **Dean First Name** and **Division Phone** fields in a similar manner. In the **Division E-mail** field, click in the first record—the data in the field displays on two lines. Increase the width of the field slightly so that each record's data in the field displays on one line. Be sure that the width of the report is within the dotted boundaries.

   c. Click the **Division Name** field name. On the Ribbon, click the **Home tab**. In the **Sort & Filter group**, click

the **Ascending** button to sort the report in alphabetic order by Division Name.

   d. **Save** the report as **Lastname Firstname 1C Divisions Report** and then click **OK**. Display the report in **Print Preview**. In the **Zoom group**, click the **Two Pages** button, and notice that the report will print on two pages because the page number is beyond the right margin of the report. **Close Print Preview**. With the report displayed in **Layout** view, scroll down and to the right to display the page number— **Page 1 of 1**. Click the page number, press ⎯Del⎯, and then **Save** the changes to the report.

   e. Display the report in **Print Preview**, and notice that the report will print on one page. In the **Zoom group**, click the **One Page** button. Create a paper or electronic printout of the report as directed. Click **Close Print Preview**. Along the top of the object window, right click any **object tab**, and then click **Close All** to close all of the open objects, leaving the object window empty.

   f. **Open** the **Navigation Pane**. If necessary, increase the width of the **Navigation Pane** so that all object names display fully. Display **Backstage** view, click **Close Database**, and then click **Exit**. As directed by your instructor, submit your database and the five paper or electronic printouts—two tables, one query, one form, and one report—that are the results of this project.

End **You have completed Project 1C** ──────────────────

Access | Chapter 1

Project 1C: Work Study Students Database | **Access** 219

Content-Based Assessments

Apply 1B skills from these Objectives:

- **6** Create a Database Using a Template
- **7** Organize Objects in the Navigation Pane
- **8** Create a New Table in a Database Created with a Template
- **9** Print a Report and a Table in a Database Created with a Template

Skills Review | Project **1D** Benefits Events

In the following Skills Review, you will create a database to store information about Employee Benefit Events at Capital Cities Community College. Your completed report and table will look similar to Figure 1.50.

Project Files

For Project 1D, you will need the following files:

> New Access database using the Events template
> a01D_Benefits_Events (Excel workbook)

You will save your database as:

> Lastname_Firstname_1D_Benefits_Events

Project Results

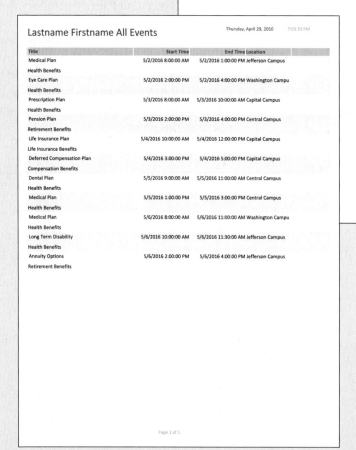

Figure 1.50

(Project 1D Benefits Events continues on the next page)

Content-Based Assessments

Skills Review | Project **1D** Benefits Events (continued)

1 **Start** Access. Under **Available Templates**, click **Sample templates**, and then click **Events**. On the right, to the right of the **File Name** box, click the **Browse** button, and then navigate to your **Access Chapter 1** folder.

a. Select the text in the **File name** box, and then using your own information, type **Lastname_Firstname_ 1D_Benefits_Events** and then press Enter. In the lower right corner of your screen, click the **Create** button. If necessary, click Enable Content.

b. Click in the first empty **Title** field, type **Medical Plan** and then press Tab. In the **Start Time** field, type **5/2/16 8a** and then press Tab.

c. In the **End Time** field, type **5/2/16 1p** and then press Tab. In the **Description** field, type **Health Benefits** and then press Tab. In the **Location** field, type **Jefferson Campus** and then press Tab three times to move to the **Title** field in the new record row.

d. Directly above the field names row, click **New Event**, and then using Tab to move from field to field, enter the record shown in **Table 1** by using the single-record form, which is another way to enter records into a table.

e. **Close** the single-record form. Using either the rows on the Multiple Items form or the New Event single-record form, enter the records shown in **Table 2**.

f. **Close** the **Event List** form. On the Ribbon, click the **External Data tab**, and in the **Import & Link group**, click the **Excel** button. In the **Get External Data – Excel Spreadsheet** dialog box, click the **Browse** button. Navigate to your student data files, and then double-click **a01D_Benefits_Events**. Click the second option button—**Append a copy of the records to the table**—and then click **OK**.

g. Click **Next**, click **Finish**, and then **Close** the dialog box. **Open** the **Navigation Pane**, and then double-click **Event List** to open the form that displays data stored in the Events table—11 total records display.

2 At the top of the **Navigation Pane**, click the **Navigation arrow**. In the list, under **Navigate To Category**, click **Tables and Related Views**.

a. In the **Navigation Pane**, point to the **Events** *table*, right-click, and then click **Open** to display the records in the underlying table.

b. In the **Navigation Pane**, double-click the *report* named **Current Events** to view this predesigned report. From the **Navigation Pane**, open the **Events By Week** report to view this predesigned report.

c. **Close** the **Events By Week** report, and then **Close** the remaining three open objects. **Close** the **Navigation Pane**.

3 On the **Create tab**, in the **Tables group**, click the **Table** button.

a. Click the **Click to Add arrow**, click **Text**, type **Campus/Location** and then press Enter. In the third column, click **Text**, type **Room** and then press Enter. In the fourth column, click **Text**, type **Seats** and then press Enter. In the fifth column, click **Text**, type **Room Arrangement** and then press Enter. In the sixth column, click **Text**, type **Equipment** and then press ↓.

b. Right-click the **ID** field name, and then click **Rename Field**. Type **Room ID** and then press Enter. On the **Fields tab**, in the **Formatting group**, click the **Data Type arrow**, and then click **Text**.

c. In the new record row, click in the **Room ID** field, type **CAP-01** and then press Tab. In the **Campus/Location** field, type **Capital Campus** and then press Tab. In the **Room** field, type **C14** and then press Tab. In the **Seats** field, type **150** and then press Tab. In the **Room Arrangement** field, type **Theater** and then press Tab. In the **Equipment** field, type **Computer Projector, Surround Sound, & Microphones** and then press Tab to move to the new record row.

Table 1

Title	Location	Start Time	End Time	Description	
Eye Care Plan	Washington Campus	5/2/16 2p	5/2/16 4p	Health Benefits	- - - ▸ (Return to Step 1-e)

Table 2

ID	Title	Start Time	End Time	Description	Location	
3	Prescription Plan	5/3/16 8a	5/3/16 10a	Health Benefits	Capital Campus	
4	Pension Plan	5/3/16 2p	5/3/16 4p	Retirement Benefits	Central Campus	- - - ▸ (Return to Step 1-f)

(Project 1D Benefits Events continues on the next page)

Skills Review | Project **1D** Benefits Events (continued)

d. In the **Views group**, click the **View** button to switch to **Design** view. In the **Save As** dialog box, save the table as **Lastname Firstname 1D Event Locations** and then click **OK**. Notice that the **Room ID** field is the **Primary Key**.

e. On the **Design tab**, in the **Views group**, click the **View** button to switch to **Datasheet** view. Enter the records in the table as shown in **Table 3**.

f. To the left of the **Room ID** field name, click the **Select All** button to select all of the columns. On the **Home tab**, in the **Records group**, click the **More** button. In the **Column Size** dialog box, click **Best Fit**.

g. Click in any record to cancel the selection of the columns, and then **Save** the table. **Open** the **Navigation Pane**, and then widen the pane to view the full names of all objects.

4 **Open** the **All Events** report, and then **Close** the **Navigation Pane**. In the lower right corner, click the **Layout View** button. At the top of the report, click the text *All Events* to surround the title with a colored border, and then click to the left of the letter *A* to place the insertion point there. Using your own name, type **Lastname Firstname** and then press Spacebar and Enter. **Save** the report.

a. Display **Backstage** view, click **Print**, and then click **Print Preview**. Notice that the entire report will print on one page in portrait orientation. Create a paper or electronic printout if instructed to do so, and then click **Close Print Preview**. **Close** the **All Events** report.

b. With the **1D Event Locations** table open in **Datasheet** view, display **Backstage** view, click **Print**, and then click **Print Preview**. On the **Print Preview tab**, in the **Page Layout group**, click the **Landscape** button, and then notice that the entire table will print on one page.

c. Create a paper or electronic printout if instructed to do so, and then click **Close Print Preview**. **Close** the **1D Event Locations** table.

d. **Open** the **Navigation Pane**. Display **Backstage** view, click **Close Database**, and then click **Exit**. As directed by your instructor, submit your database and the two paper or electronic printouts—one report and one table—that are the results of this project.

Table 3

Room ID	Campus/Location	Room	Seats	Room Arrangement	Equipment
CEN-01	Central Campus	H212	35	Lecture/Classroom	Computer Projector, 3 screens
JEFF-01	Jefferson Campus	J520	50	Lecture/Classroom	Smart Board
WASH-01	Washington Campus	A150	40	U-shaped	White Board & Computer Projector
CEN-02	Central Campus	C14	25	Computer Lab	25 Computers & Projector

(Return to Step 3-f)

End **You have completed Project 1D**

Content-Based Assessments

- ◼ Identify Good Database Design
- ◼ Create a Table and Define Fields in a New Database
- ◼ Change the Structure of Tables and Add a Second Table
- ◼ Create and Use a Query, Form, and Report
- ◼ Save and Close a Database

Mastering Access | Project **1E** Kiosk Inventory

In the following Mastering Access project, you will create a database to track information about the inventory of items for sale in the kiosk located on the quad at the Central Campus of Capital Cities Community College. Your completed database objects will look similar to those in Figure 1.51.

Project Files

For Project 1E, you will need the following files:

New blank Access database
a01E_Inventory (Excel workbook)
a01E_Inventory_Storage (Excel workbook)

You will save your database as:

Lastname_Firstname_1E_Inventory

Project Results

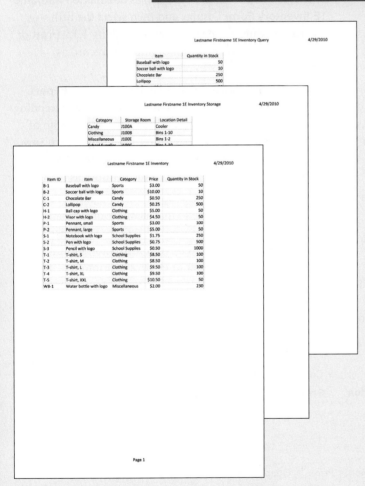

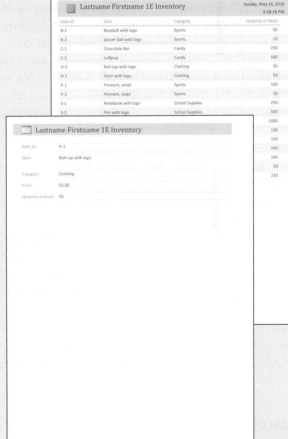

Figure 1.51

(Project 1E Kiosk Inventory continues on the next page)

Content-Based Assessments

Mastering Access | Project **1E** Kiosk Inventory (continued)

1 **Start** Access. Create a new **Blank database** in your **Access Chapter 1** folder. Name the database **Lastname_Firstname_1E_Inventory** and then **Close** the **Navigation Pane**. Create additional fields as shown in **Table 1**.

2 Change the **Data Type** of the **ID** field to **Text**, rename the field to **Item ID** and then enter the records as shown in **Table 2**.

3 **Save** the table as **Lastname Firstname 1E Inventory** and then **Close** the table. From your student data files, **Import** and then **Append** the **a01E_Inventory** Excel file to the **1E Inventory** table. Then, from the **Navigation Pane**, open your **1E Inventory** table—17 records display. Widen and then **Close** the **Navigation Pane**.

4 In **Design** view, delete the **Storage Location** field. Click in the **Category** field, change the **Field Size** to **25** and in the **Description** box, type **Enter the category of the Item** Click in the **Item ID** field, and then change the **Field Size** to **10 Save** the changes to the design of your table, click **Yes**, and then switch to **Datasheet** view. Apply **Best Fit** to all of the fields in the table, **Save** the table, and then display the table in **Print Preview**—one page results. Create a paper or electronic printout as directed by your instructor. **Close** the table.

5 From your student data files, **Import** the **a01E_Inventory_Storage** Excel file into the database as a new table; use the first row as the column headings and the **Category** field as the primary key. As the last step in the Wizard, name the table **Lastname Firstname 1E Inventory Storage** and then **Open** the **Navigation Pane**. **Open** your **1E Inventory Storage** table, and then **Close** the **Navigation Pane**. Display the new table in **Design** view, click in the **Location Detail** field, change the **Field Size** to

30 and then as the **Description**, type **Enter room and bin numbers or alternate location of inventory item.** In **Datasheet** view, apply **Best Fit** to all of the fields, **Save** the table, and then display the table in **Print Preview**. Create a paper or electronic printout as directed—one page results. **Close** the table.

6 **Create**, by using the **Query Wizard**, a **Simple Query** based on your **1E Inventory** table. Include only the fields that will answer the question *For all Items, what is the Quantity in Stock?* **Save** the query with the default name. Create a paper or electronic printout as directed and then **Close** the query.

7 Display the **1E Inventory** table, and then **Create** a **Form** for this table. **Save** the form as **Lastname Firstname 1E Inventory Form** Display and then select the fifth record. By using the instructions in Activity 1.15, print or create an electronic printout of only this record as directed. **Close** the form object.

8 With the **1E Inventory** table open, **Create** a **Report**. **Delete** the **Price** field, and then sort the records in **Ascending** order by the **Item ID** field. Scroll down to the bottom of the report and delete the page number—**Page 1 of 1**. **Save** the report as **Lastname Firstname 1E Inventory Report** and then create a paper or electronic printout as directed.

9 **Close All** open objects. **Open** the **Navigation Pane**. If necessary, widen the pane so that all of the object names display fully. In **Backstage** view, click **Close Database** and then click **Exit**. As directed by your instructor, submit your database and the five paper or electronic printouts—two tables, one query, one form, and one report—that are the results of this project.

Table 1

Data Type		Text	Text	Text	Currency	Number	
Field Name	ID	Item	Category	Storage Location	Price	Quantity in Stock	- - - ▶ (Return to Step 2)

Table 2

Item ID	Item	Category	Storage Location	Price	Quantity in Stock	
C-1	Chocolate Bar	Candy	J100A	.5	250	
C-2	Lollipop	Candy	J100A	.25	500	
T-1	T-shirt, S	Clothing	J100B	8.5	100	- - - ▶ (Return to Step 3)

End You have completed Project 1E ——————

Content-Based Assessments

6 Create a Database Using a Template

7 Organize Objects in the Navigation Pane

8 Create a New Table in a Database Created with a Template

9 Print a Report and a Table in a Database Created with a Template

Mastering Access | Project **1F** Recruiting Events

In the following Mastering Access project, you will create a database to store information about the recruiting events that are scheduled to attract new students to Capital Cities Community College. Your completed report and table will look similar to those in Figure 1.52.

Project Files

For Project 1F, you will need the following files:

New Access database using the Events template
a01F_Recruiting_Events (Excel workbook)

You will save your database as:

Lastname_Firstname_1F_Recruiting_Events

Project Results

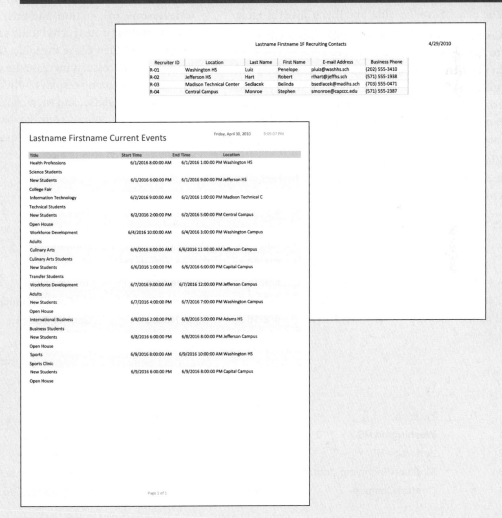

Figure 1.52

(Project 1F Recruiting Events continues on the next page)

Mastering Access | Project **1F** Recruiting Events (continued)

1 **Start** Access, click **Sample templates**, and then click **Events**. In your **Access Chapter 1** folder, save the database as **Lastname_Firstname_1F_Recruiting_Events** If necessary, enable the content.

2 In the Multiple Items form or the New Event single-record form, enter the records shown in **Table 1** into the Events table.

3 **Close** the **Event List** form, and then click the **External Data tab**. **Import** and **Append** the **Excel** file **a01F_Recruiting_Events** to the **Events** table. **Open** the **Navigation Pane**, organize the objects by **Tables and Related Views**, and then **Open** your **Events** table to view 13 records. **Close** the **Navigation Pane**. Apply **Best Fit** to all of the fields, **Save** the table, and then **Close** the table.

4 **Create** a new table using the **Table** button. Click the **Click to Add arrow**, click **Text**, type **Location** and then press Enter. In the third column, click **Text**, type **Last Name** and then press Enter. In the fourth column, click **Text**, type **First Name** and then press Enter. In the fifth column, click **Text**, type **E-mail Address** and then press Enter. In the sixth column, click **Text**, type **Business Phone** and then press ↓.

5 Right-click the **ID** field name, and then **Rename** the field to **Recruiter ID** Change the **Data Type** to **Text**, and then enter the records as shown in **Table 2**.

6 Apply **Best Fit** to all of the columns. **Save** the table as **Lastname Firstname 1F Recruiting Contacts** and then **Close** the table.

7 From the **Navigation Pane**, open the **Current Events Report**. In the lower right corner of the status bar, click the **Layout View** button, click the title *Current Events*, and then click to position your insertion point to the left of *C*. Type your own name in the format **Lastname Firstname** Display the report in **Print Preview**, and then create a paper or electronic printout if instructed to do so. **Close** the **Print Preview**. **Close** the report and save the changes.

8 From the **Navigation Pane**, open your **1F Recruiting Contacts** table. Display the table in **Print Preview**, change to **Landscape** orientation, and then create a paper or electronic printout if instructed to do so. **Close** the **Print Preview**, and then **Close** the table. **Open** the **Navigation Pane** and, if necessary, increase the width of the pane so that your table name displays fully. From **Backstage** view, click **Close Database**, and then click **Exit**. As directed by your instructor, submit your database and the two paper or electronic printouts—one report and one table—that are the results of this project.

Table 1

ID	Title	Start Time	End Time	Description	Location
1	Health Professions	6/1/16 8a	6/1/16 1p	Science Students	Washington HS
2	New Students	6/1/16 6p	6/1/16 9p	College Fair	Jefferson HS
3	Information Technology	6/2/16 9a	6/2/16 1p	Technical Students	Madison Technical Center
4	New Students	6/2/16 2p	6/2/16 5p	Open House	Central Campus

(Return to Step 3)

Table 2

Recruiter ID	Location	Last Name	First Name	E-mail Address	Business Phone
R-01	Washington HS	Luiz	Penelope	pluiz@washhs.sch	(202) 555-3410
R-02	Jefferson HS	Hart	Robert	rlhart@jeffhs.sch	(571) 555-1938
R-03	Madison Technical Center	Sedlacek	Belinda	bsedlacek@madihs.sch	(703) 555-0471
R-04	Central Campus	Monroe	Stephen	smonroe@capccc.edu	(571) 555-2387

(Return to Step 6)

End **You have completed Project 1F**

Content-Based Assessments

Apply 1A and 1B skills from these Objectives:

1. Identify Good Database Design
2. Create a Table and Define Fields in a New Database
3. Change the Structure of Tables and Add a Second Table
4. Create and Use a Query, Form, and Report
5. Save and Close a Database
6. Create a Database Using a Template
7. Organize Objects in the Navigation Pane
8. Create a New Table in a Database Created with a Template
9. Print a Report and a Table in a Database Created with a Template

Mastering Access | Project 1G Campus Expansion

In the following Mastering Access project, you will create one database to store information about the campus expansion for Capital Cities Community College and a second database to store information about the public events related to the expansion projects. Your completed database objects will look similar to Figure 1.53.

Project Files

For Project 1G, you will need the following files:

New blank Access database
a01G_Projects (Excel workbook)
a01G_Contractors (Excel workbook)
New Access database using the Events template

You will save your databases as:

Lastname_Firstname_1G_Campus_Expansion
Lastname_Firstname_1G_Public_Events

Project Results

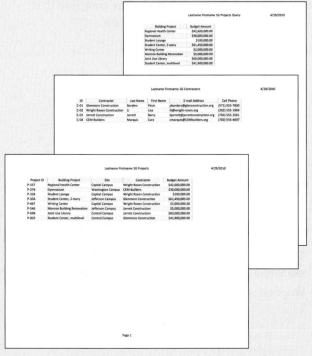

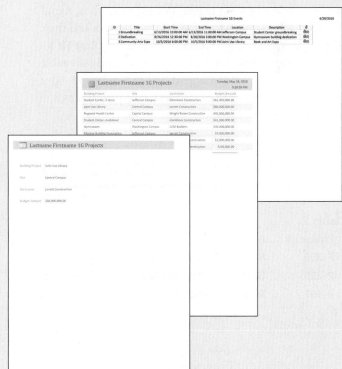

Figure 1.53

(Project 1G Campus Expansion continues on the next page)

(Project 1G Campus Expansion continues on the next page)

Access | Chapter 1

Content-Based Assessments

1 **Start** Access. Create a new **Blank database** in your **Access Chapter 1** folder. Name the database **Lastname_ Firstname_1G_Campus_Expansion** and then **Close** the **Navigation Pane**. Create the additional fields shown in **Table 1**.

2 Change the **ID** field name to **Project ID** and change its **Data Type** to **Text**. Add the three records shown in **Table 2**.

3 **Save** the table as **Lastname Firstname 1G Projects** and then **Close** the table. **Import** and **Append** the **Excel** file **a01G_Projects** to the **1G Projects** table. Then, from the **Navigation Pane**, open your **1G Projects** table—8 total records display. **Close** the **Navigation Pane**.

4 In **Design** view, click in the **Project ID** field, change the **Field Size** to **5** and as the **Description** type **Enter Project ID using the format P-###** Switch to **Datasheet** view, and save by clicking **Yes** two times. Apply **Best Fit** to all of the fields in the table, **Save** the table, and then display it in **Print Preview**. Set the orientation to **Landscape**—one page results. Create a paper or electronic printout as directed by your instructor, and then **Close** the table.

5 From the **External Data tab**, import the **Excel** file **a01G_Contractors** into the database as a new table; use the first row as the column headings and set the **ID** field as the primary key. In the final Wizard dialog box, name the table **Lastname Firstname 1G Contractors** and then **Open** the new table in **Datasheet** view. Apply **Best Fit** to all of the fields, **Save** the table, and then display the table in **Print Preview**. Set the orientation to **Landscape**—one page results. Create a paper or electronic printout as directed, and then **Close** the table.

6 **Create**, by using the **Query Wizard**, a **Simple Query** based on your **1G Projects** table. Include only the appropriate fields to answer the question *For every Building Project, what is the Budget Amount?* Create the query and save it with the default name. Create a paper or electronic printout as directed, and then **Close** the query.

7 Open your **1G Projects** table, and then **Create** a **Form** for this table. Save the form as **Lastname Firstname 1G Projects Form** Display and select the seventh record, and then by using the instructions in Activity 1.15, print or create an electronic printout of this record as directed. **Close** the form object, saving changes to it.

8 With the **1G Projects** table open and active, **Create** a **Report**. **Delete** the **Project ID** field. Sort the records in **Descending** order by the **Budget Amount** field—Access automatically totals this field. Adjust the field widths on the left and right as necessary so that the fields display within the margins of the report. At the bottom of the report, delete the **page number**, and then delete the total that displays in the **Budget Amount** column. **Save** the report as **Lastname Firstname 1G Projects Report** and then create a paper or electronic printout as directed.

9 **Close All** open objects. If necessary, **Open** the **Navigation Pane** and widen the pane so that all object names display fully. Display **Backstage** view, and then click **Close Database**. Do *not* exit Access.

Table 1

Data Type		Text	Text	Text	Currency	
Field Name	ID	Building Project	Site	Contractor	Budget Amount	- - - ▶ (Return to Step 2)

Table 2

Project ID	Building Project	Site	Contractor	Budget Amount
P-356	Student Center, 2-story	Jefferson Campus	Glenmore Construction	61450000
P-823	Student Center, multilevel	Central Campus	Glenmore Construction	41900000
P-157	Regional Health Center	Capital Campus	Wright Rosen Construction	42600000

(Return to Step 3)

(Project 1G Campus Expansion continues on the next page)

Content-Based Assessments

10 From **Sample templates**, create a new database using the **Events** template. **Save** the database in your **Access Chapter 1** folder, and as the file name, type **Lastname_Firstname_1G_Public_Events** If necessary, enable the content. Enter the records in **Table 3** by using the displayed Multiple Items Event List form or the single-record form, which is available by clicking New Event above the field names row.

11 **Close** the **Event List** form. Open the **Navigation Pane**, and then by using the **Navigation Pane arrow**, arrange the database objects by **Tables and Related Views**. Point to the **Events: Table** object, right-click, click **Rename**, and then using your own name, type **Lastname**

Firstname 1G Events Press Enter and then widen the Navigation Pane if necessary.

12 **Open** the 1G Events table, **Close** the **Navigation Pane**, and then apply **Best Fit** to all of the columns. **Save** the table, display it in **Print Preview**, change the orientation to **Landscape**, set the **Margins** to **Normal**, and then create a paper or electronic printout as directed. **Close** all open objects. **Open** the **Navigation Pane**, display **Backstage** view, click **Close Database**, and then click **Exit**. As directed by your instructor, submit your database and the six paper or electronic printouts—three tables, one query, one form, and one report—that are the results of this project.

Table 3

ID	Title	Start Time	End Time	Description	Location
1	Groundbreaking	6/13/16 10a	6/13/16 11a	Student Center groundbreaking	Jefferson Campus
2	Dedication	8/26/16 12:30p	8/26/16 2p	Gymnasium building dedication	Washington Campus
3	Community Arts Expo	10/5/16 6p	10/5/16 9p	Book and Art Expo	Joint Use Library

(Return to Step 11)

End You have completed Project 1G

Content-Based Assessments

GO! Fix It | Project **1H** Scholarships

Project Files

For Project 1H, you will need the following file:

a01H_Scholarships

You will save your database as:

Lastname_Firstname_1H_Scholarships

In this project, you will make corrections to and update an Access database that will store information about scholarships awarded to students. Start Access. In Backstage view, click Open, navigate to your student files, and then open the file a01H_Scholarships. With the database open, display Backstage view. Click Save Database As, and in the Save As dialog box, navigate to your Access Chapter 1 folder, name the file **Lastname_Firstname_1H_Scholarships** and then click Save. In the message bar, click the Enable Content button.

To complete the project you must find and correct errors in field names, data types, data design, and column widths. You should know:

- The table name should be renamed **Lastname Firstname 1H Scholarships**
- In the table, all of the data in the fields and the field names should display fully.
- Three fields in the table have incorrect data types.
- The field that represents the unique value for each record should be set as the primary key.
- In one of the records, there is a data entry error involving an athlete's name; after correcting the entry, be sure to click in another record so that the record you edit is saved.
- When open, the Navigation Pane should fully display the table name.
- A query should be created for the 1H Scholarships table that answers the question *What is the Amount, Sport, First Name, and Last Name of every athlete receiving a scholarship?* Apply Best Fit to the query results.
- Using the table, a report should be created that includes the Amount, Sport, Award Date, and the last and first name of the athlete. Sort the report in descending order by the amount and then adjust the column widths so that the fields display within the margins of the report. At the bottom of the report, delete the total for the Amount field, and then delete the page number and save with the default name.

If directed to do so, create a paper or electronic printout of the table, the query, and the report. The table should use Landscape orientation, and the query and report should use Portrait orientation. Be sure that the report prints on one page.

End You have completed Project 1H ⎯⎯⎯⎯⎯⎯⎯⎯⎯⎯

Apply a combination of the 1A and 1B skills.

GO! Make It | Project 1I Theater Events

Project Files

For Project 1I, you will need the following file:

New Access database using the Events template

You will save your database as:

Lastname_Firstname_1I_Theater_Events

Using the Events database template, create the table of theater events shown in Figure 1.54 that the Performing Arts department will present or host for April. Name the database **Lastname_ Firstname_1I_Theater_Events** Arrange the Navigation Pane by Tables and Related Views, rename the Events table **Lastname Firstname 1I Theater Events** and then widen the Navigation Pane so that all object names display fully. Open the table, apply Best Fit to all the columns, save the table, and then create a paper or electronic printout of the table as directed by your instructor. Use Landscape orientation and Normal margins.

Project Results

Figure 1.54

Lastname Firstname 1I Theater Events   4/29/2010

ID	Title	Start Time	End Time	Location	Description	🔗
1	Symphony Orchestra Concert	4/2/2016 7:30:00 PM	4/2/2016 10:00:00 PM	Jefferson Campus	Opera soprano Barbara Botillini	🔗(0)
2	The Big Band Concert	4/4/2016 7:30:00 PM	4/4/2016 9:00:00 PM	Capital Campus	The Ruth Mystic Big Band Concert	🔗(0)
3	Chaos in the House	4/6/2016 3:00:00 PM	4/6/2016 5:00:00 PM	Central Campus	Gospel Show	🔗(0)
4	Tom Sawyer	4/7/2016 7:00:00 PM	4/7/2016 10:00:00 PM	Washington Campus	CapCCC Players	🔗(0)
5	Tom Sawyer	4/8/2016 3:00:00 PM	4/8/2016 6:00:00 PM	Washington Campus	CapCCC Players	🔗(0)
6	Virginia Arts Festival	4/16/2016 8:00:00 PM	4/16/2016 10:00:00 PM	Jefferson Campus	Anika Shankar	🔗(0)
7	Virginia Arts Festival	4/17/2016 7:00:00 PM	4/17/2016 9:00:00 PM	Central Campus	Music from the Crooked Elbow	🔗(0)
8	College Awards Ceremony	4/22/2016 1:00:00 PM	4/22/2016 4:00:00 PM	Washington Campus	CapCCC Faculty and Staff Awards	🔗(0)
9	Virginia Arts Festival	4/23/2016 7:30:00 PM	4/23/2016 10:00:00 PM	Capital Campus	Russian Folk Dance Spectacular	🔗(0)
10	Music in Motion Dance	4/29/2016 1:00:00 PM	4/29/2016 3:00:00 PM	Central Campus	Dancing to Modern Music	🔗(0)

Page 1

End You have completed Project 1I

Access | Chapter 1

Content-Based Assessments

GO! Solve It | Project **1J** Student Activities

Project Files

For Project 1J, you will need the following files:

New Access database using the Events template
a01J_Student_Activities (Word document)

You will save your database as:

Lastname_Firstname_1J_Student_Activities

Create a new database from the Events database template and name the database **Lastname_Firstname_1J_Student_Activities** Using the data in the a01J_Student_Activities Word document, enter the data into the Multiple Items form. Each event begins at 7 p.m. and ends at 9 p.m. After entering the records, close the form, arrange the Navigation Pane by Tables and Related Views, rename the table that stores the records as **Lastname Firstname 1J Activities** and then widen the Navigation Pane so that all object names display fully. Open the table, apply Best Fit to the columns, and then save the table. Display the table in Print Preview, and then use the proper commands to be sure that the table prints on one page with the table name at the top of the page. Print the table or submit electronically as directed.

Performance Elements		**Performance Level**		
		Exemplary: You consistently applied the relevant skills	**Proficient:** You sometimes, but not always, applied the relevant skills	**Developing:** You rarely or never applied the relevant skills
	Create database and enter data	Database was created using the correct template and correct name. Data entered correctly.	Some but not all of the data was entered correctly.	Most of the data was entered incorrectly.
	Rename table and format table	Table named correctly and Best Fit applied to all columns.	Table named incorrectly and/or Best Fit not properly applied.	Incorrect table name and inadequate formatting applied to all columns.
	Create table printout	Printout displays on one page in Landscape orientation and the table name displays at the top.	The printout displays on two pages or the table name does not display at the top.	The printout displays on two pages and the table name does not display at the top of the page.

End **You have completed Project 1J** ——————————————

Apply a combination of the 1A and 1B skills.

GO! Solve It | Project 1K Media Contacts

Project Files

For Project 1K, you will need the following files:

New blank Access database
a01K_Media_Contacts (Excel workbook)

You will save your database as:

Lastname_Firstname_1K_Media_Contacts

Create a new blank database and name the database **Lastname_Firstname_1K_Media_Contacts** Close the default Table1. Create a table by importing the a01K_Media_Contacts Excel workbook, use the first row as the column headings, and use Media ID as the Primary Key. Name the table **Lastname Firstname 1K Media Contacts** Modify the table design by creating separate fields for the Contact's first name and last name, and then adjust the data accordingly. Apply Best Fit to the columns, and then save the table. Display the table in Print Preview, and then use the Page Layout commands to display the table on one page, being sure the table name prints at the top of the page. Print the table or submit electronically as directed.

Create a simple query that answers the following question: *What are the Publication name, first name, last name, and E-mail address for all of the media contacts?* Accept the default name, apply Best Fit to all of the columns, and then create a paper or electronic printout on one page as directed.

Create a report and delete the Media ID column. Adjust the widths of the remaining fields so that all of the data displays within the margins of the report. Sort the report in ascending order by the Publication field. In Layout View, select the report title, and then on the Format tab, in the Font group, change the font of the title of the report to 14. At the bottom of the report, delete the page number. Save the report as **Lastname Firstname 1K Media Contacts Report** and then create a paper or electronic printout as directed. Arrange the Navigation Pane by Tables and Related Views, and then widen the Navigation Pane so that all object names display fully.

Performance Elements	Performance Level: Exemplary: You consistently applied the relevant skills	Proficient: You sometimes, but not always, applied the relevant skills	Developing: You rarely or never applied the relevant skills
Create database, import data to create a table, and then modify the table design	Table created by importing from an Excel workbook, fields correctly modified, and primary key field identified.	Table created by importing from an Excel workbook, but fields are incorrect, or primary key field is incorrect.	Table created by importing from an Excel workbook, but both fields and primary key are incorrect.
Create query	Query created, named correctly, answers the question, formatted correctly.	Query created, but does not completely answer the question or formatted incorrectly.	Query does not answer the question and also includes errors in formatting.
Create report	Report created, Media ID field deleted, field sizes adjusted, sorted by Publication, correctly named, and formatted.	Report created with some errors in fields, report name, sorting, or formatting.	Report created with numerous errors in fields, report name, sorting, or formatting.

End You have completed Project 1K

Outcomes-Based Assessments

Rubric

The following outcomes-based assessments are *open-ended assessments*. That is, there is no specific correct result; your result will depend on your approach to the information provided. Make *Professional Quality* your goal. Use the following scoring rubric to guide you in *how* to approach the problem, and then to evaluate *how well* your approach solves the problem.

The *criteria*—Software Mastery, Content, Format and Layout, and Process—represent the knowledge and skills you have gained that you can apply to solving the problem. The *levels of performance*—Professional Quality, Approaching Professional Quality, or Needs Quality Improvements—help you and your instructor evaluate your result.

	Your completed project is of Professional Quality if you:	Your completed project is Approaching Professional Quality if you:	Your completed project Needs Quality Improvements if you:
1-Software Mastery	Choose and apply the most appropriate skills, tools, and features and identify efficient methods to solve the problem.	Choose and apply some appropriate skills, tools, and features, but not in the most efficient manner.	Choose inappropriate skills, tools, or features, or are inefficient in solving the problem.
2-Content	Construct a solution that is clear and well organized, contains content that is accurate, appropriate to the audience and purpose, and is complete. Provide a solution that contains no errors in spelling, grammar, or style.	Construct a solution in which some components are unclear, poorly organized, inconsistent, or incomplete. Misjudge the needs of the audience. Have some errors in spelling, grammar, or style, but the errors do not detract from comprehension.	Construct a solution that is unclear, incomplete, or poorly organized; contains some inaccurate or inappropriate content; and contains many errors in spelling, grammar, or style. Do not solve the problem.
3-Format and Layout	Format and arrange all elements to communicate information and ideas, clarify function, illustrate relationships, and indicate relative importance.	Apply appropriate format and layout features to some elements, but not others. Overuse features, causing minor distraction.	Apply format and layout that does not communicate information or ideas clearly. Do not use format and layout features to clarify function, illustrate relationships, or indicate relative importance. Use available features excessively, causing distraction.
4-Process	Use an organized approach that integrates planning, development, self-assessment, revision, and reflection.	Demonstrate an organized approach in some areas, but not others; or, use an insufficient process of organization throughout.	Do not use an organized approach to solve the problem.

Outcomes-Based Assessments

GO! Think | Project 1L Student Clubs

Project Files

For Project 1L, you will need the following files:

> New blank Access database
> a01L_Clubs (Word file)
> a01L_Student_Clubs (Excel file)
> a01L_Club_Presidents (Excel file)

You will save your database as:

> Lastname_Firstname_1L_Student_Clubs

Kirsten McCarty, Vice President of Student Services, needs a database that tracks information about student clubs. The database should contain two tables, one for club information and one for contact information for the club presidents.

Create a new blank database and name it **Lastname_Firstname_1L_Student_Clubs** Using the information provided in the a01L_Clubs Word document, create the first table with two records to store information about the clubs. Then import 23 records from the a01L_Student_Clubs Excel file. Create a second table by importing 25 records from the a0lL_Club_Presidents Excel file. Name the tables appropriately and include your name. Be sure the data types are correct and the records are entered correctly. Apply Best Fit to all of the columns.

Create a simple query based on the Clubs table that answers the following question: *What are the Club Name, Meeting Day, Meeting Time, and Room ID for all of the clubs?* Based on the Clubs table, create a form. Create a report based on the Presidents of the clubs that lists the Last Name (in ascending order), First Name, and Phone number of every president. Print the two tables, the seventh record in Form view, the query, and the report being sure that each object prints on one page, or submit electronically as directed. Group objects on the Navigation Pane by Tables and Related Views. On the Navigation Pane, be sure that all object names display fully.

 You have completed Project 1L ————————————————

GO! Think | Project 1M Faculty Training

Project Files

For Project 1M, you will need the following file:

> New Access database using the Events template
> a01M_Faculty_Training (Word file)

You will save your database as:

> Lastname_Firstname_1M_Faculty_Training

Use the information provided in the a01M_Faculty_Training Word file to create a database using the Events database template. Name the database **Lastname_Firstname_1M_Faculty_Training** Use the information in the Word file to enter the records. Training times begin at 11:30 a.m. and end at 1 p.m. Arrange the Navigation Pane by Tables and Related Views, and rename the Events table appropriately to include your name. Display the All Events report in Layout View and insert your Lastname Firstname in front of the report title *All Events*. Print the table and the All Events report or submit electronically as directed.

End You have completed Project 1M ————————————————

Access | Chapter 1

Outcomes-Based Assessments

You and GO! | Project **1N** Personal Contacts

Project Files

For Project 1N, you will need the following file:

New blank Access database

You will save your database as:

Lastname_Firstname_1N_Personal_Contacts

Create a database that stores information about your personal contacts, such as friends and family members. Name the database **Lastname_Firstname_1N_Personal_Contacts** Include a field for a birthday. Enter at least 10 records in the table, and name the table **Lastname Firstname 1N Personal Contacts** Create a query that includes at least three of the fields in the table in the result; for example, a list of names and phone numbers. Create a report that includes the name and address for each contact. Print the table, query, and report, making sure that the data for each object prints on one page, or submit electronically as directed.

End **You have completed Project 1N** _____

Getting Started with Microsoft Office PowerPoint

OUTCOMES

At the end of this chapter you will be able to:

PROJECT 1A
Create a new PowerPoint presentation.

PROJECT 1B
Edit and format a PowerPoint presentation.

OBJECTIVES

Mastering these objectives will enable you to:

1. Create a New Presentation (p. 239)
2. Edit a Presentation in Normal View (p. 243)
3. Add Pictures to a Presentation (p. 250)
4. Print and View a Presentation (p. 253)

5. Edit an Existing Presentation (p. 259)
6. Format a Presentation (p. 263)
7. Use Slide Sorter View (p. 266)
8. Apply Slide Transitions (p. 269)

© Steve Murray / Alamy

In This Chapter

In this chapter you will study presentation skills, which are among the most important skills you will learn. Good presentation skills enhance your communications—written, electronic, and interpersonal. In this technology-enhanced world, communicating ideas clearly and concisely is a critical personal skill. Microsoft PowerPoint 2010 is presentation software with which you create electronic slide presentations. Use PowerPoint to present information to your audience effectively. You can start with a new, blank presentation and add content, pictures, and themes, or you can collaborate with colleagues by inserting slides that have been saved in other presentations.

The projects in this chapter relate to **Lehua Hawaiian Adventures**. Named for the small, crescent-shaped island that is noted for its snorkeling and scuba diving, Lehua Hawaiian Adventures offers exciting but affordable adventure tours. Hiking tours go off the beaten path to amazing remote places on the islands. If you prefer to ride into the heart of Hawaii, try the cycling tours. Lehua Hawaiian Adventures also offers Jeep tours. Whatever you prefer—mountain, sea, volcano—our tour guides are experts in the history, geography, culture, and flora and fauna of Hawaii.

Project 1A Company Overview

myitlab
Project 1A Training

Project Activities

In Activities 1.01 through 1.13, you will create the first four slides of a new presentation that Lehua Hawaiian Adventures tour manager Carl Kawaoka is developing to introduce the tour services that the company offers. Your completed presentation will look similar to Figure 1.1.

Project Files

For Project 1A, you will need the following files:

> New blank PowerPoint presentation
> p01A_Helicopter
> p01A_Beach

You will save your presentation as:

> Lastname_Firstname_1A_LHA_Overview

Project Results

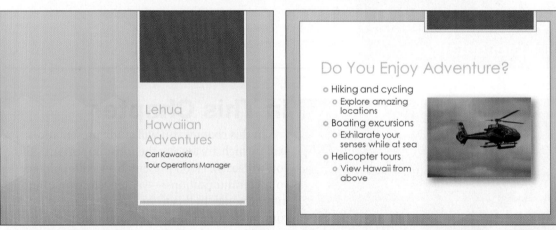

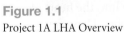

Figure 1.1
Project 1A LHA Overview

Objective 1 | Create a New Presentation

Microsoft PowerPoint 2010 is software with which you can present information to your audience effectively. You can edit and format a blank presentation by adding text, a presentation theme, and pictures.

Activity 1.01 | Identifying Parts of the PowerPoint Window

In this activity, you will start PowerPoint and identify the parts of the PowerPoint window.

1 Start PowerPoint to display a new blank presentation in Normal view, and then compare your screen with Figure 1.2.

Normal view is the primary editing view in PowerPoint where you write and design your presentations. Normal view includes the Notes pane, the Slide pane, and the Slides/Outline pane.

Figure 1.2

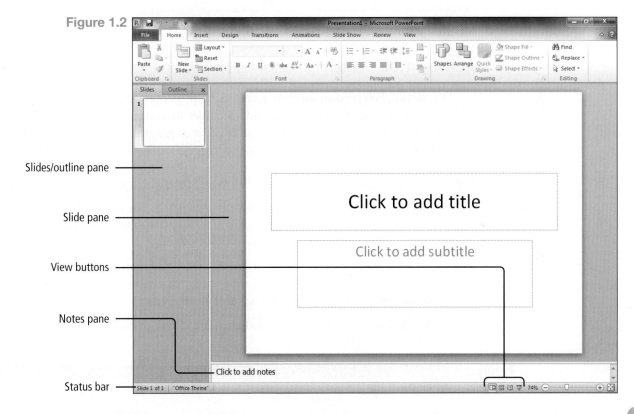

Slides/outline pane —

Slide pane —

View buttons —

Notes pane —

Status bar —

2 Take a moment to study the parts of the PowerPoint window described in the table in Figure 1.3.

PowerPoint | Chapter 1

Microsoft PowerPoint Screen Elements

Screen Element	Description
Notes pane	Displays below the Slide pane and provides space for you to type notes regarding the active slide.
Slide pane	Displays a large image of the active slide.
Slides/Outline pane	Displays either the presentation in the form of miniature images called *thumbnails* (Slides tab) or the presentation outline (Outline tab).
Status bar	Displays, in a horizontal bar at the bottom of the presentation window, the current slide number, number of slides in a presentation, theme, View buttons, Zoom slider, and Fit slide to current window button; you can customize this area to include additional helpful information.
View buttons	Control the look of the presentation window with a set of commands.

Figure 1.3

Activity 1.02 | Entering Presentation Text and Saving a Presentation

On startup, PowerPoint displays a new blank presentation with a single *slide*—a *title slide* in Normal view. A presentation slide—similar to a page in a document—can contain text, pictures, tables, charts, and other multimedia or graphic objects. The title slide is the first slide in a presentation and provides an introduction to the presentation topic.

1 In the **Slide pane**, click in the text *Click to add title*, which is the title *placeholder*.

A placeholder is a box on a slide with dotted or dashed borders that holds title and body text or other content such as charts, tables, and pictures. This slide contains two placeholders, one for the title and one for the subtitle.

2 Type **Lehua Hawaiian Adventures** point to *Lehua*, and then right-click. On the shortcut menu, click **Ignore All** so *Lehua* is not flagged as a spelling error in this presentation. Compare your screen with Figure 1.4.

Recall that a red wavy underline indicates that the underlined word is not in the Microsoft Office dictionary.

Figure 1.4

Red wavy underline no longer displays

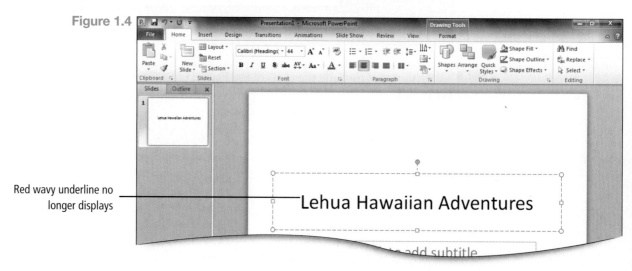

3 Click in the subtitle placeholder, and then type **Carl Kawaoka**

4 Press ⟨Enter⟩ to create a new line in the subtitle placeholder. Type **Tour Manager**

5 Right-click **Kawaoka**, and then on the shortcut menu, click **Ignore All**. Compare your screen with Figure 1.5.

Figure 1.5

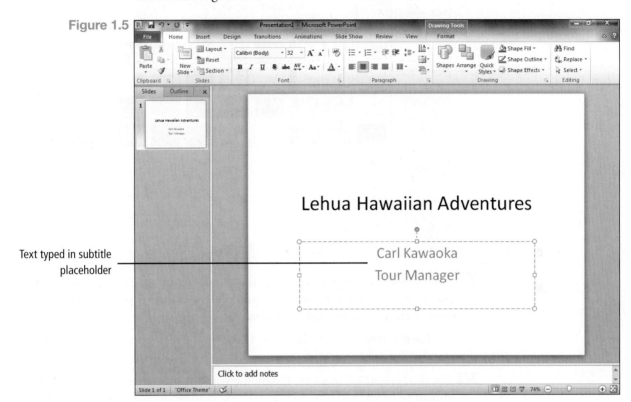

Text typed in subtitle placeholder

6 In the upper left corner of your screen, click the **File tab** to display **Backstage** view, click **Save As**, and then in the **Save As** dialog box, navigate to the location where you will store your files for this chapter. Create a new folder named **PowerPoint Chapter 1** In the **File name** box, replace the existing text with **Lastname_Firstname_1A_LHA_Overview** and then click **Save**.

Activity 1.03 | Applying a Presentation Theme

A *theme* is a set of unified design elements that provides a look for your presentation by applying colors, fonts, and effects.

1 On the Ribbon, click the **Design tab**. In the **Themes group**, click the **More** button ⬇ to display the **Themes** gallery. Compare your screen with Figure 1.6.

Figure 1.6

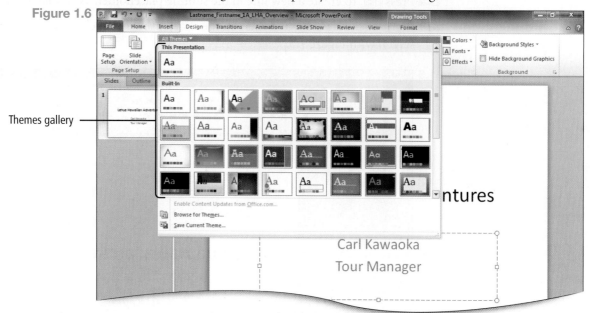

Themes gallery

2 Under **Built-In**, point to several of the themes and notice that a ScreenTip displays the name of each theme and the Live Preview feature displays how each theme would look if applied to your presentation.

> The first theme that displays is the Office theme. Subsequent themes are arranged alphabetically.

3 Use the ScreenTips to locate the theme with the green background—**Austin**—as shown in Figure 1.7.

Figure 1.7

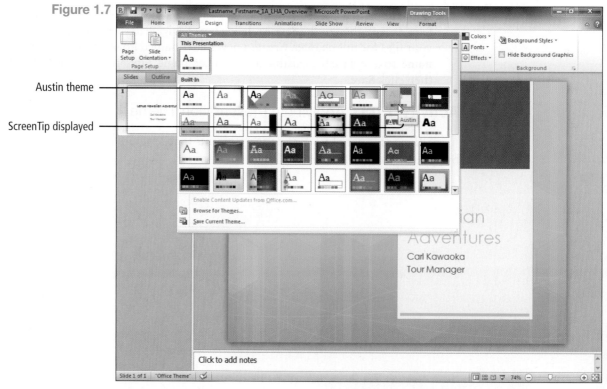

Austin theme

ScreenTip displayed

4 Click the **Austin** theme to change the presentation theme and then **Save** 🖫 your presentation.

Objective 2 | Edit a Presentation in Normal View

Editing is the process of modifying a presentation by adding and deleting slides or by changing the contents of individual slides.

Activity 1.04 | Inserting a New Slide

To insert a new slide in a presentation, display the slide that will precede the slide that you want to insert.

1 On the **Home tab**, in the **Slides group**, point to the **New Slide** button. Compare your screen with Figure 1.8.

The New Slide button is a split button. Recall that clicking the main part of a split button performs a command and clicking the arrow opens a menu, list, or gallery. The upper, main part of the New Slide button, when clicked, inserts a slide without displaying any options. The lower part—the New Slide button arrow—when clicked, displays a gallery of slide *layouts*. A layout is the arrangement of elements, such as title and subtitle text, lists, pictures, tables, charts, shapes, and movies, on a slide.

Figure 1.8

New Slide button

New Slide button arrow

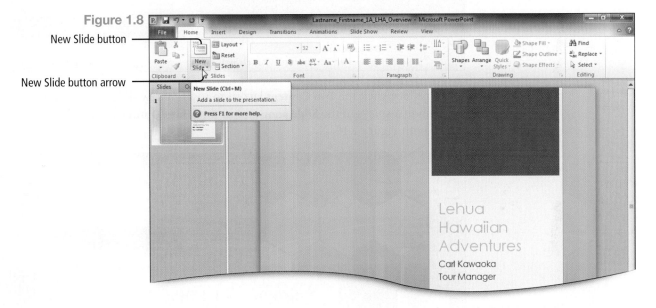

2 In the **Slides group**, click the lower portion of the New Slide button—the **New Slide button arrow**—to display the gallery, and then compare your screen with Figure 1.9.

Figure 1.9

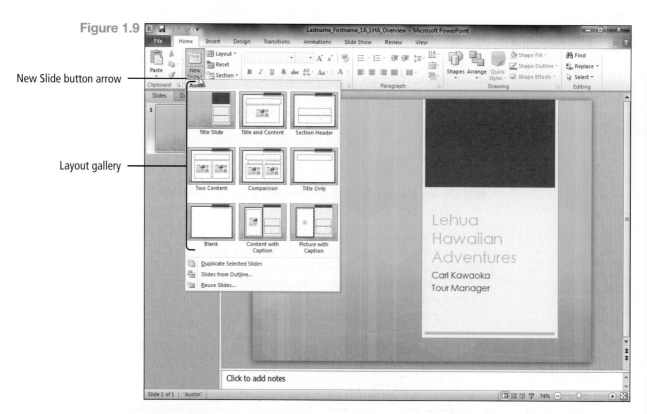

New Slide button arrow —

Layout gallery —

3 In the gallery, click the **Two Content** layout to insert a new slide. Notice that the new blank slide displays in the **Slide pane** and in the **Slides/Outline pane**. Compare your screen with Figure 1.10.

Figure 1.10

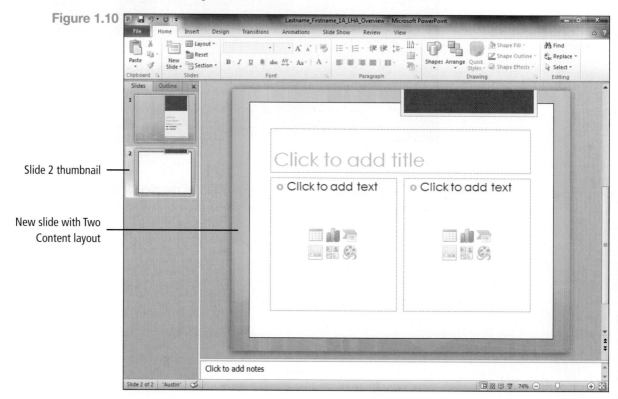

Slide 2 thumbnail —

New slide with Two Content layout —

4 In the **Slide pane**, click the text *Click to add title*, and then type **Do You Enjoy Adventure?**

5 On the left side of the slide, click anywhere in the content placeholder. Type **Hiking and cycling** and then press Enter.

6 Type **Explore locations** and then compare your screen with Figure 1.11.

Figure 1.11

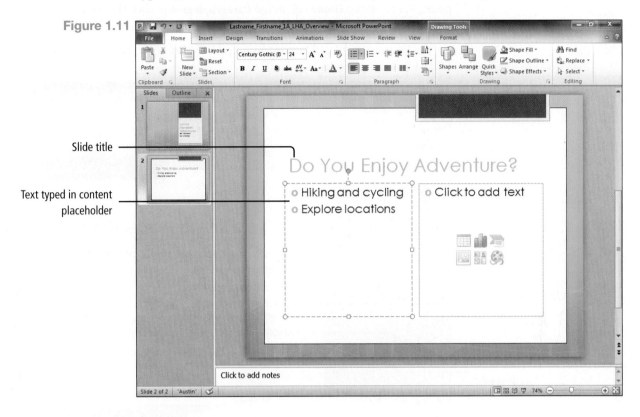

Slide title

Text typed in content placeholder

7 Save your presentation.

Activity 1.05 | Increasing and Decreasing List Levels

Text in a PowerPoint presentation is organized according to *list levels*. List levels, each represented by a bullet symbol, are similar to outline levels. On a slide, list levels are identified by the bullet style, indentation, and the size of the text.

The first level on an individual slide is the title. Increasing the list level of a bullet point increases its indent and results in a smaller text size. Decreasing the list level of a bullet point decreases its indent and results in a larger text size.

1 On **Slide 2**, if necessary, click at the end of the last bullet point after the word *locations*, and then press Enter to insert a new bullet point.

2 Type **Boating excursions** and then press Enter.

3 Press Tab, and then notice that the green bullet is indented. Type **Exhilarate your senses while at sea**

By pressing Tab at the beginning of a bullet point, you can increase the list level and indent the bullet point.

4 Press Enter. Notice that a new bullet point displays at the same level as the previous bullet point. Then, on the **Home tab**, in the **Paragraph group**, click the **Decrease List Level** button ⬛. Type **Helicopter tours** and then compare your screen with Figure 1.12.

> The Decrease List Level button promotes the bullet point. The text size increases and the text is no longer indented.

Figure 1.12
Decrease List Level button —

List level of bullet point increased —

List level of bullet point decreased —

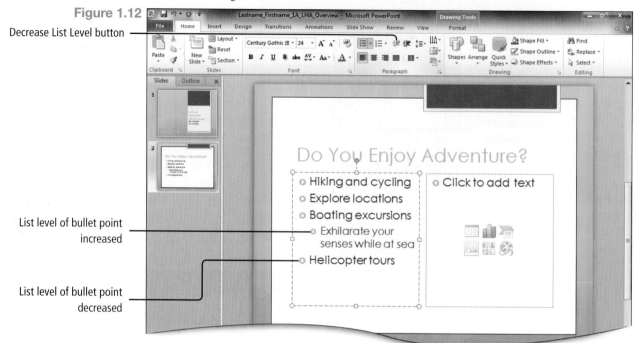

5 Press Enter, and then press Tab to increase the list level. Type **View Hawaii from above**

6 Click anywhere in the second bullet point—*Explore locations*. On the **Home tab**, in the **Paragraph group**, click the **Increase List Level** button ⬛. Compare your screen with Figure 1.13.

> The bullet point is indented and the size of the text decreases.

Figure 1.13
Increase List Level button —

List level of two bullet points increased —

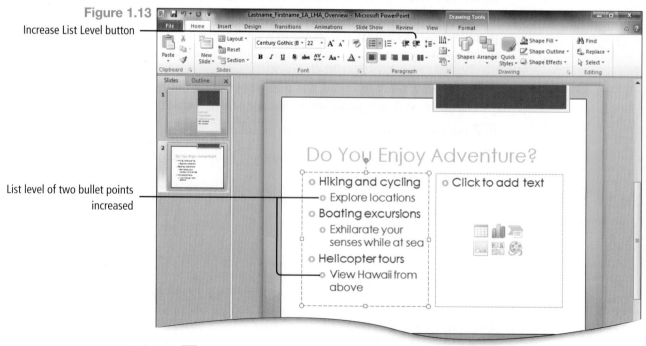

7 Save 💾 your presentation.

Activity 1.06 | Adding Speaker's Notes to a Presentation

Recall that when a presentation is displayed in Normal view, the Notes pane displays below the Slide pane. Use the Notes pane to type speaker's notes that you can print below a picture of each slide. Then, while making your presentation, you can refer to these printouts while making a presentation, thus reminding you of the important points that you want to discuss during the presentation.

1 With **Slide 2** displayed, on the **Home tab**, in the **Slides group**, click the **New Slide button arrow** to display the **Slide Layout** gallery, and then click **Section Header**.

The section header layout changes the look and flow of a presentation by providing text placeholders that do not contain bullet points.

2 Click in the title placeholder, and then type **About Our Company**

3 Click in the content placeholder below the title, and then type **Named for the crescent-shaped island noted for scuba diving, Lehua Hawaiian Adventures offers exciting and affordable tours throughout Hawaii.** Compare your screen with Figure 1.14.

Figure 1.14

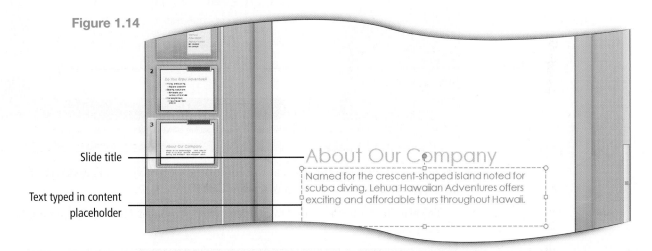

Slide title

Text typed in content placeholder

4 Below the slide, click in the **Notes pane**. Type **Lehua Hawaiian Adventures is based in Honolulu but has offices on each of the main Hawaiian islands.** Compare your screen with Figure 1.15, and then **Save** your presentation.

Figure 1.15

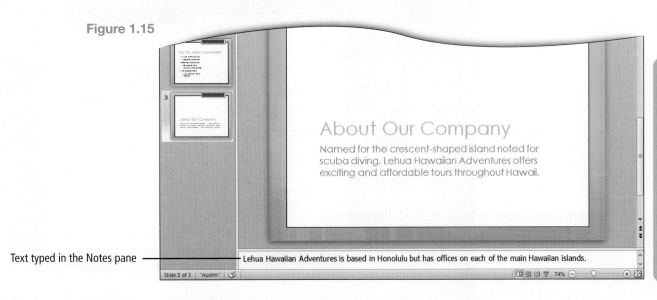

Text typed in the Notes pane

PowerPoint | Chapter 1

Activity 1.07 | Displaying and Editing Slides in the Slide Pane

To edit a presentation slide, display the slide in the Slide pane.

1 Look at the **Slides/Outline pane**, and then notice that the presentation contains three slides. At the right side of the PowerPoint window, in the vertical scroll bar, point to the scroll box, and then hold down the left mouse button to display a ScreenTip indicating the slide number and title.

2 Drag the scroll box up until the ScreenTip displays *Slide: 2 of 3 Do You Enjoy Adventure?* Compare your slide with Figure 1.16, and then release the mouse button to display **Slide 2**.

Figure 1.16

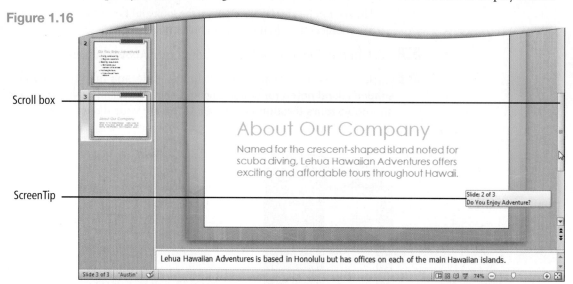

Scroll box

ScreenTip

3 In the second bullet point, click at the end of the word *Explore*. Press Spacebar, and then type **amazing** Compare your screen with Figure 1.17.

The placeholder text is resized to fit within the placeholder. The AutoFit Options button displays.

Figure 1.17

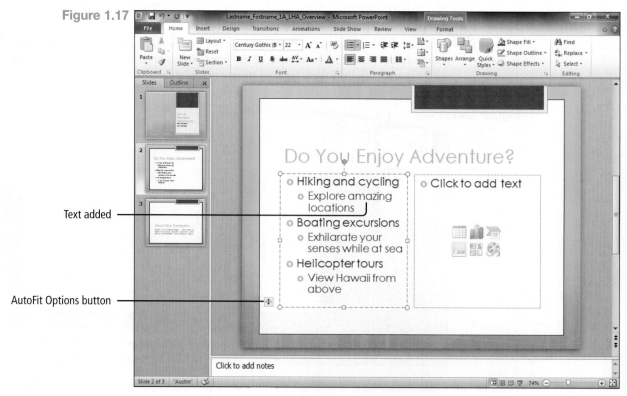

Text added

AutoFit Options button

4 Click the **AutoFit Options** button, and then click **AutoFit Text to Placeholder**.

The *AutoFit Text to Placeholder* option keeps the text contained within the placeholder by reducing the size of the text. The *Stop Fitting Text to This Placeholder* option turns off the AutoFit option so that the text can flow beyond the placeholder border; the text size remains unchanged.

5 Below the vertical scroll bar, locate the **Previous Slide** 🔼 and **Next Slide** 🔽 buttons as shown in Figure 1.18.

Figure 1.18

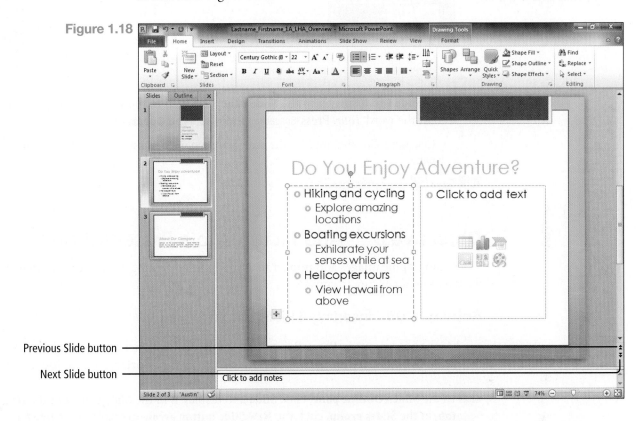

Previous Slide button
Next Slide button

6 In the vertical scroll bar, click the **Previous Slide** button 🔼 so that **Slide 1** displays. Then click the **Next Slide** button 🔽 two times until **Slide 3** displays.

By clicking the Next Slide or the Previous Slide buttons, you can scroll through your presentation one slide at a time.

7 On the left side of the PowerPoint window, in the **Slides/Outline pane**, point to **Slide 1**, and then notice that a ScreenTip displays the slide title. Compare your screen with Figure 1.19.

In the Slides/Outline pane, the slide numbers display to the left of the slide thumbnails.

Figure 1.19

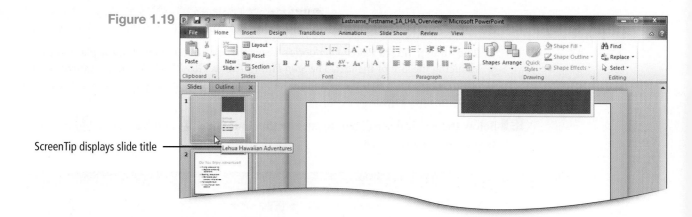

ScreenTip displays slide title

8 Click **Slide 1** to display it in the **Slide pane**, and then in the slide subtitle, click at the end of the word *Tour*. Press ⟨Spacebar⟩, and then type **Operations**

Clicking a slide thumbnail is the most common method used to display a slide in the Slide pane.

9 **Save** 🖫 your presentation.

Objective 3 | Add Pictures to a Presentation

Photographic images add impact to a presentation and help the audience visualize the message you are trying to convey.

Activity 1.08 | Inserting a Picture from a File

Many slide layouts in PowerPoint accommodate digital picture files so that you can easily add pictures you have stored on your system or on a portable storage device.

1 In the **Slides/Outline pane**, click **Slide 2** to display it in the **Slide pane**. On the **Home tab**, in the **Slides group**, click the **New Slide button arrow** to display the **Slide Layout** gallery. Click **Picture with Caption** to insert a new **Slide 3**. Compare your screen with Figure 1.20.

In the center of the large picture placeholder, the *Insert Picture from File* button displays.

Figure 1.20

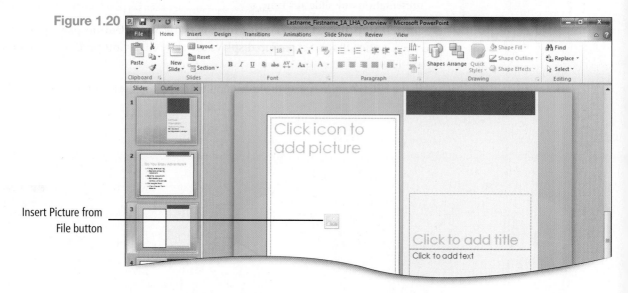

Insert Picture from
File button

2 In the picture placeholder, click the **Insert Picture from File** button 🖼 to open the **Insert Picture** dialog box. Navigate to the location in which your student files are stored, click **p01A_Beach**, then click **Insert** to insert the picture in the placeholder.

3 To the right of the picture, click in the title placeholder. Type **Prepare to be Amazed!**

4 Below the title, click in the caption placeholder, and then type **Mountain, sea, volcano. Our tour guides are experts in the history, geography, culture, and flora and fauna of Hawaii.** Compare your screen with Figure 1.21.

Figure 1.21

Inserted picture ———

Title ———

Caption ———

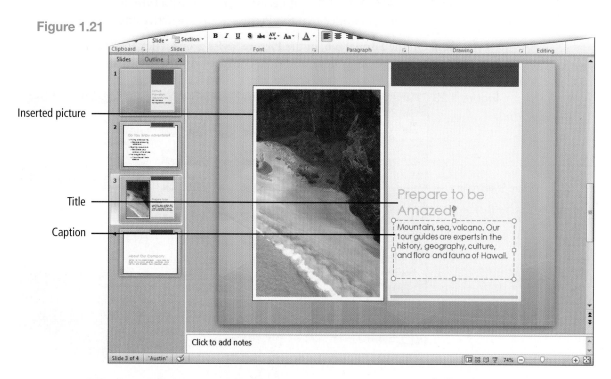

5 Display **Slide 2**. In the placeholder on the right side of the slide, click the **Insert Picture from File** button 🖼. Navigate to your student files, and then click **p01A_Helicopter**. Click **Insert**, and then compare your screen with Figure 1.22.

Small circles and squares—*sizing handles*—surround the inserted picture and indicate that the picture is selected and can be modified or formatted. The *rotation handle*—a green circle above the picture—provides a way to rotate a selected image.

Figure 1.22

Rotation handle ———

Sizing handles ———

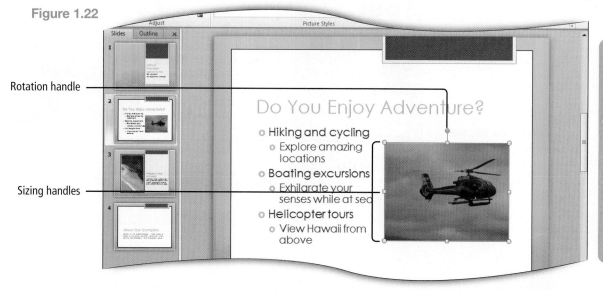

6 **Save** 🔲 the presentation.

Activity 1.09 | Applying a Style to a Picture

The Picture Tools add the Format tab to the Ribbon, which provides numerous *styles* that you can apply to your pictures. A style is a collection of formatting options that you can apply to a picture, text, or an object.

1 With **Slide 2** displayed, if necessary, click the picture of the helicopter to select it. On the Ribbon, notice that the Picture Tools are active and the Format tab displays.

2 On the **Format tab**, in the **Picture Styles group**, click the **More** button 🔻 to display the **Picture Styles** gallery, and then compare your screen with Figure 1.23.

Figure 1.23

Picture Styles gallery ——

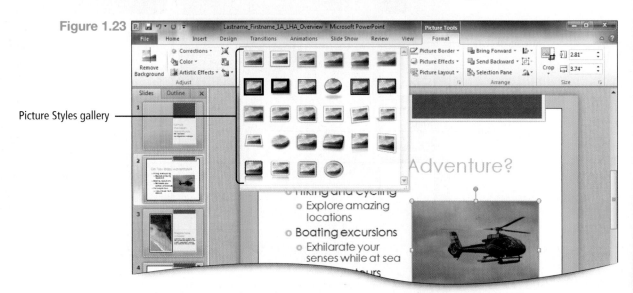

3 In the gallery, point to several of the picture styles to display the ScreenTips and to view the effect on your picture. In the first row, click **Drop Shadow Rectangle**.

4 Click in a blank area of the slide, and then compare your screen with Figure 1.24.

Figure 1.24

Drop Shadow Rectangle
picture style applied to picture

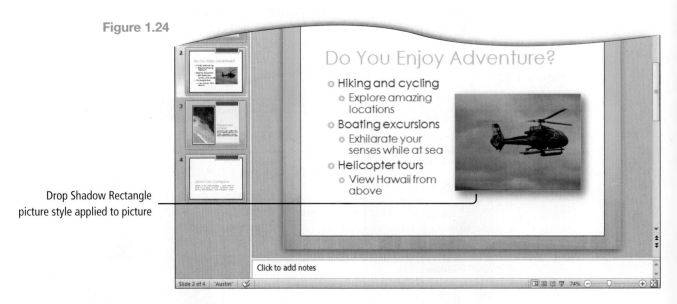

5 Save ![save icon] the presentation.

Activity 1.10 | Applying and Removing Picture Artistic Effects

Artistic effects are formats applied to images that make pictures resemble sketches or paintings.

1 With **Slide 2** displayed, select the picture of the helicopter.

2 Click the **Format tab**, and then in the **Adjust group**, click the **Artistic Effects** button to display the **Artistic Effects** gallery. Compare your screen with Figure 1.25.

Figure 1.25

Artistic Effects button

Artistic Effects gallery

3 In the gallery, point to several of the artistic effects to display the ScreenTips and to have Live Preview display the effect on your picture. Then, in the second row, click the **Paint Strokes** effect.

4 With the picture still selected, on the **Format tab**, in the **Adjust group**, click the **Artistic Effects** button to display the gallery. In the first row, click the first effect—**None**—to remove the effect from the picture and restore the previous formatting.

5 Save ![save icon] the presentation.

Objective 4 | Print and View a Presentation

Activity 1.11 | Viewing a Slide Show

When you view a presentation as an electronic slide show, the entire slide fills the computer screen, and an audience can view your presentation if your computer is connected to a projection system.

1 On the Ribbon, click the **Slide Show tab**. In the **Start Slide Show group**, click the **From Beginning** button.

> The first slide fills the screen, displaying the presentation as the audience would see it if your computer was connected to a projection system.

Another Way

Press [F5] to start the slide show from the beginning. Or, display the first slide you want to show and click the Slide Show button on the lower right side of the status bar; or press [Shift] + [F5].

PowerPoint | Chapter 1

2 Click the left mouse button or press Spacebar to advance to the second slide.

3 Continue to click or press Spacebar until the last slide displays, and then click or press Spacebar one more time to display a black slide.

> After the last slide in a presentation, a ***black slide*** displays, indicating that the presentation is over.

4 With the black slide displayed, click the left mouse button or press Spacebar to exit the slide show and return to the presentation.

Activity 1.12 | Inserting Headers and Footers

A ***header*** is text that prints at the top of each sheet of ***slide handouts*** or ***notes pages***. Slide handouts are printed images of slides on a sheet of paper. Notes pages are printouts that contain the slide image on the top half of the page and notes that you have created on the Notes pane in the lower half of the page.

In addition to headers, you can insert ***footers***—text that displays at the bottom of every slide or that prints at the bottom of a sheet of slide handouts or notes pages.

1 Click the **Insert tab**, and then in the **Text group**, click the **Header & Footer** button to display the **Header and Footer** dialog box.

2 In the **Header and Footer** dialog box, click the **Notes and Handouts tab**. Under **Include on page**, select the **Date and time** check box, and as you do so, watch the Preview box in the lower right corner of the Header and Footer dialog box.

> The Preview box indicates the placeholders on the printed Notes and Handouts pages. The two narrow rectangular boxes at the top of the Preview box indicate placeholders for the header text and date. When you select the Date and time check box, the placeholder in the upper right corner is outlined, indicating the location in which the date will display.

3 If necessary, click the Update automatically option button so that the current date prints on the notes and handouts each time the presentation is printed.

4 If necessary, *clear* the Header check box to omit this element. Notice that in the **Preview** box, the corresponding placeholder is not selected.

5 Select the **Page number** and **Footer** check boxes, and then notice that the insertion point displays in the **Footer** box. Using your own name, type **Lastname_Firstname_ 1A_LHA_Overview** so that the file name displays as a footer, and then compare your dialog box with Figure 1.26.

Figure 1.26

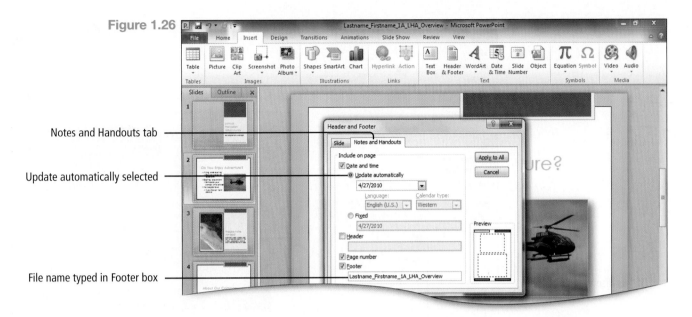

Notes and Handouts tab

Update automatically selected

File name typed in Footer box

6 In the upper right corner of the dialog box, click **Apply to All. Save** 🖫 your presentation.

> **More Knowledge** | **Adding Footers to Slides**
>
> You can also add footers to the actual slides, which will display during your presentation, by using the Slide tab in the Header and Footer dialog box. Headers cannot be added to individual slides.

Activity 1.13 | Printing a Presentation

Use Backstage view to preview the arrangement of slides on the handouts and notes pages.

1 Display **Slide 1**. Click the **File tab** to display **Backstage** view, and then click the **Print tab**.

The Print tab in Backstage view displays the tools you need to select your settings and also to view a preview of your presentation. On the right, Print Preview displays your presentation exactly as it will print.

2 In the **Settings group**, click **Full Page Slides**, and then compare your screen with Figure 1.27.

The gallery displays either the default print setting—Full Page Slides—or the most recently selected print setting. Thus, on your system, this button might indicate the presentation Notes Pages, Outline, or one of several arrangements of slide handouts—depending on the most recently used setting.

Figure 1.27

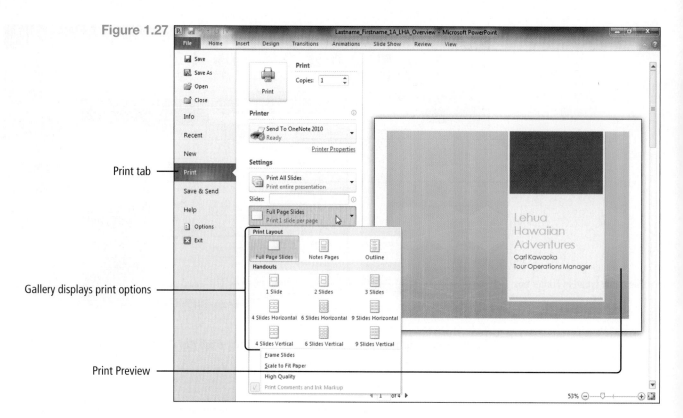

Print tab

Gallery displays print options

Print Preview

3 In the gallery, under **Handouts**, click **4 Slides Horizontal**. Notice that the **Print Preview** on the right displays the slide handout, and that the current date, file name, and page number display in the header and footer.

> In the Settings group, the Portrait Orientation option displays so that you can change the print orientation from Portrait to Landscape. The Portrait Orientation option does not display when Full Page Slides is chosen.

4 To print your handout, be sure your system is connected to a printer, and then in the **Print group**, click the **Print** button.

> The handout will print on your default printer—on a black and white printer, the colors will print in shades of gray. Backstage view closes and your file redisplays in the PowerPoint window.

5 Click the **File tab** to display **Backstage** view, and then click the **Print tab**. In the **Settings group**, click **4 Slides Horizontal**, and then under **Print Layout**, click **Notes Pages** to view the presentation notes for **Slide 1**; recall that you created notes for **Slide 4**.

> Indicated below the Notes page are the current slide number and the number of pages that will print when Notes page is selected. You can use the Next Page and Previous Page arrows to display each Notes page in the presentation.

6 At the bottom of the **Print Preview**, click the **Next Page** button ▶ three times so that **Page 4** displays. Compare your screen with Figure 1.28.

> The notes that you created for Slide 4 display below the image of the slide.

Figure 1.28

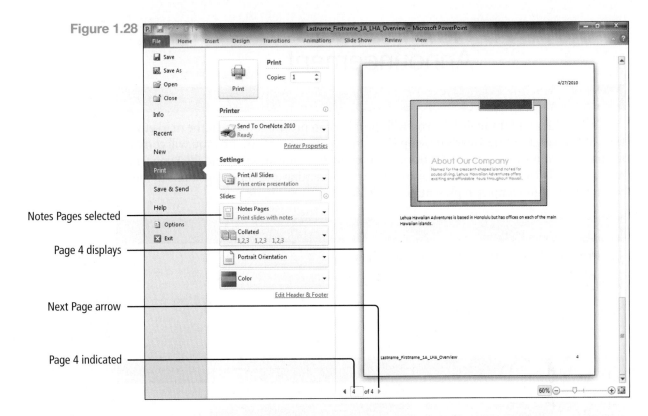

Notes Pages selected

Page 4 displays

Next Page arrow

Page 4 indicated

7 In the **Settings group**, click in the **Slides** box, and then type **4** so that only the Notes pages for **Slide 4** will print. In the **Settings group**, click **Notes Pages**, and then below the gallery, select **Frame Slides**. In the **Print group**, click the **Print** button to print the Notes page.

8 Click the **File tab** to redisplay **Backstage** view, be sure the **Info tab** is active, and then in the third panel, click **Properties**. Click **Show Document Panel**, and then in the **Author** box, delete any text and type your firstname and lastname.

9 In the **Subject** box, type your course name and section number. In the **Keywords** box, type **company overview** and then **Close** ☒ the Document Information Panel.

10 **Save** 🖫 your presentation. On the right end of the title bar, click the **Close** button ☒ to close the presentation and close PowerPoint.

End **You have completed Project 1A**

Project 1B New Product Announcement

myitlab

Project 1B Training

Project Activities

In Activities 1.14 through 1.23, you will combine two presentations that the marketing team at Lehua Adventure Travels developed describing their new Ecotours. You will combine the presentations by inserting slides from one presentation into another, and then you will rearrange and delete slides. You will also apply font formatting and slide transitions to the presentation. Your completed presentation will look similar to Figure 1.29.

Project Files

For Project 1B, you will need the following files:

p01B_Ecotours
p01B_Slides

You will save your presentation as:

Lastname_Firstname_1B_Ecotours

Project Results

Figure 1.29

Project 1B—Ecotours

Objective 5 | Edit an Existing Presentation

Recall that editing refers to the process of adding, deleting, and modifying presentation content. You can edit presentation content in either the Slide pane or the Slides/Outline pane.

Activity 1.14 | Displaying and Editing the Presentation Outline

You can display the presentation outline in the Slides/Outline pane and edit the presentation text. Changes that you make in the outline are immediately displayed in the Slide pane.

1 **Start** PowerPoint. From your student files, open **p01B_Ecotours**. On the **File tab**, click **Save As**, navigate to your **PowerPoint Chapter 1** folder, and then using your own name, save the file as **Lastname_Firstname_1B_Ecotours**

2 In the **Slides/Outline pane**, click the **Outline tab** to display the presentation outline. If necessary, below the Slides/Outline pane, drag the scroll box all the way to the left so that the slide numbers display. Compare your screen with Figure 1.30.

The outline tab is wider than the Slides tab so that you have additional space to type your text. Each slide in the outline displays the slide number, slide icon, and the slide title in bold.

Figure 1.30

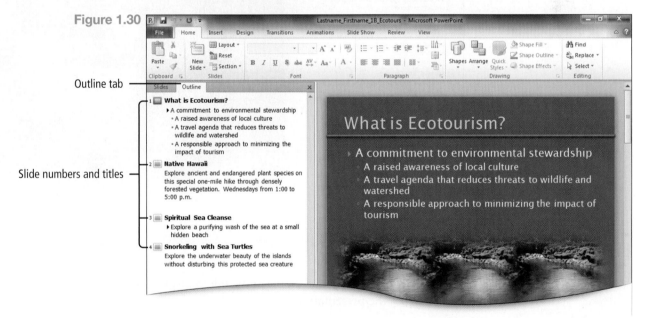

Outline tab

Slide numbers and titles

3 In the **Outline tab**, in **Slide 1**, select the last three bullet points, and then compare your screen with Figure 1.31.

Figure 1.31

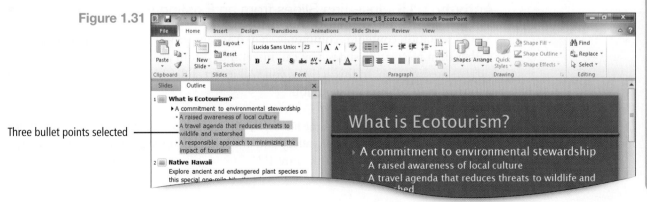

Three bullet points selected

4 On the **Home tab**, in the **Paragraph group**, click the **Decrease List Level** button one time to decrease the list level of the selected bullet points.

> When you type in the outline or change the list level, the changes also display in the Slide pane.

5 In the **Outline tab**, click anywhere in **Slide 3**, and then click at the end of the last bullet point after the word *beach*. Press Enter to create a new bullet point at the same list level as the previous bullet point. Type **Offered Tuesdays and Thursdays one hour before sunset, weather permitting**

6 Press Enter to create a new bullet point. Type **Fee: $30** and then compare your screen with Figure 1.32.

Figure 1.32

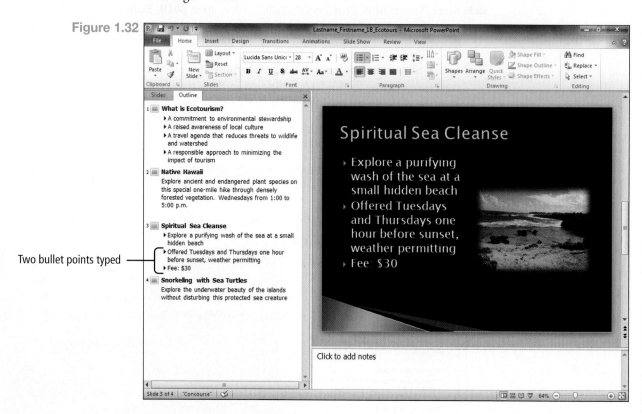

Two bullet points typed

7 In the **Slides/Outline pane**, click the **Slides tab** to display the slide thumbnails, and then **Save** the presentation.

> You can type text in the Slide tab or in the Outline tab. Displaying the Outline tab enables you to view the entire flow of the presentation.

Activity 1.15 | Inserting Slides from an Existing Presentation

Presentation content is commonly shared among group members in an organization. Rather than re-creating slides, you can insert slides from an existing presentation into the current presentation. In this activity, you will insert slides from an existing presentation into your 1B_Ecotours presentation.

1 Display **Slide 1**. On the **Home tab**, in the **Slides group**, click the **New Slide button arrow** to display the **Slide Layout** gallery and additional commands for inserting slides. Compare your screen with Figure 1.33.

Figure 1.33

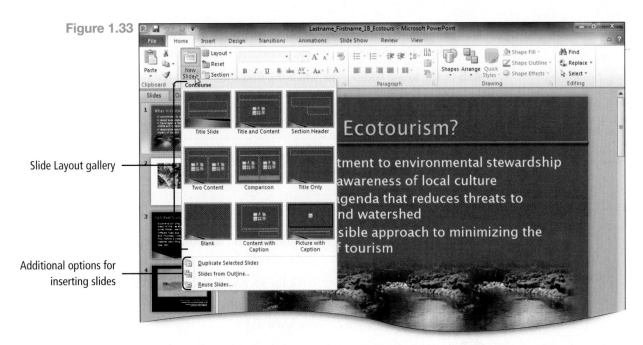

Slide Layout gallery

Additional options for inserting slides

[2] Below the gallery, click **Reuse Slides** to open the Reuse Slides pane on the right side of the PowerPoint window.

[3] In the **Reuse Slides** pane, click the **Browse** button, and then click **Browse File**. In the **Browse** dialog box, navigate to the location where your student files are stored, and then double-click **p01B_Slides** to display the slides in the Reuse Slides pane.

[4] At the bottom of the **Reuse Slides** pane, select the **Keep source formatting** check box, and then compare your screen with Figure 1.34.

> By selecting the *Keep source formatting* check box, you retain the formatting applied to the slides when inserted into the existing presentation. When the *Keep source formatting* check box is cleared, the theme formatting of the presentation in which the slides are inserted is applied.

Figure 1.34

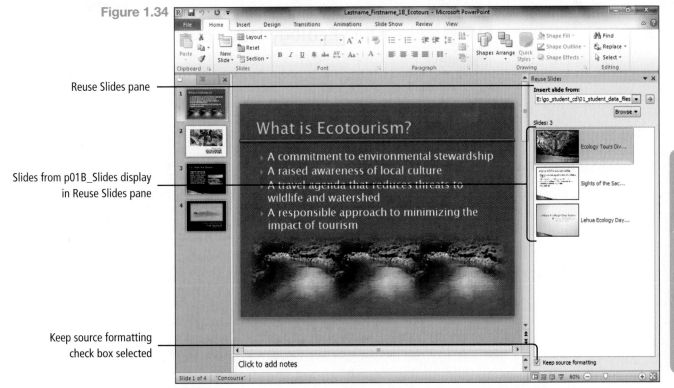

Reuse Slides pane

Slides from p01B_Slides display in Reuse Slides pane

Keep source formatting check box selected

PowerPoint | Chapter 1

5 In the **Reuse Slides** pane, point to each slide to view a zoomed image of the slide and a ScreenTip displaying the file name and the slide title.

6 In the **Reuse Slides** pane, click the first slide—**Ecology Tours Division**—to insert the slide into the current presentation after Slide 1, and then notice that the original slide background formatting is retained.

> **Note** | Inserting Slides
>
> You can insert slides into your presentation in any order; remember to display the slide that will precede the slide that you want to insert.

7 In your **1B_Ecotours** presentation, in the **Slides/Outline pane**, click **Slide 5** to display it in the **Slide pane**.

8 In the **Reuse Slides** pane, click the second slide and then click the third slide to insert both slides after **Slide 5**.

Your presentation contains seven slides.

9 On **Slide 7**, point to *Lehua*, and then right-click to display the shortcut menu. Click **Ignore all**. Use the same technique to ignore the spelling of the word *Ecotour*. Compare your screen with Figure 1.35.

Figure 1.35

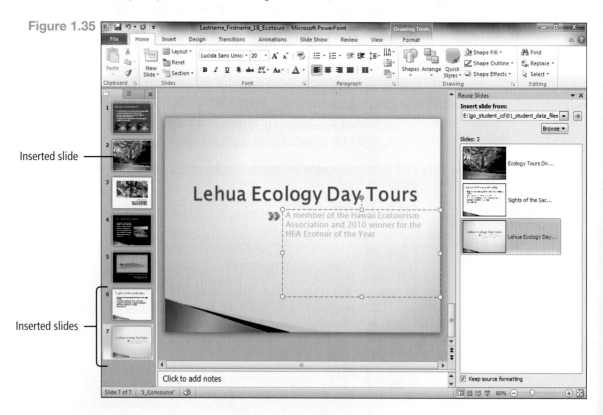

Inserted slide

Inserted slides

10 **Close** ☒ the **Reuse Slides** pane; click **Save** 🖫.

> **More Knowledge** | Inserting All Slides
>
> You can insert all of the slides from an existing presentation into the current presentation at one time. In the Reuse Slides pane, right-click one of the slides that you want to insert, and then click Insert All Slides.

Activity 1.16 | Finding and Replacing Text

The Replace command enables you to locate all occurrences of specified text and replace it with alternative text.

1 Display **Slide 1**. On the **Home tab**, in the **Editing group**, click the **Replace** button. In the **Replace** dialog box, in the **Find what** box, type **Ecology** and then in the **Replace with** box, type **Eco** Compare your screen with Figure 1.36.

Figure 1.36

Replace button

Find what box

Replace with box

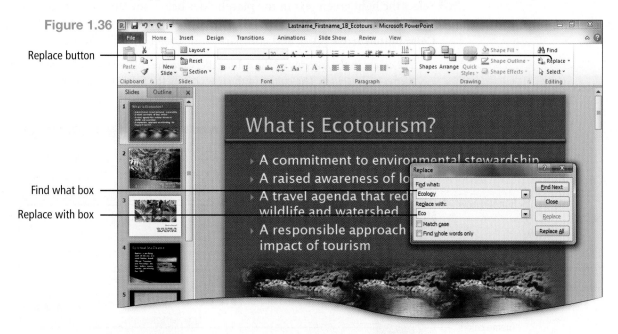

2 In the **Replace** dialog box, click the **Replace All** button.

A message box displays indicating the number of replacements that were made.

3 In the message box, click **OK**, **Close** the **Replace** dialog box, and then click **Save**.

Objective 6 | Format a Presentation

Formatting refers to changing the appearance of the text, layout, and design of a slide. You will find it easiest to do most of your formatting changes in PowerPoint in the Slide pane.

Activity 1.17 | Changing Fonts, Font Sizes, Font Styles, and Font Colors

Recall that a font is a set of characters with the same design and shape and that fonts are measured in points. Font styles include bold, italic, and underline, and you can apply any combination of these styles to presentation text. Font styles and font color are useful to provide emphasis and are a visual cue to draw the reader's eye to important text.

1 On the right side of the **Slides/Outline pane**, drag the scroll box down until **Slide 7** displays, and then click **Slide 7** to display it in the **Slides** pane.

> When a presentation contains a large number of slides, a scroll box displays to the right of the slide thumbnails so that you can scroll and then select the thumbnails.

2 Select the title text—*Lehua Eco Day Tours*. Point to the Mini toolbar, and then click the **Font button arrow** to display the available fonts. Click **Arial Black**.

3 Select the light green text in the placeholder below the title, and then on the Mini toolbar, change the **Font** to **Arial Black** and the **Font Size** to **28**. Then, click the **Font Color button arrow** [A·], and compare your screen with Figure 1.37.

> The colors in the top row of the color gallery are the colors associated with the presentation theme—*Concourse*. The colors in the rows below the first row are light and dark variations of the theme colors.

Figure 1.37

Font Color button arrow

Font size changed to 28

Title Font changed to Arial Black

Theme colors

Theme color variations

4 Point to several of the colors and notice that a ScreenTip displays the color name and Live Preview displays the selected text in the color to which you are pointing.

5 In the second column of colors, click the first color—**Black, Text 1**—to change the font color. Notice that on the Home tab and Mini toolbar, the lower part of the Font Color button displays the most recently applied font color—Black.

> When you click the Font Color button instead of the Font Color button arrow, the color displayed in the lower part of the Font Color button is applied to selected text without displaying the color gallery.

6 Display **Slide 2**, and then select the title *Eco Tours Division*. On the Mini toolbar, click the **Font Color button** [A·] to apply the font color **Black, Text 1** to the selection. Select the subtitle—*Lehua Adventure Tours*—and then change the **Font Color** to **Black, Text 1**. Compare your screen with Figure 1.38.

Figure 1.38

Font color changed
to black

7 Display **Slide 3**, and then select the title—*Native Hawaii*. From the Mini toolbar, apply **Bold** **B** and **Italic** **I**, and then **Save** 🖫 your presentation.

Activity 1.18 | Aligning Text and Changing Line Spacing

In PowerPoint, ***text alignment*** refers to the horizontal placement of text within a placeholder. You can align left, centered, right, or justified.

1 Display **Slide 2**. Click anywhere in the title—*Eco Tours Division*.

2 On the **Home tab**, in the **Paragraph group**, click the **Align Text Right** button 🔳 to right align the text within the placeholder.

3 Display **Slide 7**. Click anywhere in the text below the title. In the **Paragraph group**, click the **Line Spacing** button 🔳. In the list, click **1.5** to change from single-spacing between lines to one-and-a-half spacing between lines. **Save** 🖫 your presentation, and then compare your screen with Figure 1.39.

Figure 1.39

Line Spacing button

Line Spacing
changed to 1.5

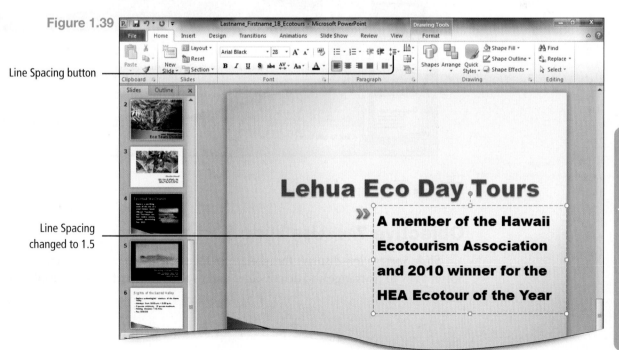

PowerPoint | **Chapter 1**

Activity 1.19 | Modifying Slide Layout

Recall that the slide layout defines the placement of the content placeholders on a slide. PowerPoint includes predefined layouts that you can apply to your slide for the purpose of arranging slide elements.

For example, a Title Slide contains two placeholder elements—the title and the subtitle. When you design your slides, consider the content that you want to include, and then choose a layout with the elements that will display the message you want to convey in the best way.

1 Display **Slide 3**. On the **Home tab**, in the **Slides group**, click the **Layout** button to display the **Slide Layout** gallery. Notice that *Content with Caption* is selected.

The selection indicates the layout of the current slide.

2 Click **Picture with Caption** to change the slide layout, and then compare your screen with Figure 1.40.

The Picture with Caption layout emphasizes the picture more effectively than the Content with Caption layout.

Figure 1.40

3 Save your presentation.

Objective 7 | Use Slide Sorter View

Slide Sorter view displays thumbnails of all of the slides in a presentation. Use Slide Sorter view to rearrange and delete slides and to apply formatting to multiple slides.

Activity 1.20 | Deleting Slides in Slide Sorter View

Another Way

On the Ribbon, click the View tab, and then in the Presentation Views group, click Slide Sorter.

1 In the lower right corner of the PowerPoint window, click the **Slide Sorter** button to display all of the slide thumbnails.

2 Compare your screen with Figure 1.41.

Your slides may display larger or smaller than those shown in Figure 1.41.

Figure 1.41

Slides display in Slide Sorter view

Slide Sorter button selected

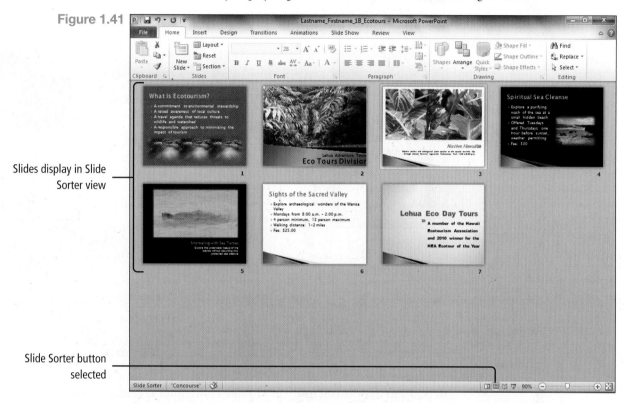

3 Click **Slide 6**, and notice that a thick outline surrounds the slide, indicating that it is selected. On your keyboard, press Del to delete the slide. Click **Save**.

Activity 1.21 | Moving Slides in Slide Sorter View

1 With the presentation displayed in Slide Sorter view, point to **Slide 2**. Hold down the left mouse button, and then drag the slide to the left until the vertical move bar and pointer indicating the position to which the slide will be moved is positioned to the left of **Slide 1**, as shown in Figure 1.42.

Figure 1.42

Vertical move bar

Pointer positioned to the left of Slide 1

Selected slide

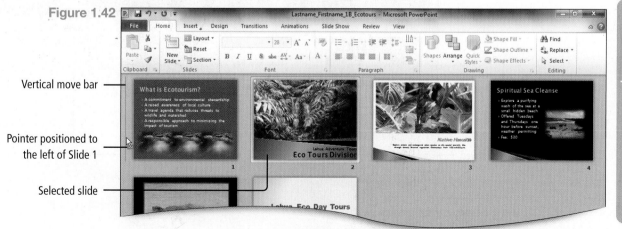

2 Release the mouse button to move the slide to the Slide 1 position in the presentation.

3 Click **Slide 4**, hold down Ctrl, and then click **Slide 5**. Compare your screen with Figure 1.43.

Both slides are outlined, indicating that both are selected. By holding down Ctrl, you can create a group of selected slides.

Figure 1.43

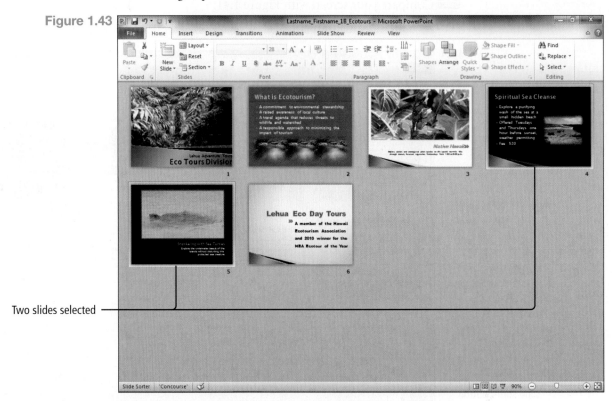

Two slides selected

4 Point to either of the selected slides, hold down the left mouse button, and then drag to position the vertical move bar to the left of **Slide 3**. Release the mouse button to move the two slides, and then compare your screen with Figure 1.44.

Figure 1.44

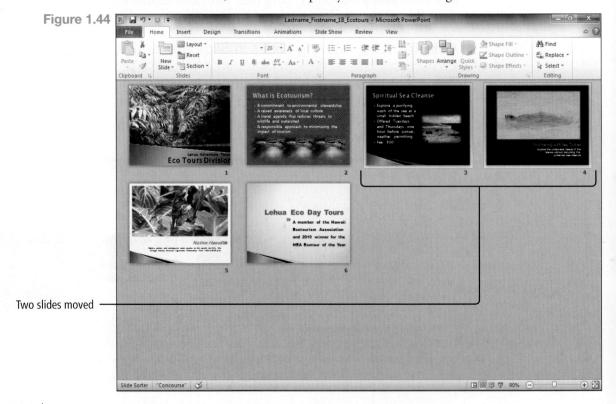

Two slides moved

5 In the status bar, click the **Normal** button ▣ to return to Normal view. **Save** 🔒 your presentation.

Objective 8 | Apply Slide Transitions

Slide transitions are the motion effects that occur in Slide Show view when you move from one slide to the next during a presentation. You can choose from a variety of transitions, and you can control the speed and method with which the slides advance.

Activity 1.22 | Applying Slide Transitions to a Presentation

1 Display **Slide 1**. On the **Transitions tab**, in the **Transition to This Slide group**, click the **More** button ▾ to display the **Transitions** gallery. Compare your screen with Figure 1.45.

Figure 1.45

Transitions gallery

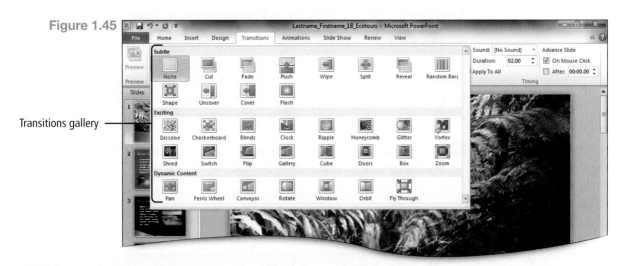

2 Under **Exciting**, click **Doors** to apply and view the transition. In the **Transition to This Slide group**, click the **Effect Options** button to display the directions from which the slide enters the screen. Click **Horizontal**.

The Effect Options vary depending upon the selected transition and include the direction from which the slide enters the screen or the shape in which the slide displays during the transition.

3 In the **Timing group**, notice that the **Duration** box displays *01.40*, indicating that the transition lasts 1.40 seconds. Click the **Duration** box **up spin arrow** two times so that *01.75* displays. Under **Advance Slide**, verify that the **On Mouse Click** check box is selected; select it if necessary. Compare your screen with Figure 1.46.

When the On Mouse Click option is selected, the presenter controls when the current slide advances to the next slide by clicking the mouse button or by pressing Spacebar.

Figure 1.46

On Mouse Click check box selected

Doors transition selected

Duration changed to *01.75*

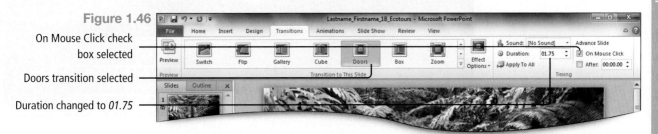

PowerPoint | Chapter 1

4 In the **Timing group**, click the **Apply To All** button so that the Doors, Horizontal with a Duration of 1.75 seconds transition is applied to all of the slides in the presentation. Notice that in the Slides/Outline pane, a star displays below the slide number providing a visual cue that a transition has been applied to the slide.

5 Click the **Slide Show tab**. In the **Start Slide Show group**, click the **From Beginning** button, and then view your presentation, clicking the mouse button to advance through the slides. When the black slide displays, click the mouse button one more time to display the presentation in Normal view. **Save** your presentation 🔲.

> **More Knowledge** | **Applying Multiple Slide Transitions**
>
> You can apply more than one type of transition in your presentation by displaying the slides one at a time, and then clicking the transition that you want to apply instead of clicking the Apply To All button.

Activity 1.23 | Displaying a Presentation in Reading View

Organizations frequently conduct online meetings when participants are unable to meet in one location. The *Reading view* in PowerPoint displays a presentation in a manner similar to a slide show but the taskbar, title bar, and status bar remain available in the presentation window. Thus, a presenter can easily facilitate an online conference by switching to another window without closing the slide show.

Another Way

On the View tab, in the Presentation Views group, click Reading View.

1 In the lower right corner of the PowerPoint window, click the **Reading View** button 📖. Compare your screen with Figure 1.47.

In Reading View, the status bar contains the Next and Previous buttons, which are used to navigate in the presentation, and the Menu button which is used to print, copy, and edit slides.

Figure 1.47

Slide displays in Reading View

Reading View button

Next button

Menu button

Previous button

2 In the status bar, click the **Next** button to display **Slide 2**. Press Spacebar to display **Slide 3**. Click the left mouse button to display **Slide 4**. In the status bar, click the **Previous** button to display **Slide 3**.

Another Way

Press Esc to exit Reading view and return to Normal view.

3 In the status bar, click the **Menu** button to display the Reading view menu, and then click **End Show** to return to Normal view.

4 On the **Insert tab**, in the **Text group**, click the **Header & Footer** button, and then click the **Notes and Handouts tab**. Under **Include on page**, select the **Date and time** check box, and if necessary, select **Update automatically**. Clear the **Header** check box, and then select the **Page number** and **Footer** check boxes. In the **Footer** box, using your own name, type **Lastname_Firstname_1B_Ecotours** and then click **Apply to All**.

5 Display **Backstage** view, and then on the right, click **Properties**. Click **Show Document Panel**, and then in the **Author** box, delete any text and type your firstname and lastname. In the **Subject** box, type your course name and section number, and in the **Keywords** box, type **ecotours, ecotourism Close** ☒ the Document Information Panel.

6 **Save** your presentation 🖫. Submit your presentation electronically or print **Handouts, 6 Slides Horizontal**, as directed by your instructor.

7 **Close** the presentation and **Exit** PowerPoint.

More Knowledge | Broadcasting a Slide Show

You can broadcast a slide show to remote viewers by using the PowerPoint Broadcast Service or another broadcast service. To broadcast a slide show, on the Slide Show tab, in the Start Slide Show group, click Broadcast Slide Show, and then follow the instructions in the Broadcast Slide Show dialog box to start the broadcast.

End **You have completed Project 1B** ─────────────

Content-Based Assessments

Summary

In this chapter, you created a new PowerPoint presentation and edited an existing presentation by reusing slides from another presentation. You entered, edited, and formatted text in Normal view; worked with slides in Slide Sorter view; and viewed the presentation as a slide show. You also added emphasis to your presentations by inserting pictures, applying font formatting, and modifying layout, alignment, and line spacing.

Key Terms

Artistic effects 253	**Notes page** 254	**Slide Sorter view**............266
Black slide.....................254	**Notes pane** 240	**Slide transitions** 269
Editing 243	**Placeholder** 240	**Slides/Outline pane** 240
Footer 254	**Reading view** 270	**Style**.................................252
Formatting.....................261	**Rotation handle** 251	**Text alignment** 265
Header...........................254	**Sizing handles**...............251	**Theme** 241
Layout 243	**Slide**................................240	**Thumbnails** 240
List level 245	**Slide handouts** 254	**Title slide**........................240
Normal view 239	**Slide pane** 240	

Matching

Match each term in the second column with its correct definition in the first column by writing the letter of the term on the blank line in front of the correct definition.

A Black slide

B Formatting

C List level

D Normal view

E Notes page

F Placeholder

G Rotation handle

H Sizing handles

I Slide

J Slide handouts

K Slide transitions

L Style

M Text alignment

N Theme

O Title slide

_____ 1. The PowerPoint view in which the window is divided into three panes—the Slide pane, the Slides/Outline pane, and the Notes pane.

_____ 2. A presentation page that can contain text, pictures, tables, charts, and other multimedia or graphic objects.

_____ 3. The first slide in a presentation, the purpose of which is to provide an introduction to the presentation topic.

_____ 4. A box on a slide with dotted or dashed borders that holds title and body text or other content such as charts, tables, and pictures.

_____ 5. A set of unified design elements that provides a look for your presentation by applying colors, fonts, and effects.

_____ 6. An outline level in a presentation represented by a bullet symbol and identified in a slide by the indentation and the size of the text.

_____ 7. Small circles and squares that indicate that a picture is selected.

_____ 8. A green circle located above a selected picture with which you can rotate the selected image.

_____ 9. A collection of formatting options that can be applied to a picture, text, or object.

_____ 10. A slide that displays at the end of every slide show to indicate that the presentation is over.

_____ 11. Printed images of slides on a sheet of paper.

_____ 12. A printout that contains the slide image on the top half of the page and notes that you have created in the Notes pane on the lower half of the page.

_____ 13. The process of changing the appearance of the text, layout, and design of a slide.

_____ 14. The term that refers to the horizontal placement of text within a placeholder.

_____ 15. Motion effects that occur in Slide Show view when you move from one slide to the next during a presentation.

Multiple Choice

Circle the correct answer.

1. In Normal view, the pane that displays a large image of the active slide is the:
   A. Slide pane   **B.** Slides/Outline pane   **C.** Notes pane

2. In Normal view, the pane that displays below the Slide pane is the:
   A. Slide Sorter pane   **B.** Slides/Outline pane   **C.** Notes pane

3. The buttons in the lower right corner that control the look of the presentation window are the:
   A. Normal buttons   **B.** View buttons   **C.** Thumbnails buttons

4. The process of modifying a presentation by adding and deleting slides or by changing the contents of individual slides is referred to as:
   A. Editing   **B.** Formatting   **C.** Aligning

5. The arrangement of elements, such as title and subtitle text, lists, pictures, tables, charts, shapes, and movies, on a PowerPoint slide is referred to as:
   A. Theme modification   **B.** Editing   **C.** Layout

6. Text that prints at the top of a sheet of slide handouts or notes pages is a:
   A. Header   **B.** Footer   **C.** Page number

7. Text that displays at the bottom of every slide or that prints at the bottom of a sheet of slide handouts or notes.
   A. Header   **B.** Footer   **C.** Page number

8. The command that locates all occurrences of specific text and replace it with alternative text is:
   A. Replace   **B.** Find   **C.** Edit

9. The view in which all of the slides in your presentation display in miniature is:
   A. Slide Sorter view   **B.** Normal view   **C.** Reading view

10. A view similar to Slide Show view but that also displays the title bar, status bar, and taskbar is:
    A. Slide Sorter view   **B.** Normal view   **C.** Reading view

Content-Based Assessments

Apply **1A** skills from these Objectives:

1. Create a New Presentation
2. Edit a Presentation in Normal View
3. Add Pictures to a Presentation
4. Print and View a Presentation

Skills Review | Project **1C** Tour Hawaii

In the following Skills Review, you will create a new presentation by inserting content and pictures, adding notes and footers, and applying a presentation theme. Your completed presentation will look similar to Figure 1.48.

Project Files

For Project 1C, you will need the following files:

New blank PowerPoint presentation
p01C_Harbor
p01C_View

You will save your presentation as:

Lastname_Firstname_1C_Tour_Hawaii

Project Results

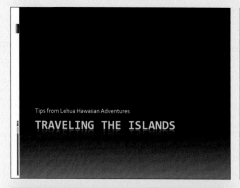

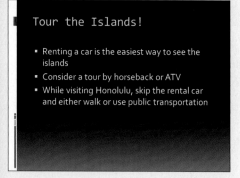

Figure 1.48

(Project 1C Tour Hawaii continues on the next page)

Content-Based Assessments

1 **Start** PowerPoint to display a new blank presentation in Normal view.

a. In the **Slide pane**, click in the title placeholder, which contains the text *Click to add title*. Type **Traveling the Islands**

b. Click in the subtitle placeholder, and then type **Tips from Lehua Hawaiian Adventures**

c. Right-click *Lehua*, and then on the shortcut menu, click **Ignore All**.

d. On the Ribbon, click the **Design tab**. In the **Themes group**, click the **More** button to display the **Themes gallery**. Recall that the themes display alphabetically. Using the ScreenTips, locate and then click **Metro** to apply the Metro theme to the presentation.

e. On the Quick Access Toolbar, click the **Save** button, navigate to your **PowerPoint Chapter 1** folder, and then **Save** the presentation as **Lastname_Firstname_1C_Tour_Hawaii**

2 On the **Home tab**, in the **Slides group**, click the **New Slide button arrow**. In the gallery, click the **Picture with Caption** layout to insert a new slide.

a. In the **Slide pane**, click the text *Click to add title*, and then type **Plan Ahead!**

b. Click in the text placeholder below the title, and then type **A little planning will go a long way toward creating a memorable and trouble-free vacation to the islands.**

c. In the picture placeholder, click the **Insert picture from File** button, and then navigate to your student data files. Click **p01C_View**, and then press [Enter] to insert the picture.

d. With the picture selected, on the **Format tab**, in the **Picture Styles group**, click the **More** button to display the **Picture Styles** gallery. Use the ScreenTips to locate, and then click the style **Soft Edge Oval**.

e. In the **Adjust group**, click the **Artistic Effects** button, and then in the fourth row, click the second effect—**Texturizer**.

3 On the **Home tab**, in the **Slides group**, click the **New Slide button arrow**. In the gallery, click the **Comparison** layout to insert a new slide. In the title placeholder, type **Destination Hawaii!**

a. Below the title, on the left side of the slide, click in the placeholder containing the pink words *Click to add text*. Type **Arriving by Air**

b. On the right side of the slide, click in the placeholder containing the pink words *Click to add text*. Type **Arriving by Sea**

c. On the left side of the slide, click in the content placeholder. Type **Western U.S. flight times are approximately 5–7 hours** and then press [Enter]. Type **Eastern U.S. flight times are approximately 12–14 hours**

d. On the right side of the slide, click in the content placeholder. Type **Embark typically from Western U.S. or Hawaii** and then press [Enter]. Type **Cruises last 10 to 14 days**

e. Press [Enter], and then on the **Home tab**, in the **Paragraph group**, click the **Increase List Level** button, and then type **Ports of call include Honolulu, Lahaina, Kona, and Hilo**

f. Right-click *Lahaina*, and then on the shortcut menu, click **Ignore All**. **Save** your presentation.

4 On the **Home tab**, in the **Slides group**, click the **New Slide button arrow**. In the gallery, click **Title and Content** to insert a new slide. In the title placeholder, type **Tour the Islands!**

a. In the content placeholder, type the following three bullet points:

Renting a car is the easiest way to see the islands

Consider a tour by horseback or ATV

While visiting Honolulu, skip the rental car and either walk or use public transportation

b. Below the slide, click in the **Notes pane**, and then type **Rental car company offices are located at each major airport.**

5 Insert a **New Slide** using the **Picture with Caption** layout.

a. In the title placeholder, type **Explore!** In the text placeholder, type **Regardless of the mode of transportation that you choose, explore Hawaii for an unforgettable vacation!**

b. In the center of the large picture placeholder, click the **Insert Picture from File** button. Navigate to your student files, and then insert **p01C_Harbor**.

c. With the picture selected, on the **Format tab**, in the **Picture Styles group**, click the **More** button to display the **Picture Styles** gallery. In the first row, click the sixth style—**Soft Edge Rectangle**.

(Project 1C Tour Hawaii continues on the next page)

PowerPoint | Chapter 1

Content-Based Assessments

6 On the Ribbon, click the **Slide Show tab**. In the **Start Slide Show group**, click the **From Beginning** button.

a. Click the left mouse button or press Spacebar to advance to the second slide. Continue to click or press Spacebar until the last slide displays, and then click or press Spacebar one more time to display a black slide.

b. With the black slide displayed, click the left mouse button or press Spacebar to exit the slide show and return to the presentation.

7 Click the **Insert tab**, and then in the **Text group**, click the **Header & Footer** button to display the **Header and Footer** dialog box.

a. In the **Header and Footer** dialog box, click the **Notes and Handouts tab**. Under **Include on page**, select the **Date and time** check box. If necessary, click the Update automatically option button so that the current date prints on the notes and handouts.

b. If necessary, clear the Header check box to omit this element. Select the **Page number** and **Footer** check boxes. In the **Footer** box, type **Lastname_Firstname_1C_Tour_Hawaii** and then click **Apply to All**.

c. Click the **File tab** to display **Backstage** view, and then on the right, click **Properties**. Click **Show Document Panel**, and then in the **Author** box, delete any text and type your firstname and lastname. In the **Subject** box, type your course name and section number, and in the **Keywords** box, type **travel tips, tour tips, trip planning Close** the Document Information Panel.

d. **Save** your presentation. Submit your presentation electronically or print **Handouts, 6 Slides Horizontal** as directed by your instructor. **Close** the presentation.

End You have completed Project 1C _____

Content-Based Assessments

Apply **1B** skills from these Objectives:

- **5** Edit an Existing Presentation
- **6** Format a Presentation
- **7** Use Slide Sorter View
- **8** Apply Slide Transitions

Skills Review | Project **1D** Luau Information

In the following Skills Review, you will edit an existing presentation by inserting slides from another presentation, applying font and slide formatting, and applying slide transitions. Your completed presentation will look similar to Figure 1.49.

Project Files

For Project 1D, you will need the following files:

    p01D_Luau_Information
    p01D_History_of_Luaus

You will save your presentation as:

    Lastname_Firstname_1D_Luau_Information

Project Results

Figure 1.49

(Project 1D Luau Information continues on the next page)

PowerPoint | Chapter 1

1 **Start** PowerPoint. From your student files, open **p01D_Luau_Information**. Click the **File tab** to display **Backstage** view, click **Save As**, navigate to your **PowerPoint Chapter 1** folder, and then using your own name, **Save** the file as **Lastname_Firstname_1D_Luau_Information** Take a moment to examine the content of the presentation.

a. In the **Slides/Outline pane**, click the **Outline tab** to display the presentation outline.

b. In the **Outline tab**, in **Slide 2**, click anywhere in the last bullet point, which begins with the text *Luaus were celebrated*.

c. On the **Home tab**, in the **Paragraph group**, click the **Decrease List Level** button one time.

d. In the **Outline tab**, click at the end of the second bullet after the word *journeys*. Press Enter to create a new bullet point at the same list level as the previous bullet point. Type **Today, luaus celebrate events such as weddings, graduations, and first birthdays**

e. In the **Slides/Outline pane**, click the **Slides tab** to display the slide thumbnails.

2 Display **Slide 1**. On the **Home tab**, in the **Slides group**, click the **New Slide button arrow** to display the **Slide Layout** gallery and additional options for inserting slides.

a. Below the gallery, click **Reuse Slides** to open the **Reuse Slides** pane on the right side of the PowerPoint window.

b. In the **Reuse Slides** pane, click the **Browse** button, and then click **Browse File**. In the **Browse** dialog box, navigate to your student files, and then double-click **p01D_History_of_Luaus**.

c. At the bottom of the **Reuse Slides** pane, select the **Keep source formatting** check box.

d. In the **Reuse Slides** pane, click the first slide—*Luau Information*—to insert the slide into the current presentation after **Slide 1**. In the **Reuse Slides** pane, click the second slide—**Celebrating a Luau** to insert it as the third slide in your presentation.

e. In your **1D_Luau_Information** presentation, in the **Slides/Outline pane**, click **Slide 5** to display it in the **Slide pane**.

f. In the **Reuse Slides** pane, click the third slide—*History of the Luau*—and then click the fourth slide—*Luau Delicacies*—to insert both slides after **Slide 5**. In the **Reuse Slides** pane, click the **Close** button.

3 Display **Slide 1**, and then select the title—*Feasting Polynesian Style*.

a. Point to the Mini toolbar, and then click the **Font arrow** to display the available fonts. Click **Arial**, and then click the **Font Size arrow**. Click **44** to change the font size. Use the Mini toolbar to apply **Bold** and **Italic** to the title.

b. Select the subtitle—*A History of the Luau*. Use the Mini toolbar to change the **Font** to **Arial** and the **Font Size** to **28**.

c. On the **Home tab**, in the **Editing group**, click the **Replace** button. In the **Replace** dialog box, click in the **Find what** box. Type **Polynesian** and then in the **Replace with** box, type **Hawaiian**

d. In the **Replace** dialog box, click the **Replace All** button to replace three occurrences of *Polynesian* with *Hawaiian*. Click **OK** to close the message box, and then in the **Replace** dialog box, click the **Close** button.

e. Display **Slide 6**, and then select the second bullet point, which begins *Originally*. On the Mini toolbar, click the **Font Color button arrow**. Under **Theme Colors**, in the sixth column, click the first color—**Teal, Accent 2**.

f. Select the last bullet point, which begins *Taro leaves*. On the Mini toolbar, click the **Font Color button** to apply **Teal, Accent 2** to the selection.

4 With **Slide 6** displayed, click anywhere in the title.

a. On the **Home tab**, in the **Paragraph group**, click the **Center** button to center the text within the placeholder.

b. Display **Slide 7**, and then **Center** the slide title.

c. Display **Slide 5**, and then click anywhere in the text in the lower portion of the slide. In the **Paragraph group**, click the **Line Spacing** button. In the list, click **1.5** to change from single-spacing between lines to one-and-a-half spacing between lines.

d. Display **Slide 3**. On the **Home tab**, in the **Slides group**, click the **Layout** button to display the **Slide Layout** gallery. Click **Title and Content** to change the slide layout.

5 In the lower right corner of the PowerPoint window, in the **View** buttons, click the **Slide Sorter** button to display the slide thumbnails in Slide Sorter view.

(Project 1D Luau Information continues on the next page)

a. Click **Slide 2**, and then notice that a thick outline surrounds the slide, indicating that it is selected. Press Del to delete the slide.

b. Point to **Slide 5**, hold down the mouse button, and then drag to position the vertical move bar to the left of **Slide 2**. Release the mouse button to move the slide.

c. Point to **Slide 5**, hold down the mouse button, and then drag so that the vertical move bar displays to the right of **Slide 6**. Release the mouse button to move the slide so that it is the last slide in the presentation.

d. Point to **Slide 4**, hold down the mouse button, and then drag so that the vertical move bar displays to the left of **Slide 3**. Release the mouse button to move the slide.

e. In the **View** buttons, click the **Normal** button to return the presentation to Normal view.

6 Display **Slide 1**. On the **Transitions tab**, in the **Transition to This Slide group**, click the **Wipe** button to apply the Wipe transition to the slide.

a. In the **Transition to This Slide group**, click the **Effect Options** button, and then click **From Top**.

b. In the **Timing group**, click the **Duration** box **up spin arrow** twice to change the Duration to *01.50*.

c. In the **Timing group**, under **Advance Slide**, verify that the **On Mouse Click** check box is selected, and select it if necessary.

d. In the **Timing group**, click the **Apply To All** button so that the transition settings are applied to all of the slides in the presentation.

e. Click the **Slide Show tab**. In the **Start Slide Show group**, click the **From Beginning** button, and then view your presentation, clicking the mouse button to advance through the slides. When the black slide displays, click the mouse button one more time to display the presentation in Normal view.

f. On the **Insert tab**, in the **Text group**, click the **Header & Footer** button to display the **Header and Footer** dialog box. Click the **Notes and Handouts tab**. Under **Include on page**, select the **Date and time** check box, and then if necessary, select Update automatically.

g. Clear the **Header** check box if necessary, and then select the **Page number** and **Footer** check boxes. In the **Footer** box, using your own name, type **Lastname_Firstname_1D_Luau_Information** and then click **Apply to All**.

h. Click the **File tab**, and then on the right side of the window, click **Properties**. Click **Show Document Panel**, and then in the **Author** box, delete any text and type your firstname and lastname. In the **Subject** box, type your course name and section number, and in the **Keywords** box, type **luau, Hawaiian history, Hawaiian culture Close** the Document Information Panel.

i. **Save** your presentation. Submit your presentation electronically or print **Handouts, 6 Slides Horizontal** as directed by your instructor. **Close** the presentation.

End **You have completed Project 1D**

Content-Based Assessments

Mastering PowerPoint | Project **1E** Boat Tours

In the following Mastering PowerPoint project, you will create a new presentation describing the types of boat tours offered by Lehua Hawaiian Adventures. Your completed presentation will look similar to Figure 1.50.

Project Files

For Project 1E, you will need the following files:

> New blank PowerPoint presentation
> p01E_Catamaran
> p01E_Raft

You will save your presentation as:

> Lastname_Firstname_1E_Boat_Tours

Project Results

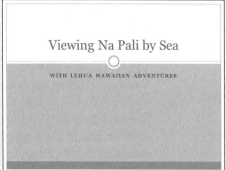
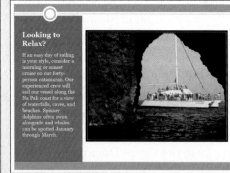
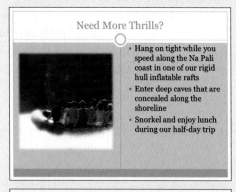

Figure 1.50

(Project 1E Boat Tours continues on the next page)

Content-Based Assessments

Mastering PowerPoint | Project 1E Boat Tours (continued)

1 **Start** PowerPoint to display a new blank presentation, and then change the **Design** by applying the **Civic** theme. As the title of this presentation type **Viewing Na Pali by Sea** and as the subtitle type **With Lehua Hawaiian Adventures**

2 Correct spelling errors on this slide by choosing the **Ignore All** option for the words *Pali* and *Lehua*. Save the presentation in your **PowerPoint Chapter 1** folder as **Lastname_Firstname_1E_Boat_Tours**

3 Insert a **New Slide** using the **Content with Caption** layout. In the title placeholder, type **Looking to Relax?** In the large content placeholder on the right side of the slide, from your student files, insert the picture **p01E_Catamaran**. Format the picture with the **Compound Frame, Black** picture style and the **Texturizer** artistic effect.

4 In the text placeholder, type **If an easy day of sailing is your style, consider a morning or sunset cruise on our forty-person catamaran. Our experienced crew will sail our vessel along the Na Pali coast for a view of waterfalls, caves, and beaches. Spinner dolphins often swim alongside and whales can be spotted January through March.**

5 Insert a **New Slide** using the **Two Content** layout. In the title placeholder, type **Need More Thrills?** In the content placeholder on the left side of the slide, from your student files, insert the picture **p01E_Raft**. Format the picture with the **Soft Edge Rectangle** picture style and the **Glow Diffused** artistic effect. In the content placeholder on the right side of the slide, type the following three bullet points:

Hang on tight while you speed along the Na Pali coast in one of our rigid hull inflatable rafts

Enter deep caves that are concealed along the shoreline

Snorkel and enjoy lunch during our half-day trip

6 Insert a **New Slide** using the **Comparison** layout. In the title placeholder, type **Which Trip is Right for You?** In the orange placeholder on the left side of the slide, type

Rigid Hull Inflatable Tour and in the orange placeholder on the right side of the slide, type **Catamaran or Sailing Tour**

7 In the content placeholder on the left, type each of the following bullet points, increasing the list level for the last three bullet points as indicated:

Good choice if you are:

> **Interested in adventure**

> **Free from recent back injuries**

> **Not prone to motion sickness**

8 In the content placeholder on the right, type each of the following bullet points, increasing the list level for the last two bullet points as indicated:

Good choice if you are:

> **Interested in a leisurely cruise**

> **Looking forward to an overall smooth ride**

9 On **Slide 4**, type the following notes in the **Notes pane**: **If you need assistance deciding which boat tour is right for you, we'll be happy to help you decide.** Insert a **New Slide** using the **Section Header** layout. In the title placeholder, type **Book Your Trip Today!** In the text placeholder, type **Contact Lehua Hawaiian Adventures**

10 Insert a **Header & Footer** on the **Notes and Handouts**. Include the **Date and time** updated automatically, the **Page number**, and a **Footer**—using your own name—with the text **Lastname_Firstname_1E_Boat_Tours** and apply to all the slides.

11 Display the **Document Information Panel**. Replace the text in the **Author** box with your own firstname and lastname. In the **Subject** box, type your course name and section number, and in the **Keywords** box, type **Na Pali, boat tours, sailing Close** the Document Information Panel.

12 **Save** your presentation, and then view the slide show from the beginning. Submit your presentation electronically or print **Handouts, 6 Slides Horizontal** as directed by your instructor. **Close** the presentation.

End **You have completed Project 1E**

Mastering PowerPoint | Project **1F** Helicopter Tour

In the following Mastering PowerPoint project, you will edit a presentation describing the helicopter tours offered by Lehua Hawaiian Adventures. Your completed presentation will look similar to Figure 1.51.

Project Files

For Project 1F, you will need the following files:

> p01F_Helicopter_Tour
> p01F_Aerial_Views

You will save your presentation as:

> Lastname_Firstname_1F_Helicopter_Tour

Project Results

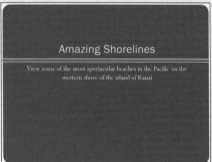

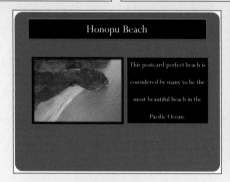

Figure 1.51

(Project 1F Helicopter Tour continues on the next page)

Content-Based Assessments

1 **Start** PowerPoint, and then from your student data files, open the file **p01F_Helicopter_Tour**. In your **PowerPoint Chapter 1** folder, **Save** the file as **Lastname_Firstname_1F_Helicopter_Tour**

2 Display the presentation **Outline**. In the **Outline tab**, in **Slide 2**, increase the list level of the bullet point that begins *Formed by erosion*. In the **Outline tab**, click at the end of the second bullet point after the word *Kauai*. Press [Enter], and then decrease the list level of the new bullet point. Type **Lava flows changed the canyon landscape over the course of centuries**

3 In the **Slides/Outline pane**, click the **Slides tab** to display the slide thumbnails, and then display **Slide 1**. Display the **Reuse Slides** pane, and then click the **Browse** button. Click **Browse File**, and then in the **Browse** dialog box, from your student files, open **p01F_Aerial_Views**. Select the **Keep source formatting** check box, and then from this group of slides, insert the first and second slides—*Aerial View of Kauai* and *Dramatic Overhead*.

4 In the **Slides/Outline pane**, click **Slide 4** to display it in the **Slide pane**, and then from the **Reuse Slides** pane, insert the third, fourth, fifth, and sixth slides—*Na Pali Coast*, *Honopu Beach*, *Amazing Shorelines*, *Tunnels Beach*. **Close** the **Reuse Slides** pane.

5 Display **Slide 1**, and then select the title—*Maui from the Sky*. Change the **Font** to **Arial**, and the **Font Size** to **44**. Change the **Font Color** to **White, Text 1**. Display the **Replace** dialog box. **Replace All** occurrences of the word **Maui** with **Kauai** and then **Close** the **Replace** dialog box.

6 Display **Slide 5**, and then select the paragraph in the content placeholder. Apply **Bold** and **Italic**, and then **Center** the text. Change the **Line Spacing** to **1.5**. Display **Slide 7**, and then change the **Slide Layout** to **Section Header**. **Center** the text in both placeholders.

7 In **Slide Sorter** view, delete **Slide 2**. Then select **Slides 6** and **7** and move both slides so that they are positioned after **Slide 3**. In **Normal** view, display **Slide 1**. Apply the **Split** transition and change the **Effect Options** to **Horizontal Out**. Apply the transition to all of the slides in the presentation. View the slide show from the beginning.

8 **Insert** a **Header & Footer** on the **Notes and Handouts**. Include the **Date and time** updated automatically, the **Page number**, and a **Footer** with the text **Lastname_Firstname_1F_Helicopter_Tour** Apply to all the slides.

9 Check spelling in the presentation. If necessary, select the Ignore All option if proper names are indicated as misspelled.

10 Display the **Document Information Panel**. Replace the text in the **Author** box with your own firstname and lastname. In the **Subject** box, type your course name and section number, and in the **Keywords** box, type **helicopter, Kauai Close** the Document Information Panel.

11 **Save** your presentation, and then submit your presentation electronically or print **Handouts, 4 Slides Horizontal** as directed by your instructor. **Close** the presentation.

End **You have completed Project 1F**

Content-Based Assessments

Apply **1A** and **1B** skills from these Objectives:

1. Create a New Presentation
2. Edit a Presentation in Normal View
3. Add Pictures to a Presentation
4. Print and View a Presentation
5. Edit an Existing Presentation
6. Format a Presentation
7. Use Slide Sorter View
8. Apply Slide Transitions

Mastering PowerPoint | Project **1G** Volcano Tour

In the following Mastering PowerPoint project, you will edit an existing presentation that describes the tour of Volcanoes National Park offered by Lehua Hawaiian Adventures. Your completed presentation will look similar to Figure 1.52.

Project Files

For Project 1G, you will need the following files:

  p01G_Crater_Information
  p01G_Lava
  p01G_Volcano_Tour

You will save your presentation as:

  Lastname_Firstname_1G_Volcano_Tour

Project Results

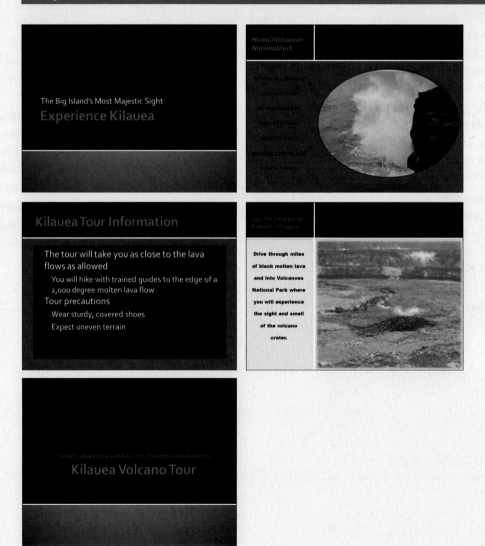

Figure 1.52

(Project 1G Volcano Tour continues on the next page)

Content-Based Assessments

Mastering PowerPoint | Project 1G Volcano Tour (continued)

1 **Start** PowerPoint, and then from your student files, open the file **p01G_Volcano_Tour**. In your **PowerPoint Chapter 1** folder, **Save** the file as **Lastname_Firstname_1G_Volcano_Tour**

2 Replace all occurrences of the text **Diamond Head** with **Kilauea** Display **Slide 3**, open the **Reuse Slides** pane, and then from your student files browse for and display the presentation **p01G_Crater_Information**. If necessary, clear the Keep source formatting check box, and then insert both slides from the **p01G_Crater_Information** file. **Close** the **Reuse Slides** pane.

3 Display the presentation outline, and then in **Slide 3**, increase the list level of the bullet point beginning *You will hike*. In either the **Slide pane** or the **Outline**, click at the end of the last bullet point after the word *flow*, and then insert a new bullet point. Decrease its list level. Type **Tour precautions** and then press Enter. Increase the list level, and then type the following two bullet points.

Wear sturdy, covered shoes

Expect uneven terrain

4 Display the slide thumbnails. In **Slide 1**, select the subtitle—*The Big Island's Most Majestic Sight*—and then change the **Font Color** to **White, Text 1** and the **Font Size** to **28**. On **Slide 2**, center the caption text located below the slide title and apply **Bold** and **Italic**. Change the **Line Spacing** to **2.0**. Click in the content placeholder on the right, and then from your student files, insert the picture

p01G_Lava. Format the picture with the **Beveled Oval, Black** picture style and the **Paint Brush** artistic effect.

5 In **Slide Sorter** view, move **Slide 5** between **Slides 3** and **4**. In **Normal** view, on **Slide 5**, change the slide **Layout** to **Title Slide**, and then type the following notes in the **Notes pane: Recent volcanic activity at the national park site may result in changes to the tour itinerary.** Apply the **Uncover** transition and change the **Effect Options** to **From Top**. Change the **Timing** by increasing the **Duration** to **01.50**. Apply the transition effect to all of the slides. View the slide show from the beginning.

6 **Insert** a **Header & Footer** on the **Notes and Handouts**. Include the **Date and time** updated automatically, the **Page number**, and a **Footer**, using your own name, with the text **Lastname_Firstname_1G_Volcano_Tour**

7 Check spelling in the presentation. If necessary, select the Ignore All option if proper names are indicated as misspelled.

8 Display the **Document Information Panel**. Replace the text in the **Author** box with your own firstname and lastname. In the **Subject** box, type your course name and section number, and in the **Keywords** box, type **Kilauea, volcano Close** the Document Information Panel.

9 **Save** your presentation. Submit your presentation electronically or print **Handouts, 6 Slides Horizontal** as directed by your instructor. **Close** the presentation.

End You have completed Project 1G

Content-Based Assessments

GO! Fix It | Project **1H** Hawaii Guide

Project Files

For Project 1H, you will need the following files:

> p01H_Hawaii_Guide
> p01H_Islands

You will save your presentation as:

> Lastname_Firstname_1H_Hawaii_Guide

In this project, you will edit a presentation prepared by Lehua Hawaiian Adventures that describes some of the activities on each of the Hawaiian Islands. From the student files that accompany this textbook, open the file p01H_Hawaii_Guide, and then save the file in your chapter folder as **Lastname_Firstname_1H_Hawaii_Guide**

To complete the project, you should know:

- All of the slides in the p01H_Islands presentation should be reused in this presentation and inserted after Slide 2. Correct two spelling errors and ignore all instances of proper names that are indicated as misspelled.

- The Opulent theme should be applied.

- Slides 3 through 8 should be arranged alphabetically according to the name of the island

- On the Maui and Molokai slides, the list level of the second bullet points should decreased.

- The Layout for Slide 2 should be Section Header, the slide should be moved to the end of the presentation, and the Flip transition using the Left effect option should be applied to all of the slides in the presentation.

- Document Properties should include your name, course name and section, and the keywords **guide, islands** A Header & Footer should be inserted on the Notes and Handouts that includes the Date and time updated automatically, the Page number, and a Footer with the text **Lastname_Firstname_1H_Hawaii_Guide**

Save your presentation and submit electronically or print Handouts, 4 Slides Horizontal as directed by your instructor. Close the presentation.

End **You have completed Project 1H** ————————

Content-Based Assessments

GO! Make It | Project 1I Dolphin Encounter

Project Files

For Project 1I, you will need the following files:

> p01I_Dolphin_Encounters
> p01I_Dolphin

You will save your presentation as:

> Lastname_Firstname_1I_Dolphin_Encounters

From your student files, open p01I_Dolphin_Encounters, and then save it in your PowerPoint Chapter 1 folder as **Lastname_Firstname_1I_Dolphin_Encounters**

By using the skills you practiced in this chapter, create the slide shown in Figure 1.53 by inserting a new Slide 2 with the layout and text shown in the figure. The title font size is 36, and the font color is Black, Background 1. The caption text font is Arial, and the font size is 16 with bold and italic applied. To complete the slide, from your student files, insert the picture p01H_Dolphin. Insert the date and time updated automatically, the file name, and a page number in the Notes and Handouts footer. In the Document Information Panel, add your name and course information and the keyword **dolphin** Save your presentation, and then print or submit electronically as directed by your instructor.

Project Results

Dolphin Encounters!

Learn about dolphins during our 30-minute training program. Then join the trainers in our pool as you swim and play with our dolphin friends!

Figure 1.53

End **You have completed Project 1I**

Content-Based Assessments

GO! Solve It | Project 1J Planning Tips

Project Files

For Project 1J, you will need the following file:

p01J_Planning_Tips

You will save your presentation as:

Lastname_Firstname_1J_Planning_Tips

Open the file p01J_Planning_Tips and save it as **Lastname_Firstname_1J_Planning_Tips** Complete the presentation by applying a theme and by correcting spelling errors. Format the presentation attractively by applying appropriate font formatting and by changing text alignment and line spacing. Change the layout of at least one slide to a layout that will accommodate a picture. Insert a picture that you have taken yourself, or use one of the pictures in your student data files that you inserted in other projects in this chapter. On the last slide, insert an appropriate picture, and then apply picture styles to both pictures. Apply slide transitions to all of the slides in the presentation, and then insert a header and footer that includes the date and time updated automatically, the file name in the footer, and the page number. Add your name, your course name and section number, and the keywords **planning, weather** to the Properties area. Save and print or submit as directed by your instructor.

		Performance Level	
	Exemplary: You consistently applied the relevant skills	**Proficient:** You sometimes, but not always, applied the relevant skills	**Developing:** You rarely or never applied the relevant skills
Apply a theme	An appropriate theme was applied to the presentation.	A theme was applied but was not appropriate for the presentation.	A theme was not applied.
Apply font and slide formatting	Font and slide formatting is attractive and appropriate.	Adequately formatted but difficult to read or unattractive.	Inadequate or no formatting.
Use appropriate pictures and apply styles attractively	Two appropriate pictures are inserted and styles are applied attractively.	Pictures are inserted but styles are not applied or are inappropriately applied.	Pictures are not inserted.

Performance Elements (left vertical label)

End **You have completed Project 1J**

Content-Based Assessments

GO! Solve It | Project **1K** Hikes

Project Files

For Project 1K, you will need the following file:

p01K_Hikes

You will save your presentation as:

Lastname_Firstname_1K_Hikes

Open the file p01K_Hikes and save it as **Lastname_Firstname_1K_Hikes** Complete the presentation by applying an appropriate theme. Move Slide 2 to the end of the presentation, and then change the layout to one appropriate for the end of the presentation. Format the presentation attractively by applying font formatting and by changing text alignment and line spacing. Review the information on Slide 3, and then increase list levels appropriately on this slide. Apply picture styles to the two pictures in the presentation and an artistic effect to at least one picture. Apply slide transitions to all of the slides. Insert a header and footer that includes the date and time updated automatically, the file name in the footer, and the page number. Add your name, your course name and section number, and the keywords **hiking Akaka Falls, Waimea Canyon** to the Properties area. Save and print or submit as directed by your instructor.

	Performance Level		
	Exemplary: You consistently applied the relevant skills	**Proficient:** You sometimes, but not always, applied the relevant skills	**Developing:** You rarely or never applied the relevant skills
Apply a theme	An appropriate theme was applied to the presentation.	A theme was applied but was not appropriate for the presentation.	A theme was not applied.
Apply appropriate formatting	Formatting is attractive and appropriate.	Adequately formatted but difficult to read or unattractive.	Inadequate or no formatting.
Apply appropriate list levels	List levels are applied appropriately.	Some, but not all, list levels are appropriately applied.	Changes to list levels were not made.

(left margin label: Performance Elements)

End **You have completed Project 1K** ————————————

Outcomes-Based Assessments

Rubric

The following outcomes-based assessments are *open-ended assessments*. That is, there is no specific correct result; your result will depend on your approach to the information provided. Make *Professional Quality* your goal. Use the following scoring rubric to guide you in *how* to approach the problem, and then to evaluate *how well* your approach solves the problem.

The *criteria*—Software Mastery, Content, Format and Layout, and Process—represent the knowledge and skills you have gained that you can apply to solving the problem. The *levels of performance*—Professional Quality, Approaching Professional Quality, or Needs Quality Improvements—help you and your instructor evaluate your result.

	Your completed project is of Professional Quality if you:	Your completed project is Approaching Professional Quality if you:	Your completed project Needs Quality Improvements if you:
1-Software Mastery	Choose and apply the most appropriate skills, tools, and features and identify efficient methods to solve the problem.	Choose and apply some appropriate skills, tools, and features, but not in the most efficient manner.	Choose inappropriate skills, tools, or features, or are inefficient in solving the problem.
2-Content	Construct a solution that is clear and well organized, contains content that is accurate, appropriate to the audience and purpose, and is complete. Provide a solution that contains no errors in spelling, grammar, or style.	Construct a solution in which some components are unclear, poorly organized, inconsistent, or incomplete. Misjudge the needs of the audience. Have some errors in spelling, grammar, or style, but the errors do not detract from comprehension.	Construct a solution that is unclear, incomplete, or poorly organized; contains some inaccurate or inappropriate content; and contains many errors in spelling, grammar, or style. Do not solve the problem.
3-Format and Layout	Format and arrange all elements to communicate information and ideas, clarify function, illustrate relationships, and indicate relative importance.	Apply appropriate format and layout features to some elements, but not others. Overuse features, causing minor distraction.	Apply format and layout that does not communicate information or ideas clearly. Do not use format and layout features to clarify function, illustrate relationships, or indicate relative importance. Use available features excessively, causing distraction.
4-Process	Use an organized approach that integrates planning, development, self-assessment, revision, and reflection.	Demonstrate an organized approach in some areas, but not others; or, use an insufficient process of organization throughout.	Do not use an organized approach to solve the problem.

Outcomes-Based Assessments

Apply a combination of the **1A** and **1B** skills.

GO! Think | Project **1L** Big Island

Project Files

For Project 1L, you will need the following files:

New blank PowerPoint presentation
p01L_Fishing
p01L_Monument

You will save your presentation as:

Lastname_Firstname_1L_Big_Island

Carl Kawaoka, Tour Operations Manager for Lehua Hawaiian Adventures, is developing a presentation describing sea tours on the Big Island of Hawaii to be shown at a travel fair on the mainland. In the presentation, Carl will be showcasing the company's two most popular sea excursions: The Captain Cook Monument Snorkeling Tour and the Kona Deep Sea Fishing Tour.

On the Captain Cook Monument Snorkeling Tour, guests meet at 8:00 a.m. at the Lehua Hawaiian Adventures Kona location and then board a 12-passenger rigid hull inflatable raft. Captained by a U.S. Coast Guard licensed crew, the raft is navigated along the Hawaii coastline, exploring sea caves, lava tubes, and waterfalls. Upon arrival at the Monument, guests snorkel in Hawaii's incredible undersea world of colorful fish, sea turtles, and stingrays. Lehua Hawaiian Adventures provides the lunch, snacks, drinks, and snorkeling equipment and asks that guests bring their own towels, sunscreen, swim suits, and sense of adventure. This tour lasts 5 hours and the fee is $85.

On the Kona Deep Sea Fishing Tour, guests meet at 7:00 a.m. at the Lehua Hawaiian Adventures Kona location and then board a 32-foot Blackfin fishing boat. The boat is captained by a U.S. Coast Guard licensed crew of three. A maximum of six guests are allowed on each trip, which sails, weather permitting, every Wednesday, Friday, and Saturday. For deep sea fishing, there is no better place than the Kona coast. On full-day adventures, it is common for guests to catch marlin, sailfish, ahi, ono, and mahi-mahi. This tour lasts 8 hours and the fee is $385.

Using the preceding information, create a presentation that Carl can show at the travel fair. The presentation should include four to six slides describing the two tours. Apply an appropriate theme and use slide layouts that will effectively present the content. From your student files, insert the pictures p01L_Fishing and p01L_Monument on appropriate slides and apply picture styles or artistic effects to enhance the pictures. Apply font formatting and slide transitions, and modify text alignment and line spacing as necessary. Save the file as **Lastname_Firstname_1L_Big_Island** and then insert a header and footer that include the date and time updated automatically, the file name in the footer, and the page number. Add your name, your course name and section number, and the keywords **sea tours, deep sea fishing, snorkeling tours** to the Properties area. Save and print or submit as directed by your instructor.

End You have completed Project 1L —————————————

Outcomes-Based Assessments

GO! Think | Project **1M** Beaches

Project Files

For Project 1M, you will need the following files:

New blank PowerPoint presentation
p01M_Black_Sand
p01M_Kite_Surf
p01M_Lithified_Cliffs
p01M_Reef
p01M_Tide_Pools

You will save your presentation as:

Lastname_Firstname_1M_Beaches

Katherine Okubo, President of Lehua Hawaiian Adventures, is making a presentation to groups of tourists at a number of hotels on the Hawaiian Islands. She would like to begin the presentation with an introduction to the beaches of Hawaii before discussing the many ways in which her company can assist tourists with selecting the places they would like to visit. The following paragraphs contain some of the information about the shorelines and beaches that Katherine would like to include in the presentation.

The shorelines of Hawaii vary tremendously, from black sand beaches with pounding surf to beaches of pink and white sand with calm waters perfect for snorkeling. Many of the shorelines provide picturesque hiking, shallow tide pools for exploring, beautiful reef where fish and turtles delight snorkelers, and waves that the most adventurous kite and board surfers enjoy. The terrain and the water make it easy for visitors to find a favorite beach in Hawaii.

The northern shore of Oahu is famous for its surfing beaches, while the southern shores of Kauai provide hikers with amazing views of the lithified cliffs formed by the power of the ocean. Black sand beaches are common on Hawaii, formed by the lava flows that created the islands. The reef that buffers many beaches from the open ocean is home to a wide variety of sea life that can be enjoyed while scuba diving and snorkeling.

Using the preceding information, create the first four to six slides of a presentation that Katherine can show during her discussion. Apply an appropriate theme and use slide layouts that will effectively present the content. Several picture files listed at the beginning of this project have been provided that you can insert in your presentation. Apply font formatting, picture styles, and slide transitions, and modify text alignment and line spacing as necessary. Save the file as **Lastname_Firstname_1M_Beaches** and then insert a header and footer that include the date and time updated automatically, the file name in the footer, and the page number. Add your name, your course name and section number, and the keywords **beaches, Black Sands beach, tide pools, lithified cliffs, scuba, snorkeling** to the Properties area. Save and print or submit as directed by your instructor.

End **You have completed Project 1M** ————————————————

You and GO! | Project **1N** Travel

Project Files

For Project 1N, you will need the following files:

New blank PowerPoint presentation

You will save your presentation as:

Lastname_Firstname_1N_Travel

Choose a place to which you have traveled or would like to travel. Create a presentation with at least six slides that describes the location, the method of travel, the qualities of the location that make it interesting or fun, the places you can visit, and any cultural activities in which you might like to participate. Choose an appropriate theme, slide layouts, and pictures, and then format the presentation attractively. Save your presentation as **Lastname_Firstname_1N_Travel** and submit as directed.

End **You have completed Project 1N**

Glossary

Absolute cell reference A cell reference that refers to cells by their fixed position in a worksheet; an absolute cell reference remains the same when the formula is copied.

Accounting Number Format The Excel number format that applies a thousand comma separator where appropriate, inserts a fixed U.S. Dollar sign aligned at the left edge of the cell, applies two decimal places, and leaves a small amount of space at the right edge of the cell to accommodate a parenthesis for negative numbers.

Active cell The cell, surrounded by a black border, ready to receive data or be affected by the next Excel command.

Address bar The bar at the top of a folder window with which you can navigate to a different folder or library, or go back to a previous one.

Alignment The placement of paragraph text relative to the left and right margins.

All Programs An area of the Start menu that displays all the available programs on your computer system.

Anchor The symbol that indicates to which paragraph an object is attached.

Append To add on to the end of an object; for example, to add records to the end of an existing table.

Application Another term for a program.

Arithmetic operators The symbols +, −, *, /, %, and ^ used to denote addition, subtraction (or negation), multiplication, division, percentage, and exponentiation in an Excel formula.

Artistic effects Formats applied to images that make pictures resemble sketches or paintings.

Auto Fill An Excel feature that generates and extends values into adjacent cells based on the values of selected cells.

AutoComplete (Excel) A feature that speeds your typing and lessens the likelihood of errors; if the first few characters you type in a cell match an existing entry in the column, Excel fills in the remaining characters for you.

AutoFit An Excel feature that adjusts the width of a column to fit the cell content of the widest cell in the column.

AutoNumber data type A data type that describes a unique sequential or random number assigned by Access as each record is entered and that is useful for data that has no distinct field that can be considered unique.

AutoPlay A Windows feature that displays when you insert a CD, a DVD, or other removable device, and which lets you choose which program to use to start different kinds of media, such as music CDs, or CDs and DVDs containing photos.

AutoSum Another name for the *SUM* function.

Back and Forward buttons Buttons at the top of a folder window that work in conjunction with the address bar to change folders by going backward or forward one folder at a time.

Backstage tabs The area along the left side of Backstage view with tabs to display various pages of commands.

Backstage view A centralized space for file management tasks; for example, opening, saving, printing, publishing, or sharing a file. A navigation pane displays along the left side with tabs that group file-related tasks together.

Bar tab stop A vertical bar that displays at a tab stop.

Best Fit An Access command that adjusts the width of a column to accommodate the column's longest entry.

Black slide A slide that displays at the end of an electronic slide show indicating that the presentation is over.

Blank database A database that has no data and has no database tools— you must create the data and the tools as you need them.

Bulleted list A list of items with each item introduced by a symbol such as a small circle or check mark, and which is useful when the items in the list can be displayed in any order.

Bullets Text symbols such as small circles or check marks that precede each item in a bulleted list.

Caption A property setting that displays a name for a field in a table, query, form, or report other than that listed as the field name.

Category axis The area along the bottom of a chart that identifies the categories of data; also referred to as the *x-axis*.

Category labels The labels that display along the bottom of a chart to identify the categories of data; Excel uses the row titles as the category names.

Cell The intersection of a column and a row.

Cell address Another name for a *cell reference*.

Cell content Anything typed into a cell.

Cell reference The identification of a specific cell by its intersecting column letter and row number.

Cell style A defined set of formatting characteristics, such as font, font size, font color, cell borders, and cell shading.

Center alignment An arrangement of text in which the text is centered between the left and right margins.

Center alignment The alignment of text or objects that is centered horizontally between the left and right margin.

Center tab stop A tab stop in which the text centers around the tab stop location.

Chart (Excel) The graphic representation of data in a worksheet; data presented as a chart is usually easier to understand than a table of numbers.

Chart layout The combination of chart elements that can be displayed in a chart such as a title, legend, labels for the columns, and the table of charted cells.

Chart Layouts gallery A group of predesigned chart layouts that you can apply to an Excel chart.

Chart style The overall visual look of a chart in terms of its graphic effects, colors, and backgrounds; for example, you can have flat or beveled columns, colors that solid or transparent, and backgrounds that are dark or light.

Chart Styles gallery A group of predesigned chart styles that you can apply to an Excel chart.

Chart types Various chart formats used in a way that is meaningful to the reader; common examples are column charts, pie charts, and line charts.

Click The action of pressing the left button on your mouse pointing device one time.

Column A vertical group of cells in a worksheet.

Column chart A chart in which the data is arranged in columns and which is useful for showing data changes over a period of time or for illustrating comparisons among items.

Column heading The letter that displays at the top of a vertical group of cells in a worksheet; beginning with the first letter of the alphabet, a unique letter or combination of letters identifies each column.

Comma Style The Excel number format that inserts thousand comma separators where appropriate and applies two decimal places; Comma Style also leaves space at the right to accommodate a parenthesis when negative numbers are present.

Command An instruction to a computer program that causes an action to be carried out.

Common dialog boxes The set of dialog boxes that includes Open, Save, and Save As, which are provided by the Windows programming interface, and which display and operate in all of the Office programs in the same manner.

Common field A field in one or more tables that stores the same data.

Compressed file A file that has been reduced in size and thus takes up less storage space and can be transferred to other computers quickly.

Constant value Numbers, text, dates, or times of day that you type into a cell.

Context sensitive A command associated with activities in which you are engaged; often activated by right-clicking a screen item.

Context sensitive command A command associated with activities in which you are engaged.

Contextual tabs Tabs that are added to the Ribbon automatically when a specific object, such as a picture, is selected, and that contain commands relevant to the selected object.

Copy A command that duplicates a selection and places it on the Clipboard.

Currency data type An Access data type that describes monetary values and numeric data that can be used in mathematical calculations involving data with one to four decimal places.

Cut A command that removes a selection and places it on the Clipboard.

Data Facts about people, events, things, or ideas.

Data (Excel) Text or numbers in a cell.

Data marker A column, bar, area, dot, pie slice, or other symbol in a chart that represents a single data point; related data points form a data series.

Data point A value that originates in a worksheet cell and that is represented in a chart by a data marker.

Data series Related data points represented by data markers; each data series has a unique color or pattern represented in the chart legend.

Data source (Word) A list of variable information, such as names and addresses, that is merged with a main document to create customized form letters or labels.

Data type The characteristic that defines the kind of data that can be entered into a field, such as numbers, text, or dates.

Database An organized collection of facts about people, events, things, or ideas related to a specific topic or purpose.

Database management system Database software that controls how related collections of data are stored, organized, retrieved, and secured; also known as a *DBMS*.

Database template A preformatted database designed for a specific purpose.

Datasheet view The Access view that displays data organized in columns and rows similar to an Excel worksheet.

DBMS An acronym for *database management system*.

Decimal tab stop A tab stop in which the text aligns with the decimal point at the tab stop location.

Default The term that refers to the current selection or setting that is automatically used by a computer program unless you specify otherwise.

Deselect The action of canceling the selection of an object or block of text by clicking outside of the selection.

Design view An Access view that displays the detailed structure of a query, form, or report; for forms and reports, may be the view in which some tasks must be performed, and only the controls, and not the data, display in this view.

Desktop In Windows, the opening screen that simulates your work area.

Destination table (Access) The table to which you import or append data.

Details pane The area at the bottom of a folder window that displays the most common file properties.

Dialog box A small window that contains options for completing a task.

Dialog Box Launcher A small icon that displays to the right of some group names on the Ribbon, and which opens a related dialog box or task pane providing additional options and commands related to that group.

Displayed value The data that displays in a cell.

Document properties Details about a file that describe or identify it, including the title, author name, subject, and keywords that identify the document's topic or contents; also known as *metadata*.

Dot leader A series of dots preceding a tab that guides the eye across the line.

Double-click The action of clicking the left mouse button two times in rapid succession.

Drag The action of holding down the left mouse button while moving your mouse.

Drawing objects Graphic objects, such as shapes, diagrams, lines, or circles.

Edit The actions of making changes to text or graphics in an Office file.

Editing The process of modifying a presentation by adding and deleting slides or by changing the contents of individual slides.

Ellipsis A set of three dots indicating incompleteness; when following a command name, indicates that a dialog box will display.

Enhanced ScreenTip A ScreenTip that displays more descriptive text than a normal ScreenTip.

Expand Formula Bar button An Excel window element with which you can increase the height of the Formula Bar to display lengthy cell content.

Expand horizontal scroll bar button An Excel window element with which you can increase the width of the horizontal scroll bar.

Extract To decompress, or pull out, files from a compressed form.

Field A single piece of information that is stored in every record and formatted as a column in a database table.

Field (Word) A placeholder that displays preset content, such as the current date, the file name, a page number, or other stored information.

Field properties Characteristics of a field that control how the field displays and how data can be entered in the field.

File A collection of information stored on a computer under a single name, for example a Word document or a PowerPoint presentation.

File list In a folder window, the area on the right that displays the contents of the current folder or library.

Fill The inside color of an object.

Fill handle The small black square in the lower right corner of a selected cell.

First principle of good database design A principle of good database design stating that data is organized in tables so that there is no redundant data.

Flat database A simple database file that is not related or linked to any other collection of data.

Floating object A graphic that can be moved independently of the surrounding text characters.

Folder A container in which you store files.

Folder window In Windows, a window that displays the contents of the current folder, library, or device, and contains helpful parts so that you can navigate.

Font A set of characters with the same design and shape.

Font styles Formatting emphasis such as bold, italic, and underline.

Footer (PowerPoint) Text that displays at the bottom of every slide or that prints at the bottom of a sheet of slide handouts or notes pages.

Footer A reserved area for text or graphics that displays at the bottom of each page in a document.

Form A database object used to enter data, edit data, or display data from a table or query.

Form view The Access view in which you can view the records, but you cannot change the layout or design of the form.

Format (Excel) Changing the appearance of cells and worksheet elements to make a worksheet attractive and easy to read.

Format Painter An Office feature that copies formatting from one selection of text to another.

Formatting The process of establishing the overall appearance of text, graphics, and pages in an Office file—for example, in a Word document.

Formatting (PowerPoint) The process of changing the appearance of the text, layout, and design of a slide.

Formatting marks Characters that display on the screen, but do not print, indicating where the Enter key, the Spacebar, and the Tab key were pressed; also called *nonprinting characters*.

Formula An equation that performs mathematical calculations on values in a worksheet.

Formula Bar An element in the Excel window that displays the value or formula contained in the active cell; here you can also enter or edit values or formulas.

Function A predefined formula—a formula that Excel has already built for you—that performs calculations by using specific values in a particular order or structure.

Gallery An Office feature that displays a list of potential results instead of just the command name.

General format The default format that Excel applies to numbers; this format has no specific characteristics—whatever you type in the cell will display, with the exception that trailing zeros to the right of a decimal point will not display.

Graphics Pictures, clip art images, charts, or drawing objects.

Groups On the Office Ribbon, the sets of related commands that you might need for a specific type of task.

Header (PowerPoint) Text that prints at the top of each sheet of slide handouts or notes pages.

Header A reserved area for text or graphics that displays at the top of each page in a document.

Horizontal window split box (Excel) An Excel window element with which you can split the worksheet into two horizontal views of the same worksheet.

Icons Pictures that represent a program, a file, a folder, or some other object.

Import The process of copying data from another file, such as a Word table or an Excel workbook, into a separate file, such as an Access database.

Info tab The tab in Backstage view that displays information about the current file.

Information Data that is organized in a useful manner.

Inline object An object or graphic inserted in a document that acts like a character in a sentence.

Insert Worksheet button Located on the row of sheet tabs, a sheet tab that, when clicked, inserts an additional worksheet into the workbook.

Insertion point A blinking vertical line that indicates where text or graphics will be inserted.

Justified alignment An arrangement of text in which the text aligns evenly on both the left and right margins.

Keyboard shortcut A combination of two or more keyboard keys, used to perform a task that would otherwise require a mouse.

KeyTips The letter that displays on a command in the Ribbon and that indicates the key you can press to activate the command when keyboard control of the Ribbon is activated.

Labels Another name for a text value, and which usually provides information about number values.

Landscape orientation A page orientation in which the paper is wider than it is tall.

Layout The arrangement of elements, such as title and subtitle text, lists, pictures, tables, charts, shapes, and movies, on a PowerPoint slide.

Layout view The Access view in which you can make changes to a form or report while the object is running—the data from the underlying data source displays.

Leader characters Characters that form a solid, dotted, or dashed line that fills the space preceding a tab stop.

Left alignment An arrangement of text in which the text aligns at the left margin, leaving the right margin uneven.

Left alignment (Excel) The cell format in which characters align at the left edge of the cell; this is the default for text entries and is an example of formatting information stored in a cell.

Left tab stop A tab stop in which the text is left aligned at the tab stop and extends to the right.

Legend A chart element that identifies the patterns or colors that are assigned to the categories in the chart.

Lettered column headings The area along the top edge of a worksheet that identifies each column with a unique letter or combination of letters.

Library In Windows, a collection of items, such as files and folders, assembled from various locations that might be on your computer, an external hard drive, removable media, or someone else's computer.

Line spacing The distance between lines of text in a paragraph.

Link A connection to data in another file.

List level An outline level in a presentation represented by a bullet symbol and identified in a slide by the indentation and the size of the text.

Live Preview A technology that shows the result of applying an editing or formatting change as you point to possible results—*before* you actually apply it.

Location Any disk drive, folder, or other place in which you can store files and folders.

Margins The space between the text and the top, bottom, left, and right edges of the paper.

Merge & Center A command that joins selected cells in an Excel worksheet into one larger cell and centers the contents in the new cell.

Metadata Details about a file that describe or identify it, including the title, author name, subject, and keywords that identify the document's topic or contents; also known as *document properties*.

Microsoft Access A database program, with which you can collect, track, and report data.

Microsoft Communicator An Office program that brings together multiple modes of communication, including instant messaging, video conferencing, telephony, application sharing, and file transfer.

Microsoft Excel A spreadsheet program, with which you calculate and analyze numbers and create charts.

Microsoft InfoPath An Office program that enables you to create forms and gather data.

Microsoft Office 2010 A Microsoft suite of products that includes programs, servers, and services for individuals, small organizations, and large enterprises to perform specific tasks.

Microsoft OneNote An Office program with which you can manage notes that you make at meetings or in classes.

Microsoft Outlook An Office program with which you can manage e-mail and organizational activities.

Microsoft PowerPoint A presentation program, with which you can communicate information with high-impact graphics.

Microsoft Publisher An Office program with which you can create desktop publishing documents such as brochures.

Microsoft SharePoint Workspace An Office program that enables you to share information with others in a team environment.

Microsoft Word A word processing program, also referred to as an authoring program, with which you create and share documents by using its writing tools.

Mini toolbar A small toolbar containing frequently used formatting commands that displays as a result of selecting text or objects.

Multiple Items form A form that enables you to display or enter multiple records in a table.

Name Box An element of the Excel window that displays the name of the selected cell, table, chart, or object.

Navigate The process of exploring within the organizing structure of Windows.

Navigation area An area at the bottom of the Access window that indicates the number of records in the table and contains controls (arrows) with which you can navigate among the records.

Navigation Pane (Access) An area of the Access window that displays and organizes the names of the objects in a database; from here, you open objects for use.

Navigation pane (Windows) In a folder window, the area on the left in which you can navigate to, open, and display favorites, libraries, folders, saved searches, and an expandable list of drives.

Nonprinting characters Characters that display on the screen, but do not print, indicating where the Enter key, the Spacebar, and the Tab key were pressed; also called *formatting marks*.

Normal view (Excel) A screen view that maximizes the number of cells visible on your screen and keeps the column letters and row numbers close to the columns and rows.

Normal view (PowerPoint) The primary editing view in PowerPoint in which you write and design your presentations; consists of the Notes pane, Slide pane, and the Slides/Outline pane.

Normalization The process of applying design rules and principles to ensure that your database performs as expected.

Notes page A printout that contains the slide image on the top half of the page and notes that you have created on the Notes pane in the lower half of the page.

Notes pane The PowerPoint screen element that displays below the Slide pane with space to type notes regarding the active slide.

Nudge The action of moving an object on the page in small precise increments.

Number format A specific way in which Excel displays numbers in a cell.

Number values Constant values consisting of only numbers.

Numbered list A list of items in which each item is introduced by a consecutive number to indicate definite steps, a sequence of actions, or chronological order.

Numbered row headings The area along the left edge of a worksheet that identifies each row with a unique number.

Object window An area of the Access window that displays open objects, such as tables, forms, queries, or reports; by default, each object displays on its own tab.

Objects The basic parts of a database that you create to store your data and to work with your data; for example, tables, forms, queries, and reports.

Office Clipboard A temporary storage area that holds text or graphics that you select and then cut or copy.

Open dialog box A dialog box from which you can navigate to, and then open on your screen, an existing file that was created in that same program.

Operators The symbols with which you can specify the type of calculation you want to perform in an Excel formula.

Option button A round button that allows you to make one choice among two or more options.

Options dialog box A dialog box within each Office application where you can select program settings and other options and preferences.

Page Layout view A screen view in which you can use the rulers to measure the width and height of data, set margins for printing, hide or display the numbered row headings and the lettered column headings, and change the page orientation; this view is useful for preparing your worksheet for printing.

Paragraph symbol The symbol ¶ that represents a paragraph.

Paste The action of placing text or objects that have been copied or moved from one location to another location.

Paste Options Icons that provide a Live Preview of the various options for changing the format of a pasted item with a single click.

PDF (Portable Document Format) file A file format that creates an image that preserves the look of your file, but that cannot be easily changed; a popular format for sending documents electronically, because the document will display on most computers.

Picture element A point of light measured in dots per square inch on a screen; 64 pixels equals 8.43 characters, which is the average number of digits that will fit in a cell in an Excel worksheet using the default font.

Picture styles Frames, shapes, shadows, borders, and other special effects that can be added to an image to create an overall visual style for the image.

Pixel The abbreviated name for a *picture element*.

Placeholder A box on a slide with dotted or dashed borders that holds title and body text or other content such as charts, tables, and pictures.

Point The action of moving your mouse pointer over something on your screen.

Point and click method The technique of constructing a formula by pointing to and then clicking cells; this method is convenient when the referenced cells are not adjacent to one another.

Pointer Any symbol that displays on your screen in response to moving your mouse.

Points A measurement of the size of a font; there are 72 points in an inch, with 10-12 points being the most commonly used font size.

Populate The action of filling a database table with records.

Portrait orientation A page orientation in which the paper is taller than it is wide.

Preview pane button In a folder window, the button on the toolbar with which you can display a preview of the contents of a file without opening it in a program.

Primary key The field that uniquely identifies a record in a table; for example, a Student ID number at a college.

Print Preview A view of a document as it will appear when you print it.

Program A set of instructions that a computer uses to perform a specific task, such as word processing, accounting, or data management; also called an *application*.

Program-level control buttons In an Office program, the buttons on the right edge of the title bar that minimize, restore, or close the program.

Protected view A security feature in Office 2010 that protects your computer from malicious files by opening them in a restricted environment until you enable them; you might encounter this feature if you open a file from an e-mail or download files from the Internet.

Pt. The abbreviation for *point*; for example when referring to a font size.

Query A database object that retrieves specific data from one or more database objects—either tables or other queries—and then, in a single datasheet, displays only the data you specify.

Quick Access Toolbar In an Office program, the small row of buttons in the upper left corner of the screen from which you can perform frequently used commands.

Quick Commands The commands Save, Save As, Open, and Close that display at the top of the navigation pane in Backstage view.

Range Two or more selected cells on a worksheet that are adjacent or nonadjacent; because the range is treated as a single unit, you can make the same changes or combination of changes to more than one cell at a time.

Range finder An Excel feature that outlines cells in color to indicate which cells are used in a formula; useful for verifying which cells are referenced in a formula.

Read-Only A property assigned to a file that prevents the file from being modified or deleted; it indicates that you cannot save any changes to the displayed document unless you first save it with a new name.

Reading view A view in PowerPoint that displays a presentation in a manner similar to a slide show but in which the taskbar, title bar, and status bar remain available in the presentation window.

Record All of the categories of data pertaining to one person, place, thing, event, or idea, and which is formatted as a row in a database table.

Record selector bar The bar at the left edge of a record when it is displayed in a form, and which is used to select an entire record.

Record selector box The small box at the left of a record in Datasheet view that, when clicked, selects the entire record.

Redundant In a database, information that is repeated in a manner that indicates poor database design.

Relational database A sophisticated type of database that has multiple collections of data within the file that are related to one another.

Relative cell reference In a formula, the address of a cell based on the relative position of the cell that contains the formula and the cell referred to.

Report A database object that summarizes the fields and records from a table or query in an easy-to-read format suitable for printing.

Ribbon The user interface in Office 2010 that groups the commands for performing related tasks on tabs across the upper portion of the program window.

Ribbon tabs The tabs on the Office Ribbon that display the names of the task-oriented groups of commands.

Right alignment An arrangement of text in which the text aligns at the right margin, leaving the left margin uneven.

Right tab stop A tab stop in which the text is right aligned at the tab stop and extends to the left.

Right-click The action of clicking the right mouse button one time.

Rotation handle A green circle that provides a way to rotate a selected image.

Rounding A procedure in which you determine which digit at the right of the number will be the last digit displayed and then increase it by one if the next digit to its right is 5, 6, 7, 8, or 9.

Row A horizontal group of cells in a worksheet.

Row heading The numbers along the left side of an Excel worksheet that designate the row numbers.

Run The process in which Access searches the records in the table(s) included in the query design, finds the records that match the specified criteria, and then displays the records in a datasheet; only the fields that have been included in the query design display.

Sans serif A font design with no lines or extensions on the ends of characters.

Scaling (Excel) The process of shrinking the width and/or height of printed output to fit a maximum number of pages.

ScreenTip A small box that that displays useful information when you perform various mouse actions such as pointing to screen elements or dragging.

Scroll bar A vertical or horizontal bar in a window or a pane to assist in bringing an area into view, and which contains a scroll box and scroll arrows.

Scroll box The box in the vertical and horizontal scroll bars that can be dragged to reposition the contents of a window or pane on the screen.

Search box In a folder window, the box in which you can type a word or a phrase to look for an item in the current folder or library.

Second principle of good database design A principle stating that appropriate database techniques are used to ensure the accuracy of data entered into a table.

Select To highlight, by dragging with your mouse, areas of text or data or graphics, so that the selection can be edited, formatted, copied, or moved.

Select All box A box in the upper left corner of the worksheet grid that, when clicked, selects all the cells in a worksheet.

Select query A type of Access query that retrieves (selects) data from one or more tables or queries, displaying the selected data in a datasheet; also known as a *simple select query*.

Series A group of things that come one after another in succession; for example, January, February, March, and so on.

Serif font A font design that includes small line extensions on the ends of the letters to guide the eye in reading from left to right.

Shapes Lines, arrows, stars, banners, ovals, rectangles, and other basic shapes with which you can illustrate an idea, a process, or a workflow.

Sheet tab scrolling buttons Buttons to the left of the sheet tabs used to display Excel sheet tabs that are not in view; used when there are more sheet tabs than will display in the space provided.

Sheet tabs The labels along the lower border of the Excel window that identify each worksheet.

Shortcut menu A menu that displays commands and options relevant to the selected text or object.

Simple select query Another name for a select query.

Single-record form A form that enables you to display or enter one record at a time in a table.

Sizing handles Small circles and squares that indicate that a picture is selected.

Slide A presentation page that can contain text, pictures, tables, charts, and other multimedia or graphic objects.

Slide handouts Printed images of slides on a sheet of paper.

Slide pane A PowerPoint screen element that displays a large image of the active slide.

Slide Sorter view A presentation view that displays thumbnails of all of the slides in a presentation.

Slide transitions The motion effects that occur in Slide Show view when you move from one slide to the next during a presentation.

Slides/Outline pane A PowerPoint screen element that displays the presentation either in the form of thumbnails (Slides tab) or in outline format (Outline tab).

SmartArt A designer-quality visual representation of your information that you can create by choosing from among many different layouts to effectively communicate your message or ideas.

Source file When importing a file, refers to the file being imported.

Sparkline A tiny chart in the background of a cell that gives a visual trend summary alongside your data; makes a pattern more obvious.

Spin box A small box with an upward- and downward-pointing arrow that lets you move rapidly through a set of values by clicking.

Split button A button divided into two parts and in which clicking the main part of the button performs a command and clicking the arrow opens a menu with choices.

Spreadsheet Another name for a *worksheet*.

Start button The button on the Windows taskbar that displays the Start menu.

Start menu The Windows menu that provides a list of choices and is the main gateway to your computer's programs, folders, and settings.

Status bar (Excel) The area along the lower edge of the Excel window that displays, on the left side, the current cell mode, page number, and worksheet information; on the right side, when numerical data is selected, common calculations such as Sum and Average display.

Status bar The area along the lower edge of an Office program window that displays file information on the left and buttons to control how the window looks on the right.

Structure In Access, the underlying design of a table, including field names, data types, descriptions, and field properties.

Style (PowerPoint) A collection of formatting options that can be applied to a picture, text, or an object.

Subfolder A folder within a folder.

Subpoints Secondary-level information in a SmartArt graphic.

SUM function A predefined formula that adds all the numbers in a selected range of cells.

Tab stop Specific locations on a line of text, marked on the Word ruler, to which you can move the insertion point by pressing the Tab key, and which is used to align and indent text.

Table (Access) The database object that stores data organized in an arrangement of columns and rows, and which is the foundation of an Access database.

Tables and Related Views An arrangement in the Navigation Pane that groups objects by the table to which they are related.

Tabs On the Office Ribbon, the name of each activity area in the Office Ribbon.

Tags Custom file properties that you create to help find and organize your own files.

Task pane A window within a Microsoft Office application in which you can enter options for completing a command.

Text alignment (PowerPoint) The horizontal placement of text within a placeholder.

Text box A movable resizable container for text or graphics.

Text box (PowerPoint) An object within which you can position text anywhere on a slide.

Text data type An Access data type that describes text, a combination of text and numbers, or numbers that are not used in calculations, such as a number that is an identifier like a Student ID.

Text effects Decorative formats, such as shadowed or mirrored text, text glow, 3-D effects, and colors that make text stand out.

Text values Constant values consisting of only text, and which usually provides information about number values; also referred to as *labels*.

Text wrapping The manner in which text displays around an object.

Theme A predesigned set of colors, fonts, lines, and fill effects that look good together and that can be applied to your entire document or to specific items.

Theme (PowerPoint) A set of unified design elements that provides a look for your presentation by applying colors, fonts, and effects.

Thumbnails (PowerPoint) Miniature images of presentation slides.

Title bar The bar at the top edge of the program window that indicates the name of the current file and the program name.

Title slide The first slide in a presentation the purpose of which is to provide an introduction to the presentation topic.

Toggle button A button that can be turned on by clicking it once, and then turned off by clicking it again.

Toolbar In a folder window, a row of buttons with which you can perform common tasks, such as changing the view of your files and folders or burning files to a CD.

Top-level points The main text points in a SmartArt graphic.

Triple-click The action of clicking the left mouse button three times in rapid succession.

Truncated Refers to data that is cut off or shortened.

Trusted Documents A security feature in Office 2010 that remembers which files you have already enabled; you might encounter this feature if you open a file from an e-mail or download files from the Internet.

Underlying formula The formula entered in a cell and visible only on the Formula Bar.

Underlying value The data that displays in the Formula Bar.

USB flash drive A small data storage device that plugs into a computer USB port.

Value Another name for a *constant value*.

Value axis A numerical scale on the left side of a chart that shows the range of numbers for the data points; also referred to as the *y-axis*.

Vertical window split box (Excel) A small box on the vertical scroll bar with which you can split the window into two vertical views of the same worksheet.

Views button In a folder window, a toolbar button with which you can choose how to view the contents of the current location.

Window A rectangular area on a computer screen in which programs and content appear, and which can be moved, resized, minimized, or closed.

Windows Explorer The program that displays the files and folders on your computer, and which is at work anytime you are viewing the contents of files and folders in a window.

Windows taskbar The area along the lower edge of the Windows desktop that contains the Start button and an area to display buttons for open programs.

Wizard A feature in Microsoft Office that walks you step by step through a process.

Wordwrap The feature that moves text from the right edge of a paragraph to the beginning of the next line as necessary to fit within the margins.

Workbook An Excel file that contains one or more worksheets.

Workbook-level buttons Buttons at the far right of the Ribbon tabs that minimize or restore a displayed workbook.

Worksheet The primary document that you use in Excel to work with and store data, and which is formatted as a pattern of uniformly spaced horizontal and vertical lines.

x-axis Another name for the horizontal *(category)* axis.

y-axis Another name for the vertical *(value)* axis.

Zoom The action of increasing or decreasing the viewing area on the screen.

Index

F

fields (tables)
    definition, 173
    deleting, 186–187
    footers, 62
    modifying, 187–188
    naming, 177–180
    properties, 187
    renaming, 180
File list, 5
File name box, 17
File tab, 8
files
    compressing, 44–45
    definition, 3
    extracting compressed files, 45
    finding, 3–6
    management, Backstage view, 14
    names, adding to footers, 62–64
    opening, 22–25
    printing, 18–20
    properties, Read-Only, 23
    saving, 13–18, 22–25
    source, definition, 183
    storing, 14
fill handles, copying formulas, 118–119
Fill Series option, context sensitive, 112
fills, 12
financial numbers, formatting, 121–122
finding
    files, 3–6
    folders, 3–6
    text, 263
First Line Indent tab alignment option, 78
first principle of good database design,
    definition, 174
flash drives, USB, 6
flat databases, definition, 173
floating objects, 55
folder window, 4–5
Folder window toolbar, 5
folders
    creating, 13–18
    definition, 3
    finding, 3–6
Font Color button, 36, 264
font size setting, 51
fonts, 35, 51
    font styles, 36
    points (pt), 35
    presentations, 263–265
    sans serif, 35
    serif, 35
    styles, 36
footers, 33
    adding file names to, 62–64
    creating, 127–129
    fields, 62
    objects, 195
    presentations
      adding, 254–255
      definition, 254
    slides, 255
Form view, definition, 200
Format Painter, 37

formats, typing telephone numbers, 181
formatting, 32–34
    cells
      financial numbers, 121–122
      Merge & Center command, 120–121
      Percent Style, 142
      styles, 120–121
    presentations, 263–266
      fonts, 263–265
      layouts, 266
      line spacing, 265
      text alignment, 265
    shapes, 60–62
    slides, Keep source formatting check box, 261
    sparklines, 126–127
    text, 34–38, 53–54
    text boxes, 60–62
formatting marks
    definition, 25, 51
    Show/Hide button, 27
forms
    definition, 196
    printing, 198–200
Formula Bar, 108, 115
formulas
    absolute cell references, 138–140
    arithmetic operators, 136–138
    AutoSum button, 118
    copying, 118–119
    definition, 110
    displaying, 130–131
    hiding, 130–131
    point and click method, 117
    printing, 130–131
    range finder, 138
    relative cell references, 119, 377
    status bar calculations, 138
    worksheets, 116–118
Formulas Bar, underlying formulas, 117
Forward button, 5
functions
    definition, 116
    SUM, 116–118

G

galleries
    Artistic Effects, 253
    Chart Layouts, 125
    definition, 12
    Paste Options, 40
    Themes, 242
General format, 115, 136
graphics, 53. *See also* **clip art; pictures**
    size, 55
    SmartArt
      bullets, 83
      definition, 80
      inserting into documents, 80–81
      modifying, 81–83
    spin boxes, 55
grid area, 108
groups
    Clipboard, commands, 39
    definition, 26

Dialog Box Launcher, 39
names, 8
size, 30

H

Hanging Indent tab alignment option, 78
headers, 33
    adding, 254–255
    definition, 254
    objects (Access), 195
headings (column), worksheets, 109
Help, 43–44
hiding formulas, 130–131
Horizontal window split box, 109

I

icons, definition, 5
importing
    definition, 183
    Excel worksheets, 183–185, 189–191
Increase List Level button, 246
increasing list levels, 245–246
indentation, text, 71–73
Info tab, 14
InfoPath, 7
information, definition, 173
inline objects, 54
Insert Picture from File button, 250
Insert Worksheet button, 108
inserting
    columns into worksheets, 142–144
    data by ranges, 135–136
    data into worksheets, Auto Fill, 112–113
    descriptions into table fields, 187–188
    file names into footers, 62–64
    footers into presentations, 254–255
    headers into presentations, 254–255
    numbers into worksheets, 114–115
    pictures into documents, 54–55
    pictures into presentations from files, 250–252
    records into tables, 181–183
    rows into worksheets, 142–144
    shapes into documents, 58–59
    slides into presentations, 243–245, 260–262
    SmartArt graphics into documents, 80–81
    speaker notes into presentations, 247
    tables into databases, 186–196
    text, 9–11, 51–53, 240–241
    text boxes into documents, 58–59
    text into worksheets, 110–111
insertion point, 9

J-K

justification (text alignment), 68

Keep source formatting check box, 261
keyboard keys
    controlling Ribbon, 31–32
    nudging, 57

keyboard shortcuts, 10, 38
    inserting data into worksheets, 110–111
    navigating worksheets, 113
KeyTips, 31–32

L

labels
    category labels, 123
    worksheets, 110
landscape orientation, 33, 256
Layout view, definition, 199
layouts, 243–244
    charts, 125
    section headers, 247
    slides, 266
leader characters, 80
left alignment, 68, 111
Left Indent tab alignment option, 78
Left tab alignment option, 78
legends, 123
Lettered column headings, 109
libraries, definition, 4
line spacing, 51, 70–71, 265
links, definition, 183
list levels
    decreasing, 245–246
    increasing, 245–246
lists. See bulleted lists; numbered lists
Live Preview
    definition, 31
    Paste Options gallery, 40
locations, 13

M

margins, 51, 67–68
    alignment, 34
    center alignment, 34
    rulers, 27
menus
    shortcut menus, 11
    Start, All Programs, 7
Merge & Center command, 120–121
metadata, 14
Microsoft Access Database window, 177
Microsoft Access Opening window, 175
Microsoft InfoPath, 7
Microsoft Office 2010, 6
    Help, 43–44
    starting programs, 6–8
Microsoft Office Access 2010, 7
    content-based assessments, 214–233
    outcomes-based assessments, 234–236
Microsoft Office Excel 2010, 7
    content-based assessments, 148–165
    outcomes-based assessments, 166–169
    starting, 107–108
Microsoft Office Outlook 2010, 7
Microsoft Office PowerPoint 2010, 7
    content-based assessments, 272–289
    outcomes-based assessments, 290–293
    starting, 239–240
Microsoft Office Word 2010, 7
    content-based assessments, 84–101
    outcomes-based assessments, 102–104

deleting, 142–144
scaling, 131
spelling, checking, 133–135
text
  alignment, 113–114
  inserting, 110–111
  left alignment, 111
  wrapping text, 144–146
text values, 110

views, 127–129
wrapping text, 55–56, 144–146

X-Z

x-axis, 123
y-axis, 123
zooming, definition, 33

SINGLE PC LICENSE AGREEMENT AND LIMITED WARRANTY

READ THIS LICENSE CAREFULLY BEFORE OPENING THIS PACKAGE. BY OPENING THIS PACKAGE, YOU ARE AGREEING TO THE TERMS AND CONDITIONS OF THIS LICENSE. IF YOU DO NOT AGREE, DO NOT OPEN THE PACKAGE. PROMPTLY RETURN THE UNOPENED PACKAGE AND ALL ACCOMPANYING ITEMS TO THE PLACE YOU OBTAINED THEM. *THESE TERMS APPLY TO ALL LICENSED SOFTWARE ON THE DISK EXCEPT THAT THE TERMS FOR USE OF ANY SHAREWARE OR FREEWARE ON THE DISKETTES ARE AS SET FORTH IN THE ELECTRONIC LICENSE LOCATED ON THE DISK:*

1. GRANT OF LICENSE and OWNERSHIP: The enclosed computer programs ("Software") are licensed, not sold, to you by Prentice-Hall, Inc. ("We" or the "Company") and in consideration of your purchase or adoption of the accompanying Company textbooks and/or other materials, and your agreement to these terms. We reserve any rights not granted to you. You own only the disk(s) but we and/or our licensors own the Software itself. This license allows you to use and display your copy of the Software on a single computer (i.e., with a single CPU) at a single location for academic use only, so long as you comply with the terms of this Agreement. You may make one copy for back up, or transfer your copy to another CPU, provided that the Software is usable on only one computer.

2. RESTRICTIONS: You may not transfer or distribute the Software or documentation to anyone else. Except for backup, you may not copy the documentation or the Software. You may not network the Software or otherwise use it on more than one computer or computer terminal at the same time. You may not reverse engineer, disassemble, decompile, modify, adapt, translate, or create derivative works based on the Software or the Documentation. You may be held legally responsible for any copying or copyright infringement which is caused by your failure to abide by the terms of these restrictions.

3. TERMINATION: This license is effective until terminated. This license will terminate automatically without notice from the Company if you fail to comply with any provisions or limitations of this license. Upon termination, you shall destroy the Documentation and all copies of the Software. All provisions of this Agreement as to limitation and disclaimer of warranties, limitation of liability, remedies or damages, and our ownership rights shall survive termination.

4.DISCLAIMER OF WARRANTY: THE COMPANY AND ITS LICENSORS MAKE NO WARRANTIES ABOUT THE SOFTWARE, WHICH IS PROVIDED "AS-IS." IF THE DISK IS DEFECTIVE IN MATERIALS OR WORKMANSHIP, YOUR ONLY REMEDY IS TO RETURN IT TO THE COMPANY WITHIN 30 DAYS FOR REPLACEMENT UNLESS THE COMPANY DETERMINES IN GOOD FAITH THAT THE DISK HAS BEEN MISUSED OR IMPROPERLY INSTALLED, REPAIRED, ALTERED OR DAMAGED. THE COMPANY DISCLAIMS ALL WARRANTIES, EXPRESS OR IMPLIED, INCLUDING WITHOUT LIMITATION, THE IMPLIED WARRANTIES OF MERCHANTABILITY AND FITNESS FOR A PARTICULAR PURPOSE. THE COMPANY DOES NOT WARRANT, GUARANTEE OR MAKE ANY REPRESENTATION REGARDING THE ACCURACY, RELIABILITY, CURRENTNESS, USE, OR RESULTS OF USE, OF THE SOFTWARE.

5. LIMITATION OF REMEDIES AND DAMAGES: IN NO EVENT, SHALL THE COMPANY OR ITS EMPLOYEES, AGENTS, LICENSORS OR CONTRACTORS BE LIABLE FOR ANY INCIDENTAL, INDIRECT, SPECIAL OR CONSEQUENTIAL DAMAGES ARISING OUT OF OR IN CONNECTION WITH THIS LICENSE OR THE SOFTWARE, INCLUDING, WITHOUT LIMITATION, LOSS OF USE, LOSS OF DATA, LOSS OF INCOME OR PROFIT, OR OTHER LOSSES SUSTAINED AS A RESULT OF INJURY TO ANY PERSON, OR LOSS OF OR DAMAGE TO PROPERTY, OR CLAIMS OF THIRD PARTIES, EVEN IF THE COMPANY OR AN AUTHORIZED REPRESENTATIVE OF THE COMPANY HAS BEEN ADVISED OF THE POSSIBILITY OF SUCH DAMAGES. SOME JURISDICTIONS DO NOT ALLOW THE LIMITATION OF DAMAGES IN CERTAIN CIRCUMSTANCES, SO THE ABOVE LIMITATIONS MAY NOT ALWAYS APPLY.

6. GENERAL: THIS AGREEMENT SHALL BE CONSTRUED IN ACCORDANCE WITH THE LAWS OF THE UNITED STATES OF AMERICA AND THE STATE OF NEW YORK, APPLICABLE TO CONTRACTS MADE IN NEW YORK, AND SHALL BENEFIT THE COMPANY, ITS AFFILIATES AND ASSIGNEES. This Agreement is the complete and exclusive statement of the agreement between you and the Company and supersedes all proposals, prior agreements, oral or written, and any other communications between you and the company or any of its representatives relating to the subject matter. If you are a U.S. Government user, this Software is licensed with "restricted rights" as set forth in subparagraphs (a)-(d) of the Commercial Computer-Restricted Rights clause at FAR 52.227-19 or in subparagraphs (c)(1)(ii) of the Rights in Technical Data and Computer Software clause at DFARS 252.227-7013, and similar clauses, as applicable.

Should you have any questions concerning this agreement or if you wish to contact the Company for any reason, please contact in writing:

Multimedia Production,
Higher Education Division,
Prentice-Hall, Inc.,
1 Lake Street,
Upper Saddle River NJ 07458.